D1376623

PUBLIC LAW AND PRIVATE POWER

A volume in the series

CORNELL STUDIES IN POLITICAL ECONOMY

edited by Peter J. Katzenstein

A list of titles in this series is available at

www.cornellpress.cornell.edu.

PUBLIC LAW AND PRIVATE POWER

Corporate Governance Reform

in the Age of Finance Capitalism

· JOHN W. CIOFFI

Cornell University Press   ·   Ithaca and London

First published 2010 by Cornell University Press

Printed in the United States of America

Library of Congress Cataloging-in-Publication Data

Cioffi, John W.
    Public law and private power : corporate governance reform in the age of finance capitalism / John W. Cioffi.
        p. cm. — (Cornell studies in political economy)
    Includes bibliographical references and index.
    ISBN 978-0-8014-4904-8 (cloth : alk. paper)
    1. Corporate governance—Political aspects—United States. 2. Corporate governance—Political aspects—Germany. 3. Corporate governance—Law and legislation—United States. 4. Corporate governance—Law and legislation—Germany. 5. International finance. 6. Financial crises. I. Title. II. Series: Cornell studies in political economy.

    HD2741.C56 2010
    338.60943—dc22

2010018405

Cloth printing 10 9 8 7 6 5 4 3 2 1

For Bronwyn, Teo, and Nadia

CONTENTS

FIGURES AND TABLES

ACKNOWLEDGMENTS

I have had an unusually personal connection to several of the historical events that occupy a central place in this book. I was a law student when the hostile takeover wave and the savings and loan crisis of the 1980s signaled the transition to a new, financially driven form of capitalism. I was a young lawyer clerking for a federal judge and practicing law in a large New York law firm as many of the legal disputes generated by these developments were flooding the courts. Leaving the practice of law (though not necessarily the associated habits of mind) in the mid-1990s for the University of California, Berkeley, I found myself with a ringside seat for the great dot-com bubble and subsequent crash that triggered the Enron-era corporate governance reforms.

Leaving Berkeley for a teaching position at the University of California, Riverside, I moved to what became the epicenter of subprime mortgage lending and the real estate bubble it produced. One need not have been an economic genius to see a market bubble swelling to historic proportions. I watched the value of my own home inflate and then plummet as the bubble ran its course. My drive to work passes through neighborhoods devastated by the wave of foreclosures that followed.

The effects of the catastrophic financial crisis and the Great Recession that followed the real estate crash have been particularly severe in California. The University of California, the institution that educated and now employs me, is now in extreme crisis as a result of the economic downturn, compounded by state dysfunction. One of the great institutional legacies of an era in which government built institutions that supplied critical public goods, rather than bailing out private interests that have wreaked so much economic destruction, is teetering. We certainly are living in a new world of finance capitalism.

These events confirmed me in the conclusion, reached many years ago, that political and economic developments since the 1980s had not only privileged financial interests but also wrought a structural change in the political economy that had increased the importance and power of financial markets and corporate firms. All I have witnessed since has reinforced my view that the postwar political economy has been transformed into a new, financially driven and increasingly volatile form of capitalism. My training in law and political science made me acutely aware that this transformation was not merely the aggregate outcome of market processes but the product of profound political shifts and legal changes in the structures of firms and financial markets. I resolved to study the dangerous boom-bust cycles that resulted in order to understand the accelerating, and often disorienting, changes of the last three decades. This book is the result.

In the research and writing, I have benefited more than I can say from more people than I can thank. I have been fortunate over the years to have had mentors, colleagues, and collaborators around the world who unstintingly gave me their time, ideas, and insight. At the University of California, Berkeley, Bob Kagan, John Zysman, Jonah Levy, Nick Ziegler, Steve Vogel, and Richard Buxbaum helped and inspired me over more years than I'd like to recount. Bob Kagan has been a wonderful friend and mentor over many years, and this book bears many of the traces of his integration of the study of law and politics. John Zysman has also been a great friend and mentor who provided me with a supportive and congenial home at the Berkeley Roundtable on the International Economy. He fundamentally shaped my thinking about political and economic institutions, and his work has been a tremendous influence on this book.

The group of scholars in political science studying issues of finance and corporate governance provided constant discussion, information, professional growth, provocation, intellectual curiosity, and goodwill. Martin Höpner, Richard Deeg, Yves Tiberghien, Gregory Jackson, Pepper Culpepper, Sussane Lütz, Britta Rehder, and Sig Vitols generously afforded me with a wealth of intellectual stimulation and personal collegiality. Special thanks go to Peter Gourevitch, a model citizen of the academy, who has been extraordinarily helpful to me and many other younger scholars, helping to blaze a trail in studying the political economy of corporate governance and to create a community among those who followed. Wolfgang Streeck welcomed me to the Max Planck Institute in Cologne and has been both an intellectual inspiration and source of insight into recent developments in the German political economy. Peer Zumbansen's generosity in sharing his broad and deep knowledge of comparative and German law was invaluable in clarifying many difficult legal and conceptual issues. I benefited greatly from conversations and comments from David Soskice and Peter Hall, who at various times helped sharpen my thinking about political economic analysis and national models of capitalism. I am grateful to Marty Levin, Martin Shapiro, Mark Landy, Jonah Levy, and David Levi-Faur for invitations to participate in collaborative projects that have informed this work. I am honored to be associated with such exceptional scholars, researchers, and thinkers. I owe a vast debt of gratitude to Peter Katzenstein and Roger Haydon for their confidence in this project, hard work to improve it, and patience with its author. I have been extraordinarily fortunate to work with them, and this book is much improved as a consequence.

My thanks also go to the many people, too numerous to name, in the United States and Germany who gave their time in interviews and discussions related to this research. Their thoughtful and patient responses to my questions provided an understanding of matters that are not easily grasped outside highly specialized professional circles but are absolutely vital for understanding how politics, law, finance, and governance interact. Many very busy and very accomplished people were extremely generous with their time and knowledge.

All the above individuals contributed in many ways to my thinking, research, and writing. All remaining errors, of course, are my own.

Research and writing would have been impossible without financial assistance and other support over the years from the U.C. Riverside Academic Senate and Department of Political Science; the Max Planck Institute for the Study of Societies, Cologne; the Wissenschaftszentrum Berlin für Sozialforschung, the National Science Foundation; the Sharlin and Stimson funds of the Institute of International Studies at U.C. Berkeley; and the U.C. Berkeley Department of Political Science.

And finally, I express my immense gratitude to my wife, Bronwyn, and our two wonderful children, Teo and Nadia. I could not have completed this book without Bronwyn's tireless help, warm encouragement, sharp editorial eye, and sharper mind.

CHAPTER I

Corporate Governance Reform and the Age of Finance Capitalism

eginning in 2007, the most devastating economic crisis since the Great Depression undermined the economic, ideological, and political foundations of the neoliberal model of corporate governance and political economic organization. Although it was in many respects a banking and financial market crisis, with further probing one quickly finds underlying failures of corporate governance. The crisis cast a harsh light not only on the deficiencies of underregulated market-driven financial systems but also on the consistent failures of governance regimes to control the structurally entrenched agency problems, conflicts of interest, and rapacious opportunism within the large public corporation—particularly within the financial sector.[1] Paradoxically, corporate governance reforms ostensibly designed to protect shareholders and advance the development of financial markets helped to foster an unhealthy and unsustainable economic order. They encouraged many managers and investors to pursue higher short-term shareholder returns, and this ultimately contributed to the destruction of trillions of dollars in shareholder value. Whereas in recent decades the United States had exported juridical and ideological elements of its corporate governance model, it was now exporting an economic crisis in large part born of this model. The world was left to confront the appalling costs of getting corporate governance wrong.

The past politics of corporate governance and financial regulation is prologue to the future politics of reform and political economic development. We

---

1. By public corporation, I refer to corporations with shares traded on public securities markets, not to state-owned enterprises. It is perhaps a sign of the times that the latter, a staple of Shonfield's (1965) account of the postwar "mixed" economy, has been almost entirely eclipsed by the private, but publicly traded, corporation.

must understand the political origins of corporate governance reforms that began in the 1990s if we are to understand the nature of the later global economic crisis and the capacities of political actors to address it.

This book examines politics and legal change in the United States and Germany, two countries widely viewed as exemplifying sharply divergent forms of political economic organization, in order to advance four interrelated arguments regarding contemporary corporate governance. First, the reform of national corporate governance regimes reflects the emergence of a broader political economic paradigm of finance capitalism marked by internationalized financial markets and services, the increasing size of the financial sector and its influence over economic activities, and the increasing political centrality of financial interests in matters of law and policy. Second, pro-shareholder corporate governance reform is fundamentally a political process largely driven, in the United States and Germany, by Center-*Left* politicians seeking to construct new political coalitions within the constraints of interest group pressures shaped by established law and institutional arrangements. Third, the era of finance capitalism is also the age of the resurgent regulatory state as corporate governance reform expands legal and regulatory intervention into the public corporation and financial markets—a trend only likely to accelerate now that underregulation has proved disastrous. Fourth, in addition to its regulative role, law performs a *constitutive* function in establishing corporate governance structures that embody norms, institutional arrangements, and power relations characteristic of distinctive national governance regimes and that influence the future trajectories of reform.

Taken together, these arguments explain the legal development of corporate governance and elucidate its importance as a juridical and institutional dimension of political economic organization. They show not only how law and regulation are *produced* but also how legal rules *work* by constituting the institutional arrangements that define markets and firms. The arguments help explain how juridical structures frame the intersection of partisan politics with shifting interest group alignments and market conditions. An integrated political and legal analysis of corporate governance regimes, often lacking in the scholarly literature and policy debates, aids our understanding of a set of norms and institutionalized relationships that have become increasingly politicized in an era of reform yet remain highly resilient even amid financial crises.

The economic and legal model of the financially driven corporate firm with shareholder returns as its preeminent value has animated corporate governance reform and financial system development around the world in recent decades. This form of corporate governance, combined with the deepening of financial globalization and the growing financialization of the advanced industrial economies, led to the emergence of a new and crisis-prone form of international finance capitalism. Politics drove these profound changes in policy and economic organization. In important respects, this politics was practiced more by the Left than by the Right. It represented a triumph of neoliberalism's fixation on markets, skepticism toward regulation, and bias in favor of financial interests. The depth and scope of the global economic crisis delivered a brutal blow, in practical and ideological terms, to the appeal, and perhaps the legitimacy, of this shareholder-centric model of corporate governance and the politics that made manifest the vision of a financially driven economy.

The public corporation and the equity markets on which it depends are foundational institutions of modern capitalism and principal drivers of economic growth, innovation, restructuring, and adjustment. The decline of direct economic management by the state since the 1980s only magnified the importance of politics in structuring markets and firms through law and regulation. As a consequence, economic governance increasingly has become a matter of corporate governance. By allocating power over the governance of the firm among private actors and corporate stakeholder groups, corporate governance law confers substantial economic and political power. Not surprisingly, corporate governance reform has become increasingly central to economic policy and politics.

The increasing destructiveness of governance failures in recent decades is striking. In neither the United States nor Germany did ostensibly pro-shareholder corporate governance reforms place adequate checks on managerial recklessness, incompetence, dishonesty, and/or opportunism. Governance failures contributed to the destruction of vast amounts of shareholder value, inflicted immense and lasting damage to the "real economy," and compelled public bailouts of the financial sector valued at trillions of dollars to stave off catastrophic domestic and global economic collapse. Take, for example, the insurance giant American International Group (AIG), the most emblematic and perhaps the most costly corporate casualty of the crisis. Long notorious for its organizational complexity and financial opacity, AIG was mired in accounting scandals during the Enron era that began in 2001 and was targeted in a lawsuit by the AFSCME union pension fund to improve its poor governance.[2] Unknown to most observers, within AIG's complex web of (profitable) insurance subsidiaries and other holdings was a London-based financial services division that issued over $500 billion worth of risky credit default swaps (essentially unregulated insurance contracts on mortgage-backed securities) that triggered massive losses during the nadir of the financial crisis in late 2008 and threatened to bring down not only the firm but much of the world's financial system. To stave off systemic collapse, the United States effectively nationalized the company, and the Federal Reserve and Treasury Department

2. *American Federation of State, County & Municipal Employees v. American International Group*, 462 F.3d 121 (2d Cir. 2006) (compelling inclusion of dissident board candidates in company proxy materials).

issued loans and guarantees on AIG debt and derivatives contracts totaling over $180 billion as of mid-2009. In a stunning manifestation of governance gone awry, the company's management *still* awarded multimillion-dollar bonuses to its senior staff, including those in the division that destroyed the firm, and the U.S. government professed itself powerless to stop them.

AIG exemplified the absence of transparency, risk management, and accountability that are the hallmarks of bad governance—and dramatically illustrates the costliness of such failures—but the roots of this governance crisis reach farther back in time and entangle a far broader array of companies. In the Enron scandal, for example, managers extracted vast personal benefits from highly leveraged shady business dealings that were hidden off the corporate balance sheet in "special purpose vehicles" that destroyed the firm with devastating consequences to its shareholders, employees, and retirees. Little more than half a decade later, notwithstanding an array of post-Enron reforms, fundamental failures of corporate governance, this time at the commanding heights of the financial sector, brought down much of the American financial system. Once again, overleveraged financial institutions paid senior managers extravagant compensation packages while hiding ruinous aggregate exposure to trillions of dollars' worth of toxic debt and derivatives obligations in "storage facilities" or special investment vehicles.

In Germany, corporate managers, encouraged by government policy, adopted financially driven pro-shareholder value business strategies that veered away from their traditional focus on production. As the Enron-era scandals were breaking in the United States, forays by German firms into American-style market-driven finance and shareholder-centered corporate governance were largely disastrous. During the first decade of the twenty-first century, Germany suffered from the bursting of its own high-tech stock market bubble, the collapse of the country's high-tech stock market (the Neue Markt), and the poor performance of many large banks that stumbled in moving into market-based financial services. Allegations of fraudulent financial disclosures by the recently privatized Deutsche Telekom, leading to large shareholder losses, sullied the government's elaborate attempts to create a national "equity culture." The legal fiasco of the Vodafone-Mannesmann takeover and subsequent criminal prosecution of Mannesmann's former directors for payment of golden-parachute severance packages (discussed in chapter 5) reflected the intense ambivalence toward elements of the Anglo-American governance model, even as bribery scandals involving employee representatives at Siemens and Volkswagen tainted Germany's stakeholder governance. As in the United States, the defects of corporate governance and market-based finance festered. The financial sector's continued drive to increase shareholder value led to excessive risk taking and the accumulation of bad debts estimated in excess of €850 billion that inflicted grievous damage on the banking system at the core of the country's economy.

One of the tragedies underlying the economic crisis was that the politics and law of corporate governance (and of financial regulation more broadly) failed to keep pace with financial developments and in some ways contributed to the deep structural flaws in firm governance that drove the global economy to the brink of disaster. But this crisis did not mark the end of finance capitalism. To the contrary, it intensified the political debate over the reform of national corporate governance regimes and the future of international finance capitalism. The emergence of finance capitalism was inevitably accompanied by political struggles over the proper balance of the interests, influence, and autonomy of corporate stakeholders—namely managers, shareholders, and employees—battles that are ultimately fought over the allocation of private power and the scope of public legal authority.[3] The economic crisis of 2007–10, even more than those preceding it, intensified these conflicts.

Still, the political forces and institutional arrangements that shaped neoliberal finance capitalism and shareholder-oriented corporate governance reforms have remained intact to a surprising degree. The American market-driven financial system and nominally shareholder-centered corporate governance regime self-destructed twice within a decade, yet the policy responses of the Bush and Obama administrations were, at best, halting in addressing its flawed legal and institutional foundations. In Germany, a senior Social Democratic minister in the Red-Green Schröder government denounced activist hedge fund investors as "locusts" even as his government pursued pro-shareholder reforms that empowered them. The succeeding Grand Coalition government advocated vigorously for regulatory reforms in response to the crisis but did little. The assiduous cultivation of market-based financial services, securitized finance, and shareholder-oriented corporate governance via law and public policy left these features of contemporary capitalism well entrenched in both countries, even though they contributed to spiraling economic crises. The gravity of the crisis pointed to the need for fundamental reforms of governance processes that would enable corporate stakeholders to monitor and check abuses of managerial power. This book's analysis of corporate governance regimes suggests that domestic politics will likely frustrate such reforms. We are all heirs to the consequences.

CORPORATE GOVERNANCE AT THE INTERSECTION OF LAW AND POLITICS

Corporate governance and its reform are intensely politicized and juridified. Analysis of the roles of politics and law reveals not only the political sensitivity of corporate governance law but the implications of political, juridical, and

3. Cf. Shonfield (1965); Zysman (1983).

institutional legacies for the future of desperately needed reforms. The book's central arguments sketch the political and juridical logic of corporate governance reform and, by extension, modern finance capitalism between 1990 and 2010. These arguments do not stand in isolation; they build on and reinforce one another in ways that reveal the systemic character of national corporate governance regimes and how they evolve through political and legal processes.

Finance Capitalism and the Problem of Corporate Governance

At the highest level of generality, corporate governance reform reflects the emergence of a new paradigm of finance capitalism that relies increasingly on financial markets and shareholding as mechanisms of savings, investment, and economic restructuring.[4] This ongoing transformation of capitalism at the national and international levels represents a departure from the established models of the postwar era and the role of the state in economic governance and organization.[5] Political and economic changes inverted the postwar world of "embedded liberalism," in which markets were stabilized and legitimated by social and governmental institutions, into one in which institutions are embedded in markets that play a far more prominent role in the course of economic development and social life.[6] During the "golden age" of postwar capitalism, financial actors, institutions, and markets were means of enabling productive economic activity. During the succeeding golden age of finance capitalism, abetted by politics, policy, and law, they increasingly drove political economic development and organization in ways that magnified the wealth and power of the financial sector.

The liberalization of international financial markets followed the collapse of the original Bretton Woods regime in the 1970s. In countries as divergent as the United States and Germany, subsequent changes in domestic economic conditions, partisan coalitional alignments, and ideologies shifted the established balance of power in favor of managerial elites and financial capital. The globalization of capital markets and the internationalization of financial services and investment profoundly altered the comparative advantages, benefits, and opportunity costs of established national financial systems and corporate

4. Among the numerous recent scholars who have addressed the financialization of capitalism in recent decades, see, e.g., Moran (1991), O'Brien (1992), Helleiner (1994), Strange (1998), Boyer (2000), Lazonick and O'Sullivan (2000), Dore (2000), and Lütz (2005).
5. Cioffi (2006a, 2006b). For classic works in the literature on national models of political economy, see, e.g., Schonfield (1965), Katzenstein (1985, 1987), Goldthorpe (1984), Zysman (1983), and Berger and Dore (1996). For more contemporary variations on this general approach to comparative political economy, see, e.g., Levy (2006), Hall and Soskice (2001), and Kitschelt et al. (1999).
6. For the original theoretical treatment of "embedded liberalism," see Ruggie (1982).

governance regimes. These changed incentive structures opened up new business strategies for internationally oriented firms and new opportunities for political entrepreneurs seeking to adapt to an altered economic and interest group environment.

The forces driving corporate governance reform were political. Reform was not driven by the need to attract investment capital within an increasingly porous and liquid international financial environment. If the genesis of the financial and economic crises of 2007–10 tells us anything, it is that the world was awash in an excess of investment capital during the 1990s and the following decade. Contrary to theories of path dependence and neoliberal convergence alike, corporate governance reforms reveal both the common structural characteristics and the divergent developmental trajectories of the American and German varieties of finance capitalism. These persistent differences cannot be attributed to economic forces and financial market changes. Variations in politics, law, and institutional legacies at the national level channeled reform in distinct ways and directions. The international phenomenon of finance capitalism is grounded on national financial systems and corporate governance regimes—and the domestic politics that drives their development.

The Political Construction of Corporate Governance Regimes

The Primacy of Politics and the Role of State Actors

The primacy of politics in corporate governance reform should come as no surprise. The corporation, by definition, is a creation of law; law, in turn, is a product of politics. Politics produced the legal order necessary for corporate capitalism, and the rise of the large public corporation—the institutional product of law—profoundly reshaped the politics and law of corporate governance. This relationship between corporate and political power has become increasingly fraught during the past twenty years as corporate governance emerged worldwide as an increasingly central and politicized area of economic policy.[7]

The political salience of corporate governance soared as the advanced industrial countries grappled with the consequences of the 1973 economic crisis, the ascendance of neoliberalism, and the explosive growth of liberalized international financial markets after the 1980s. Corporate governance had long been a technical domain of professionals and business elites largely hidden from the public eye. Its varying forms across countries were well

---

7. Cf. Buxbaum (1987).

established and stable. No longer. The public corporation and securities markets have been at the center of controversies over economic change and the policies and legal rules that shape it. Waves of corporate restructuring, the globalization of investment and financial services, and the increasing economic power and political influence of financial interests transformed capitalism around the world. Sharpening conflicts over political economic power, rents, legal reform, and institutional change inevitably reached the foundational institution of capitalism: the corporation.

Struggles over the form and functioning of the corporation became most visible and intense in the politics of corporate governance reform. The structure of the corporation and the allocation of power within it substantially determine the speed and form of economic change, who benefits from it, and who bears its costs. Notwithstanding persistent and significant cross-national differences, state actors across the industrialized countries have undertaken major legal reforms of corporate governance. These changes have largely favored financial capital. Struggles for power in both the public and the private spheres underlie these structural changes.

This view of corporate governance reform and, more broadly, the construction of contemporary finance capitalism, emphasizes the centrality of national politics over international or transnational politics and economics. This is not an ex ante assumption but a conclusion derived from careful case studies. In the United States and Germany, despite substantial differences in political economic organization and positions within the global economy, domestic imperatives drove the politics of reform. Where international politics and market pressures came into conflict with the logic of domestic politics, the latter prevailed in the framing and implementation of reform. In the United States, for example, the Sarbanes-Oxley Act of 2002, enacted as part of a raft of post-Enron reforms, was harshly (and excessively) criticized as contrary to emerging international norms and bound to debilitate American firms and securities markets. Yet the reforms not only were passed but proved resilient against an antiregulation backlash by powerful business interests and conservative politicians. Likewise, domestic politics entrenched Germany's resistance to weakening its codetermination laws and drove its retreat from the European Union's original neoliberal Takeover Directive in 2001, despite intense international pressure. The nation-state remains the primary locus of political power and lawmaking, far outpacing international bodies and, where politically sensitive issues are concerned, limiting the authority of the European Union.

The Paradox of the Center-Left

Corporate governance reform in the United States and Germany displays another striking parallel: it was largely the product of Center-Left politicians with the support of large, sophisticated financial institutions.[8] Pro-shareholder policy agendas and supporting political coalitions and major policy agendas were fashioned by actors and parties with the capacity to frame reform narratives and to overcome the collective action problems faced by interest groups and individuals. They were not driven by economic logic or by bottom-up pressures from interest groups. Hence, corporate governance reform reveals the primacy of politics over self-organization of coalitions based on the intersection of narrow economic interests. In both countries, individual and institutional shareholders as a group were too weak and beset by collective-action problems to drive reform. Center-Left politicians took advantage of financial scandals and perceptions of economic crisis to mobilize and/or coordinate interest group coalitions—and successfully frame legal reforms in normative and legislative terms. The interest group politics of reform turned on the preferences of powerful segments of the financial sector that recognized the need for pro-shareholder legal reforms to promote and maintain a market-based financial system.

Pro-shareholder reforms from the Left appear deeply paradoxical and contrary to the historical allegiances of Center-Left parties. However, this shift followed a political logic. During the 1990s, the Democrats in the United States and the Social Democrats and Greens in Germany embraced much of the ascendant neoliberal conception of finance capitalism as the route to economic modernization and growth. The promise of faster economic growth and innovation fostered by rapid capital formation and reallocation via well-developed financial markets and facilitated by financially driven corporate restructuring appealed to Center-Left parties in an era marked by chronic budget constraints and the limits of industrial policy. Belief in the potential of financial markets and shareholder-oriented corporate governance to deliver prosperity spread from liberal market economies, led by the United States, to nonliberal economies such as Germany, and it provided the ideological foundation that held together the coalitional and partisan politics of reform.

The repositioning of the Center-Left on financial market and corporate governance issues coincided with the weakening of organized labor, the decline of postwar working class politics, and shifting interest group alignments. The reform agenda appealed to the Center-Left's traditional skepticism toward unfettered markets and managerial power. As a matter of political strategy, these parties championed the causes of shareholders and corporate governance reform as a way to exploit economic and legitimacy crises and appeal to nontraditional constituencies, such as segments of the financial sector and middle-class investors. At the same time, they secured the support of their traditional labor constituencies, who saw reform as a spur to growth, a

8. See Cioffi and Höpner (2006a, 2006b).

means of constraining managerial misconduct, and a source of economic benefits.[9]

Political Constraints and the Limits of Reform

However, the politics of corporate governance reform in the United States and Germany differed in vitally important respects. In the first place, the two countries began with very different forms of political economic organization, corporate structures, and financial development. Accordingly, in responding to an increasingly liberalized international financial system and globalizing financial markets, Germany had to engage in a far more wrenching systemic reform of its traditionally bank-based financial system and stakeholder governance regime. The country's policymakers sought to embrace the new market reality of international finance while retaining much of the legal and institutional architecture of stakeholder governance. The United States, in contrast, pioneered the development of market-driven finance and a corporate governance regime far more devoted to the norm of shareholder value. American corporate governance reform did not seek to accommodate international financial developments; it responded to its own endogenously generated crises of corruption and systemic instability.

Second, the partisan character of reform politics differed considerably between the two countries. German corporate governance reform was the product of a more consensual form of politics, as required by the depth of the changes these reforms embodied. In the United States, partisan conflict permeated the politics of reform, which could overcome resistance by managerial and financial-sector interests only in the context of serious scandal and economic crisis. Even then the reforms adopted proved limited, incomplete in critical respects, and only modestly effective.

Consequently, politics limited—and continues to limit—reform in both the United States and Germany, but in different ways. First, the Center-Left's need to accommodate managerial interests constrained reform and frustrated attempts to divide business interests by cleaving financial institutions and investors from corporate managers. Given the weakness of shareholders as a constituency, the Center-Left remained reliant on the managers of large financial institutions and other firms with an interest in financial market development. Parties on the right remained closely allied with managerial elites, and they could exploit the interests of managers, including those of financial firms,

---

9. These benefits were defined substantially by established legal and institutional arrangements in each country. American unions sought to increase the governance leverage of and returns to private pension funds that they controlled and that workers relied upon for retirement security. In Germany, unions saw reform as a way to enhance their governance role via codetermination and their collective bargaining strength through greater corporate financial transparency.

where they conflicted with shareholder interests in curbing managerial power and autonomy. The interests of managers qua managers in maintaining intracorporate control within the financial sector thus constrained the proshareholder reform agenda.

Second, and more broadly, the pro-shareholder strategy failed to mobilize electorates as appeals to working-class identity had once done. Despite the increasing proportion of households holding shares, "shareholder" is not a salient political identity. Consequently, the promotion of shareholder interests as part of the "New Democrat" and "Neue Mitte" policy agendas has not proved an effective long-term electoral or coalitional strategy for the Center-Left. These limitations on the political efficacy of pro-shareholder reform appear especially problematic in the wake of the 2007–8 global financial collapse and ensuing recession. Ties to the financial sector have become politically toxic, and policy commitments to the interests of financial capital appear to have come down on the wrong side of history. There is no escape from the resulting political quandary. Politicians on the right and left confront enormous pressures for legal reform, and they are as intense now as at any time since the 1930s. On the right, resistance to reform runs the risk of a public backlash and electoral repudiation. On the center-left, alliances with financial interests complicate the crafting and pursuit of a responsive policy agenda. What is clear is that, consistent with the recent history of corporate governance reform, regulatory expansion again has become the order of the day.

Juridification and the Expansion of the Regulatory State

Even prior to the current economic crisis, corporate governance reforms during the past two decades have been characterized by a *proliferation* of legal rules and an *expansion* of state regulatory power.[10] The political sensitivity of corporate governance makes the reforms that have swept over most of the advanced industrialized countries during the past twenty years all the more striking. The politics of reform has increased and centralized regulatory authority at the national level while extending legal intervention into the private sphere through rules that reconfigure internal power relations of the corporation. Liberalized financial markets and firm-driven growth and adjustment strategies have been buttressed by a formidable and expanding regulatory framework. As Steven Vogel has argued, freer markets require more rules.[11] Just as the proponents of deregulation appeared to be reaching the zenith of their power, national corporate governance regimes became the subjects of

10. Cioffi (2004b, 2006a, 2006b); cf. Keleman and Sibbit (2004).
11. Vogel (1996).

increasingly visible—and often bitter—political battles over reform and *re*-regulation. In an era of resurgent liberalism and globalized market capitalism, two institutional pillars of modern capitalism—the public corporation and securities markets—have been subjected to *increased* regulatory intervention. The financial and economic crises of 2007–2010 have accelerated this process. The age of finance capitalism is also the age of legalism, juridification, and the regulatory state.

Corporate governance, at least in the advanced industrial countries, is law-intensive. The comparative analysis developed here captures this by conceiving of national corporate governance regimes as a "juridical nexus" of securities, company, and governance-related aspects of labor relations law. Because of the varying political configurations underpinning them, the degree of legal change has been uneven across these areas of law. Despite important convergent aspects, the legal reforms described in the case studies of the United States and Germany have left the two countries on divergent developmental trajectories towards distinctive forms of finance capitalism. Securities law and disclosure regulation have undergone the most pronounced pro-shareholder reforms, and these are the areas in which Germany has most clearly converged on the American model, dating back to the New Deal, of a national securities regulator overseeing rule-based transparency. Indeed, Germany has overtaken the United States in terms of regulatory centralization. Formal law and mandatory regulation have displaced much of the prior regime of voluntary self-regulation. Disclosure regulation has grown more stringent, and state regulatory authority has expanded—though it still proved insufficient to prevent a financial meltdown driven not only by the continued opacity of much of the financial sector but also by poor governance and pervasive conflicts of interest.

Efforts to reform company and labor relations law, however, threatened vested interests in established intracorporate allocations of power more directly than did transparency regulation under securities law. Consequently, company law has experienced more limited change than securities regulation, and it has also seen intense political conflict over the substance and extent of reform. Notably, there have been virtually no reforms of governance-related aspects of labor law, the area of law in which the United States and Germany are most sharply differentiated, and few serious political initiatives to either strengthen or diminish the role of labor as stakeholder in governance matters. Reform proponents on the center-left were wary of antagonizing their labor base, and their newly cultivated financial-sector constituencies were hostile to any recognition or expansion of labor's governance role.[12]

12. The weakening economic position of labor also contributed to the essential stability of labor law. Business interests had little reason to expend substantial political capital on divisive political fights over legal reform while the market was shifting power and wealth toward managers and financial interests—and away from employees and unions.

Where transparency and disclosure regulation represents the *expansion* of law and regulation over market relations, efforts to reform the rules governing corporate boards, shareholder voting rights, and stakeholder governance mechanisms indicate the increasing *penetration* of law into the institutional structure of the corporation. On the one hand, company law reform represents an increased use of "structural regulation" that reconfigures the corporate form and the power relations that it embodies for regulatory ends. This self-executing form of law and economic governance is well suited to an era of pronounced skepticism toward detailed prescriptive regulation and discretionary industrial policy. On the other hand, the political and economic sensitivity of these structural power relations generates resistance to reform precisely because it disrupts the legal mechanisms by which they are institutionalized within the corporate form and its governance processes.

The Constitutive Dimension of Law and Regulation

Law and regulation are not only regulative but also *constitutive* in their effects on both economics and politics.[13] Consequently, a focus on the politics of juridification and the growth of the regulatory state, as important as those phenomena are, tends to underestimate the significance of legal change. If, to quote E. E. Schattschneider, "new government policy creates new politics," we may reasonably extend that classic insight to infer that legal reforms make new politics.[14] Law defines not only the subject matter of political contestation over corporate governance but also the actors, coalition groups, power relations, and interests that drive politics. The corporation is, of course, a legal construct. Its internal constituencies (or stakeholders) and the relations among them are therefore also largely constituted by law. On the one hand, the legal foundations of national corporate governance regimes reinforce their resilience and thus contribute to the path dependence of their developmental trajectories. Law informs, and may define, the identities and positional interests of actors and groups. On the other, the technical complexity and normative tensions of corporate governance law reflects conflicting conceptions of economic interests and social values. These conflicts tend to cleave interest groups, fracture coalitional alignments, and render their policy preferences uncertain and susceptible to political manipulation. This enhances the role of political agency by governmental actors in reform processes and thus the constitutive function of politics.

13. See Edelman and Suchman (1997).
14. Schattschneider (1963).

Despite the analytical affinity and causal linkages between the constitutive roles of law and institutional arrangements, constitutive law and regulation remain largely foreign to institutionalist theories of political economy. Law and regulation certainly influence political and economic action through legal proscription, prescription, and sanctions. But legally constituted norms, rules, and institutional structures also alter politics and economics by shaping the identities, interests, policy preferences, and relative power of influential political constituencies such as managers, financial institutions, investors, and workers. Consistent with much institutionalist theory and empirical research, this constitutive conception of law helps elucidate the self-reinforcing tendencies of juridical and institutional structures. Constitutive law goes further, however, in contributing to our understanding of reform by revealing the importance of law in the politics of institutional change.

Legal rules and norms redefine the terrain on which the battles of reform politics are fought. They are both the *objects* of political contestation and *substantial determinants* of the interests, demands, and strategies pursued by political protagonists. The established forms of corporate governance law contributed to the distinctive limitations that partisan politics and the interest group dynamics imposed on the development of "shareholder capitalism." Viewed cross-nationally, managers, employees, and investors wanted different reforms and accepted different policy outcomes in the United States and Germany. Historically, the juridical nexus of American corporate governance empowered managers, weakened shareholders, and exiled labor. Subsequent struggles over corporate governance conceived governance as a balance of power between managers and shareholders. Despite favoring the expansion of shareholder protection since the 1980s, the politics of legal reform could not overcome managerial and political resistance to changes that would grant shareholders more power within core governance processes. Board elections and managerial compensation remained largely beyond the reach of reform.

The German stakeholder model was the product of a legal framework that encouraged concentrated stock ownership and buttressed the strong governance position of blockholders and large banks while incorporating formal governance roles for labor through codetermination law. The more complex legal and institutional balance of power within the German corporation gave rise to distinctly different politics of corporate governance reform. Managers were willing to accept a more active role for shareholders because they were already constrained by blockholders and banks. Managers and shareholders had largely adapted to and internalized the norms of Germany's stakeholder governance. To the extent that they had not, they were unwilling to expend the enormous amount of political capital necessary to roll back codetermination law. The consensualist norms embodied in this stakeholder model also militated against the extractive, financially driven relations common in

American corporate governance such as hostile takeovers or grossly inflated managerial compensation.

But attention to the constitutive effects of law also indicates how reform and regulation can be made more effective by altering the power relations within the corporation—and the broader political economy. Legal reforms altering the rights and powers of shareholders and employees in firm governance implicate the way in which state power is deployed and its effectiveness in pursuit of policy goals. Hence, this book presents the legal constitution of the corporate form and its governance processes as a potentially effective—if politically contentious—mode of governance reform and regulation. Pervasive failures by governmental regulatory agencies leading up to the financial crisis of 2007–9 demonstrate the importance of reform via structural regulation. Structural regulation as a means of deliberately enhancing the powers of shareholders, and perhaps other stakeholders, raises the possibility of improving intracorporate accountability, equity, and efficiency in order to secure sustainable growth and systemic financial stability. This also underscores the two basic dimensions of reform: one altering the institutional governance structure of the firm, the other regulating transparency and information flows to the external financial market. The argument advanced here maintains that reform through structural regulation is both more difficult and more fundamental to the constitution of the political economy.

Given the depth of the global financial collapse and ensuing economic crisis, we might expect fundamental reform. The severity of this crisis in the United States and its spread around the world have again unleashed a rethinking of how economies, financial systems, and corporations should be governed. However, new thinking does not amount to new politics. One can only speculate on the outcomes, but an appreciation of the politics and law of corporate governance during the era of finance capitalism is essential for an understanding of the policy issues, the juridical possibilities for resolving them, and the political dynamics that will determine what paths we travel.

INSTITUTIONALIST ANALYSIS AND
JURIDICAL POLITICS

This book uses qualitative case studies to analyze the political and juridical dynamics of corporate governance reform in two critically important countries, the United States and Germany. The data marshaled here were compiled over nearly a decade of extensive fieldwork in addition to much primary and secondary research. Intensive interviews of politicians and their staffs, regulators, lobbyists, bankers, lawyers and other corporate governance professionals, labor leaders, institutional investors, and policy experts endow these case studies with the empirical detail needed to elucidate the politics underlying an extraordinarily complex and often opaque area of reform. The historical and analytical narratives developed in the studies accomplish three goals. First, they provide a baseline historical and analytical description of the American and German corporate governance regimes from which we can assess the significance of legal reforms and institutional change. Second, these chapters show the importance of state actors, political conflict, and historical contingency in a largely endogenous process of reforming corporate governance regimes in response to economic crisis and financial globalization. Third, they show how the formal legal and institutional dimensions of corporate governance contribute to the development of nationally distinctive forms of finance capitalism, each with its own characteristic flaws and vulnerabilities.

These case studies analyze the legal and institutional aspects of corporate governance reform in the United States and Germany from a historical institutionalist perspective. The treatment of this subject is in some respects consistent with well-established preoccupations of historical institutionalist literature. Policymaking has long been a preoccupation of historical institutionalism.[15] Likewise, institutional change has become an area of intense interest during the past decade.[16] Law and legal change, however, have not received the attention appropriate to an age in which regulatory politics has become a central preoccupation of state actors, economic governance is ever more law-intensive, and the legal reform of corporate governance has become a global trend.[17] Because, as a practical matter, law plays an important role in the structuring of institutional arrangements, it should be a prominent subject in institutionalist research.[18]

There are also compelling theoretical reasons to focus on law and legal change. The juridification of economic relations, the expansion of the regulatory state, and the constitutive function of law all point to the necessity of addressing law and legal change within institutionalist theory. Law is an instrumental mechanism of policy but also inherently normative and ideological in character.[19] Hence, analyzing the politics of legal change provides an excellent way to assess both the practical and the ideational dimensions of political economic organization and their interplay in the process of reform. Legal rules and frameworks are generally difficult to alter because of political impediments such as institutional veto points and the resistance of powerful

15. See, e.g., Weir, Orloff, and Skocpol (1988) and Steinmo, Thelen, and Longstreth (1992).
16. See, e.g., Campbell (2004), Pierson (2004), Streeck and Thelen (2005), and Levy (2006).
17. See Milhaupt and Pistor (2008).
18. See Smith (1988); cf. Levi-Faur (2005) and Levi-Faur and Jordana (2005).
19. Smith (1988).

vested interests in both the state and the private sphere. These inertial tendencies thus contribute to the path dependence of institutional arrangements, including governance regimes.[20] Conversely, the study of legal reforms provides a means of gauging the direction and degree of systemic change in institutional arrangements. Corporate governance regimes are highly complex and integrated juridical frameworks that implicate intensely held interests of powerful groups. They often exhibit substantial path dependence born of domestic politics—and yet have been subject to repeated and often systemically consequential reforms. When reform politics overcomes potent sources of resistance to change, significant corporate governance reforms signal important developments in the underlying dynamics of a political economy.

In addition, the analysis of law, legal change, and the politics of reform complements the ways in which historical institutionalist theories problematize interests, and it is particularly well suited to analyzing the constitutive effects of institutional arrangements on the identities and interests of actors. As discussed above, the study of law as a constitutive mechanism traces the translation of values and ideas into norms and norms into institutional arrangements and practices. Further, law routinely embodies and adjudicates among competing, often conflicting, values, normative commitments, and conceptions of interest. Consequently, law as a social phenomenon calls into question the homogenization of interests and hierarchical ordering of values in economic theory. It compels a more realistic recognition of normative pluralism in political and economic life.

My analysis of corporate governance and its reform thus departs from the "shareholder primacy" view, common to most work in law and economics, and its hierarchy of values that prioritizes shareholder value over other competing values and stakeholder interests. The treatment of law and politics as constitutive of institutional forms problematizes economic interests and functionalist assumptions underlying much economic theory. Even in the United States, where scholars, policymakers, and judges have embraced the norm of shareholder primacy to a greater extent than elsewhere, the architecture of corporate governance retains managerialist features in tension with shareholders' interests. The German stakeholder governance regime, even after adopting numerous pro-shareholder reforms, still stands in contrast to the idea that shareholder interests are paramount. Shareholder primacy is an outcome of politics embodied in legal change—and a contested one at that. With the onset of a metastasizing economic crisis that originated in the American financial sector and corporate governance failures, political conflict over social values and economic structures is once again intensifying.

20. See, e.g., Licht (2001) and Roe (1995).

CRITICAL CASES: THE AMERICAN AND GERMAN CORPORATE GOVERNANCE REGIMES

The United States and Germany are two of the most important national models of corporate governance and political economic organization in the advanced industrial world. Both are large, wealthy, and highly sophisticated economies. Policy developments in each are consequential beyond their borders. The United States, as global hegemon of the post–cold war era, has wielded disproportionate influence on the development of the global economy and particularly on the international financial system. Germany is not only the third largest and the most successful export-oriented manufacturing economy in the world but is also at the political and economic core of the European Union, which plays an increasingly important role on the world stage.

The United States and Germany both possess historically strong yet divergent legal traditions and well-established, distinctive corporate governance regimes. Both countries have undertaken substantial reforms during the past two decades that offer fertile grounds for comparison. These reforms, in the context of the two countries' substantial *dissimilarities*, make the United States and Germany especially illuminating cases for comparative analysis. They represent contrasting "liberal" and "nonliberal" models of political economic organization and corporate governance.[21] Substantially dissimilar cases provide a robust test of convergent and path-dependent trajectories of political economic development. They also offer insight into the political dynamics of reform, not only across nations but across the juridical elements of these divergent regimes.

The United States is, to use Peter Hall and David Soskice's terminology, the preeminent liberal market economy (2001). Because it is the hub of the international financial system, policy decisions, legal reforms, and institutional changes in the United States have a profound influence around the world.[22] The American model has become the polestar for the neoliberal vision of pro-shareholder corporate governance reform and market-driven corporate restructuring. The United States has a corporate governance model defined by well-developed and extremely dynamic securities markets, diffuse shareholding, strong shareholder protections, an active market for corporate control, and the near total exclusion of labor and stakeholder interests from firm decision making and governance. However, the American liberal market order elevates the importance of law and legal institutions. In the absence or underdevelopment of alternative forms of governance, formal legal rules, rights, and enforcement mechanisms have long played a crucial role in economic ordering

---

21. See Streeck and Yamamura (2001) and Yamamura and Streeck (2003); cf. Hall and Soskice (2001) and Pontusson (2005).
22. Dore (2000).

and are tailored to a liberal, market-driven economy either by enabling contractual relations or by correcting perceived market failures.[23] The dominant mode of economic interaction in labor, financial, and other markets therefore tends to take the form of short-term and arm's-length contractual transactions embedded in regulatory frameworks.

Described variously as a "nonliberal," "coordinated market," or "social market" economy, Germany remains the most important alternative model to the neoliberalism of the United States.[24] In addition to being the world's premier manufacturing and export economy, Germany wields substantial influence over the European Union. The postwar German corporate governance regime features a stakeholder model that incorporates and protects the interests of banks and labor. Germany's long-established bank-centered financial system, concentrated stock ownership (or blockholding), and extensive corporate cross-shareholdings complemented the stakeholder model by encouraging industrial enterprises to adopt long-term adjustment and growth strategies. German economic relations are also often highly legalistic. However, German legalism embodies a long tradition of using law to fashion representational structures and institutional frameworks that channel opposing interests into negotiation rather than into formal contestation or enforcement.

Codetermination laws incorporate employees into the formal institutions of corporate governance, while German company law empowers banks, which historically have been both prominent blockholders and the principal source of debt finance, by giving them substantial control over proxy voting. German politics and law have fashioned the corporation into a "microcorporatist" institution to facilitate negotiation among the conflicting interests of management, finance, and labor. As a consequence, the German corporate governance model has tended to encourage long-term planning and incremental improvements in corporate performance that underpin the country's successful high-wage, high-skill, and high-value-added manufacturing economy.

The United States and Germany are also marked by sharp differences in state institutional structures. The American two-party system, which prevents the emergence of new party competitors, combined with the decline of organized labor and social movement politics on the left, has resulted in two pro-business parties. The multiple veto points created by the Constitution, congressional rules, and the administrative process, combined with the pluralist fragmentation of the country's interest groups, impair deliberation and

---

23. See generally Kagan (2001).

24. Following the prolonged economic malaise in Japan and the abandonment of *dirigiste* economic governance and policy in France, the American and German models are the remaining exemplars of the divergent forms taken by contemporary capitalism in large-scale economies (thus excluding much smaller Scandinavian countries with more highly centralized forms of corporatism). By focusing intensively on the German case, much of the varieties-of-capitalism literature appears to share this view.

impede coherent and sustained policymaking. The problem of coherence is compounded by a form of federalism that allocates legislative and judicial control over corporate law to the states.

In contrast, Germany's proportional representation electoral system and multiparty coalition governments allow for representation of and bargaining among a broader range of interests. It also creates a credible threat of defection from established parties should they fail to respond to the demands of significant constituencies—as shown by the rise of the Green Party in the 1980s and, more recently, the Left Party. Policy bargains are facilitated by centralized peak associations representing managers, organized labor, and banks. There are also structural factors that impede policymaking, including federalism, countervailing peak associations, strong courts, and sharply limited federal jurisdiction over collective bargaining. These features of German politics impair policymaking at the federal level to the extent that the Germans have coined the term *Reformstau* for policy paralysis. However, Germany's more centralized policymaking structures foster linkages among public and private actors and provide institutional channels for more coherent and comprehensive policy deliberations and reforms, even as they limit their speed and scope.

ORGANIZATION OF THE BOOK

The next chapter sets out the "juridical nexus" model of corporate governance and the essential role of politics in constituting it. The chapter theorizes that corporate governance regimes are a core feature of national political economies and critiques alternative approaches to the study of corporate governance and comparative political economy.

The next three chapters are the empirical core of the book and provide detailed case studies of the development and reform of the American and German corporate governance regimes. Chapter 3 presents these regimes as exemplars of the liberal market and nonliberal organized (or coordinated) forms of political economic organization. The stylized descriptions of the American and German regimes set out analytical models of the structural and juridical components that defined them during the postwar era and thus establish bases for cross-country comparison and the assessment of subsequent reforms.

Chapter 4 examines the politics of corporate governance reform in the United States from 1992 to 2005. Chapter 5 is a detailed case study of corporate governance reform in Germany from the early 1990s to 2005 that draws out the political and economic logics of reform in a nonliberal political economy with strong neocorporatist features. These chapters each leave off in

2005, when, for very different reasons, the domestic politics of both countries turned against continued reform.

Chapter 6 then turns to the corporate governance dimensions and implications of the global economic crisis that began in 2007. This discussion is necessarily speculative, given that the crisis is still unfolding and that its extraordinary severity makes its ramifications difficult to discern. What can be identified with certainty are how flaws in governance structures contributed to the crisis and its spread and how the politics of recent reforms is framing future reforms at a potentially critical juncture in political economic history.

Finally, chapter 7 returns to the theoretical analysis of corporate governance reform to set out the political and economic preconditions of reform. It explains convergent and divergent reform outcomes as the product of different strategies adopted by Center-Left state actors and of differences in interest group alignments, both cross-nationally and across juridical components of corporate governance regimes. Coalitional tensions ultimately harden resistance to reform and splinter pro-reform coalitions, leaving the underlying conflict over the transformation of power within the national political economies unresolved.

These patterns of conflict and change reveal the emergence of varieties of finance capitalism that are far from complete, fixed, or final. What is clear is not only that crises are drivers of reform but that they are substantially generated by the institutional arrangements at the foundation of national political economies. Even the economic crisis discussed here, despite its obvious international scope, cannot be understood as an exogenous shock. The origins and spread of the crisis, like those that preceded it, are rooted in *domestic* institutional arrangements and juridical frameworks and in the politics that created and maintained them.

This new financially driven economic order *may* yet foster greater innovation, efficiency, and productivity, but it may also sharpen distributional conflict, erode political economic legitimacy, and herald an era of greater stagnation and instability. The credit crisis that engulfed the United States in 2007–9 and spilled out into financial markets and institutions around the world belatedly drew attention to the deep flaws in finance capitalism and the legal and institutional arrangements of corporate governance. The stage is set for a new round of conflict, reform, and structural change in response to the deficiencies of finance capitalism. But it is inevitable that any further reforms will be built on the legal and regulatory foundations created during this most recent era of pro-shareholder and pro-market reforms. What has been done in political economies as divergent as the United States and Germany may be modified, perhaps in dramatic ways, but it will not be undone. We can be sure, however, that the corporation and its governance will be a critical field of battle in these future struggles.

CHAPTER 2

Corporate Governance as Juridical Nexus and the Politics of Reform

INTERNATIONAL FINANCE CAPITALISM AND THE FINANCIAL SECTOR TRANSFORMED

The corporation is a legal construct, and law is politically constructed. It follows from these two prosaic propositions that any understanding and explanation of corporate governance reform must integrate legal and political analysis. This synthesis of theoretical and analytical perspectives emphasizes and illuminates the central substantive concerns of this book. It situates corporate governance regimes—the formal rules, institutional arrangements, and norms that structure stakeholder power relations—in their juridical and political context and thus provides an excellent foundation for comparative analysis. The combined perspectives of law and politics sharpen our focus on the juridical foundations of governance and how its reform reflects changing power relations among interest groups and in partisan politics, struggles over the expansion and form of regulation, and the increasing financialization of advanced industrial economies. The focus on legal change and its constitutive effects requires recognition of both the partisan politics of reform, driven largely by the center-left, and the consequent reallocation of stakeholder power in favor of financial interests that alter the political terrain going forward.

This chapter sets out a theoretical framework to analyze national corporate governance regimes as the juridical nexus of company, securities, and labor relations law. These bodies of law constitute the basic institutional features of such regimes and influence the relationships among shareholders, managers, and employees as the primary stakeholders in the corporation. Political conflict drives the development of these areas of law with respect to the institutional attributes of the corporation, the rights of stakeholders within it, and the transparency of corporate finances and decision making. At the same time, established legal frameworks and institutional arrangements described by the juridical nexus shape the politics of corporate governance reform by configuring power relationships and altering the interests of stakeholder groups within the corporation. Viewing a corporate governance regime as a juridical nexus integrates comparative legal and political analysis within institutionalist theory and provides a framework that emphasizes the constitutive function of law. The nexus provides a framework to assess the politics of legal change affecting important institutional arrangements that are increasingly characterized by juridification.

The American and German corporate governance regimes and the dynamics that shaped them have been unsettled by political conflict, economic crisis, and financial globalization. During the past thirty years, globalization and the changing role of finance have transformed capitalism. These changes magnified the practical importance of corporate governance law and intensified political conflict over its reform. The recurrent crises of finance capitalism lend increasing urgency to the task of understanding the relationships among politics, law, and the corporation that contribute to the production and reproduction of this unstable political economic order.

In the early 1980s, John Zysman analyzed the relationships among states, financial systems, and firms in terms that provide a foundation for the comparative analysis of more recent corporate governance reforms. He developed a three-part typology that distinguished among (1) capital market-based financial systems, (2) credit-based systems in which the state administers prices as part of ongoing interventions in industrial affairs, and (3) credit-based systems dominated by financial institutions.[1] This typology clarified cross-national differences in institutional arrangements and state capacities in order to explain divergent modes of industrial adjustment during the postwar period and particularly in response to the wrenching economic changes of the 1970s and early 1980s.[2] The market-based financial model present in the American and British cases reinforced "arm's-length relations between government and industry" and, depriving the state and banks alike of coordinating capacity, favored "company led" industrial adjustment.[3] In contrast, finance in France and Japan conferred broad interventionist capacities on bureaucrats that favored processes of "state led" adjustment toward politically determined

---

1. Zysman (1983, 18, 69–75). For more recent analyses of national corporate governance regimes using this typology, see Cioffi (2000a, 2004b).

2. Zysman (1983, 85–91).

3. Ibid., 91–93.

economic goals.[4] In credit-based financial systems dominated by financial institutions, exemplified by West Germany, large banks performed a coordinating function in industrial development that allowed for a "tripartite negotiated" model of adjustment through negotiation among stakeholders.[5]

A quarter century later, this seminal account of national financial systems and the politics of industrial adjustment remains indispensable for understanding the political economy of finance and its influence on corporate and macroeconomic performance. Zysman explained how state capacities and politics shaped the institutional character of finance as a tool of economic policy and how the form taken by the financial system determined the mechanisms of firm-level adjustment. Comparative analysis of the structure and development of national corporate governance regimes begins with his distinction between bank-based and market-based finance. In many respects, Zysman's elucidation of the complex cross-national differences in the relationships among the state, the financial system, and the firm pioneered the comparative political analysis of corporate governance.[6]

However, understanding the implications of the extraordinary changes in financial markets and economic policy over the past twenty-five years requires a new theoretical framing of comparative political economy that accounts for the increasing importance of legal change and corporate governance reform. The world of discrete financial systems began to unravel in the 1970s, and the transformation of the financial sector has only accelerated since the mid-1980s. The erosion and collapse of the Bretton Woods regime was a consequence of the relative deterioration of American dominance in international trade.[7] The international monetary and financial regime that replaced it (often dubbed Bretton Woods II) forced the opening of the semiclosed national financial systems of the postwar international order.[8] This environment posed new political challenges for economic adjustment even more profound than those presented by the intensification of competition in international trade.

The globalization and marketization of finance during the 1980s and 1990s, enabled by the steady opening of national financial systems, fundamentally changed the relationships among politics, law, and economic governance. The emergence of open international and domestic financial markets undermined the state-led model of finance and deprived state industrial policy, already suffering declining (or negative) returns, of its most potent lever.

---

4. Ibid.
5. Ibid.
6. It is noteworthy, however, that Zysman did not use the term "corporate governance." The later ubiquity of the term is an indication of the increasing focus on the corporate firm in legal and policy debates since the early 1980s.
7. See Zysman (1983, 15).
8. See Helleiner (1994).

These conditions made negotiation of neocorporatist coordination increasingly difficult and spurred calls for greater contractual and market flexibility. This transformation of finance at the domestic and international levels unleashed political forces that altered not only the rules governing the relationships among the state, finance, industry, and labor but also the *role* of legal rules in ordering the political economy. Law became an increasingly important means of pursuing policy objectives as states withdrew from discretionary intervention in the economy yet often expanded the regulation of markets and firms. To understand how finance capitalism and its different national variants have developed, one must look to the constitutive juridical foundations of corporate governance regimes and the politics of their reform.

Recent reforms reflect the rise of a new paradigm of international finance capitalism. Rudolph Hilferding, the German socialist and finance minister during the Weimar Republic, coined the term "finance capitalism" in the early twentieth century to describe a protectionist German economy dominated by monopolistic enterprises and cartels with strong financial linkages to major banks, a political economic order that structurally anticipated the centralization and nonmarket relations of socialism.[9] In many ways, contemporary finance capitalism emerged as the antithesis of Hilferding's conception. Markets encroach upon and erode institutionalized relationships. The primacy of industrial manufacturing is displaced by the increasing dominance of finance. Competition trumps cooperation; arm's-length contracting predominates over informal and relational means of coordination. Finance capitalism today connotes a political economic order characterized by an expansion and deepening of financial markets, a loosening of ties between financial and industrial capital, and a reallocation of political and economic power toward the financial sector. It is built on a growing class of private investors, robust and expanding international capital markets, and sophisticated financial services. Legal reforms of corporate governance and financial market regulation facilitate the growth of market-driven finance as a means of channeling investment and driving economic restructuring and ultimately as a profitable end in itself.

If the postwar Bretton Woods era was one of "embedded liberalism," the era of finance capitalism could be described as one of embedded *neo*liberalism. The collapse of the Bretton Woods fixed exchange rate regime in the early 1970s precipitated the erosion of the protective semi-enclosure of national financial systems and enabled the explosive growth of international currency, securities, and derivatives markets from the 1970s through the first decade of the twenty-first century. Nationally distinctive market and bank-based financial systems endured, along with their accompanying governance regimes, but were embedded in a new and volatile financial environment that altered the power relations and incentives of political and economic actors.

9. Hilferding (1910/1981); see Höpner (2003) and Cioffi and Höpner (2006a, 2006b).

National financial systems integrated into an increasingly porous, competitive, and crisis-prone international financial marketplace.

Finance capitalism not only stoked increasing tensions between financial and industrial capital, and hence between investors and managers, but also strained the institutional and juridical foundations of stakeholder governance. The emergence of global capital markets and financial services firms transformed financial markets, firms, and sectors across the industrialized countries. The opening of domestic financial systems impaired the ability of governments to pursue Keynesian demand-side management and associated full-employment policies. The deflationary monetary policies of the 1980s, intensifying competition in international trade, and rapid growth in cross-national capital flows destabilized relationships among employers, employees, and investors.

Financial globalization became an important feature of the international economy during the 1990s and into the next decade. The burgeoning size, liquidity, and complexity of the new international financial markets were both the cause and the consequence of a rapidly growing and increasingly lucrative international financial services industry. National financial centers competed to attract capital and maintain their status in the new global financial landscape, while major financial institutions internationalized to compete for foreign market share in the most lucrative areas of finance. This dual competition altered political and economic incentives in favor of legal reforms favoring financial elites. Some observers viewed the new markets and the financial institutions that navigated them as the engines of neoliberal convergence.[10] In fact, national economic models and corporate governance regimes retained much of their distinctiveness amid the ferment and change surrounding finance. The market and bank-based financial systems identified by Zysman went through wrenching legal and structural changes, but national institutional and juridical legacies channeled them along different developmental paths.

Corporate governance reform became integral to the regulatory framework of the new finance capitalism as political elites saw its potential to promote economic adjustment and new partisan coalitions. Pro-shareholder reforms held the potential to promote financially driven corporate restructuring, along with productivity and innovation-enhancing investment at a time when state industrial policies and negotiated adjustment appeared incapable of reversing lagging growth, profits, and employment. At the same time, an increasingly market-oriented financial services sector depended on the growth and development of securities markets that, in turn, generated more political support for pro-shareholder reform by the largest, most sophisticated, and most powerful financial institutions—so long as the benefits of reform

---

10. See Rajan and Zingales (2004), Hansmann and Kraakman (2000), Strange (1996, 1998); cf. Dore (2000).

outweighed the constraints on these firms and their managers. But successful reform required these institutions to join with other groups and policy entrepreneurs to form new and often unstable alignments within fractious coalitional and partisan politics.

The juridification of economic relations has accompanied marketization, and both phenomena have steadily displaced informal, relational, and state-mediated forms of market, sectoral, and corporate governance.[11] As Steven Vogel has shown, the era of globalization and neoliberalism was one of "freer markets and more rules."[12] As the legal constitution of the corporation and the securities markets became more central to economic performance, conflicts over economic policy took the form of regulatory politics. Not surprisingly, as corporate governance reform has taken on a higher political profile, partisan and interest group struggles over the legal limits and reallocation of power within the corporation have become increasingly contentious. Understanding corporate governance reform, and the development of finance capitalism more broadly, requires analysis of the juridical subject matter of regulatory politics and the political dynamics driving legal change.

POLITICAL COALITIONS AND PARTISAN POLITICS

The comparative analysis of corporate governance has built on the dichotomy between bank-centered stakeholder-oriented regimes and market-driven shareholder-centered regimes. The influential "varieties of capitalism" theory incorporates this distinction between types of financial systems in its analytical synthesis of market-driven "liberal market economies" (LMEs) and the more institutionally mediated "coordinated market economies" (CMEs).[13] Peter Hall and David Soskice point out that corporate governance complements other institutional components of national political economic systems—such as bank-based or market-based financial systems, labor relations and employee training systems, and sectoral governance arrangements—that endow domestic firms with different core competencies and comparative competitive advantages characteristic of LMEs and CMEs.[14] In theory, economic benefits conferred by these arrangements and the intricate functional relationships among their components reinforce the interests and policy preferences of business

11. See Cioffi (2009).
12. Vogel (1996).
13. See, e.g., Hall and Soskice (2001), Gourevitch and Shinn (2005), and Vitols (2001b). However, this LME-CME typology ignores the significant institutional and operational differences Zysman identified between historically bank-centered financial systems, such as the German model, and more statist or state-directed financial systems, such as those of postwar France and Japan. Cf. Tiberghien (2007, 27–28).
14. Hall and Soskice (2001, 21–24, 27–29).

interests in favor of maintaining established institutional arrangements. Because the benefits of complementarity accrue from the systemic whole of these institutional components, the path dependence that is so prominent in the varieties-of-capitalism literature should maintain the corporate governance arrangements that form a part of these national systems.[15] However, the prevalence of pro-shareholder corporate governance reforms across the advanced industrial countries is hard to reconcile with this theoretical account.

The significant changes in national corporate governance regimes since the 1980s contradict the logics of complementarity, comparative competitive advantage, and path dependence. This discrepancy arises for two reasons. First, the theory largely ignores politics and the state in the creation, maintenance, and transformation of institutional arrangements and governance regimes. In the absence of politics, institutional complementarities are viewed as self-sustaining by virtue of their provision of nonmarket public goods, the reduction of transaction costs in coordinating different factors of production, and consequent efficiencies in sectoral and firm core competencies. Second, the assumption of unitary and coherent "business interests" underpinning the broad institutional structure of the national political economy is empirically questionable. Recent corporate governance reforms are not the product of generic business interests or even stable interest group coalitions. Interest groups generally lack the internal cohesion and coalitional stability necessary to drive the adoption of formal corporate governance reform.

To understand these reform processes, we must disaggregate the structural components and politics of corporate governance. We must deconstruct what is meant by "business" if we are to "bring business back in" to political economic analysis.[16] The corporate firm and its governance are broken down into the opposing, intersecting, and interacting interests of managers, shareholders, and employees, whose identities and interests are, in turn, substantially constituted by their legal and institutional environment. The political strength, policy preferences, and alliances of these three groups vary across the component areas of corporate governance law and across nations. Predictably, these differences in interests and political demands produce divergent policy outcomes and patterns of legal change that describe distinctive national trajectories of development even as they accommodate the new form of finance capitalism.

Reform hinges on the relationship between shifting interest group alignments and the strategies of state actors in partisan political conflict. If institutional change is viewed solely from the bottom up, as the product of interest

15. See Hall and Soskice (2001); cf. Gourevitch and Shinn (2005). Law and economics scholars have also recognized and elaborated upon the importance of path dependence in the development of corporate governance regimes. See Licht (2001), Bebchuk and Roe (1999), and Roe (1995, 2003a).
16. Cf. Hart (2004).

group pressures, the prospects for reform look daunting. However, political support for reform may be coordinated in a more top-down fashion by state actors with the resources of state power to overcome collective action problems and the capacity to draw on legal authority to legitimate new policies. From this perspective, reform appears more plausible but will tend to follow a more political and less economistic logic than in conventional interest group theories. State actors with their own interests and policy preferences can exert a substantial influence on the configuration of interest group coalitions and on the technical, normative, and ideological formulation of reform.

Yves Tiberghien, studying Japanese, French, and South Korean corporate governance reforms, makes a persuasive case that understanding the process of change in these historically statist political economies requires greater attention to the "entrepreneurial" role, policy agendas, and relative autonomy of bureaucrats.[17] He further argues that these state actors pursue reform as part of a "golden bargain" in which countries seek to attract "abundant and cheap capital flows . . . in exchange for corporate reforms that guarantee the rights of minority shareholders and a high return on investment through the facilitation of corporate restructuring."[18] The Millstein Commission's report to the Organization for Economic Cooperation and Development (OECD) advanced a similar argument that the need to attract financial capital and increase the supply of domestic investment drives (or should drive) corporate governance reforms across the advanced industrialized countries.[19] Policymakers have promoted reforms to develop and maintain the attractiveness of national equity markets. However, the reasons for this are only indirectly related to increasing the amount of foreign capital channeled into domestic equity financing. Until the credit crisis of 2007–9, the world was awash in capital, and most established firms continued to rely on debt and retained earnings for financing over more expensive equity capital.

Likewise, administrative agencies and bureaucrats are undoubtedly important in policy formulation and implementation (witness the importance of the Securities and Exchange Commission in the United States), but in liberal and more neocorporatist political economies they do not have the kind of autonomous influence they do (or did) in countries such as Japan and France, where bureaucrats have traditionally wielded broader discretionary powers. Accordingly, in the United States and Germany, partisan conflict and interest group alignments loom larger in the politics of corporate governance. The entrepreneurial role played by state actors under these conditions consists in their framing and formulating legislative reform agendas and mobilizing supportive interest group coalitions.

17. Tiberghien (2007, 13–27).
18. Ibid., xii.
19. Millstein (1998).

TABLE 2.1: COALITIONAL LOGIC OF COMPARATIVE CORPORATE GOVERNANCE (WINNERS LISTED FIRST)

Coalitional Alignments	Governance Regime	Shareholding Pattern
Managers-shareholders vs. employees	Investor	Diffusion (Separation of ownership and control)
Managers-employees vs. shareholders	Corporatist compromise	Blockholding (Unity of ownership and control)
Shareholders-employees vs. managers	Transparency coalition	Diffusion
Managers vs. Shareholders-employees	Managerial	Diffusion
Shareholders vs. managers-employees	Oligarchy	Blockholding
Employees vs. managers-shareholders	Labor	Blockholding

Source: Adapted from Gourevitch and Shinn (2005, 23, 60, tables 2.3 and 4.1).

Peter Gourevitch and James Shinn have recognized the importance of interest group politics by describing corporate governance as a set of institutionalized relationships among managers, shareholders, and employees. They synthesize theories of interest group coalitions, principal-agent problems within the firm, and varieties of capitalism to explain cross-national differences in stock ownership patterns and the separation of ownership and control.[20] This coalitional model has the virtue of providing an elegant theoretical map of the interest group foundations of different corporate governance regimes—and their relation to broader institutional arrangements in national political economies. Using a rational-choice framework, Gourevitch and Shinn set out the array of coalitional possibilities and specify their predicted effect on patterns of shareholding and corporate control (table 2.1).

Of particular interest are the three coalitional arrangements in which there is a victorious pairing of corporate constituencies. These not only are politically plausible; they also highlight the complexities of coalitional dynamics in shaping governance regimes. The political logic of the "investor" and "corporatist compromise" coalitions closely resembles the dichotomy between LMEs and CMEs in the varieties-of-capitalism literature. In the investor coalition, managers and shareholders align against employees to advance policies and rules that favor the maximization of returns to capital

20. Gourevitch and Shinn (2005).

and divide rents between shareholders and managers (leading to higher executive compensation). They exclude labor from firm governance, excepting employees in their capacity as shareholders through individual, mutual fund, or pension investments. Legal constraints on managerial shirking and opportunism should encourage both the maximization of shareholder value and more diffuse shareholding—but at the expense of longer-term planning and relative income equality.

The corporatist compromise between managers and employees strengthens managerial autonomy against investor threats and protects employees' interests by strengthening their bargaining position and shielding them from the brunt of firm restructuring and adjustment costs. Blockholding patterns of concentrated ownership counter the corporatist alliance and reduce managerial insulation from shareholder monitoring and influence. The corporatist compromise therefore should discourage equity financing in favor of lower-risk bank and debt financing that yields the sort of patient capital, long-term financial ties, and cooperative relations between management and labor characteristic of CMEs. This is precisely the sort of complementarity of institutions and economic relationships at the center of the varieties-of-capitalism theory. Alterations of institutional structures that would change investment patterns and time horizons threaten the complementarities that underpin the comparative economic advantages of these divergent models.

The "transparency coalition" of shareholders and employees helps explain substantial reforms of regimes that favor shareholder interests and are deliberately designed to foster the development of securities markets and market-driven financial services in nonliberal political economies. This alliance favors strong disclosure rules with respect to corporate finances, profits, and risk profiles. Shareholders want to ensure the flows of information they need to accurately value their investments and increase market pressures on managers to raise share values. Employees and organized labor also favor transparency to constrain inept or opportunistic managers, to protect their pension assets and other shareholdings, or to glean information useful in bargaining with employers. But the transparency coalition raises more questions than it answers. How, why, and when does it form? Is it stable and enduring? Does it actually account for the pro-shareholder reforms that have become so widespread and pronounced?

The coalitional politics of corporate governance reform plays out in ways that are considerably more complicated than those suggested by Gourevitch and Shinn. My departure from their account in my analysis of reform is grounded on four analytical propositions.

First, corporate governance as a legal and policy construct cannot be viewed as an undifferentiated whole. Rather, it is a composite construct of company, securities, and labor relations law—the juridical nexus of corporate governance. This presents a serious problem in terms of political analysis. No single coalition necessarily dominates reform across all three bodies of law. Managers, shareholders, and employees do not have the same preferences or intensity of interest across these areas of law and policy.[21] Managers are particularly sensitive to changes in the allocation of power and authority under company and labor law that might threaten their autonomy. Shareholders are keenly interested in enhanced transparency regulation (to which managers may be amenable), but they also have an interest in company law reform to increase managerial accountability, which is more likely to spark conflict between these two groups. Labor is most intensely interested in governance-related aspects of labor relations law, though it may have lower intensity interests in increasing transparency and managerial accountability—so long as reform does not increase the threat of rent extraction at employee expense (e.g., takeovers). Consequently, stakeholder groups may have common ground to form an alliance with respect to one legal policy area but may form alternative—and potentially opposing—coalitions regarding others.

Further, not all coalitions are created equal. Some are more stable, potent, and enduring. For example, manager-shareholder coalitions tend to encompass wide areas of agreement and should endure over time (at least where managers receive high levels of compensation in de facto exchange for their loss of autonomy and job security). In contrast, the shareholder-employee transparency coalition is founded on the narrowest of grounds and should prove the most unstable. The areas of conflict between the partners—encompassing takeover law, norms of shareholder primacy, stakeholder rights and employee representation, and distributional issues—are likely to outweigh their agreement on stronger disclosure regulation, at least once securities regulation has been reformed. Hence, the shareholder-employee transparency coalition may have a significant impact on policymaking, particularly when cultivated by state actors, but it is likely to be unstable and difficult to sustain.

Second, institutionalist and comparative analysis of politics compels recognition of the contingency and variation in the identities, power, and interests of actors and groups. Their interests, policy preferences, and influence vary across institutional, and thus national, contexts. Characterizing shareholders as a *politically* salient stakeholder constituency is especially problematic. Shareholders as a group are politically weak because of relatively low levels of shareholding and equity finance in most countries, and because of serious collective-action problems where securities markets are well developed and shareholding is widespread and diffuse. Accordingly, corporate governance reform relies more on the support of powerful financial institutions with an economic stake in promoting securities markets and shareholding than on shareholders themselves. Yet this introduces a cross-cutting cleavage into the coalitional picture: large financial institutions may advocate some shareholder

---

21. See Mabe (2004).

interests, but they are run by managers whose support for reform is tempered by their own interests in autonomy and income maximization.

Labor's interests and influence in reform vary cross-nationally. American organized labor is politically and economically feeble but financially strong as a result of its role in the public and private employee pension systems. Organized labor is a powerful and influential constituency in Germany, inside both the corporation and the political system, but in a country with an extensive welfare state and predominantly public pensions it has had few direct ties to the financial system and shareholders. For institutional reasons, labor's interests overlap with those of shareholders to a greater degree in the United States than in Germany, with significant implications for the plausibility, stability, and policy agendas of shareholder-labor alliances.

Third, coalitional politics presents the problem (duly acknowledged by Gourevitch and Shinn) of *conflict within stakeholder groups*.[22] Interest groups frequently display internal divisions that complicate the prediction of their preferences and alignments. Managers are not a unified group but span sectors, including financial services, a situation that informs their policy preferences. Managers of different types of firms, from large, internationalized publicly traded companies to small and medium-sized enterprises, have very different interests and preferences regarding the regulation and structure of the financial sector. Labor is not a unified class but a group fractured by unionization status, sector, skill level, and—not least—stock ownership in various forms. Shareholders are divided among different types and sizes of financial institutions, different types of institutional investors, blockholders, and small minority investors. As the predominant mix within stakeholder groups varies cross-nationally, so too will the possibilities for coalition formation.

The unstable and shifting coalitional foundations of corporate governance regimes risk destroying the institutional complementarities central to the varieties-of-capitalism theory, and they drive constant reform and change instead of producing a stable institutional and policy equilibrium. Stakeholder groups and coalitions contain latent cleavages that can be exploited by opponents and policymakers. The struggle over reform is therefore not a three-way battle among managers, shareholders, and labor but one among a larger array of subgroups, which may form shifting alliances in favor of or in opposition to reform, depending upon the juridical area in question. This also suggests the potential of these different areas of law and the institutions they shape to become mismatched, their development characterized by political tendencies toward systemic incoherence and dysfunction.

Fourth, the fractious character of interest group politics increases the importance and centrality of state actors in the process of reform. In order to create and preserve the coalitional configurations that will help maintain their

22. Gourevitch and Shinn (2005, 25).

power and authority, state actors must mobilize and align interest group coalitions. In the corporate governance context, this function is particularly important because of the collective weakness of shareholders, leaving them in need of coalition partners and political advocates, and the uncertainty and ambivalence group members may have regarding their interests and policy preferences. State actors take on a more central and autonomous role in reform as interest group politics become more fractious and interests more uncertain. The strategic and ideological interests of state actors therefore have a substantial effect on the course of reform.

The political logic of corporate governance reform remains primarily domestic as state actors actively cultivate interest group support for their preferred policies and as the resulting coalitional alliances, in turn, influence the substantive content of specific changes in law and policy. In part, this is a supply-side argument. Politicians and parties frame and advance governance reform agendas to strengthen their base of coalitional support and increase their electoral appeal. They advocate legal reforms that promise to solve perceived economic problems and foster the legitimacy of political economic arrangements. There is also a demand side to the argument. The *interests of powerful financial institutions,* not those of shareholders (or managers, as argued by Culpepper [forthcoming, 2010]), have been politically pivotal in reform. The reform agenda has encompassed three mutually reinforcing goals. Obviously, it entails greater legal protections for shareholders. Second, the reforms help develop large and liquid securities markets that have potentially enormous value to large financial institutions. Third, many reform advocates viewed stronger shareholder rights and more developed markets as means to facilitate financially driven corporate restructuring, and thus improved economic performance and the growth of financial services.

Highlighting the centrality of partisan and interest group politics in structuring corporate governance raises questions of what political configurations produced the legal and institutional foundations of different types of governance regimes and which political dynamics drive reform. Mark Roe has advanced the argument that social democratic politics precludes both the development of extensive equity financing through securities markets and the separation of ownership and control characteristic of the American corporate governance model.[23] The "social democracy thesis" shares with the varieties-of-capitalism literature an emphasis on the path dependence of national models of capitalism at the expense of minimizing the significance and political provenance of the corporate governance and securities market reforms of recent decades. Roe argues that strong labor unions and social democratic parties prevent shareholders from maximizing their returns. This is by contrast with the situation in liberal market economies, like those of the United

23. Roe (2003b).

States and United Kingdom, where labor is weaker and the political Right stronger or, perhaps more accurate, where the entire political spectrum is shifted rightward. Because of limited returns to equity under social democracy, shareholding is less attractive, stock markets languish, and firms rely largely on retained earnings and turn to loans and other forms of debt for external finance. Where shareholders are poorly protected by law, less capital flows into stock markets, and self-protection is secured by greater use of block-holding by controlling shareholders. Roe elaborates on the famous Berle and Means analysis of the separation of ownership and control and finds that separation occurs and securities markets flourish where labor is weak and where national politics favors the containment of managerial agency costs to shareholders. The quality of corporate governance law cannot explain cross-national divergence; it is a proxy for politics.[24]

The social democracy thesis gets the postwar politics of corporate governance backward.[25] Social democracy, a political economic order fashioned and maintained by a strong Center-Left party and labor movement, did not retard the development of securities markets and the dispersion of shareholding; postwar *conservative* politics did. The error is in misunderstanding the ideological and coalitional character of nonliberal conservatism. Conservative parties in industrialized countries like Germany, Japan, France, and Italy fashioned and maintained political economic orders characterized to varying degrees by bank-based finance, concentrated shareholding, cross-shareholding within networks of firms, strong legal protections for employees, and relatively egalitarian distributions of income.[26] Outside the Anglo-American democracies, conservatism cannot be equated with neoliberalism. Even in the United States conservative politics supported a pre-Depression bank-based system of concentrated stock ownership, interlocking directorates, and financial networks that was finally uprooted by the post-New Deal regulatory regime.

The social democracy thesis obscures both the origins of nonliberal capitalism and the partisan politics and substantive outcomes of corporate governance reform of recent decades. Conservative parties in liberal and nonliberal political economies alike have long maintained close ties to managerial and financial elites, just as Center-Left parties have been allied with labor. The destabilization of this tripartite alliance on the right is one of the most important political aspects of corporate governance reform. The postwar national models of capitalism embodied a capital-labor accord, but they also institutionalized relations between financial and managerial elites in ways that contained conflicts over corporate control. Once an economic peace was

24. Ibid. (critiquing the "legal family" theory of equity market development and the separation of ownership and control).
25. Cioffi (2004a) and Cioffi and Höpner (2006a, 2006b).
26. Cioffi and Höpner (2006a, 2006b); see also the essays collected in Streeck and Yamamura (2001), especially those by Streeck, Jackson, and Vitols.

established between management and finance capital, both groups could be incorporated into a stable political coalition on the right.

The post-1973 economic crises afflicting the Western industrialized countries and the subsequent transformation of international capital markets and finance undermined these economic relations along with the political alliances that reinforced them. Consequently, many of the same economic pressures that weakened postwar social democracy also eroded the political foundations of conservatism. This placed conservative parties in a dilemma: whether to support managers or financial interests when these groups came into conflict. In general, they supported managers, thereby giving Center-Left parties an opening to cultivate the support of the financial sector and shareholders.[27] Seizing this political opportunity, the Center-Left made peace with financial globalization and the marketization of finance.[28] The politics of corporate governance reform was driven by this shift.

At first glance, it appears paradoxical that corporate governance reform has largely been a project of the Center-Left, often against resistance from the Right. Center-Left parties championed reform as a way to foster more dynamic financial systems. They hoped to deliver higher rates of growth, innovation, and employment in an era in which Keynesian fine-tuning had fallen to stagflation and industrial policy had become increasingly ineffective and difficult to finance. This striking development was in part attributable to Center-Left parties' turn to the right. It was part of a broader political trend embodied in the rise of the neoliberal Democratic Leadership Council and President Bill Clinton's legislative "triangulation" strategy in the United States, Chancellor Gerhard Schröder's Neue Mitte in Germany, and Prime Minister Tony Blair's New Labor agenda in the United Kingdom. However, economic and political changes also created new opportunities for Center-Left parties to pursue their programmatic (or at least rhetorical) preferences for constraining managerial power, expanding regulation of business, and democratizing the economy. They used securities market and corporate governance reform to mobilize the support of, and forge alliances among, large financial institutions, institutional investors, and unions while appealing to the growing number of middle-class shareholders. The reform agenda helped achieve these political ends. The active role of the Center-Left in reform produced new variants of finance capitalism, rather than retarding its development.[29]

In political economies as disparate as the United States and Germany (as well as in the rest of the European Union Big Four: France, Italy, and, to a lesser extent, the United Kingdom), the Center-Left repositioned itself to press

---

27. Cioffi and Höpner (2006a, 2006b).

28. See Abdelal (2007, 16–17, 31–32).

29. The affinity between social democracy and finance capitalism is also indicated by high stock market capitalization rates in Scandinavia and the Netherlands.

for corporate governance reform.[30] The Democratic Party in the United States used the post-bubble scandals and the collapse of share prices to attack the Republican Party with an appeal to the approximately one-half of middle-class voters who were also investors.[31] The reforms of the German Social Democratic Party (SPD) reforms satisfied left-wing and populist constituencies by targeting managerial and (to some extent) banking elites.[32] They also formed part of a strategy to lure political and electoral support from the middle class and financial sector by promoting policies that promised higher returns to savings, greater efficiency in capital allocation, more rapid rates of growth and innovation, and economic restructuring at the corporate level. In each case, economic crisis and scandal weakened the opponents of reform. In both countries, conservative parties tended to defend a managerial elite and corporate status quo increasingly brought into disrepute by systemic dysfunction.

Corporate governance reform also fit surprisingly well within the emerging contours of Center-Left ideology. The Democratic Party and the SPD were both committed to the development of the regulatory state as a counterweight to managerial authority, corporate power, and market failures. Both parties had a strategic and ideological interest in shoring up the perceived fairness and equity of markets that absorbed increasing shares of working- and middle-class pension and retirement savings. The rhetoric of shareholder democracy was equated with broader and more venerable notions of economic democracy. Governance and securities law reform thus appealed to both the Center-Left's egalitarian ideology and its welfare state agendas—even as the practical consequences of these reforms often undermined such commitments. The general point holds: corporate governance reform has been largely a project of the political Left—not the ostensibly pro-business or neoliberal Right.

This analysis of partisan and coalitional politics helps explain the incidence and general direction of corporate governance reform but cannot account for or even describe its legal character or significance. Corporate governance is inherently law-intensive. After all, by definition the corporation (as opposed to the generic business firm) exists only as the creation of law. Corporate governance reflects the necessity of complex legal frameworks as a foundation for capitalism and the increasing juridification of political economic organization. Just as its political determinants vary cross-nationally, its juridical form varies across legal systems. These legal forms are outcomes of politics, and they also play a significant constitutive role in shaping the institutional context, interests, and even the identities of the groups that drive reform. Understanding both the *substance* and the trajectory of corporate governance reform requires comparative analysis of both law and politics.

30. See Cioffi and Höpner (2006a, 2006b).
31. Cioffi (2007).
32. Cioffi (2002), Höpner (2003), Cioffi and Höpner (2006a), and Lütz and Eberle (2007).

CORPORATE GOVERNANCE AS JURIDICAL NEXUS

The Juridical Nexus

Corporate governance, as the term is used here, is constituted by a juridical nexus of securities, company, and labor relations law that structurally allocates power among managers, shareholders, and employees within the corporation.[33] Each of these stakeholder groups is a "corporate insider." Economically, each bears a significant level of residual risk regarding the performance of the corporation.[34] From an institutional perspective, each plays an important role in the corporation's patterns of hierarchical authority, organizational structure, business strategies, core competitive competencies, distribution of income, and internal norms of obligation and trust (or the lack thereof). Politically, these groups are the most important protagonists—and often antagonists—in contests for control over corporate decision making and resources. As these conflicts spill over into politics and law, they are resolved by state actors in widely varying ways that reflect the configuration of interests and allocation of power within the broader political economy.

This restriction of corporate governance to corporate insiders excludes suppliers, customers, local communities, and members of the general public, all of whom are outside the firm's boundaries.[35] Perhaps more controversially, it also excludes creditors, such as lenders and bondholders, on the grounds that they protect their interests via collateralization and risk-adjusted interest rates. Established legal frameworks of corporate governance distinguish between shareholders and debt holders by recognizing the former as participants in governance processes while giving debt holders priority protection and the lead role in bankruptcy proceedings. This distinction reflects the importance of legal structures in defining the relevant actors within corporate governance regimes.

The tripartite group structure of corporate governance corresponds to a tripartite juridical nexus of company (or corporate), securities, and labor relations law. These bodies of law share a common attribute of defining the status and power relations of insider constituencies within corporate governance. Traditional, and rather anachronistic, conceptions of public and private law would locate these legal areas within the bounds of private law, as their core concerns are the relationships among private parties rather than internal operations of the state or relations between the state and private citizens or

---

33. Cioffi (2002, 574) and Fligstein and Choo (2005, 62).

34. In fact, managers and especially employees may bear more concentrated residual risk of corporate failure than would a rationally well-diversified shareholder (Blair 1995).

35. The legal interests of these groups are defined and protected through contract and/or forms of social and economic regulation outside the domain of corporate governance.

entities. The components of the juridical nexus are bodies of *public* law both by virtue of their authoritative allocation of values to achieve governmental (i.e., public) purposes and because they constitute an institutional form that would not otherwise exist.[36] They jointly define the essential formal institutional attributes of the corporation, its internal power relations, and its decision-making procedures. They not only regulate conduct through enabling, pre-scriptive, and prohibitive provisions but also shape, order, and mediate the interests of the principal internal stakeholder groups involved in corporate affairs. In short, the juridical nexus establishes the boundaries and internal structural relations of corporate governance. Together, these bodies of law constitute distinctive and enduring national governance regimes.

Figure 2.1 illustrates the relationships among these bodies of public law and how they together constitute corporate governance regimes by delimiting and informing the governance relations among shareholders, managers, and employees. Each of these bodies must reconcile the competing normative claims, interests, and demands of clashing corporate—and political—constit-uencies. Company law creates the governance structure of the firm that addresses the contentious relationships and conflicts among all three stake-holder groups. In contrast with the functional specialization of securities and labor law, company law performs a mediating function by providing an institu-tional structure for corporate decision making and conflict resolution.[37] It must reconcile the competing demands and interests of multiple corporate constituencies, and this is reflected in its position between securities law and labor relations law. Elements of labor relations law pertaining to corporate governance mediate manager-labor conflict by creating, or effectively pre-cluding, formal mechanisms of employee participation in corporate decision making.[38] Securities law primarily regulates the conflict between managers and shareholders through prescriptive transparency and disclosure rules (including accounting rules and principles) that address the pervasive infor-mation asymmetries in securities markets and decision making.

These bodies of law function jointly, often with explicit reference to each other, to define the structure of the corporation as an institutional form and to shape the incentives and interests of its stakeholders. Ideally, the juridical nexus produces a governance framework that promotes the productive long-term allocation and use of resources by limiting the threats of opportunism from all stakeholders. The priority, of course, is to constrain managerial

36. Shapiro (1972, 413).
37. Cf. Pound (1993), elaborating on the "political" model of the corporation.
38. As discussed in chapter 3, even in the United States, where employees and labor law would appear to be irrelevant to corporate governance, judicial decisions have implicitly recog-nized the importance of labor by explicitly excluding employees from "managerial" decision making.

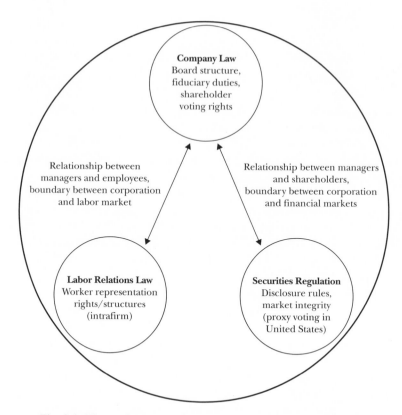

Company Law
Board structure,
fiduciary duties,
shareholder
voting rights

Relationship between
managers and employees,
boundary between corporation
and labor market

Relationship between managers
and shareholders,
boundary between corporation
and financial markets

Labor Relations Law
Worker representation
rights/structures
(intrafirm)

Securities Regulation
Disclosure rules,
market integrity
(proxy voting in
United States)

Fig. 2.1 *The juridical nexus of national corporate governance regimes*

discretion to maximize power via insulation from stakeholder, shareholder, and capital market pressures.

This legal-institutional model of corporate governance excludes antitrust, bankruptcy, pension and mutual fund, and contract law. It likewise excludes social regulation such as employment, environmental, and workplace safety law. None of these areas regulate or modify the firm's internal governance relationships. Antitrust law remains outside the analytical field of corporate governance because it addresses the size of the corporation relative to its market(s) and its behavior vis-à-vis the *external* environment (whether defined by product or geographical markets, consumer interests, competitors, or relations with other firms). It does not per se structure the corporation's *internal* governance relations.[39] Likewise, managerial, entrepreneurial, and investment

39. The Clayton Act prohibits interlocking directorates, but this has had a negligible effect on American corporate governance. Neil Fligstein (1990) has argued persuasively that American antitrust law had a significant impact on corporate governance, indirectly encouraging a financial conception of corporate control. However, Mark Roe (1996) observes that corporate governance largely usurped the centrality of antitrust as the relaxation of antitrust enforcement in the 1980s enabled successive waves of takeovers and mergers.

behavior may be shaped in the shadow of bankruptcy law, but it does not define the formal governance relations within the firm.[40] The same may be said of pension and mutual fund regulation (and the tax rules that powerfully shape the funds' investment strategies).[41]

The division of corporate governance into company, securities, and labor relations law has significant functional, jurisprudential, and political consequences. These bodies of law may be under the control of different levels of government in federal systems.[42] Legislative, oversight, and regulatory responsibilities regarding these bodies of law may be vested in different parts of the state (e.g., legislative committees, ministries or executive departments, and regulatory authorities). Rule making, interpretation, and enforcement may be entrusted to different entities as well, including independent and non-independent regulatory agencies, private quasi-autonomous self-regulatory bodies, and prosecutors and/or private litigants before courts.

Different interest group configurations among management, labor, and shareholders may underlie each of these bodies of law as well. These alliances are informed by the interests and policy preferences of these groups as shaped by the existing legal regime, just as their political strategies regarding reform are shaped by the available channels of policy and legal change—including institutional capacities for deliberation, negotiation, coordination, and/or litigation among actors and groups. Accordingly, the tripartite juridical nexus of company, securities, and labor relations law is not merely a manifestation of legal formalism. Both its form and its substance reflect political, as well as legal, conditions that affect the trajectories of corporate governance reform.

The juridical nexus conception of corporate governance departs from the dominant neoclassical economic theory of the firm as a "nexus of contracts" and the closely related normative commitment to shareholder primacy.[43] Most important, the nexus-of-contracts conception is a theory of the *firm* as the product of individual, economically rational transactions, *not* of the *corporation*

40. The passage of a firm into bankruptcy creates a new legal entity with separate rights, interests, and a distinct governance structure designed to balance the goals of salvaging troubled enterprises and protecting the firm's creditors.
41. Mark Roe (1991) has shown how legal regulation and taxation of institutional investors encouraged or compelled dispersion of shareholding, and thus deliberately separated ownership and control, in the post-New Deal United States. These rules did not directly alter firm governance structures or practices, and the dispersion of shareholding has become self-perpetuating. Later attempts to legally compel institutional activism in governance were defeated politically or were disappointing in practice.
42. For example, American federalism traditionally left most, if not all, corporate law to the states, while federal law and independent agencies predominated in securities and labor law. Conversely, Germany has long had a uniform federal labor and company law, while securities law was, until the mid-1990s, under the control of the *Länder* (states).
43. Jensen and Meckling (1976). Variations on the neoclassical theory of the firm that derived, for example, from transaction cost economics or property rights theories are beyond the scope of this discussion. For a critique of the contractualist view, see Eisenberg (1999).

as inherently a creation of law and politics. Even under highly permissive enabling rules, the corporation is an institutional form fashioned from a set of legally established structural attributes, internal procedures, and the allocation of authority, rights, and obligations. These features, including choices between mandatory and enabling approaches to corporate governance law, are the product of politics.[44]

In contrast, the contractarian paradigm doubly dissolves the corporation. First, the corporation as a complex hierarchical entity vanishes into innumerable component contracts; its qualitative organizational and institutional characteristics become unrecognizable. Second, many of these discrete transactions dissolve into *incomplete* contracts, in which substantive terms largely evaporate. Emptied of content, they represent authority relations that are the hallmark of institutional organization. The nexus-of-contracts theory therefore becomes self-annihilating at the level of the contractual transaction, its basic unit of analysis. In this light, the legal rules and institutional norms that structure the corporation become *more* important, not less, in defining the organizational form and its internal patterns of authority. Contracting occurs in the space left it by the legal framework described by the juridical nexus of corporate governance law.

The nexus-of-contracts conception of the firm also tends to collapse normative and empirical claims. The corporate structures and the disclosure and transactional practices mandated by law, even in its most permissive manifestations, are viewed as either contracts that the parties *would have* negotiated in the absence of legal rules but for market failures or as *unwarranted departures* from a hypothetically efficient baseline of bilateral contracting. Moreover, the incomplete contracts comprising the corporation render indeterminate the identities of principal and agent. In the case of the manager-employee, the ambiguity is more theoretical than real. But in the case of investors, is the shareholder the principal or are managers "hiring" capital via shareholder agents who can exit, as can employees, if they become dissatisfied with the relationship?

Shareholder primacy provides a normative answer to this question by designating shareholders as principals and provides the baseline against which legal rules are assessed. This norm is justified, again theoretically, as optimizing both efficiency and welfare. But shareholder primacy is hardly a universal characteristic of actual corporate governance regimes and does not appear in unadulterated form even in the most shareholder-friendly liberal

---

44. Enabling or default rules allow for greater flexibility in modifying firm governance via the corporate charter and bylaws, giving rise to debates over the propensity of such permissive rules to promote efficient bargaining or rent-seeking by managers and/or controlling shareholders. Default rules still influence outcomes because they inform identities, initial negotiating positions, and normative expectations of the parties and because bargaining to replace them is costly.

market political economies. As noted above, law reflects the interests and values of rival groups, and comparative analysis of corporate governance compels recognition of this basic fact, especially in light of cross-national variation in the governance role of labor. Even where shareholder primacy is recognized as a legal principle, the norm is the product of politics and could not persist absent political support. Shareholder primacy also does not adequately capture the structural features of corporate governance, variations in governance and disclosure rights, or the effectiveness of enforcement mechanisms. The political analysis of corporate governance and its reform explains how these juridical and institutional features developed as products of different domestic power relations.

Market-Enabling Law and Structural Regulation

A second dimension of analysis relies on the distinction between types of legal rules underlying the tripartite-juridical-nexus conception of corporate governance.[45] Legal scholars have classified the various approaches to governance regulation into the heuristically useful (though non-exhaustive) taxonomy set forth in table 2.2. These categories may overlap. The distinction between rules and standards is porous—legal mechanisms such as mandatory disclosure or fiduciary duties may take the form of either. Similarly, "governance strategies" may take the form of regulation and *vice versa*. Some of these mechanisms, such as the moral and reputational components of the "trusteeship" approach, are not even properly considered legal. But setting out the various approaches to the problems of corporate governance provides a useful overview of the legal mechanisms available to policymakers and a point of entry in analyzing the structures of governance and the politics underlying them.

I condense and reclassify these rule types into a fundamental distinction between "market-enabling rules" and "structural regulation."[46] To illustrate the categories, a non-exhaustive list of market-enabling rules and forms of

45 The distinction among securities, company, and labor relations law can be criticized as excessively legalistic and the artifact of historical divisions that have become ever more blurred and overlapping. Arguably, this is an analytically imprecise way of distinguishing among the legal mechanisms of governance and regulation. Further analytical distinctions among different mechanisms of regulation address these objections.

46. This differentiation between market-enabling rules and structural regulation owes a debt to Hirschmann's (1970/1981) conceptions of "exit" and "voice" as organizational principles. It is also similar to Zetzsche's distinction between "implicit" and "explicit" systems of corporate control. Implicit systems rely on market prices and pressures to constrain behavior and thus favor legal rules that enhance market liquidity and the ability of shareholders to exit the firm via selling shares at fair market price (2004, 19–29). Explicit systems rely on shareholder voice through legal structures that allow their direct influence or participation in corporate decisions. Ibid.

TABLE 2.2: TAXONOMY OF JURIDICAL APPROACHES TO GOVERNANCE	
Regulatory Strategies	
Rules	Specific mandatory ex ante behavioral prescription or prohibitions
Standards	General ex ante norms of behavior defined by ex post application and adjudication
Affiliation terms	Rules or standards governing ex ante disclosure to potential investors; ex post rights of financial withdrawal/share transfer and delisting
Governance Strategies	
Appointment rights	Rights and procedures regarding selection and removal of directors and managers
Decision rights	Rights and procedures regarding initiation and ratification of major corporate decisions
Material incentives	Compensation structures ("pay for performance," equity stakes, and stock options) to align stakeholder interests
Trusteeship	Moral suasion and reputational incentives limiting opportunism by directors, managers, and controlling shareholders

structural regulation is set forth in table 2.3.[47] Market-enabling rules, most prominently disclosure and transparency rules, redress asymmetric information and other agency problems that inhibit or impair efficient market functioning. They may mandate ex ante conduct, such as the timely and public disclosure of financial information, conflicts of interest, or specific decision-making procedures, but they are typically enforced by ex post rights-based claims for damages or other forms of compensation. Securities law, in particular, imposes substantial disclosure obligations, but the principal remedy is through suits for securities fraud or breach of fiduciary duty. Underlying market-enabling rules is the recognition that sophisticated financial markets do not arise naturally and, in fact, require supportive legal and regulatory frameworks to function in an efficient and socially legitimate fashion.

Market-segmentation regulation is a second variant of market-enabling rules. These rules define and limit entry to different markets and functionally differentiated lines of business. For example, the Glass-Steagall Act (prior to its erosion and repeal) mandated the separation of commercial and investment banking, while post-Enron reforms restricted accounting firms from performing consulting services for audit clients. Market- and business-segmentation rules historically played a more important role in the United States, with its deliberately fragmented financial system, than in most countries with forms of

---

47. Adapted and modified from Kraakman et al. (2004, 23–28, table 2-1). Focusing on company law, Kraakman et al. largely exclude disclosure rights and remedies under securities regulation from their taxonomy, though they do touch upon their importance elsewhere in the volume. See ibid., chap. 8.

TABLE 2.3: ILLUSTRATIVE FORMS OF MARKET ENABLING AND STRUCTURAL REGULATION	
Market-enabling rules	
Financial reporting and disclosure rules	Transparency of financial information and governance practices; form and timing of disclosure
Accounting rules and principles	Accuracy of financial disclosure
Fiduciary duties	Duties regarding conflicts of interest and disclosure of financial information
Share transferability rules	Insider trading; bearer versus registered shares; restrictions on timing of share trading (blackout periods imposed on all or some shareholders)
Market segmentation	Definition and separation of markets and lines of business (e.g., commercial and investment banking, auditing and consulting)
Structural regulation	
Board composition and elections	Procedures for board nominations and election; mandatory independent director rules; board codetermination (employee representation)
Board role and capacities	Independent director requirements; functionally specialized committees (e.g., auditing, nomination, compensation); Power to amend corporate charter/bylaws; hiring/oversight of auditor, counsel, board staff; responsibilities for risk controls, legal compliance
Works council codetermination	Formation/election rules; employee codecision and consultation rights
Shareholder communication and voting	Proxy voting rules; voting rights (e.g., voting caps, one share–one vote, supermajority/blocking minority)
Takeovers	Fiduciary duties defining permissible defenses, decision-making standards/procedures, and "change of control" compensation packages
Shareholders' meeting	Decisional powers of shareholders; requirements for calling shareholder meetings

universal banking. In recent decades, however, pressures from deregulation and financial-sector consolidation have diminished the importance of market- and business-segmentation rules in financial system organization and corporate governance, placing greater stress on other regulatory mechanisms.

Structural regulation fashions the corporation into a self-regulating institution by altering its internal structure and power relations through the allocation of control rights and the creation of formal institutional channels for information flows and negotiation among stakeholder groups. This intervention into the private sphere of the corporation provides ex ante rules allocating control over decision making, often with formal ex post enforcement mechanisms in reserve to reinforce bargaining relationships. Structural regulation may recognize (or exclude) groups as participants in governance processes, expand (or limit) their participation in corporate decision making, or define and assign the legal duties of governance participants.

Structural regulation may be used to promote a wide array of objectives and values. It may advance shareholder primacy by addressing the conflicts of interest and principal-agent problems endemic to the corporate form, address coordination problems that affect economic functionality, or promote values such as economic and industrial democracy. For example, German shareholders have the right to vote on a wider range of business decisions in the shareholders' meeting than do U.S. shareholders, and major issues must decided by a supermajority vote, creating a 25 percent blocking minority threshold. In contrast to the American system, under which managers control proxy votes and the voting patterns of stockbrokers are traditionally pro-management, German law gives universal banks the right to vote the large number of shares their brokerage clients deposit with them. Likewise, employees are formally incorporated into the governance of the German corporation through codetermination laws that provide for worker representation on boards and works councils. Conversely, decision making by American managers and directors is more constrained by complex fiduciary duties in takeover situations—and shareholders have the right to enforce them in court.

Both types of rules may be found within company, securities, and labor relations law. Moreover, the same doctrinal area may take on the form and functions of market-enabling rules and structural regulation.[48] Fiduciary duties under company law can be viewed as structural (e.g., as requiring boards to fashion risk management and regulatory compliance policies) or market-enabling (e.g., as the basis for insider trading liability, duties of disclosure, or challenging takeover defenses). However, the two types of rules are not evenly distributed across the three areas. Market-enabling disclosure rules are the dominant mode of regulation in modern securities law and regulation. Structural regulation is more prominent in the corporate governance provisions of company and labor law, which establish the basic institutional arrangements of the corporation.

---

48. Some legal mechanisms are not clearly in either category. Under American and German law appraisal rights and actions for an accounting or for fair valuation of minority shares reduce private benefits of control and in doing so create a check on managerial discretion, but via adjudication rather than financial transparency or institutional governance procedures. Neither remedy fits comfortably within the market-enabling or structural category.

The distinction between market-enabling rules, particularly disclosure regulation, and structural regulation takes on practical significance in two related ways, one regulatory and the other political. Paradoxically, market-enabling law and regulation generally rely on expanding the scope and prescriptive detail of formal regulation and the role of state institutions. Such rules require legalistic articulation and formal enforcement by agencies and courts. Structural regulation, however, offers a potential means of reducing legalism via legally structured self-regulation while also avoiding the significant conflict of interest and rent-seeking problems created by delegating self-regulation to higher-level organizations such as trade or business associations. Ideally, it provides a responsive and flexible form of regulation that exploits the potential efficacy of negotiation while rejecting laissez faire contractualism. It allows for juridification without judicialization or administrative bureaucratization. By fashioning the countervailing power relations within the firm and the forums in which bargaining is situated, structural regulation devolves regulatory functions to the level of stakeholders and diminishes the need for more formal regulations and adjudicative proceedings.

The political sensitivity of structural regulation, however, renders it more resistant to change than disclosure rules and fosters continued cross-national variation. Because it directly and deliberately alters institutionalized power relations within the company, structural regulation may generate far more political opposition from powerful groups than disclosure regulation. Governmental administration of formal transparency and disclosure rules has diffused internationally from liberal to traditionally nonliberal economies. Yet in cases as disparate as the United States and Germany, the politics of corporate governance reform pushed beyond the strengthening of disclosure and federal regulatory authority to take up more controversial reforms of structural regulation favoring shareholders and financial capital. By integrating the perspectives of comparative law and comparative political economy, we can more fully appreciate the depth of the reform.

COMPARATIVE LAW, POLITICAL ECONOMY, AND INSTITUTIONAL CHANGE

The study of comparative political economy has much to gain from comparative legal analysis and vice versa. Unfortunately, law has not been central in the institutionalist theory and empirical study of comparative political economy.[49] Political science as a field has largely marginalized the study of law, while the rich literature of comparative political economy seldom influences academic

49. For an earlier plea to incorporate law in institutionalist theory, see Smith (1988).

legal analysis.[50] Comparative law and comparative political economy share complementary analytical and substantive concerns. Both seek to develop broad classificatory schemes as modes of comparison and analysis (e.g., common versus civil law systems or liberal versus coordinated economies). Likewise, both bodies of scholarship frequently resort to stylized microanalytics as the bases for constructing broader classifications, such as abstract conceptions of rights, behavioral assumptions underlying collective action or principal-agent problems, and institutional typologies. While these tools aid in articulating general propositions, they also may obscure important features of law, politics, and economic relations. Accordingly, scholars of comparative law and political economy often problematize ideal type classifications as reflecting a thin, if analytically elegant, description of complex social processes. Where comparative law scholars recognize problems of excessive legal formalism, those in comparative political economy confront the distorting effects of reductionist theories and analytical frameworks. These ostensibly distinct difficulties derive from the common problem of oversimplification.

Comparative law and political economy also share a concern with excessive functionalism, one that has intensified with widespread adoption of neoclassical economic theory in the study of law and politics. One of the central preoccupations of historical institutional theory is its critique of economic functionalism and assumptions regarding interests, strategic and collective action, and normative commitments. Similarly, debates over functionalism have long preoccupied comparative law theorists.[51] Functionalist theory in comparative law presumes that "the legal system of every society faces essentially the same problems, and solves these problems by quite different means though very often with similar results."[52] The functionalist approach to comparative law focuses on finding which "legal norms, concepts or institutions in one system perform the equivalent functions performed by certain legal norms, concepts or institutions in another system."[53] Functionalism entails an instrumental conception of law, but the ends served by law are defined a priori as only those found *across* legal systems.[54] This approach to legal comparison thus narrows analysis with respect to both the policy ends served by law (and politics) and the juridical means identifiable as similar or analogous across legal systems. Differences tend to be screened out in favor of what is identifiable as similar or analogous across legal systems. Functionalism imposes a homogenizing normative orientation, regardless of the ambiguities and

50. For prominent exceptions integrating comparative political economy within legal scholarship, see Pistor (2006), Milhaupt and Pistor (2008), Zumbansen (2007), and Zumbansen and Saam (2007).
51. See Frankenberg (1985) and Hill (1989).
52. Zweigert and Kötz (1998, 34).
53. Kamba (1974, 517).
54. Cf. ibid.

tensions among legal norms and rules. We lose the systemic particularism of these norms and rules and what they actually *mean* to actors within a specific legal system.[55] For example, framing the functionality of corporate governance regimes in terms of minority shareholder protection or maximization of shareholder value is hardly normatively or politically neutral. A more abstract framing may produce the same problems. If the function of law is deemed the reduction of agency costs, stakeholder governance mechanisms such as codetermination often appear dysfunctional and their social and ideological functions unrecognized.

The integration of political economic analysis with comparative legal theory can ameliorate these theoretical problems by showing how the functions and meanings of law vary according to systemic differences in politics and economic organization. The substantial literature on the political economy of capitalism has shown how national models of capitalism develop distinctive comparative advantages (and disadvantages) in economic performance that derive from and perpetuate divergent institutional arrangements. This explanation of comparative advantages implies that cross-national variations in institutional and legal mechanisms serve different functional ends. Legal comparisons across different national models of capitalism reveal that the form and normative content of the legal mechanisms deployed and the ends served by law are often dissimilar, not analogous. Conversely, comparative law can enrich our understanding of the political economy by revealing the locally fashioned epistemic, ideological, and normative meanings of law that may alter social, political, and economic conduct.[56] As Peer Zumbansen notes, "By stressing the production of 'solutions' through legal regulations, the functionalist dismisses as irrelevant or does not even recognize that law also produces and stocks interpretive patterns and visions of life which shape people's ways of organizing social experience, giving it meaning, qualifying it as normal and just or as deviant or unjust."[57]

Legal rules reflect, albeit imperfectly, the policy preferences, values, and normative orientations of political actors and groups. The normative content of law illuminates the ideological and ideational dimensions of institutions, politics, and policy. Corporate governance law embodies norms of social solidarity, group identity, individual self-interest, competition, economic efficiency, hierarchical or egalitarian power relations, and equity. Politics, along with adjudication, translates these social values into public law and imposes them on the private sphere. This process of legal articulation and normative imposition is inherently political. As Peter Hall has noted, "Politics is intimately

55. Cf. Zumbansen (2005, 1075–76), discussing Frankenberg's critique of functionalism as a perspective of false objectivity that obscures important dimensions of law and differences among legal systems.

56. See ibid., 1076.

57. Ibid.

bound up with governance. And governance is a fundamentally normative matter."[58] Conversely, governance is bound up with politics, and *politics* is a fundamentally normative matter.[59] And law, the product of politics, is the great repository of norms.

Formal legal rules define the basic incentive structure within which actors maneuver. Legal rules represent expressions of political power backed by the coercive and legitimation powers of the state.[60] Accordingly, they induce actors and organizations to adopt means of compliance, which can inform an array of other organizational routines and practices. Law directly influences economic action and organization through prescriptive and prohibitive rules, and indirectly by altering the allocation of power within organizations or by changing the costs of pursuing alternative courses of action. Formal legal rules not only supplant or override private contractual ordering but also shape it by framing the bargaining power of the parties and legitimating forms of contracting.[61] As one organization theorist has noted, "Efforts to regulate the behavior of professionals . . . [and] corporations must be legitimated in terms of societal institutions, the most important of which is the law."[62] Through law's threat of sanctions and legitimation functions, "[a]ction at the microlevel is constrained by the opportunities and limitations defined at the macroorder."[63]

In this sense, legal rules do not serve merely as regulative instruments of politics and the state; they are also often *constitutive* of institutions and thus of broader socioeconomic relations. Institutions are, broadly speaking, "the formal rules, compliance procedures, and standard operating practices that structure the relationship between individuals in various units of the polity and economy."[64] Law is an important source of behavioral constraints and incentives, but it also configures institutional forms and validates norms that order political and economic activity at the levels of the state, firm, and market. These institutional arrangements shape the identities, interests, and strategies pursued by actors and groups. Formal rules are the features of institutions most explicitly defined by law and most directly linked to the state and politics. Legal rules encompass the characteristics of authority, legitimacy, obligation, and enforcement that are hallmarks of institutions and make them so important in social and economic life. Contracting, compliance procedures, rou-

58. Hall (1986, 275).
59. Cf. ibid., 276.
60. Cf. Streeck and Thelen (2005, 10–11). The implicit assumption here is that the rule of law is established and functional in the political economy.
61. Bainbridge (2008) provides an excellent overview of the neoclassical conception of the firm and its governance. For an account of the growing influence of the neoclassical contractualist conception of corporate governance in Germany, see Klages (2007).
62. Galaskiewicz (1991, 294).
63. Ibid., 295; cf. Gourevitch (1996).
64. Hall (1986, 19).

tines, and operating practices develop in the shadow of the law and thus of politics. Law can influence behavior by imposing mandatory—and enforceable—formal norms of conduct or by creating institutional forms in which particular norms and behaviors are reinforced. Both separately and in tandem, legal rules and institutions influence the behavior, interests, and preferences of individuals and groups by sanctioning conduct (both positively and negatively) and providing (or precluding) institutional mechanisms that promote the formation and empowerment of different groups.

The constitutive effect of legal rules and institutions is evident in three of the most important and ubiquitous institutions of political and economic modernity: the regulatory state, the corporate firm, and the market. Complex state institutions, sophisticated markets, and the corporation itself cannot exist in the absence of law. Government is constituted by bodies of public law ranging from constitutions to the increasingly pervasive and detailed administrative law and rules of the regulatory state. As long noted by social and economic theorists, formal legal rules define and preserve the functionality and legitimacy of the market as an institution.[65] Modern financial markets in particular, so vulnerable to the unholy trinity of speculative bubbles, panics, and manipulation, depend not only on property and contract rights but on functional regulatory frameworks of burgeoning complexity and expansiveness to address market failures. Neither the corporate form nor its internal constituencies exist in the absence of company law that fuses property, contract, and regulation in structuring the firm as an economic and social institution.

There are, of course, limits to the constitutive effects and practical efficacy of legal norms. Although law may indirectly influence private contracting and informal norms, each plays an important role in many forms of economic activity, and parties generally retain considerable discretion and autonomy. This is true even in more heavily regulated nonliberal forms of capitalism. Legal systems also typically create multiple ways to solve economic problems, including a variety of corporate forms that expand the degrees of organizational freedom enjoyed by managers and financial interests. Inevitable imperfections of legal design, compliance, and enforcement may generate unanticipated consequences or facilitate a variety of divergent behavioral and organizational outcomes. Ideological and political hostility to regulation, so pronounced on the American Right during the past thirty years, may lead to deliberate undermining of legal enforcement, even where formal deregulation has failed.

Normative tensions and ambiguities within legal rules and frameworks, particularly ones as complex as corporate governance, may weaken the practical effects of law or render them indeterminate. Law and the institutions it shapes often embody and mediate competing societal values and normative

65. See, e.g., Hurst (1970) and Horowitz (1992); cf. Polanyi (1944) and North (1990).

commitments that can be resolved in any number of ways. Further, once legally established, institutions may exercise an autonomous constitutive and regulatory influence on actors and groups that may be in tension or in direct conflict with legal norms. The corporation's institutional form may promote legal compliance but may also create perverse incentives to circumvent or systematically violate the law, as seen in repeated waves of corporate scandal and financial crisis that have intensified demands for reform.

Accordingly, legal regimes and institutional arrangements should not be fetishized as *overdeterminative* of interests, preferences, or behavior and thus as rigidly path-dependent and impervious to change. Nor should they be characterized as functionally coherent systems fashioned by political deliberation or historical logic. Law and institutions are mutable. They are formed and reformed through processes that are often chaotic and contentious. Relations within and among institutions and bodies of law may be interlocking and complementary but also unstable and contradictory. Any advanced political economy is pervaded with both types of relationships and dynamics. One of the contributions of the varieties-of-capitalism literature is its explicit focus on, and formalization of, the ways in which institutions can form complementary relationships and generate comparative economic advantages.[66] However, these same institutional components are also in a state of constant tension and flux.[67]

Institutional regimes contain conflicting normative and structural elements that cannot be readily reconciled into a coherent whole. They empower opposing groups, constitute and reinforce antagonistic interests, and legitimate discordant material and normative demands. Institutional arrangements may give rise to efficient complementarities, comparative competitive advantages, and path-dependent self-reproduction. But they may also foster dysfunction and trajectories of development driven by their distinctive internal tensions. Changes in the juridical foundations and characteristics of institutions reveal these tensions in particularly clear form. Law and regulation are thus ideal material for the analysis of both institutional complementarities and conflicts that underpin political economic stability and change.

The difficulty lies in explaining the political dynamics that drive the patterns and timing of change. Structural changes sweeping political economies around the world in recent decades have posed a particularly serious challenge to historical institutionalist theorists, who have developed compelling analytical accounts of institutional "stickiness" and path dependence. Historical institutionalist scholarship mounted an effective empirical and theoretical attack on neoliberal notions of institutional optimality and convergence. But its emphasis on path dependence and institutional resilience left the theoretical

---

66. Hall and Soskice (2001).
67. See Streeck and Thelen (2005).

framework unable to convincingly account for conflict and both the prevalence and degree of institutional change across the industrialized political
economies during last quarter century.[68] This weakness looms larger than ever
in an era marked by the expansion of the regulatory state and the rise and
catastrophic collapse of finance capitalism.

Analyzing corporate governance in terms of *legal change* directs attention
toward two important and underdeveloped areas of institutional theory: the
role of law as an instrument of politics and policy in constituting institutional
forms and the problem of institutional change.[69] Legal change provides unusually good material for tracing different forms of institutional development. To
use the conceptual categories developed by Wolfgang Streeck and Kathleen
Thelen, law creates a formal record of the "displacement" of legal rules and
mechanisms by succeeding ones.[70] Likewise, changes in legal interpretation
and formal enforcement proceedings facilitate the "conversion" of legal norms
from serving one purpose to serving another, often with elaborate justifica-
tions supplied by judges or other officials. Further, law displays a particular
affinity for change through "layering" as new rules and principles are integrated into existing legal structures.[71] The value placed on precedent, stability,
and upholding settled expectations in legal development favors incremental
change that allows for innovation while retaining much of the established
framework. Finally, the relative difficulty of legal change may produce "drift"
and, in extreme cases, "exhaustion," when the efficacy of legal rules and
enforcement erodes for failure to adapt to changing economic conditions.[72]

Last, legal change also provides a *metric* of the significance, direction, and
depth of political economic reform. Given the difficulty of accomplishing
reform amid contentious and veto-prone politics, legal change is an indication
of substantial shifts in power and interests sufficient to induce powerful actors
to change the rules of the game. Legal rules and the institutional forms they
create are therefore particularly sticky and prone to path dependence. The
articulation of complementary institutional arrangements, the interdepen-
dency of rules, and the internalization of routines and values in a given institutional environment further increase the costs associated with significant legal
change and contribute to the self-reproduction of institutional structures.[73]
Formal legal change, particularly when it alters the allocation of power and
authority among politically influential actors and groups, provides a robust

68. See ibid., 6–9.
69. See, e.g., Milhaupt and Pistor (2008), Streeck and Thelen (2005), and Campbell
(2004).
70. Streeck and Thelen (2005, 18–30, table 1.1).
71. Similarly, Milhaupt and Pistor (2008, 213–14) describe the "transplantation" of foreign legal concepts as subject to "stacking."
72. See Streeck and Thelen (2005), Hacker (2005).
73. See, e.g., Thelen (2002), Powell (1991), and North (1990)

indication of substantial systemic transformation. To explain such transformative changes we must look to the politics that underlies them.

The theoretical framework set out here calls for the fruitful synthesis of comparative political economy with comparative law. Each perspective brings different and complementary analytical and theoretical strengths. Comparative political economy focuses on the political bases and constitutive functions of institutions. It problematizes the interests of economic actors and groups while granting state actors relative autonomy in pursuing policy agendas for both strategic and substantive purposes. Further, comparative institutional analysis has developed sophisticated accounts of how national political economies form interlocking institutions that display complementary as well as contradictory elements and dynamics.

Comparative law offers a richer and more nuanced account of the formal rules that constitute institutions and shape the behavior of actors within them. By design, these rules tend to form complex structures that may be mutually reinforcing but may also contain conflicting normative and structural elements. Law reflects the political forces that formed it. It is constructed to contain and resolve conflict yet may contribute to it as well. It is only a contingent resolution of opposing political and economic forces and a frame for future conflict over policy that alters the interests of groups seeking or resisting reform. As the object of conflicting demands made through politics, legal structures become the focus of political conflict.

The conception of corporate governance as a politically constructed juridical nexus uses law as a bridge between politics and the broader institutional terrain of the political economy. This interdisciplinary approach is particularly useful in the study of corporate governance, which is both inherently legalistic and at the center of political economic institutional arrangements and conflicts. Together, political and legal analyses can identify where national corporate governance regimes have developed similar legal and institutional structures and where they differ. The law and politics of corporate governance show that the boundaries between the public and private spheres are often blurred, particularly with respect to structural regulation. Law plays a crucial role in forming institutions and their internal power relations. Although legal change is subject to political and institutional constraints, a critical dimension of agency remains. In the wake of the 2007–9 financial crisis and Great Recession, the blurring of public and private has grown dramatically. Understanding the political construction of national corporate governance regimes is more important than ever.

CHAPTER 3

Neoliberal Governance and the Neocorporatist Firm

Governance Models in the United States and Germany

During the postwar period, the American and German corporate governance regimes developed sharply differing juridical infrastructures reflecting the political forces that constituted their distinctive shareholder and stakeholder models. In each nation, corporate governance law continually evolved, sometimes quite dramatically, but these developments tended to reinforce established forms of legal ordering and corporate control while allowing for incremental change. American law relied primarily on market-enabling legal mechanisms within a disclosure-based regulatory regime buttressed by unusually pro-plaintiff litigation rules. This regime favored the protection of shareholders' interests in the monetary value of their shares, rather than in enhancing direct shareholder or stakeholder influence within the corporation. Exit trumped voice; market-enabling rules took precedence over structural regulation. German corporate governance law favored mandatory rules defining the institutional structures and governance procedures of the corporation over juridical market facilitation. The resulting "microcorporatist" firm strengthened stakeholder voice through formal representation and negotiation in firm governance.[1] During the postwar era, corporate governance law expanded the range of recognized stakeholders to include employees alongside managers, shareholders, and bankers. In each case, legal structures and political dynamics tended to reinforce each other to produce nationally distinctive developmental trajectories.

This chapter analyzes the core legal features of the American and German corporate governance regimes prior to the crises and reforms of the 1990s and

1. Cf. Assmann (1990); Streeck (1984) (describing the German firm as "microcorporatist").

first decade of the twenty-first century. It uses the juridical nexus model set out in chapter 2 to identify the core legal components of corporate governance regimes within company law, securities regulation, and labor relations law. The American and German cases illustrate how these core juridical components of corporate governance vary across different models of political economic organization. My characterization of the American and German regimes is not intended to be exhaustive.[2] The stylized rendering of their core juridical structures highlights the *systemic* character of corporate governance as a *regime* comprised of interlocking arrangements of rules, institutions, and enforcement mechanisms that mutually reinforce each other sufficiently to persist over time. This account recognizes the role of law in fashioning these normative and institutional relationships and the recursive relationships between juridical structures and politics that shaped these regimes over time. Finally, it identifies the sources of systemic instability and change that would become increasingly important with the emergence of contemporary finance capitalism beginning in the early 1990s. Against this backdrop, the political and economic dynamics of corporate governance reform can be seen more clearly as they are examined in the chapters that follow.

THE AMERICAN MODEL OF CORPORATE GOVERNANCE

Academic and policy discourses commonly identify the United States as the exemplar and the global epicenter of shareholder-centric corporate governance and neoliberal finance capitalism. By the 1990s, when corporate governance emerged as a major policy area around the world, the American model was generally perceived as defined by market-driven finance, stringent disclosure rules, strong shareholder rights, and comparatively robust enforcement of legal norms. This image would become increasingly influential in policy debates and reforms around the world.

However, this oversimplified characterization of the American regime obscures two important points. First, American "shareholder capitalism" is of much more recent vintage than commonly recognized. Only in recent decades have legal developments significantly favored shareholder interests, and investors have won, at best, only partial victories. The growing solicitude toward investors and, more important, large financial institutions in corporate governance law and policy has been powerfully influenced by financial market developments, international and domestic competitive pressures, financial innovations, hostile takeover battles, and corporate restructuring since the

---

2. For examples of the literature detailing these corporate governance regimes in historical and political economic context, see, e.g., Jackson (2001, 2003, 2009), Milhaupt and Pistor (2008), Gourevitch and Shinn (2005), Roe (1994, 2003b), Vitols (2001a, 2001b), Dore (2000), O'Sullivan (2000), and Deeg (1999).

1970s. Second, the American regime is not as protective of shareholders as it is often portrayed. Postwar corporate governance in the United States was largely managerialist—and remains significantly so. It was the product of incessant tensions between managerial and financial interests. Conflicting interests and struggles for economic power between managers and shareholders animated the regulatory and legislative politics of corporate governance and periodically burst into public view in moments of political or economic crisis. Partisan political strategies and coalitional interest group alignments produced a governance framework that favored managerial autonomy even as it buttressed the operation of financial markets.

Power relations within the American governance regime mirrored political and market arrangements in important ways. The United States possesses a highly fragmented yet porous state structure that renders both coordination of economic activity and substantial policy changes exceedingly difficult. The pluralist form of American political governance at once fostered a profusion of interest groups and privileged those with the most organizational resources. American corporate governance recapitulated this dual fragmentation and concentration of power to a striking degree. The federal securities law deliberately advanced the growth and liquidity of stock markets while encouraging, and often mandating, fragmentation of stock ownership.[3] Highly permissive state corporation laws granted broad autonomy to directors and managers, and facilitated the centralization and entrenchment of managerial authority. Federal labor law and American "business unionism," characterized by weak labor rights, low union-density and collective bargaining coverage, and adversarial labor relations, militated against any role for employees as active stakeholders in firm governance. American law framed labor relations within the narrow confines of established forms of unionization and economistic contractual bargaining. It effectively excluded firm governance and nonunion forms of employee representation and empowerment from the labor relations and corporate governance agendas. Figure 3.1 sketches the resulting institutional form of the American public corporation and its governance relationships.

Taken together, these bodies of law marginalized shareholder and employee constituencies within corporate governance and *reinforced* the separation of ownership and control originally described by Adolph Berle and Gardiner Means in the 1930s. The juridical framework contributed to self-sustaining market-based economic relations, stock market transparency and expansion, and diffuse shareholding through portfolio diversification.[4] American corporate governance preserved an expansive private sphere of managerial autonomy bounded by a highly developed framework of formal legal rights, obligations, and disclosure rules. Economic regulation generally did not *directly* modify the

3. Roe (1991, 1994).
4. Berle and Means (1932); cf. Coffee (1991).

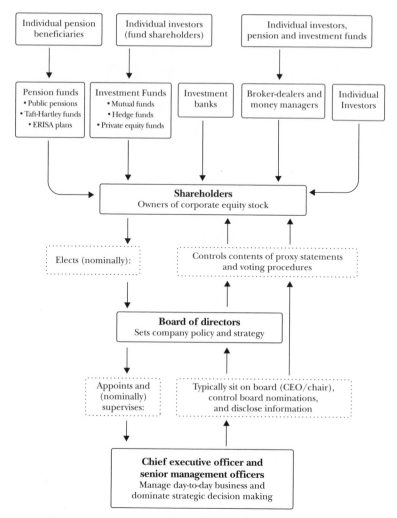

Fig. 3.1 *The American corporation and governance relationships*

corporate form by imposing mandatory self-regulating institutional structures.[5] Instead, corporate governance law generally allowed great latitude in the structuring of private institutions and relationships and used *formal prescriptive legal rules to eliminate and redress market failures.* The politics that elevated the market as the primary mechanism of economic and corporate organization also drove the development of market-reinforcing law and regulation within corporate governance. A brief examination of corporation, securities, and labor law highlights these characteristics of the American corporate governance regime.

5. This is not to say that American corporation law imposes *no* mandatory terms, but it is unusually permissive in comparative perspective. Cf. Eisenberg (1989), Gordon (1989), and Coffee (1989, discussing enabling and mandatory features in corporation law).

Company Law

American corporation law is predominantly a responsibility of state rather than federal law. The persistence of state corporation law is an artifact of federalism.[6] In light of the inexorable growth of federal regulation in the twentieth century, the absence of a federal corporation law is an arresting feature of the American corporate governance regime and distinctive among the advanced industrial countries. Prior to the New Deal, political resistance and the threat of constitutional invalidation under the Supreme Court's federalism and Commerce Clause jurisprudence protected state control over corporation law from encroachment or displacement by federal law. Post–New Deal constitutional doctrines eliminated those judicial limits on federal authority, but political constraints on federal legislation imposed by powerful and entrenched state, managerial, and financial interests still obstructed the federalization of corporation law. The emergence of large, publicly traded industrial corporations unleashed political conflicts over federal regulation of business but never resulted in the reallocation of authority over corporate law to the federal level. During the Progressive Era, a potent alliance of business and parochial state interests defeated repeated attempts to pass a federal incorporation act. Even at the height of the New Deal, economic reformers seeking to federalize corporation law could not overcome the political entrenchment of federalism.[7]

This extraordinary resilience of corporate law federalism indicates the political power of the financial and industrial elites and their preference for preserving the political market for corporation law. By the early twentieth century, interstate competition for corporate charters led states to redraft corporation laws as highly permissive enabling statutes. Delaware became the overwhelmingly dominant corporate law jurisdiction by catering to the demands of managers and financiers for maximum flexibility in business organization and merger and acquisition activities. State law established the bare minima of the corporate form: limited liability, the "corporate personality" (the capacity to contract, sue, and be sued), a board of directors, and the fiduciary duties of directors and officers. Otherwise, it granted managers and directors wide discretion over how to structure, finance, and manage the firm. It offered shareholders comparatively few rights to vote on important decisions. In fact, American law not only allowed managers to sit on the board of directors, essentially supervising themselves, but also gave them control over the nomination and election of directors.

6. See generally Bratton and McCahery (2004).
7. Proposals for a federal corporation and corporate governance law were sidelined by struggles over securities law and ultimately undone by overreaching when Congress sought to combine corporate governance, antitrust law, and the rights of employees into a single legislative package. See Seligman (2003, 205–10); see also Loss (1961, 109).

The resulting pattern of American corporate governance established the legal foundations of managerialism. A management team dominated by the chief executive officer (CEO) ran the corporation with little oversight by, or input from, shareholders or their representatives on or off the board. The board of directors provided the primary *structural* mechanism of shareholder protection under corporate law. In theory, the board was elected by the shareholders (and no other corporate stakeholders) and formally charged with selecting, monitoring, and constraining management. In practice, however, it proved a feeble restraint, with most or all directors typically either drawn from or nominated by management. Management maintained tight control over nominations, proxy voting, the flow of information, and the agenda, thereby limiting the board's effectiveness as a structural check on management.[8] The law imposed few, if any, mandatory terms on the structure or composition of the board to enhance its effectiveness.[9]

Despite a pronounced increase in the proportion of "outside" directors (i.e., individuals not part of management) from the late 1970s CEOs continued to dominate the composition of boards. Inside directors comprised 38 percent of the average board in 1972, but by 1992 the percentage decreased to 25.[10] However, the status of outsider did not necessarily translate into true independence or diligence. The dominance that managers maintained over board nominations tended to diminish the independence of outside directors, many of whom were former employees of the corporation or had other business or personal ties to the CEO. Board members typically deferred to the CEO. Nominally independent directors helped legitimate management while preserving its power. Because boards were structurally incapable of constraining managers, the legal obligations of directors gained greater prominence in corporate governance.

If the board as a *representational* body failed to adequately check managerial discretion, what of the *legal obligations* of the board to act in the best interests of the corporation? Situated "between… government regulation and private ordering through contract," fiduciary duties constitute the *normative* core of American corporate law.[11] Fiduciary duties encompass three obligations: (1) a duty of *obedience* requiring directors and officers must act consistently with the corporate charter; (2) they owe a duty of *loyalty* that obliges them to use their powers over the corporation and its assets for the benefit of the corporation

---

8. Coffee (1991, 1323–24, 1327–28).

9. In 1977, the Securities and Exchange Commission (SEC) pressured the New York Stock Exchange (NYSE) to require audit committees of outside directors under its listing rules; 90 percent of listed firms already had them. These mandatory committees proved just as passive as their voluntarily adopted predecessors. Seligman (2003, 547).

10. See Korn/Ferry International (1993, 3, 7, 13); compare Investor Responsibility Research Center (1996, 3–6) (65.8 percent of directors were independent, and over 80 percent of boards had a majority of outsiders in a 1996 sample of 435 S&P 500 companies).

11. Bratton (1993, 1100) and see (1994, 23–31).

and its shareholders; and (3) they have a duty to exercise the degree of *care* that a reasonably prudent person would be expected to exercise under the circumstances. The fiduciary duties of corporate directors and officers ostensibly counterbalanced the institutional weakness of shareholders in corporate governance with the threat of shareholder litigation. But they have proved a problematic and ultimately ineffective means of protecting shareholders.

First, fiduciary duties implicate courts in second-guessing the judgments of managers and directors in what are often enormously complex and difficult decisions involving vast financial sums. Even if courts were sufficiently competent and expeditious to undertake such inquiries, extensive judicial review of corporate decisions would tax the courts' resources and create intolerable economic disruption and uncertainty. These problems are compounded by the indeterminacy of fiduciary duties. They share a characteristic of incomplete contracts: they cannot anticipate with specificity the innumerable situations in which they might come into play. They are stated abstractly and left to the courts to apply through the adjudication of specific disputes. Unlike detailed statutes and regulatory codes, they are often too vague to provide corporate directors and managers with clear guidance in advance of adjudication.

Second, if the courts imposed fiduciary liability too readily, the threat of potentially ruinous monetary damage awards and reputational injury could (and did) cause a crisis in the price and availability of directors' and officers' insurance and keep qualified candidates from serving on boards.[12] Accordingly, the "business judgment rule" insulates directors against fiduciary liability where the director (1) is *disinterested* in the challenged judgment, (2) was informed of the relevant facts to the degree *believed to be appropriate* under the circumstances, and (3) rationally believed the decision was *in the best interests of the corporation*.[13] In practice, the business judgment rule gives directors and managers enormous latitude in decision making without meaningful threat of liability or other legal sanction.

Finally, the substantive standards of fiduciary duties are diluted by the competing demands involved in the governance of a complex corporate organization. The business judgment rule reflects this acceptance of corporate pluralism by specifying that the decision must be in the best interests of the *corporation*, not of the *shareholders*.[14] This position is also consistent with Delaware case law concerning takeovers—a context implicating fiduciary conflicts

12. *Smith v. Van Gorkum*, 488 A.2d 858 (Del. 1985), imposed a low threshold for director and officer liability and immediately triggered a crisis in the D&O insurance market until the state legislature quickly overturned the decision by statute. See Del. Code. Ann. tit. 8, § 102(b)(7).

13. American Law Institute (1994, § 4.01(c)); cf. *Aronson v. Lewis*, 473 A.2d 805 (Del. 1984); Block, Barton, and Radin (1998, 20–24). Subsumed within these criteria is the requirement that directors act in "good faith," that is, with the subjective intent to fulfill legal obligations.

14. Former SEC commissioner Steven Wallman (1999) argues that American corporate law has *never* endorsed the principle of shareholder primacy, despite some scattered, though famous, court decisions that may suggest the contrary.

of interest at their most intense. In a jointly written article, three eminent corporate law jurists note that the debate over the social role and legal character of the corporation is still very much alive and has devolved into a tension between a pro-takeover "property" conception of the firm consistent with shareholder primacy and a more protective "entity" conception closer to a stakeholder model.[15]

Given the difficulties of using either representational governance processes or normative rights-based means of protecting shareholders *within the corporation*, the post–New Deal politics of corporate governance in the United States turned toward protecting investors *within the securities markets*. This resulting emphasis on transparency and disclosure in securities regulation dampened, but did not eliminate, demands to reform the corporate structure for regulatory ends.

Securities Law

In contrast with corporation law, securities law became the responsibility of the federal government.[16] American securities regulation is one of the New Deal's great legacies. Political limitations on federal influence over company law increased the incentive for federal policymakers to use *market-reinforcing* securities regulation as a principal means of protecting shareholders from fraud, misappropriation, and abuse by managers and market intermediaries. While state law granted investors few governance rights and structural protections within the corporation, federal legislation and regulation developed a disclosure and transparency regime to protect shareholders in and through the market. The internal affairs of the public corporation continued to be governed primarily under the law of the chartering state. Its relations with investors in the securities markets, which the states had been unwilling or unable to address through corporate law, were subject to federal regulation.[17] With corporate financial disclosure and securities markets reasonably well regulated, political pressures for federalization of corporate law diminished—only to reappear sporadically in times of economic and political crisis.

The New Deal's legal and institutional reforms ushered in the first modern system of securities regulation and relaid the foundations of the American financial system with the Securities Act of 1933 and the Securities Exchange Act of 1934. The Securities Act mandated the disclosure of financial information in a prospectus prior to the initial public offering of securities.[18] The even

15. See Allen, Jacobs, and Strine (2002).
16. State "blue sky" laws also regulated securities, but they were marginalized by federal law and regulation.
17. See Loss (1961); cf. Aranow and Einhorn (1959, 306, state legislative inaction induced Congress to address proxy vote regulation under the Securities and Exchange Act of 1934).
18. Securities Act of 1933, 15 U.S.C. §§ 77a–77aa.

more far-reaching Securities Exchange Act blended populist resentment of financial elites with the progressives' faith in the regulatory state, technocratic expertise, and agency independence. It created the Securities and Exchange Commission—a strong independent regulatory agency with broad rule-making and enforcement authority to reduce information asymmetries and improve the functioning of securities markets.[19] The SEC was charged with drafting and enforcing elaborate and mandatory registration, disclosure, and securi- ties fraud rules and with overseeing the administration of stock exchanges (and their listing and disclosure rules). In short, the SEC's mission was to make the markets work.

The securities laws also charged the SEC with oversight of the stock exchanges' internal listing and disclosure rules and of the National Associa- tion of Securities Dealers' self-regulatory functions, placing it at the top of a public-private regulatory hierarchy allowing for self-regulation to complement formal regulation.[20] Likewise, the agency oversaw, albeit rather loosely, the Financial Accounting Standards Board, a private professional body respon- sible for proposing and drafting accounting rules that profoundly influenced the disclosure practices of public firms, and the Public Oversight Board, responsible for self-regulation of accounting firms. However imperfectly, stock exchange administrators, financial-sector associations, and accounting profes- sionals became private regulators in the shadow of the SEC.

Legalistic regulation, as opposed to corporatist negotiation and coordina- tion, became a central and enduring legacy of the New Deal and a dominant mode of policy implementation in the United States.[21] The transparency and disclosure regime of American securities law and regulation exemplified this legacy. Consistent with broader regulatory patterns in the United States, secu- rities regulation relied to a striking extent on highly formal and often pre- scriptive rules, along with litigious enforcement mechanisms.[22] As a result of this institutionalization of securities regulation, the United States possessed comparatively strong transparency, disclosure, and insider trading rules designed to protect minority shareholders, facilitate market transactions, and maintain the integrity of the country's securities markets. Within this regula- tory framework, the "external" capital markets in the United States became among the most developed and liquid in the world, with a high proportion of publicly traded firms, a sophisticated financial services industry, and a wide range of debt and equity financing options.

At the same time, federal law during and after the New Deal broke up con- centrated financial power within securities markets and firms to curtail the

19. Securities Exchange Act of 1934, 15 U.S.C. §§ 78a–78kk.
20. Ibid., § 19(b), as amended, 15 U.S.C. § 78s (2001).
21. See Brand (1988); cf. Kagan (2001).
22. For a comprehensive analysis of the political and ideological determinants of this reli- ance on formal law and litigious enforcement, see Kagan (2001).

risks it posed to financial market stability. Legal reforms drove the dispersion of shareholding and limited the power of financial interests, while disclosure regulation increased the transparency and enhanced the importance of securities markets and listed firms.[23] The Glass-Steagall Act segmented the financial services industry by separating investment banking and brokerage from commercial banking and traditional lending, thus barring universal banking in the United States. This hostility to concentrated financial power, a staple of American politics since the early nineteenth century, also took the form of *mandatory* portfolio diversification by institutional investors.[24] The mandatory dispersion of shareholding enhanced managerial power by minimizing the use of blockholding and exacerbating shareholders' collective action problems. Not only were dispersed shareholders hard to organize, the costs of corporate monitoring and governance activism could not be recouped from passive free-riding investors who would share the benefits of improved financial or business performance. The resulting incentive structure reinforced shareholder dispersion and passivity by making investment diversification more attractive than activism.

While transparency and disclosure regulation burgeoned under the post-New Deal regime, alternative governance mechanisms of shareholder voice withered. With the emergence of hostile tender offers during the 1960s, Congress quickly responded with yet another transparency law, the Williams Act of 1968, which required disclosure of holdings in a publicly traded firm when they exceeded statutory thresholds and mandated rules for conducting tender offers for outstanding shares to prevent coercive bidding practices.[25] The goal was to facilitate the emerging market for control, not to enhance the control rights of shareholders or other corporate stakeholders.

The emphasis of federal securities law on transparency and disclosure regulation encouraged investors to rely on exit by selling shares in response to governance and management problems rather than on the exercise of voice.[26] There arose a self-perpetuating relationship among the dispersion of shareholding, the development of robust and liquid securities markets, and the market-enabling regulatory regime. Shareholder weakness within the firm increased the importance of prescriptive disclosure regulation to protect shareholder interests. Financial institutions reliant on the securities markets favored a legal regime that fostered market development. Corporate managers

---

23. See generally McCraw (1984, especially chap. 5) and Roe (1991).

24. Following the Glass-Steagall Act of 1933, the Investment Company Act of 1940 and the Employee Retirement Income Security Act of 1974 limited the equity stakes that investment firms and funds could hold as a percentage of their own capital and of outstanding corporate equity. See generally Roe (1991, 1994).

25. Amending the Securities Exchange Act, sections 13(d) and 14(d), 15 U.S.C. §§ 78m(d), 78n(d).

26. See, e.g., Roe (1991) and Coffee (1991).

benefited from a financial and corporate governance regime that supplied plentiful equity capital while enhancing their autonomy from shareholders and financial institutions. By midcentury, interest group politics entrenched the institutional and economic logic of modern American finance and corporate governance.

Labor Law

While American corporate governance law limited shareholder influence within firm governance, it wholly excluded employees. No representational structures ever emerged in American law or labor relations practices to incorporate employees into firm decision making or assure ongoing consultation, such as that provided by board representation or works council structures in Germany (see the following section). The New Deal labor law's broad legal prohibition of company unions protected employee organization from managerial control at the expense of organizational experiments such as workplace committees dealing with safety and productivity issues. American labor law also distinguished between labor relations and firm management by limiting mandatory subjects of collective bargaining to a narrow range of bread-and-butter issues concerning the terms and conditions of employment.[27]

The National Labor Relations Board and federal courts reinforced this rigidity in interpretations of federal labor law that further impeded the formation of alternative forms of employee representation.[28] These rulings reinforced the separation between the spheres of state corporate law and federal labor law. Matters such as investment, marketing, production, design, and finance were (and are) considered within the "core of entrepreneurial control" and not subject to collective bargaining, although these issues may decisively affect the future of the workforce.[29] By strictly separating labor relations and firm management, the American legal framework came to protect managerial prerogatives from encroachment by collective bargaining and other forms of employee influence. It also fostered a form of business unionism characterized by high levels of labor-management conflict, rigid and adversarial labor relations within the enterprise, highly decentralized collective bargaining, and

27. See *NLRB v. Borg-Warner Corp.*, 356 U.S. 342 (1958); *Fibreboard Paper Products Corp. v. NLRB*, 379 U.S. 203 (1964); see also *First National Maintenance Corp. v. NLRB*, 452 U.S. 666 (1981).

28. See *Electromation, Inc.*, 309 N.L.R.B. 990 (1992), enforced sub nom. *Electromation, Inc. v. NLRB*, 35 F.3d 1148 (7th Cir. 1994); *E.I. du Pont de Nemours & Co.*, 311 N.L.R.B. 893 (1993); see also Estreicher (1994), Hyde (1993), Summers (1993).

29. *Fibreboard Paper Products Corp. v. NLRB*, 379 U.S. 203, 223 (1964) (Stewart, J., concurring); see also *Ford Motor Co. v. NLRB*, 441 U.S. 488, 498 (1979) (quoting *Fibreboard*).

detailed contracts that imposed rigid terms on the parties rather than creating governance mechanisms conducive to cooperative adjustment.[30]

The steady erosion of organized labor beginning in the 1950s and the exclusion of employees from corporate governance aided the rise of finance capitalism in the United States. Investors did not favor the development of worker participation in firm governance that might dilute shareholder power further, divert earnings from shareholders to employees, and constrain managerial strategies for the maximization of shareholder wealth. With the decline of organized labor's countervailing power within the public and private spheres, financial market pressures became central in driving the restructuring that has characterized American corporate capitalism since the 1970s. The separation of labor relations from managerial discretion and corporate governance left managers free to externalize the costs of economic adjustment on labor when pursuing mergers, acquisitions, and corporate restructuring.[31] These strategies to boost shareholder value in turn made it easier to execute additional mergers and acquisitions using stock as a form of currency.

The rise of labor-controlled pension funds did not reverse the decline in labor's power. As unionization rates collapsed, the financial holdings under union (and, more broadly, worker) control increased dramatically through the expansion of pension funds. Yet the influence of organized labor has never reflected this growing financial clout. The most financially powerful labor movement in the world was left one of the weakest. Despite the formation of the Council of Institutional Investors in 1985 by seventeen public employee pension funds and three private-sector unions, "labor's capital" did not alter the prevailing economic interests and policy preferences of financial institutions and financiers, who saw greater benefits in maximizing shareholder value than in a more stakeholder-oriented regime of "patient capital."[32] Increasingly, labor pension fund activism, by both public and private employee funds, embraced the interests of shareholders even as these interests diverged from those of employees.[33] As their activism became increasingly intertwined with that of other institutional investors, employee investment funds proved no more capable than unions of advancing the interests of employees and organized labor.[34]

30. See generally Bok (1971) and Rogers (1990).
31. Cf. Shleifer and Summers (1988).
32. See Marens (2004, 117–20).
33. Cf. ibid. (noting potential fiduciary and other legal constraints on pro-labor pension fund activism and labor support for repeal of antitakeover defenses).
34. The vast majority of shares are not held by union and public employee funds. Thus the interests of finance capital remain in tension with those of labor. When labor funds seek a voice in corporate governance through stock holdings, they must still secure the support of other shareholders. See Schwab and Thomas (1998).

THE GERMAN MODEL OF CORPORATE
GOVERNANCE

The postwar German political economy and corporate governance regime stood in sharp contrast to the neoliberal American model. Germany's model of "organized private enterprise" combined interest articulation and policy negotiation through peak associations; sectoral standard setting, worker training, and wage bargaining; and networks of bank-based relational finance and corporate cross-shareholding.[35] This form of political economic organization organized powerful interest groups within national and sectoral peak associations that allowed for bargaining over intra- and interassociational conflicts. These institutions, integral to Germany's "social-market economy," were designed to prevent the recurrence of economic instability and class conflict regarded as the root cause of the Weimar Republic's collapse and to limit state power in response to the trauma of Nazism. The institutional and juridical legacies of authoritarian corporatism were refashioned into a democratic neocorporatist order.[36] The postwar political economic order supplemented, and to some extent supplanted, markets and private contracting. It situated economic groups and embedded property rights and markets within legally constituted institutional arrangements conducive to resolving political and economic conflicts.[37] These arrangements promoted long-term stakeholder relationships, the provision of public goods, and sectoral and intrafirm coordination among stakeholders that contributed to Germany's comparative economic advantages in export-oriented manufacturing.[38]

Germany's form of organized capitalism and the stakeholder orientation of corporate governance have deep historical roots. However, its postwar incarnation was largely the creation of the nonliberal Christian democratic Center-Right, albeit under pressure from the Social Democratic Center-Left and a powerful labor movement.[39] In contrast to the American faith in contractualism and markets, the German Center-Right and Center-Left embraced a postwar economic order that tended to institutionalize economic relations in finance and labor relations.[40] Moreover, the common characterization of the German political economy as consensual tends to obscure the conflict that accompanied its development and inhered within its operation. Compromise,

35. See Shonfield (1965, chap. 11, using the term "organized private enterprise") and Zysman (1983, showing how these arrangements contributed to "negotiated adjustment").
36. See Höpner and Krempel (2004) and Lehmbruch (2001, 77–86).
37. See Lee (1983, 49, describing the subordination of private law to "an all-embracing public law").
38. See Hall and Soskice (2001, 8), Soskice (1999, 1991) and Streeck (1991, 1997).
39. See Cioffi and Höpner (2006a, 2006b), Cioffi (2004a), and Höpner (2003).
40. See generally the essays collected in Streeck and Yamamura (2001).

not consensus, was the foundation and a primary aspiration of the German political economic structure.

The German corporate governance regime reproduced these broader national and sectoral patterns of countervailing power, authority, and organization through a legal framework that created mechanisms of institutionalized representation, negotiation, and coordination among management, finance capital, and labor. The allocation of rights and decision-making power among these opposing groups served to inform and reinforce these structures and relationships. The German regime used law and regulation to structure the firm as a largely self-regulating entity, situated within a consensus-based social-market economy. This ordering of opposing interests into long-term institutional relationships was replicated at the level of the firm through a microcorporatist form that mediated the interests of shareholders and creditors, managers, and labor within a stakeholder model of governance.[41] Law played an integral role by fashioning representational structures for recognized stakeholder groups and channeling conflicts among them into negotiation.[42] The allocation of rights served to reinforce institutionalized bargaining rather than enforcement through litigation.[43]

The microcorporatist firm fit within postwar West Germany's form of organized capitalism. Short-term economic interests, including those of financiers and shareholders, were subordinated to goals of long-term stability, prosperity, and security.[44] The corporate governance regime insulated firms from demands for short-term equity returns by encouraging finance through the "patient capital" of bank loans and retained earnings. Likewise, it developed an overlapping and complementary relationship with the broader labor relations regime that incentivized improvements in labor skills and productivity. The juridical framework encouraged the negotiation of long-term adjustment strategies at the company level that allowed for flexibility in restructuring work and production while pushing industrial conflict to the sectoral level, where more centralized unions and employer associations addressed collective bargaining and strike actions. In concert with national and sectoral institutional arrangements, the corporate governance regime thus contributed to institutional preconditions for Germany's export-oriented model of "diversified quality production" characterized by high-skill, high-value-added manufacturing

41. Cf. Assmann (1990) and Streeck (1984).
42. Cf. Streeck (1990, neocorporatist law defines groups functionally for representational and coordination purposes, in contrast to the liberal individualism underlying contractual forms of governance).
43. See Cioffi (2009) and Pistor (2006).
44. See Vagts (1966, 38–48, analysis and critique of concepts of the "public interest" and "public welfare" in German company law).

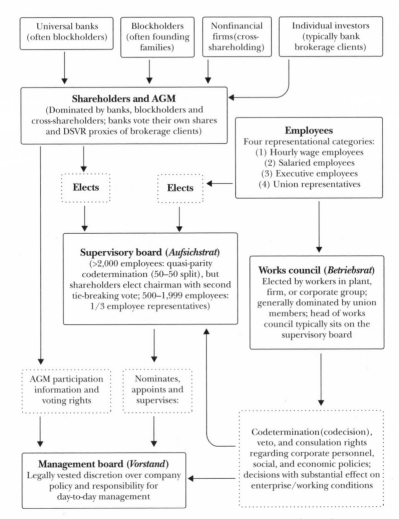

Fig. 3.2 *The German corporation and governance relationships*

and a relatively egalitarian income distribution.[45] Figure 3.2 illustrates the complex microcorporatist structure of the German stock corporation and the governance relations among its stakeholders.

45. Streeck (1992, 1991). For theoretical and empirical analyses of the institutional foundations of the German and Japanese production techniques, see also Soskice (1999, 1991), Aoki (1994), Womack (1991), and Porter (1990). For a comprehensive analysis of the relationships among corporate governance, financial and industrial organization, and management strategies in the United States and Germany, see O'Sullivan (2000), particularly chapters 5–6 (United States) and chapters 7–8 (Germany).

Company Law

The relationship between German securities and company law was the mirror image of the American model. American federalism matched centralized federal securities regulation with state corporation law. In Germany, a uniform federal company law developed amid the fragmentation of securities regulation among the *Länder* (states) and eight local self-regulating exchanges. Federal company law dates from the 1870s, when severe economic crisis and corporate collapses threatened German political and economic stability. Federal control precluded the sort of regulatory competition to appease managers or shareholders that characterized corporate law in the United States.[46] In contrast to transparency regulation and permissive corporation laws in the United States, Germany's corporate governance regime relied on *mandatory* company law rules to constitute the representational and governance structure of the corporation. The corporate structure organized stakeholder interests into self-regulating relationships within a prescribed institutional form. Self-regulation took the form of self-governance. Disclosure regulations and accounting rules remained weak, securities markets undeveloped, and company finances opaque. Company and securities law provided few effective avenues for private litigation to enforce shareholder rights.[47] The legal framework privileged the exercise of stakeholder voice within governance rather than exit through market-enabling rules and regulation.

Under German company law, a public corporation (*Aktiengesellschaft*, or AG) has a two-tiered board structure that mandates complete separation of the supervisory board (the *Aufsichtsrat*, analogous to the American board of directors) from the management board (the *Vorstand*, a more collegial version of the CEO and senior management of the American firm), with no overlapping membership between them. Theoretically, this should strengthen the supervisory board by reducing conflicts of interest. In practice, German law conferred a "massive concentration of power" on the managerial board.[48] The supervisory board appoints and nominally supervises the managing board and formulates (or at least approves) major corporate policies and strategies. However, although the supervisory board oversees general corporate strategy and policy, by law it cannot usurp the management function of the management board. And although the law bars current members of the management board from the supervisory board, *former* managers can ascend to it—and do so in growing numbers.

German company law also granted shareholders comparatively strong rights to receive relevant information and vote at the annual general meeting (AGM) on a broad range of issues, including mergers, significant acquisitions,

46. For historical overviews, see Jackson (2001) and Shonfield (1965).
47. See Cioffi (2009).
48. Charkham (1994, 19); cf. Kübler (1987, 216).

capital increases, and major changes in business strategy. In effect, company law created a disclosure and transparency regime outside securities regulation through the institution of the AGM, though disclosure was far less frequent in comparison with the continuous process under American securities law. In the absence of stringent securities regulation designed to improve the efficiency and disciplinary function of stock markets, German company law relied on the internal corporate institutions—the board and AGM—to transmit information and constrain managerial power. However, these institutional constraints were not designed to protect shareholders alone, as in the United States, but also to safeguard the interests of other stakeholders, including creditor banks and employees.

Germany's bank-centered financial system fostered stable and interlocking governance relationships based on concentrated stock ownership, extensive cross-shareholding networks, and long-term relational finance ties among banks and corporate borrowers. These financial structures reinforced the stakeholder model, and German law reinforced these relationships. Relational finance by banks alleviated pressures for maximizing short-term financial returns and encouraged the adoption of long-term adjustment and growth strategies by industrial enterprises that could balance the competing demands of capital and labor.

Large "universal banks" combined commercial lending with investment banking and securities services. These banks became important lenders to, and major shareholders in, publicly traded firms. Under German law, the banks could vote "deposited share voting rights" (DSVRs) if authorized to do so by their brokerage clients. Thus, in addition to their own equity holdings, the banks wielded disproportionate proxy voting strength and leverage over board nominations or key strategic decisions.[49] Even when German management attempted to maintain autonomy by diversifying sources of bank debt, banks adopted a practice of designating a "lead bank" to monitor the corporation, vote their aggregate DSVRs, and maintain supervisory board representation.[50] Bank representation on the supervisory board frequently cemented the combination of bank voting power, long-term relational lending, and direct shareholding.

In theory, the banks' status as shareholders aligned their interests with those of other shareholders who were protected by the banks' power and monitoring within firm governance. In practice, banks often did not play an active monitoring role, and their institutional identity as lenders first and shareholders second generated conflicts of interest that were not alleviated by law or regulation. In the absence of strong shareholder protections or incentives for major banks to cultivate equity finance, relatively few German firms became

49. Charkham (1994, 37–38) and Vagts (1966, 53–58).
50. See Deeg (1992, 208) and Vitols (1995, 6).

publicly traded, equity financing and securities markets languished, and market-enabling law remained far less developed than in the United States.

Securities Law

Until the mid-1990s, German securities regulation was the province of the eight self-regulating regional stock exchanges and the Länder in which they were located. Following financial and economic crises in the late nineteenth century, political pressures for federal securities market regulation coalesced in a contentious debate over the authority of the still new and consolidating central government. Banks, securities issues, and the exchanges allied with the Länder governments to protect local autonomy and insider control over markets against federal encroachment. In contrast with other domains of economic importance, such as company, banking, and social welfare law, the central government lost this battle for regulatory supremacy.[51] A federal exchange act adopted in 1896 vested market oversight in Länder-appointed state commissioners (*Staatskommissare*) and produced a regime of local exchange self-regulation.[52] Once in place, this regime entrenched Länder control and self-regulation of securities markets by financial insiders. It persisted for nearly a century.

After the Second World War, West Germany's Basic Law (constitution) re-entrenched this fragmented self-regulatory structure by granting the Länder codecision rights over exchange regulation.[53] The exchanges formed the Federation of Stock Exchanges in 1952 to return the nation's securities markets to the status quo ante, which included their autonomy from formal—and particularly federal—regulation.[54] Though the exchanges were considered public law bodies, the universal banks and banking associations dominated the quasi-formal cartels of issuers, stockbrokers, and exchange personnel that controlled stock exchange governance and self-regulation.[55] The exchanges were not captured; they were legally constituted creatures of the financial sector. Unlike the development of American corporation law, this was not the result of a competitive race to the bottom but a deliberate and coordinated choice of powerful financial interests. Small shareholders lacked representation and influence within a financial system dominated by banks and blockholders. Federalism and interest group politics insulated this closed, decentralized, and self-regulatory structure of exchange governance from reform. Without strong pro-shareholder constituencies, there were few calls for regulatory or

51. See Lütz (1998).
52. Nussbaum (1935, 840–41).
53. Lütz and Deeg (2000).
54. Lütz (1998).
55. Ibid.

stock exchange reform that would have to pass in the *Bundesrat*, the upper chamber of parliament, where Länder interests are represented.

Control by financial insiders and feeble parochial public authority produced weak securities market regulation and enforcement. The exchanges imposed few constraints on managers, controlling shareholders, powerful intermediary banks, and securities traders. Minority shareholders had meager means of legal redress in cases of market manipulation and fraud. Insider trading was not prohibited. Disclosure and accounting rules remained weak, public enforcement actions rare, and company finances opaque. Unsurprisingly, investors were less inclined to purchase shares when minority shareholders were vulnerable to market manipulation, artificially high trading costs, fraud, and other forms of insider opportunism. Bankruptcy law played a larger role in protecting the interests of capital than did securities and exchange regulation—and it strongly favored the protection of bank interests as secured creditors over those of shareholders. The undeveloped state of securities law and regulation reinforced the German model of bank finance, encouraged blockholding, and constrained the growth of securities markets and equity finance.[56]

Labor Law

Two forms of labor codetermination integrated employees into the firm's governance processes and embodied the stakeholder conception of the corporation.[57] Company and labor relations law created microcorporatist structures conducive to negotiation, compromise, and cooperation within firm governance. The three types of supervisory board codetermination are set out in table 3.1. The Codetermination Act of 1976 required most corporations with over two thousand employees to appoint an equal number of shareholder and employee representatives to their supervisory boards (quasi-parity codetermination), while the Industrial Constitution Act of 1952 and the Works Constitution Act of 1972 required those with five hundred to two thousand employees to set aside one-third of the board seats for employee representatives.[58] However, even quasi-parity preserved formal shareholder (or managerial)

56. This is consistent with empirical research finding significant correlations between national stock market capitalization and the effectiveness of disclosure and enforcement rules. See Coffee (2006), and La Porta, Lopez-de-Silanes, and Shleifer (2006, 19).

57. See generally Katzenstein (1987, chap. 3) and Wiedemann (1980).

58. Wiedemann (1980, 79–80). "Montan" codetermination, the third (and original) variant, applies only to firms in the coal, mining, and steel sectors employing more than one thousand workers. It provides for *full parity* of shareholder and employee representation. The decline of the mining and steel sectors in Germany has reduced the importance of Montan codetermination.

Law	Firm coverage criteria	Employee representation on supervisory board
TABLE 3.1: FORMS OF SUPERVISORY BOARD CODETERMINATION		
Coal, Iron and Steel Industry Codetermination Act of 1951 (*Montan-Mitbestimmung*)	Firms (AktG & GmbH) with >1,000 employees in the coal, iron, and steel sectors	Full parity plus one neutral representative selected by agreement of employee and shareholder representatives
Industrial Constitution Act of 1952 and Works Constitution Act of 1972	Firms (AktG & GmbH) with >500 employees	One-third employee representation
Codetermination Act of 1976	Firms (AktG & GmbH) with >2,000 employees	Quasi-parity employee representation (tie-breaking board chair selected by shareholder representatives)

dominance by giving the shareholder-elected chairman of the supervisory board a second tie-breaking vote.[59]

Board codetermination became enormously important, symbolically and ideologically, as a feature of Germany's consensus-driven social-market economy, but its practical import has been modest. Critics argue that codetermination diminished incentives to strengthen the role of supervisory boards and diluted the content of fiduciary duties by compelling the recognition of multiple stakeholder groups, including labor, in construing the "interests of the corporation" under German fiduciary law.[60] However, a large body of empirical research on board codetermination indicates that it has had little economic impact.[61] This suggests that the controversies that have long swirled around employee representation on boards are primarily struggles for power within the corporation rather than for increased efficiency.

By contrast, works council (*Betriebsrat*) codetermination has provided a second and more important form of employee representation in firm governance.[62] Originally the product of the divisive 1952 attempt by Konrad Adenauer's Center-Right government to break the unions' monopoly over worker representation, works councils wield substantial influence within the workplace,

59. Wiedemann (1980, 79).
60. See, e.g., Prigge (1998) and Roe (1998, 2003b).
61. Empirical assessment of board codetermination's impact poses difficult theoretical and methodological problems. See Sadowski, Junkes, and Lindenthal (2000, 52–56) and Prigge (1998, 1006–11, tentatively concluding that board codetermination weakens the governance role of the supervisory board but finding no significant economic impact); see also Baums and Frick (1999, event study showing no negative impact of pro-labor codetermination court decisions); *compare* Roe (2003a, 32–33 n. 9, arguing that board codetermination has a substantial negative impact on corporate share values).
62. Wiedemann (1980, 80–82). For general discussions of the political origins and impact of codetermination, see, e.g., Vagts (1966, 64–78) Streeck (1984), Katzenstein (1987, chap. 3), and Muller-Jentsch (1995). For the role of works councils in German labor relations, see Thelen (1991); cf. Turner (1991).

and often over entire corporate groups, through their wide and complex array of informational, consultation, and codetermination or codecision rights, as shown in table 3.2. Works councils can exert additional influence by using these rights to impede the implementation of managerial decisions. They also have the authority to demand compensation for economic injury caused by changes in corporate policy. Although potentially obstructionist, works council codetermination has also proved highly beneficial to firms as a way of coordinating labor relations in workplaces staffed by highly skilled and productive employees. The fact that many large firms have voluntarily instituted enterprise (or *Konzern*) works councils covering an entire corporate group, even though the law provides for the councils only at the plant level, suggests that this form of codetermination fosters beneficially stable and cooperative labor relations.

TABLE 3.2: SUMMARY OF WORKS COUNCIL RIGHTS	
Subject matter of right	*Type of right*
Enterprise alterations	
Downsizing, closure, merger, or transfers of the establishment or division	Codetermination; social compensation plan[a]
Important changes in plant or firm organization or business	Codetermination; social compensation plan[a]
Introduction of new work methods or production processes	Codetermination; social compensation plan[a]
Financial matters	
Appointment of and representative on finance committee	Information/consultation[b]
Social matters	
Operation of and conduct of employees in establishment	Codetermination[c]
Determination and changes in working hours	Codetermination[c]
Form and timing of pay	Codetermination[c]
Leave policies	Codetermination[c]
Technological monitoring of employees	Codetermination[c]
Safety and health issues and implementation of related regulations	Codetermination[c]
Firm-administered social services	Codetermination[c]
Staff policies	
Personnel planning	Information/consultation
Staff surveys	Codetermination[c]
Employment and promotion criteria	Codetermination[c]
Vocational training and appointment of training officer	Codetermination[c]
Recruitment, classification, and transfer of employees	Codetermination[d]
Dismissal of employee	Codetermination[e]

TABLE 3.2: *(CONTINUED)*	
Organization of jobs and operations	
Construction, alteration, and expansion of premises	Information/consultation
Technical plant changes	Information/consultation
Working procedures; scope of job responsibilities	Information/consultation
Structural or organizational decisions that result in "special burden" or inhumane working conditions	Codetermination[c]

[a]The works council and the employer must formally negotiate and draft the social compensation plan. Disputes over proposed alterations or compensation terms are brought to the president of the Land Labor Office for mediation and, in the absence of agreement, to the conciliation committee for binding proceedings. Works Constitution Act §§ 112–112a. Social plans may be enforced by an action in the Labor Court.
[b]Finance committee must include at least one works council member and may inquire into (1) economic, financial, production, and marketing situation of the firm; (2) investment, production, and rationalization plans (including introduction of new work methods); (3) downsizing and plant closures; (4) change in firm's structure or business objectives; (5) any other matter that may have a material impact on employees. Disputes over information requests are subject to binding conciliation committee proceedings.
[c]Codetermination requires consent of the works council regarding the management policy or decision, subject to binding conciliation committee proceedings, unless otherwise noted.
[d]Consent may be withheld only under specified circumstances.
[e]Consent may be withheld only under specified circumstances. An action challenging a dismissal may be brought in the Labor Court *by the individual employee* following the objection of the works council. This does not apply to "exceptional" dismissals or to those of works council members. Works Constitution Act §§ 103–104.

MECHANISMS OF ENFORCEMENT: LITIGIOUS SHAREHOLDERS VERSUS RELATIONAL STAKEHOLDERS

The means by which the interests of corporate stakeholders are protected is a critical component of any corporate governance regime. Without effective enforcement mechanisms, legal rights are merely markings on paper. A comparison of the specific enforcement mechanisms deployed in the United States and Germany reveals the stark differences between the litigation-driven mode of the American regime and the highly institutionalized, negotiation-centered mode typical of German corporate governance. Enforcement mechanisms and rights within these two regimes tended not only to take different forms but also to serve divergent ends. These distinct modes of enforcement not only show how law constitutes power relationships within the corporation; they also manifest fundamentally different conceptions of rights, authority, and conflict resolution underlying neoliberal and microcorporatist governance.

The American Model: Litigious Enforcement and Its Discontents

The American corporate governance regime has depended to an exceptional extent on ex post litigation-driven enforcement to remedy alleged violations of shareholder rights.[63] Given weak shareholder voting rights and the absence of effective institutional channels for representation and negotiation within the corporation, court-ordered monetary damages and injunctive relief were the principal remedial ends of enforcement. Litigation-driven enforcement as it developed within American corporate governance was congruent with managerialism and liberal market capitalism. The enabling-disclosure approach to corporate governance law and its litigation-driven enforcement substituted for more interventionist forms of regulation. This legal framework also granted managers and boards comparatively broad discretion in the contractual ordering of corporate organization and strategies.

Litigious, rights-based enforcement is a feature of what Robert A. Kagan has termed "adversarial legalism," which reached its zenith in the 1960s and 1970s.[64] Building on a long tradition of enforcing public law rights by private litigation, institutional and ideological factors enhanced the lawmaking and enforcement power of courts. Fragmentation of political authority in the United States, multiple veto points in the policymaking process, and suspicion of centralized and discretionary regulatory power all strengthened the courts and favored litigious enforcement mechanisms. The American common-law adjudicatory model served the ends of the regulatory state by means of a litigation process at once highly adversarial, formal, and coordinate in the control granted to attorneys over the litigation process.[65] This model characterized the unusually robust forms of both public and private adjudicatory enforcement proceedings that have distinguished American corporate governance from that of most other industrialized countries. However, though investigations and enforcement actions by the SEC, other regulators, and federal and state prosecutors were significant, private shareholder litigation became the most important means of enforcing legal norms and ensuring regulatory compliance in the American regime.[66]

The prevalent use of private litigation to enforce public law norms was encouraged by a variety of procedural mechanisms under federal and state law. The federal courts recognized (or implied) private rights of action to sue

63. The SEC's ex ante prospectus and registration statement approval process and "no-action letter" procedure (advance approval of proxy statements forswearing enforcement action) are exceptions to this reliance on ex post enforcement. However, they are not continuous supervisory process, and neither is conducted by the Division of Enforcement. Further, the no-action procedure is quasi-adjudicatory and initiated by the issuer.

64. See Kagan (1991, 2001) and Cioffi (2009).

65. Cioffi (2009, 238) and Kagan (1997, 167–86).

66. See Cox and Thomas (2009, 12) and Kagan (2001, 36); cf. Coffee (2006, 266–68, 273–74, post-2000 data).

under securities law for fraud and other violations of disclosure rules.[67] In one seminal case, the Supreme Court described shareholder plaintiffs as "private attorney generals."[68] Procedural rules also reinforced the use of litigation as an enforcement mechanism. State and federal law allowed contingency fees and, in some circumstances, allowed plaintiffs to recover fees from defendants. Both created class action procedures to enable the consolidation and collective litigation of large numbers of small claims sharing common nuclei of fact and law that would not be worth litigating individually. State corporation laws granted shareholders expansive rights to pursue derivative actions against directors and officers on behalf of the corporation to remedy alleged violations of fiduciary duties and other rights. Plaintiffs' attorneys assumed greater control over the conduct of litigation in the common-law tradition, in which judges typically act as referees, than in the judge-directed inquisitorial civil law tradition. Attorney control over the litigation process in complex shareholder and corporate litigation became particularly important in the conduct of discovery under permissive civil procedure rules that allowed plaintiffs to compel disclosure of often huge amounts of information in search of incriminating evidence.

Partisan and interest group politics sustained the litigation-driven enforcement model.[69] During the post–New Deal period, the Democratic Party became increasingly committed to private litigation as a means of promoting social change and enforcing legal rules and norms. For obvious reasons, shareholders (including large institutional funds and wealthy investors) and plaintiffs' attorneys supported the expansive role of litigation. In this favorable legal environment, securities and corporate governance litigation became highly lucrative and created the conditions for the emergence of a large, well-funded, and influential plaintiffs' bar that aggressively sought to protect and expand the legal structures on which it depended. It became a key constituency of the Democratic Party.[70] Reliance on private litigation of shareholder rights benefited managers and boards as well. Adversarial and litigious enforcement played a critical practical and legitimation function in the broader legal framework of American corporate governance. In comparison with statist supervision or mandatory structural regulation, this framework preserved an expansive sphere of managerial autonomy during the post–New Deal growth of the regulatory state. The prevalence of litigation was an important and

---

67. *JI Case Co. v. Borak*, 377 U.S. 426, 432 (1964) (implied right of action for proxy rule violations under Securities Exchange Act § 14(a)); *Superintendent of Insurance v. Bankers Life & Casualty Co.*, 404 U.S. 6, 13 (1971) (approving implied private right of action for securities fraud under SEC Rule 10b-5, following *Kardon v. National Gypsum Co.*, 69 F. Supp. 512 (E.D. Pa. 1946)).

68. *JI Case Co. v. Borak*, 377 U.S. 426, 432.

69. Cioffi (2009, 238).

70. See Cioffi (2007).

distinctive feature of the American liberal market order. It was also a byproduct of the political dynamics that fashioned and perpetuated that order. From this perspective, civil litigation in the United States appears to have developed as the means of enforcement most consistent with a liberal political economy and not simply a pathology that arbitrarily emerged within it.

The litigation of corporate governance disputes also played an important role in maintaining corporate law federalism. During the mid-1970s, Supreme Court decisions began to stress the primacy of state law with respect to fiduciary duties and the internal structure of the corporation and to reinforce the division of state and federal domains in corporate governance.[71] The Court ruled that state law governs internal corporate affairs and held that, in the absence of congressional intent to override established state law, breach of state law fiduciary duties is not actionable under federal securities laws.[72] This shift by the courts came as a post-Watergate anti-corporate reform movement, following the lead of former SEC Chairman William Cary, had begun to attack the pro-management "Delaware effect" of corporate law federalism. The reformers demanded federal minimum standards in corporation law and directors' duties, expanded federal litigation remedies against board members, federal incorporation of large public corporations, and even appointment of public interest directors.[73] Some eminent—and hardly radical—critics of managerialism, including former Supreme Court justice Arthur Goldberg and future SEC Commissioner Harvey Goldschmid, advocated a quasi-stakeholder regime and called for enhanced board powers, professionalism, and responsibilities in order to more actively monitor managers and protect employee, consumer, environmental, and general public interests.[74]

All these proposals failed. Proposed reforms mobilized fierce resistance from managers and were hamstrung by senators sensitive to state interests in maintaining control over corporation law. On top of this formidable political opposition, the Supreme Court's rulings restricting SEC jurisdiction limited the possibility of federalizing corporate governance and the adoption of structural regulation through SEC rulemaking. Congressional inaction and judicial limitations hardened the preferences of the SEC leadership for market-based means of controlling corporate and managerial behavior. The SEC's policy proposals jettisoned ideas of federalizing corporate governance law and sought to accommodate both sides of the debate by seeking moderate reforms

71. The SEC itself endorsed this position in the mid-1960s. See *In re Franchard Corp.*, 42 S.E.C. 163 (1964) (Securities Act "does not purport . . . to define Federal [fiduciary standards] and nowhere empowers [the SEC] to formulate administratively such regulatory standards.").

72. *Cort v. Ash*, 422 U.S. 66, 84 (1975); *Santa Fe Industries v. Green*, 430 U.S. 462 (1977); see also *Business Roundtable v. SEC*, 905 F.2d 406 (D.C. Cir. 1990) (Exchange Act did not empower SEC to impose one share–one vote rule on public stock exchanges).

73. Cary (1974); see also Sporkin (1977, SEC director of enforcement supporting federal incorporation act).

74. Goldberg (1972) and Goldschmid (1973, 17–28).

requiring more disclosure of director independence. Even this modest reform agenda generated such opposition that it was watered down.[75] Finally, the increasing severity of the post-1973 economic crisis and stock market slump had the paradoxical effect of reinforcing and expanding the most liberal elements of the American political economy.[76] In a context of economic crisis, implacable managerial opposition, and ascendant neoliberalism, fears that sweeping corporate governance reform might diminish corporate competitiveness and profitability undermined political support for the more far-reaching proposals.

Amid this conflict over federalism and structural regulation, the balance of political forces underpinning litigation-driven enforcement began to shift as well. Foreshadowing the neoliberal politics and policy to come, intensifying political and judicial attacks on shareholder litigation as an enforcement mechanism followed the defeat of the 1970s reform movement. Pro-plaintiff procedural rules aided the litigation of meritorious cases, but they also massively increased the leverage of plaintiffs' attorneys to extract settlements in more dubious "strike suits" by threatening corporate defendants (along with directors and officers) with potentially enormous litigation costs. Although empirical research is ambiguous regarding the character and effectiveness of shareholder litigation, polemical attacks on litigation that enriched lawyers and yielded little shareholder compensation had a potent impact on policy discourse.[77]

During the 1980s, an increasingly conservative federal bench, with considerable interpretive powers to shape federal law, grew hostile to litigation-driven enforcement. Securities fraud litigation came under increasingly withering criticism as wasteful and inefficient for generating extortionate strike suits and opportunistic settlements with plaintiffs' class action attorneys, imposing enormous costs in time and money, and failing to adequately compensate injured shareholders. Federal court decisions restricted the availability and scope of private rights of action to enforce securities laws.[78] By the 1990s, the federal

75. See Securities and Exchange Commission (1978a, proposed rule amending 17 C.F.R. 240.14a-1–4, 6–7, 11, and 1978b, withdrawing proposed rule).

76. Cf. Levy, Kagan, and Zysman (1999).

77. For a review focusing on post-1995 empirical literature, see Cox and Thomas (2009); see also Alexander (1991, shareholder litigation is ineffective and compromised by strike suits) and Seligman (1996, no evidence of a shareholder litigation explosion or increase in meritless suits).

78. See, e.g., *Cort v. Ash*, 422 U.S. 66, 78 (1975) ("corporations are creatures of state law" and federal causes of action should not overlap those "traditionally relegated to state law"); *Blue Chip Stamps v. Manor Drug Stores*, 421 U.S. 723, 734 (1975) (per Rehnquist, J., courts will not expand scope of civil liability beyond express terms of the statute); *Piper v. Chris-Craft Industries, Inc.*, 430 U.S. 1 (1977) (adopting restrictive approach to implying civil actions under federal securities law); *Santa Fe Industries v. Green*, 430 U.S. 462 (1977) (interpreting federal securities laws to protect the traditional core of state corporation law); *Dirks v. Securities and Exchange Commission*, 463 U.S. 646 (1983) (limiting causes of action for insider trading); *Business Roundtable v. SEC*, 905 F.2d 406 (D.C. Cir. 1990) (SEC power to regulate share classes not granted under the 1934 act).

courts would eliminate private suits for third-party liability against intermediaries like investment banks, underwriters, and accountants.[79] Outside the courts, the political tides would also turn against litigation-driven enforcement. This would in turn force corporate governance reformers to seek alternative mechanisms of enforcement and ultimately the structural reform of governance.

The German Model: Enforcement through Institutions

In contrast with the litigation-prone American model, the German corporate governance regime favored negotiation within the institutional framework of the corporation rather than enforcement of rights through adjudication.[80] Rather than relying on market-enabling rules and the litigious enforcement of rights by *individual* actors, the German form of microcorporatist governance relied to a far greater extent on structural regulation to allocate rights of group representation and participation to *institutional* actors.[81] The governance structure of the German corporation, legally mandated ex ante to a far greater degree than its American counterpart, served as an institutional enforcement mechanism to mediate the conflicting interests of powerful political constituencies. By contrast with the American governance regime, shareholder litigation played at most a minor supplementary role and tended to bolster the structural mechanisms of corporate governance and reinforce rather than substitute for institutionalized negotiation.[82]

The subordination of litigation to the imperatives of iterative bargaining relationships was reflected in both substantive and procedural law. With the exception of disclosure and voting rights in the context of the shareholders' annual general meeting (discussed below), shareholder rights were generally weak and difficult to enforce in court. If weak securities regulation reflected the closed character of the financial system and the marginality of equity finance, weak shareholder rights and enforcement mechanisms reflected both the insider-domination and stakeholder orientation of German corporate governance.

Weak Länder securities regulation rendered civil actions for materially false or misleading statements practically unavailable in all but the most egregious cases.[83] Insider trading was not prohibited and thus not a basis for

---

79. See *Central Bank of Denver v. First Interstate Bank of Denver,* 511 U.S. 164 (1994) (no civil action against third parties for aiding and abetting liability in securities fraud).
80. See Pistor (2006).
81. Cf. Teubner (1985, 155–56).
82. See Pistor (2006).
83. Plaintiffs had to satisfy the daunting standard of proof for "willful deception." See Baums and Scott (2003, 20).

shareholder litigation. The pervasive financial opacity of firms and markets shielded opportunistic dealings from shareholder view and thus from challenge. Indeed, it was common corporate practice to distribute the annual auditor's report at the beginning of a supervisory board meeting and then collect it after the managers' summary of its contents. Even under the *Konzernrecht*, the law of corporate groups that granted minority shareholders in controlled subsidiaries comparatively strong rights to challenge transactions ex post, the external auditor's report on intragroup transactions was disclosed only to the firms' supervisory boards, not to the shareholders.[84]

Substantive company law likewise discouraged claims for breach of directors' duties (*Untreue*). Shareholder litigation against directors contradicted the logic of governance through stakeholder negotiation over disputes. Further, reliance on litigation would have mired the courts in intractable conflicts over which stakeholder's rights trumped another's when company law conceived of the firm as a community of multiple stakeholder interests. German courts also implicitly imposed their own version of the American business judgment rule to sharply circumscribe liability for alleged mismanagement.[85] Even in alleged breaches of the duty of loyalty, which implicate conflicts of interest or self-dealing rather than conflicts among stakeholders, German company law relied primarily on procedural rules governing supervisory board approval of related-party transactions.[86] Whereas American mergers and takeovers frequently triggered fierce litigation (discussed below), German merger law mandated ex ante assessment of *all* merger agreements by a court-appointed expert prior to submission to the shareholders for approval. Shareholders or creditors could seek compensation for economic injury caused by a merger but only by requesting the court's appointment of a representative to assess and pursue the claims.

German procedural law also strongly discouraged private shareholder litigation. Would-be plaintiffs faced unfavorable procedural rules such as limits on discovery, a "loser pays" rule for attorney's fees and court costs, and the prohibition of contingency fee retainers.[87] These rules created powerful disincentives for plaintiffs and attorneys to initiate complex and costly corporate governance litigation. Germany had no equivalent of the American class action or the derivative shareholder suit, and their absence from the legal landscape reflected Germany's traditional hostility toward litigation as a means of protecting shareholders and resolving governance disputes. Shareholders seeking to compel a suit against the management board had to represent 10 percent of outstanding share capital (successively lowered by later reforms), and actions

84. See ibid., 13.
85. See *ARAG/Garmenbeck*, 135 BGHZ 244 (April 21, 1997) (explicit recognition of the long-established, judge-made rule).
86. Baums and Scott (2003, 14).
87. Stock Corporation Act § 147(4).

against a manager (or the management board) were presumptively under the control of the supervisory board.[88] The relationship between the two bodies posed an obvious conflict of interest, but shareholders could circumvent this requirement only in rare cases. State prosecutors could bring criminal charges against directors for breach of trust (as seen in the *Mannesmann* case discussed in chapter 5), but the number of such cases was vanishingly small.

The absence of any effective procedure for collective litigation left small shareholders unable to overcome collective action problems of dispersion, resource limitations, informational asymmetries, and disparities between the value of individual claims and litigation costs. Small minority shareholders would not finance a complex lawsuit against a deep-pocketed corporation to recover modest individual damages. Private negotiation among huge numbers of individual shareholders to share costs and recoveries was impracticable. The absence of contingency fees and the imposition of attorney's fees and costs on the losing party compounded these problems. Shareholders could not shift the costs and risks of litigation onto plaintiffs' attorneys—who could marshal more resources and spread risk across multiple cases.

In addition, Germany's hierarchical and inquisitorial form of judicial proceedings, rooted in civil law tradition, gave judges greater control over the litigation and discovery process than they had in the common-law model.[89] Courts' limitations on discovery further weakened the plaintiff's position and compounded the opacity of financial reporting. Even if sufficient publicly available information alerted shareholders to a potential violation of their rights, proving their case was difficult, if not impossible, without adequate discovery of additional information from the corporate defendants. Discovery often accounts for up to 90 percent of litigation costs in American securities cases, borne almost entirely by defendant companies but driven by plaintiffs' attorneys under permissive civil procedure rules. Strict limits placed on discovery by the courts in Germany further reduced the shareholders' settlement leverage and chances of success while raising the downside risks for plaintiffs.

However, German corporate governance did develop one significant, and increasingly controversial, form of litigation regarding the functions and proceedings of shareholder meetings. German company law vested these meetings with broad mandatory decision-making powers and imposed complex mandatory disclosure and procedural rules on their conduct to vindicate both shareholder voting rights and corporate policymaking. Shareholders could bring a private action to enjoin or nullify any corporate decision taken in violation of these rights.[90] They could also sue for a judicial declaration obliging

---

88. Ibid. § 112.
89. Cioffi (2009, 245).
90. Stock Corporation Act §§ 131–32, 241, 243.

management to put a given decision to a shareholder vote.[91] Because these cases often concerned important and time-sensitive business decisions, plaintiffs' attorneys had greater leverage to extract lucrative settlements from managers eager for quick resolution. Plaintiffs' attorneys' peculiar legal and tactical advantages in these situations account for the growth of this form of litigation, despite the disincentives to sue under German procedural rules.

Yet the prevalence of shareholder litigation over the conduct of shareholder meetings also reveals deeper differences between German and American corporate governance. American corporate law granted shareholders comparatively few rights to put corporate policies to a vote, while federal securities regulation and litigation primarily concerned issues of disclosure to the market. German shareholder litigation, in contrast, even when asserting violations of disclosure rights, reinforced the ability of shareholders to vote on corporate decisions. This articulation of shareholder rights still fit within the framework of structural regulation by strengthening the shareholder meeting as a representational and decision-making body. Even so, these suits became controversial as the source of numerous allegedly abusive lawsuits and an opportunistic plaintiffs' bar that reinforced the perception of litigation as wasteful, ineffective in the achievement of policy goals, and disruptive to the cooperation and negotiation fostered by German institutional arrangements.[92]

THE MARKET FOR CONTROL AND
CONTROL IN WEAK MARKETS

Along with the formal legal mechanisms of enforcement, private mechanisms of corporate control within the American and German governance regimes also differed. In part, divergent forms of contractual and market ordering reflected the underlying legal frameworks described above. Hence, the development of an active market for control in the United States and the dynamics of blockholder and bank influence in Germany constituted additional means of enforcing governance norms. A comparison of the two regimes' distinctive private governance processes shows how they differed in operation and also in their juridical preconditions. These processes had political, as well as legal, underpinnings and consequences. The private sphere, at least where so much wealth and economic power is implicated, cannot be disentangled from public law and politics. The emergence of hostile takeovers in

91. See the Federal Supreme Court's decision in *Holzmüller*, 83 BGHZ 122 (February 25, 1982).

92. See Cioffi (2009).

the United States heralded the emergence of a finance-driven form of capitalism and the destabilization of political, economic, and legal arrangements that raised the salience of corporate governance as a policy area. German corporate governance remained far more stable through the 1980s, but its internal dynamics revealed a sustaining constellation of interests, institutional commitments, and policy preferences that would later fragment and set the politics of reform in motion.

The United States: From Takeovers to Governance

During the 1980s, takeovers became a driving force in the reorganization of corporate firms and much of the economy. By the end of the 1980s takeover wave, more than 25 percent of the Fortune 500 had been the targets of hostile bids.[93] Nearly half of the major listed firms in the United States received either a friendly or a hostile takeover bid, and 41 percent were acquired.[94] High stock prices, driven by increasing returns to shareholders, provided not only a first line of defense against takeovers but also a means of financing acquisitions. The economic repercussions of this change were enormous. For the first time since the era of JP Morgan, financial elites challenged the preeminence of industrial managers and fashioned a new paradigm of finance capitalism in which financial markets and shareholders became driving forces in corporate restructuring and strategy. Takeovers repudiated the corporation's relational obligations to stakeholders that had formed an important, but largely informal and implicit, dimension of the post–New Deal political economy.[95] Maximizing shareholder value displaced problems of competitiveness in a new and Darwinian economic environment. American corporate governance rapidly shifted from a paradigm of "retain and reinvest" to one of "downsize and redistribute," as managers propped up short-term share prices through dividends or capital gains.[96] The age of stock market capitalism had arrived.[97]

Yet in an early iteration of finance capitalism's boom-bust cycle, the hostile takeover wave ended amid insider trading scandals, a crash in the junk bond debt market, recession, and political backlash. Economic theories rationalizing the maximization of shareholder value and the norm of shareholder primacy gained influence as a way to justify and adjudicate takeover conflicts. But fierce debates erupted over the mixed economic record of takeovers, even in

93. Lazonick and O'Sullivan (2000).
94. Mitchell and Mulherin (1996, 199–200 and table 2).
95. Cf. Shleifer and Summers (1988, takeovers break and appropriate the value of implicit contracts).
96. Lazonick and O'Sullivan (2000, 17–27).
97. Dore (2000, 1–14).

increasing shareholder value. Excessive leverage and layoffs, short-term financial engineering, and integration problems often destroyed shareholder value,
impaired longer-term corporate competitiveness, and inflicted serious negative externalities on a wide range of nonshareholder interests. Even when eval-
uated solely in terms of shareholder value, the weight of the evidence indicates
that target shareholders reap substantial takeover premiums while bidder firm
shares lose value in most cases.[98] The cyclical pattern and increasing intensity
of takeover waves raised suspicions that takeovers were driven not by business
fundamentals and poor target management but by macroeconomic and capital market conditions. A cleavage within the American business elite widened
as managers and their allies denounced takeovers as an unproductive and disruptive extraction of value by the financial sector.[99]

Litigation over the fiduciary duty of loyalty played a central role in takeover battles and the regulation of the market for control. Hostile takeovers
intensified conflicts of interest that pitted shareholders demanding immediate
maximization of share value against managers and directors seeking to preserve their positions and autonomy. Charged with deciding on takeover offers
and defense strategies, the boards of directors were placed in the middle of
these conflicts over control and conceptions of the corporation. In a highly
technical and adversarial legal context, they confronted intractable practical
problems regarding the scope of managerial and board authority, the appropriate time horizon for business strategies (and the maximization of shareholder value), and the complexities of balancing the wide range of interests
implicated by the management of the public firm.

Managers and boards adopted an inventive array of antitakeover defenses
such as "poison pills," staggered boards (depriving a successful bidder of a
board majority for years afterward), conditional assets sales and "lockup"
agreements, conditional voting caps, and recapitalizations that increased
leverage or placed shares with a friendly owner. In a series of watershed decisions, the Delaware Supreme Court upheld poison pills and other antitakeover
defenses but barred their use to wholly foreclose takeovers.[100] Poison pills were
adopted by boards, often without shareholder approval, to deter hostile bids by

98. See Bratton (2007).
99. See Andrade, Mitchell, and Stafford (2001, 105 and figure 1).
100. See *Moran v. Household International, Inc.*, 500 A.2d 1346 (Del. 1985) (upholding
poison pill defense in limited circumstances); *Unitrin v. American General Corp.*, 651 A.2d 1361
(Del. 1995) (adopting a permissive reasonableness standard for evaluating antitakeover
defenses, so long as they are not "coercive" or "preclusive"); *Revlon, Inc. v. MacAndrews & Forbes
Holdings, Inc.*, 506 A.2d 173, 182 (Del. 1986) (holding that the board may consider nonshareholder constituencies where "there are rationally related benefits accruing to the stockholders"); compare *Unocal Corp. v. Mesa Petroleum Co.*, 493 A.2d 946, 955 (Del. 1985) (prospective
change in control triggers fiduciary duties that limit defensive tactics) with *Paramount Communications v. Time*, 571 A.2d 1140 (Del. 1989) ("just say no" defense to a superior tender offer valid
to protect previously agreed change in control).

threatening massive dilution of a would-be raider's equity stake in the company in the event of a takeover attempt. Under the complex and shifting Delaware case law, poison pills and other defenses did not provide an ironclad form of defense, but they raised the control premium an acquirer would have to pay and thus lowered anticipated returns. This diminished the threat to managers, along with the stringency of fiduciary duties.

Outside the courts, managers mobilized organized labor and community groups in ad hoc cross-class coalitions pressing state legislatures to pass antitakeover statutes.[101] A 1987 Supreme Court decision upholding an antitakeover statute opened the way for the flood of laws that followed.[102] By 1988, in the words of a leading corporate law scholar, there had been "an epidemic-like character to the spread of state anti-takeover legislation" emanating from the deindustrializing "Rustbelt" states.[103] With the notable exception of Delaware, the epidemic of antitakeover statutes embodied the prevailing politics and policy at the state level.[104] "Corporate constituency" laws became the most common form of antitakeover statute. These statutes allowed managers and directors to invoke the interests of multiple constituencies, including shareholders, employees, creditors, suppliers, customers, and local communities, in responding to a hostile takeover attempt.[105] Notably, constituency statutes did not grant these constituencies any enforceable rights. Antitakeover politics reinforced managerialism in the guise of pseudo-stakeholder governance.

In contrast, Congress never passed a significant piece of legislation addressing takeovers and related financial practices, though numerous hearings were held and bills proposed.[106] Regardless of their economic merits, antitakeover defenses and laws reflected political equilibriums in which manager- and financier-led coalitions counterbalanced each other. Shareholder primacy as a legal norm proved too economically destabilizing to withstand legal and political challenge. The influence of financial and managerial elites was more evenly matched at the federal level, and broad congressional opposition to takeovers counterbalanced the largely pro-takeover Reagan administration and SEC. Congress was not so much cautious as paralyzed. Because of divisions within both parties over the issues and the veto-prone structure of

101. See Roe (1993a) and Orts (1992, nn.47, 61–63 and accompanying text).

102. *CTS Corp. v. Dynamics Corp. of America*, 481 U.S. 69 (1987) (upholding a "control share law" that limited a bidder's voting rights to a statutory threshold absent a shareholder vote to restore them).

103. Coffee (1988, 435–36).

104. For an analysis of these "second generation" antitakeover statutes, see Romano (1987).

105. See Adams and Matheson (2000, n.9 and appendix, listing thirty-three states with constituency statutes).

106. The implicit threat of federal intervention may have influenced state takeover law, especially in Delaware, but evidence of this is questionable. See Roe (2003a, 616–20, finding substantial federal influence).

the legislative process, no manager- or financier-led coalition emerged as powerful enough to push through federal takeover legislation.

Federal paralysis, federalism, and strategic positioning preserved Delaware's preeminence as the de facto national legal capital for corporate America. Its state courts and legislature were less parochial and of necessity more responsive to both financial and managerial elites. Delaware law struck an effective compromise between managers and financial interests—the two constituencies capable of undermining the state's status as the preferred jurisdiction of incorporation for publicly listed corporations. Managers and their allies could not obtain a strong antitakeover statute, but they did get partial protection under court decisions upholding antitakeover defenses and the state's "business combination" law.[107] The legal outcome simultaneously dampened the hostile market for control while allowing for an active market for mergers and acquisitions. As a result, the American corporate governance regime preserved many of its managerialist features within the emerging domestic and international order of finance capitalism. The solution defused potential threats of corporate migration and loss of Delaware's market share in corporate charters, but the hostile takeover wave and the legal changes it precipitated presented serious practical and conceptual problems for the American regime.

The American approach to corporate governance had relied on market-enabling rules and litigation-driven enforcement of shareholder rights. Capital market pressures alone had proved insufficient to redress managerial principal-agent problems, as had shareholder litigation. Yet by the beginning of the 1990s, the political and judicial reaction to takeovers had curtailed the most potent market mechanism to discipline managers to maximize shareholder value. And growing political and judicial antipathy constrained any expansion of civil litigation as an enforcement mechanism. The corporate governance regime faced a crisis of enforcement and accountability.

Policymakers and shareholder activists would focus increasing attention on the governance structures and incentive alignments within the corporation. Governance activism by institutional investors, enhanced disclosure regulation, and the ostensible "contracting away" of conflicts of interest through managerial "incentive pay" arrangements were viewed as the most promising means of addressing governance deficiencies. None would be effective. The attempt to align managerial and shareholder interests via compensation incentives, including golden parachutes, guaranteed severance and pension packages, and enormously lucrative stock option plans, would prove extremely problematic.[108] These incentives helped facilitate managerial acceptance of buyouts—in part by conferring an increasing share of equity and the control

---

107. Del. Code tit. 8, § 203 (2001).
108. See generally Bebchuk and Fried (2004).

premium on managers. But stock options also became an engine of the inexorable rise in executive compensation. Escalating managerial pay was not merely a symptom of dysfunctional governance institutions and skewed power relations. Stock option plans would *magnify* the conflicts of interest they were supposed to diminish. They became the most effective means of managerial rent seeking (or looting) ever devised. Perversely, by *successfully* inducing managers to pursue the maximization of shareholder value, stock options exacerbated the short-term orientation of American managers and heightened their incentives for financial manipulation and recklessness.

Germany: Insider Governance and Institutional Reinforcement

Hostile takeovers played no appreciable role in postwar German corporate governance.[109] Antitakeover defenses, such as voting caps, share transferability limitations, and unequal share voting rights, were legally permitted but not particularly widespread. Far more important were the capital market conditions, ownership structures, blocking minority rights, and strong stakeholder protections that virtually precluded Anglo-American-style takeovers. Hostile takeovers become common only when control can be acquired via tender offers to dispersed shareholders and where post-acquisition restructuring yields profits (returns in excess of the control premium). Germany satisfied neither condition.

First, hostile takeovers require a liquid stock market, listed firms with a large "free float" (the percentage of shares actively traded), and legal rules that enable the acquisition of full control through a tender offer to dispersed shareholders. The illiquid blockholdings and cross-shareholdings typical of German firms reduced the free float of shares. A 25 percent "blocking minority" rule under company law gave blockholders a veto over major business decisions, such as merger approval, recapitalizations, restructurings, and changes in business strategy. These blocking rights typically precluded acquisition of effective control—even where a bidder could buy a majority of shares. Second, the country's stakeholder governance regime, further buttressed by strong unions and job protection laws, empowered and protected employees. Strong unions and employee rights under codetermination, labor, and social welfare laws limited corporate restructuring and constrained managers and shareholders from imposing adjustment and restructuring costs on employees. This lowered potential returns to investors and thus diminished the economic incentives for takeovers, by contrast with the United States.

109. See, e.g., Franks and Mayer (1998).

Preemptive (or antidilution) rights under company law further reinforced blockholding and cross-shareholding by requiring firms to offer existing shareholders the chance to purchase newly issued shares in proportion to their existing holdings.[110] This prevented boards from issuing new shares to a would-be acquirer or to an acquisition target in lieu of a cash payment. This strong antidilution norm simultaneously protected existing shareholders and inhibited managerial control over merger and acquisition activity.[111] Ironically, these preemption rights barred a German version of poison pill defenses that threaten bidders with massive dilution of their equity stake. Given other potent impediments to hostile takeovers, there was no practical need for such takeover defenses. As will be discussed in chapter 5, however, preemptive rights' unintended constraints on antitakeover defenses intensified political resistance to neoliberal takeover law reforms. In contrast, the absence of mandatory preemptive rights under Delaware law facilitated *both* poison pills and control transactions.

Yet corporate control transactions were far more prevalent than is commonly appreciated. Almost invariably, they were brokered by large financial institutions through the sale of blockholdings and conducted quietly, without public fanfare or even disclosure.[112] More rarely, control blocks figured in hostile contests for control without the necessity of a public tender offer.[113] In part, the unobtrusiveness of control transactions reflected a tradition of discreet dealings among corporate and financial elites and served to mute public suspicion of concentrated financial and corporate power. There were other, more immediate, forms of self-interest underlying this mode of acquisition. Blockholders could appropriate the *entire* control premium, as opposed to a tender offer's pro rata distribution among all shareholders, while preserving blockholding patterns that might confer similar benefits in the future. A German market for corporate control existed but in a form consistent with an insider-dominated corporate governance regime.

So long as the interests and policy preferences of the principal stakeholder groups maintained this equilibrium, the postwar German corporate governance regime remained stable. Banks benefited from relational banking practices and their central position within the bank-based financial system. The

110. Stock Corporation Act § 186.

111. Preemptive rights can be waived by a 75 percent supermajority vote at the general shareholders' meeting. This supermajority requirement reflects and bolsters the 25 percent blocking minority rule in German company law by preserving the size of large but nonmajority stakes.

112. Köke (2001) found that between 1986 and 1994 block trades led to an annual control transfer rate averaging 8.3 percent of listed firms and 6 percent of nonlisted firms, with the most active buyers and sellers of control blocks being nonfinancial firms and individuals.

113. See Jenkinson and Ljungqvist (2001, seventeen cases of "hostile stakes" from the late 1980s through the mid-1990s).

regime empowered, protected, and enriched blockholders. Unions and employees championed the stakeholder model that endowed them with multiple levers of influence and levels of protection. Each of these groups opposed legal changes and governance practices that might undermine these benefits and shift rents to smaller shareholders. Without powerful allies, small shareholders remained politically and economically weak—inside the corporation but outsiders in the politics of corporate governance. The recursive logic of interest formation within the German political economy also sustained the corporate governance regime. The principal stakeholder groups were heavily invested in the institutional foundations of Germany's comparative advantages and firm-level core competencies, particularly with respect to highly competitive export-oriented manufacturing. Economic success tended to empower those groups most reliant on the country's distinctive political economic model, including its governance regime, and strengthened their interests in its reproduction.

REGIMES COMPARED: DIVERGENT STRUCTURES AND INTERNAL TENSIONS

This chapter has set out the core legal features and political underpinnings of the German and American corporate governance regimes as they had developed through the late 1980s. Tables 3.3 and 3.4 provide a summary of the main attributes of these national governance models and political economies just prior to the explosive growth of international finance capitalism and the sudden global surge in corporate governance reform during the 1990s. Table 3.3 compares the most important legal attributes of the American and German corporate governance regimes. Table 3.4 describes some of the more important economic relationships and characteristics of the two governance regimes.

The tables reveal the American regime's emphasis on transparency and disclosure rights and the use of law as a means of strengthening the market as the primary mode of economic organization. Conversely, institutional governance mechanisms and shareholder participation rights remained notably weak. Shareholders were marginalized within corporate governance, their interests framed and protected as participants in the stock market rather than in a firm. Reliance on market-enabling disclosure rules sought to discipline management by intensifying financial market pressures, but it had the effect of diminishing the constraints on managers within the corporation as a self-governing entity. The juridical framework and resulting incentive structure of corporate governance effectively pushed directed investors away from governance and into the market.

TABLE 3.3: CORPORATE GOVERNANCE MECHANISMS AND RIGHTS (CIRCA 1990)		
Legal mechanism	*Germany*	*United States*
Board	Two-tiered, separate personnel; codetermined supervisory board with employee and union representatives	One tier, typically includes CEO/chair and other managers; weak director independence and committee rules
Proxy voting	Banks and blockholders dominant (banks vote DSVRs) Shareholders must attend AGM or specify representative (enhances power of DSVRs) Supervisory board typically nominates new members, but banks and blockholders tend to dominate board	Jointly regulated under federal securities and state corporation law Managerial/board control over proxy content and solicitation Shareholder access to company proxy limited in governance matters; cannot nominate directors, alter voting rules Voting by mail (enhances power of managerial control over proxy); shareholders may solicit proxies at own expense
One share–one vote	No	Yes, mandated by stock exchange listing rules, but different share classes may have different voting rights
Share voting thresholds	Blocking minority (25%), majority (50%+), and supermajority (75%) (favors blockholding)	No blocking minority set by law (favors exit and dispersion over blockholding)
Annual general meeting	Strong, but dominated by blockholders and banks; minority shareholders empowered by disclosure and approval rights	Weak, few rights to approve major decisions; management controls content of AGM announcement and agenda
Emergency meeting	Vote of 5% of share capital required to call meeting	Vote of 1% of share capital required to call meeting.
Fiduciary duties	Relatively weak and undeveloped due to stakeholder conflicts and obstacles to litigation	Theoretically strong and highly developed but undercut by practical limitations and business judgment rule under state law
Takeover defenses	Yes (voting caps, differential voting rights); financial system and labor relations discourage takeovers Preemptive rights prohibit poison pill defenses	Yes, state law allows poison pills, staggered boards, etc. Strong antitakeover/corporate constituency statutes after 1987 (excluding Delaware)
Disclosure regulation	Weak under Länder-based self-regulation; no federal law or regulation	Stringent and regular formal disclosure federally mandated and enforced
Accounting standards	Allow substantial "earnings management" and undisclosed reserves to curb volatility in financial reporting	Comparatively stringent (prior to erosion in 1990s) but weak accounting standards for costs of stock options and mergers.

TABLE 3.3: (CONTINUED)		
Legal mechanism	*Germany*	**United States**
Insider trading	Not prohibited.	Prohibited, subject to criminal & civil action.
Derivative suits (company law)	No (supervisory board can sue management on corporation's behalf, rare exceptions for shareholder suits).	Yes (brought by shareholders on behalf of the corporation).
Private rights of action (securities law)	No	Yes (federal courts recognized implied rights of action for violations of disclosure & proxy rules).
Class actions	No	Yes
Discovery	Limited, judge-controlled	Expansive rights to information in litigation, attorney-driven, potentially very costly
Contingency fees	No	Yes, litigation costs and risk of loss shifted to plaintiffs' attorneys
Fee and cost shifting	Yes, "loser pays" rule	No, litigants bear own costs (exception: plaintiffs reimbursed for derivative suits resulting in "substantial benefit" to the corporation)

TABLE 3.4: CORPORATE GOVERNANCE AND ECONOMIC CHARACTERISTICS (CIRCA 1990)		
Attribute	*Germany*	**United States**
Planning horizons	Long-term: incremental production process-oriented innovation; labor as investment in human capital	Short-term: rapid restructuring of labor, financial, and supply-chain relations; labor as variable cost and highly stratified
Comparative advantages	Firm strategy based on diversified quality production in manufacturing, high skills, and design and quality-based competition	Firm strategy based on breakthrough technologies and cost/price-based competition in manufacturing; technical sophistication in services
Function of equity capital	Cross-shareholdings are basis of interfirm cooperation (risk-averse); management/enterprise defense mechanism	Financing and capital formation and incentive structure to encourage maximum profits, growth. and managerial effort (increased appetite for risk)

TABLE 3.4: (*CONTINUED*)		
Attribute	*Germany*	*United States*
Monitoring of management	Moderate (through blockholders and universal banks owning stakes and voting proxies) Low via securities markets due to weak disclosure and low level of market development	Low (separation of ownership and control by operation of law and market) High via securities markets due to stringent mandatory disclosure and high level of market development
Labor relations	Substantial institutional and informal powers and influence over wide range of issues; cooperative relations typical Strong unions and labor rights reinforce codetermination Sectoral bargaining removes most divisive issues from firm-level governance High investment in skills and flexible work arrangements	No role in decision making/strategy; broad managerial power and discretion, little employee voice Weak unions and labor rights; decentralized bargaining produces detailed contracts and rigid work practices Conflictual relations, little cooperation Low investment in skills, flexibility through part-time/temporary work, layoffs
Mechanisms of corporate control	Stakeholder alliances, negotiation and bargains, long-term relational ties Blockholding and bank influence (through relational finance, ownership stakes, DSVRs, and directorships) No hostile takeovers; limited market for control blocks	Market for control (tender offers, mergers and acquisitions), hostile takeovers diminished but not precluded by defenses/statutes Cost of capital determined by share price Investor influence through market exit (depressed share price, higher cost of capital, and increased threat of takeover)

Entirely absent from this framework was any mechanism or even an implicit commitment to the incorporation of labor or other stakeholder groups into corporate governance. The formal representation of opposing interests and the institutionalization of countervailing power within the German corporate structure are notably absent from the American model. If shareholders were marginalized, employees and organized labor were exiled from corporate governance, and the legal protection of their interests as actors within the labor market was conspicuously weak. Perhaps most striking of all, the American model incorporated a set of rules and legal practices that encouraged litigation-driven enforcement of shareholder rights. The market function and litigious enforcement of disclosure rights, along with the managerialist legal structure of the firm and its governance processes, reflected a governance regime that valued exit over voice and the market over governance.

As can be gleaned from table 3.3, the German corporate governance regime inverted the American pattern by pairing strong structural regulation with weak disclosure and litigation rules. The German regime emphasized mandatory ex ante institutional mechanisms that defined the corporate form and its internal governance processes. These rules protected the interests of stakeholder groups by granting them representation rights within the corporation. This use of structural regulation provided institutional channels for the flow of information and negotiation among conflicting group interests within the firm. The microcorporatist German model conferred substantial power on managers by law and by allowing them to form shifting alliances with shareholders, lenders, and employees. However, the negotiation of these alliances simultaneously constrained managers and undermined the interests of minority shareholders vis-à-vis blockholders, banks, and employees.

The substantive rights of individual shareholders (and correlative duties of board members) remained relatively weak and undeveloped. Likewise, litigation rules were highly restrictive and either precluded shareholder lawsuits or effectively discouraged them. Rights in this context tended to reinforce institutional functioning and integrity. Formal enforcement of rights typically directed the opposing parties back into the institutionalized negotiation of intrafirm governance rather than into the market. The constitutive function of law in fashioning institutional forms and relationships—rather than disclosure rules, market transparency, and litigation-driven enforcement of individual rights—characterized the dominant juridical approach to corporate governance. This legal structure constituted a governance model that valued the norm and practice of voice over exit.

As the 1990s began, the economic prospects and political foundations of the American and German corporate governance regimes appeared increasingly parlous. In the United States, the legal and institutional features of the corporate governance regime encouraged risk taking, organizational restructuring, and technological innovation. But these strengths were paired with the problem of increased managerial "short-termism" that elevated immediate financial concerns over long-term growth and stability. Even more troubling, the development of American corporate governance during the 1980s raised concerns about the potentially destabilizing and extractive power of the financial sector. The United States came to be seen as the incarnation of the neoliberal market economic model, yet American corporate governance embodied a fundamental tension between managerialism and shareholder primacy. The rise of finance capitalism in the 1980s did not resolve this tension; it intensified it. The resulting pathologies of the corporate governance regime, along with finance capitalism's extravagantly crisis-prone character, would prompt increasingly urgent demands for reform and bitter political conflict.

Disenchantment with the market for control and private litigation posed a problem for the reform of a governance regime that for decades had relied on market forces, market-enabling legal rules, and litigation-driven enforcement of rights. Structural regulation of the corporation's institutional form presented an alternative to the perceived excesses of the market and the plaintiffs' bar, and it had been advocated during prior periods of reform fervor. But these proposals had repeatedly failed. Structural regulation had at best a minimal presence and shallow roots in American corporate governance. Any reform altering power relations within the corporation would likely trigger bitter resistance, as it had in the 1970s, and the balance of political and economic power in the 1990s favored managerial interests far more than it had twenty years earlier. Even as calls for reform grew more numerous, the legal form and political logic of reform remained elusive.

Germany's stakeholder-oriented governance regime both legitimated the postwar capitalist order and conferred comparative advantages in high-quality, high-value-added manufacturing and incremental innovation in industrial production. German industry focused on market niches that rationalized high wages and investment in skill formation. But these benefits came at an increasingly steep price of high labor costs, sluggish adjustment and risk capital formation, and weak job and firm creation. By the early 1990s, the effects of reunification and declining national economic performance made economic reform increasingly urgent but not necessarily welcomed either by the electorate or by the powerful and highly organized interest groups that dominated politics and policymaking.

This secular decline in economic performance accelerated just as the globalization of finance began to alter the economic interests that had sustained the postwar corporate governance regime. As the interests of the large universal banks and managers of the largest and most internationalized firms began to shift in favor of a more market-based financial system, the banks started to withdraw from traditional governance arrangements and altered their policy preferences as well. Faced with a chronic economic crisis and a potentially unprecedented change in the banks' economic role, German politicians and parties confronted the questions of what their reform agenda should be, what coalition of interest groups might back reform, and which party or governing coalition could mobilize it. In a historic change in coalitional strategies and policy agendas, the financial sector and the Center-Left Social Democratic Party—not shareholders—would drive a prolonged and deliberate process of pro-shareholder corporate governance reform.

CHAPTER 4

U.S. Corporate Governance Reform

Boom, Bust, and Backlash

During the mid- to late 1990s, the American economy and stock markets were on an unprecedented roll. The accelerating growth rates, astonishing stock market returns, and business and technological innovations associated with the boom were the envy of the world. Perhaps at no time has the American model of capitalism exerted such fascination, envy, or influence. Shortly after the turn of the century, the financial boom turned to bust as the securities market bubble burst, mass media spotlighted vast corporate scandals and bankruptcies, and calls for regulatory reform dominated the political scene. The most important and visible product of this burst of regulatory fervor was the Sarbanes-Oxley Act of 2002.[1] Heralded as the most significant reform of American securities law since the New Deal, Sarbanes-Oxley inaugurated an era of corporate governance reform at the federal level. It is part of a long history of political struggle over the form, power, and legitimacy of the corporation and financial capital and the means of regulating them.

Yet the act also represented a break with established forms of regulation and federalism in American corporate governance. It significantly expanded federal regulatory authority over corporate accounting and sought to protect shareholders by imposing self-enforcing regulatory mechanisms that strengthened the board of directors and internal monitoring of management rather than relying on rights-based litigious mechanisms of enforcement. Consequently, Sarbanes-Oxley instituted corporate governance reform in ways that both encroached on the traditional province of state corporate law and

1. Pub. L. No. 107-204, 116 Stat. 445 (2002) (codified in scattered sections of 11, 15, 18, 28, and 29 U.S.C.).

departed from the established pattern of using courts and litigation as primary modes of enforcement. Notwithstanding these innovations, however, the act and the reforms that followed it did not address the fundamental structural problems of corporate power: the manager-dominated process of nominating and electing directors. This failure, as much as the successful reforms, offers a glimpse into the politics of American corporate governance.

Among the central puzzles presented by American corporate governance reform is how and why Congress passed such significant reform during a politically conservative era in which corporate and managerial power were at a zenith, why its form deviated from past regulatory approaches, and why it ultimately failed to address the central conflicts of interest that plagued the American corporation. In part, the answers are straightforward: the extraordinary conditions of stock market crashes and corporate financial scandals temporarily disrupted interest group politics and partisan divisions to allow substantial legal and institutional change. However, this is only the beginning of the explanation. This chapter argues that these events reflected more enduring dynamics of corporate governance reform in the United States. First, since the 1980s, reform has been an ongoing—if sporadic and contradictory—process that elevated the interests of shareholders in American politics and policymaking. Second, political constraints on the use of litigation as a means of enforcing corporate governance norms impelled legislators to embrace alternative structural mechanisms of regulation. Financial crisis and political constraints provided the conditions for regulatory innovation. But, as in the case of limits on litigation, political constraints still circumscribed legal change, and thus the extent of reform, and prevented policymakers from altering the institutional foundations of managerial power within the corporation.

Exemplified by the spectacular failure of Enron, the financial market and corporate collapses of 2001–2 were, in large part, a corporate governance crisis. The stock market crashes, seemingly endless disclosures of financial fraud and manipulation, and the largest corporate bankruptcies in American history represented massive failures of market, corporate, and regulatory institutions. A crisis of investor confidence and ultimately of the broader legitimacy of the American political economic order compelled Congress to act quickly to pass reform legislation that could never have been passed under ordinary conditions. Significant reforms followed in the wake of the post-Enron corporate governance crisis, but they *did not* expand or create new avenues for litigation. Instead, many of the Sarbanes-Oxley reforms and those later adopted by the SEC took the path of *structural regulation* of the institutional arrangements within the corporation to alter behavior with minimal, if any, recourse to legal enforcement. The politics of corporate governance reform, not economics or some internal legal logic, drove policymakers to use this mode of regulation.

Federal corporate governance reform was a deliberate, and for a time substantially successful, attempt to shore up the regulatory regime and restore investor confidence on which the securities markets relied—all within the narrow political constraints of a conservative era. These objectives reflect regulation's central purposes: providing for market efficiency and maintaining popular belief in the integrity of the market. Reform may be embodied in law or regulation, but it is the product of politics rather than economic optimality. If this story supports the argument that freer markets require more rules, to paraphrase Steven Vogel (1996), it also reveals that we get only the rules the political system can deliver. Corporate governance reform in the United States overrode interest group and partisan politics, departed from the established forms of regulation, yet remained cabined by powerful political constraints that could limit the effectiveness of regulatory innovations. Those constraints pertained to the use of private litigation to curb managerial financial misconduct. During the 1990s, hostility toward litigation as a mechanism of legal and regulatory enforcement became an entrenched feature of federal legislative politics and culminated in the passage of federal securities litigation reform laws. Faced with the post-Enron corporate governance crisis and unable to use traditional litigious mechanisms of enforcement to protect shareholder interests, proponents of reform expanded the scope of federal regulation and pursued an incremental *federalization of the structural components of corporate law* to achieve their ends. The exigencies of recent governance reform and the political legacy of anti-litigation politics produced a paradox: the political constraints on the use of litigious enforcement mechanisms led to even more extensive forms of governmental regulatory power over corporate affairs. Ultimately, federal legislative and regulatory encroachment on the institutional bases of managerial power and autonomy, by Congress and later by the SEC, mobilized business interests to resist further reforms and lash out against parts of Sarbanes-Oxley itself.

The broader historical context of corporate governance reform elucidates the political dynamics of the process. Reform consistently involves successive waves of backlash politics, in which legislators and partisan coalitions seize the initiative before the veto-prone logjam of pluralistic American politics reasserts itself. This history is presented in three stages. The first covers the politics of securities litigation reform of the early to late 1990s. The second deals with the legislative and regulatory corporate governance reforms of 2001–4. The last phase encompasses an ongoing business backlash against reform and the expanding regulatory intervention in corporate affairs. This anti-regulation backlash mobilized business groups and their political allies, but left intact the legal reforms of the corporate governance regime. It shaped the Bush administration's perversely deregulatory response to the devastating subprime credit crisis but could not contain growing pressures for further reform. Corporate governance reform reflects both a substantial change in the

American political economy and an enduring struggle for economic power within the corporation and the new finance capitalism that is nowhere near resolved.

THE SEC IN THE 1990s AND THE ANTECEDENTS
OF STRUCTURAL REGULATION

The conservative ascendancy and the takeover wave of the 1980s heightened political conflict over corporate governance reform. As a result, during the 1990s, the SEC was whipsawed between managerial and pro-shareholder groups, along with their respective political allies. In the political battles that ensued, the SEC got little effective political support from shareholders. For one thing, diffuse and fragmented shareholders faced steep collective-action problems that made unified and coherent action in opposition to managers a near impossibility. The separation of ownership and control extended from the corporate realm into the political sphere, where it again privileged managerial interests. The same problems were magnified in the much larger political arena and afflicted the political strength and effectiveness of shareholders as a class and an interest group. Second, the pro-shareholder forces were also split among themselves with respect to their preferred mode of reform. Some favored expanded formal disclosure regulation, enforced by the SEC (and to a lesser extent by private litigation). Others sought to encourage the monitoring of management and corporate governance activism by institutional investors. The vacillations of SEC policy during the 1990s reflected this political and ideological conflict. From 1992 to 2000, the SEC under Chairman Arthur Levitt, a Clinton appointee, and his Republican predecessor, Richard Breeden, initiated a series of reforms to protect shareholders by improving managerial accountability and financial transparency—with mixed political and practical success.

In 1992, after several years of pressure from institutional investors, the SEC under Breeden reformed its proxy statement rules to encourage corporate governance activism among large institutional investors. The regulatory change eliminated the requirement to disclose communications among large shareholders concerning corporate governance issues (at least where seizure of control was not at issue), thereby making it easier and cheaper for them to communicate with each other and with management.[2] The amendments

2. See Regulation of Communications among Shareholders, Exchange Act Release Nos. 34-31,326, IC-19,031, 57 Fed. Reg. 48, 276, 48, 283 (Oct. 22, 1992). See Calio and Zahralddin (1994) and Minow (1991, 149, arguing that government agencies generally had initiated previous federal corporate governance reforms but that institutional shareholders were now driving proxy reform); see also Frenchman (1993, nn. 2, 6, and 155–56 and accompanying text).

unleashed the fiercest fight over SEC rule making in the agency's history up to that time. The SEC received over 1,700 comment letters, and business attacks on the proposal were even more heated than the statements in support. The rule inflamed economic conflicts and ideological debates over the merits and legitimacy of managerialism and the potential financial and governance power of institutional shareholders.[3] In contrast to the transparency and disclosure rules common in American securities market regulation, the 1992 proxy rules reduced disclosure obligations and were an experiment in structural regulation that altered intracorporate power relations to achieve the policy goal of increased monitoring and governance activism by institutional investors. The rule changes appear to have encouraged greater activism but at the expense of transparency. Institutional investors, with some notable exceptions, preferred to voice their concerns and criticisms to management in private communications that would not depress the price of their stock holdings. These discussions no longer had to be disclosed in proxy statements, at the risk of privileging some large institutions over other (and particularly smaller) investors with respect to information access. This use of structural regulation posed problems of transparency, opportunism, and insider trading even as the SEC sought to use it to redress the balance of power between shareholders and managers.

The SEC under Levitt pursued a more activist policy agenda favoring small shareholders, but he was soundly defeated in his attempts to reform the accounting treatment of stock options, curb conflicts of interest in the accounting industry, and improve the accuracy of audits.[4] The impetus for the accounting rule change actually did not come from the SEC but from the Financial Accounting Standards Board (FASB), the accounting industry's standards body. Not known for its aggressive rule making, this body and its troubled predecessors had long been a source of frustration in the SEC's attempts to increase the accuracy of financial disclosure. But it was not completely captive either. In June of 1993, FASB reasonably, and quite correctly, noted that stock options both had discernible market value and imposed costs of dilution on existing stockholders, and it proposed a new rule requiring that these costs be written down as a liability on the balance sheet when options were granted. The response from business groups and sympathetic politicians was immediate and forceful. Managers growing rich on huge grants of stock options, along with partisans of "New Economy" technology firms that had little revenue and were thus dependent on options as a form of compensation, enlisted bipartisan congressional and executive branch support to quash the initiative. In a foreshadowing of the bipartisan politics of securities litigation reform to come, opposition to the FASB option-expensing rule was predominantly Republican but drew significant Democratic support. Though no legislation

---

3. See Cioffi (2002, 210–12).
4. See generally Levitt (2003).

passed, a Senate resolution condemning the FASB proposal introduced by Democratic senator Joseph Lieberman of Connecticut, a state home to many financial firms, passed 88–9.[5] Levitt feared that he could not protect the FASB from political attack and that continued legislative opposition might result in even worse rules if the option proposal went forward—fears that intensified after the Republic takeover of Congress in late 1994. In what he later acknowledged was a mistake, Levitt urged the FASB to back down, and it complied.

The failure to require the expensing of stock options in corporate financial statements was a politically damaging blow to Levitt and the SEC and set the stage for subsequent battles over accounting rules. In late 1995, a coalition of senior managers from some of the largest public corporations in the country attempted to take over the FASB board, alleging that the group was anti-business.[6] The SEC engineered the FASB's defense, but the episode revealed the growing tensions over accounting rules and the fragility of the industry's self-regulation. That self-regulation would prove problematic when it came to the governance of the accounting industry itself and ensuring its own integrity and independence.

Large accounting firms had steadily increased their consulting arms to the extent that their revenues from auditing had declined from approximately 70 percent in the mid-1970s to less than half that in 1998. Fearing that conflicts of interest created by accounting firms acting simultaneously as consultants and auditors would compromise the integrity of their auditing, the SEC in mid-1997 began to lay the groundwork to increase the independence of accountants. The regulation of accounting firms became an especially important issue following a 1994 Supreme Court decision that largely abolished "aiding and abetting" liability, under which accounting and law firms could be held liable for fraudulent statements and omissions by publicly traded corporate clients.[7] Without the threat of private litigation, SEC regulation was the only enforcement option remaining.[8] In September 1998, as the stock market frenzy of the late 1990s was well under way and balance sheet restatements were spiraling upwards,[9] the SEC unveiled a plan to substantially curtail the amount and types of consulting work accounting firms could do for the publicly traded corporations they audited. In a Pyrrhic victory that would prove disastrous following disclosure of the Enron-era accounting frauds (and accountant

---

5. Ibid., 114–18.

6. Levitt attributes this takeover attempt to the blue-chip corporations' hostility to a proposed change in the accounting treatment of derivatives, which had led to some substantial losses. Ibid., 119–20. As discussed in chapter 6, weak accounting for derivatives would fuel the 2007–9 credit crisis spawned by the collapse of the mortgage-backed securities markets.

7. *Central Bank of Denver v. First Interstate Bank of Denver,* 511 U.S. 164 (1994).

8. The Private Securities Litigation Reform Act (PSLRA) of 1995 authorized aiding and abetting suits brought by the SEC but not by private plaintiffs.

9. See General Accounting Office of the United States (2002, 4–5).

complicity or negligence), the accounting industry enlisted allies in Congress to fight on their behalf and bring legislative pressure on the SEC. After congressional Republicans threatened the agency's funding, the regulatory proposal was withdrawn and a far weaker compromise worked out with the major accounting firms.[10]

However, the Levitt SEC was successful in pushing through a new regulation that ended the practice of selective disclosure of important business and financial information to favored analysts and institutional investors. This move was widely perceived as a way for the SEC to claw back some of its regulatory authority over insider trading that had been limited by Supreme Court decisions over the prior fifteen years. As an indication of the intensifying public interest in corporate governance issues, the SEC received over six thousand comment letters, eclipsing the former record set by the 1992 proxy reforms.[11] In August 2000, the SEC adopted Regulation Fair Disclosure (Regulation FD).[12] The regulation prohibited selective disclosure of material information by corporate managers to favored analysts, financial institutions, and institutional investors if that information were not released to the general public. The SEC promoted formal equality among shareholders by addressing the problem of informational asymmetries that disadvantaged small investors vis-à-vis large institutions, even though the informational playing field could never be even between individuals and giant financial players. Regulation FD expressly rejected the need for private litigation by shareholders and relied exclusively on SEC enforcement, once again indicating the new political constraints on litigious enforcement. Yet there was another tension underlying the adoption of the regulation. That was the deeper conflict between structural and disclosure regulation.

The 1992 proxy reforms and Regulation FD reflected an emerging and fundamental tension in SEC policymaking. The regulation undermined the SEC's own 1992 proxy reforms by limiting the ability of institutional investors to pursue corporate governance activism through private communications with managers and board members. Monitoring by institutional investors tends to conflict with equal access to information for all shareholders. More fundamentally, the mechanisms of structural regulation may conflict with established forms of disclosure regulation. Disclosure is the favored mode of regulation in a market-driven "outsider" governance regime preoccupied with the functioning of markets comprised of dispersed shareholders. Structural regulation seeks to marshal or actively constitute the countervailing power of

10. Levitt (2003, 135–48).
11. Selective Disclosure and Insider Trading, Exchange Act Release Nos. 33-7881, 34-43,154, IC-24,599 § II A (1), esp. n. 9, 65 Fed. Reg. 51,715, 17 C.F.R. 240.10b5-1 & 2, 243.100-103 (Aug. 21, 2000).
12. See Regulation FD, 17 C.F.R. §§ 243.100–103 (2003); Selective Disclosure and Insider Trading, Exchange Act Release Nos. 33-7881, 34-43154, IC-24,599, Fed. Reg. (Aug. 21, 2000).

insiders to curb agency costs and promote desired economic outcomes. The 1992 proxy rule amendments presumed that more intensive communications between institutional investors and managers would benefit all shareholders. Regulation FD presumed that such communications fostered unfairness and insider trading. By the end of 2000, these two dominant paradigms of corporate governance reform had collided on the levels of politics, law, and corporate practice.

SECURITIES LITIGATION REFORM IN THE 1990s

Litigation, Legal Liberalism, and American Securities Regulation

By the end of the 1980s, battles over hostile takeovers and the financially driven transformation of the American corporate economy (along with its significant deindustrialization) had exhausted both corporate and financial elites. They had battled fiercely in the courts, legislatures, and boardrooms and fought to a rough draw over the legal balance of power within publicly traded corporations. Nonetheless, the tensions between these groups persisted and in some ways deepened. Out of the public glare of titanic takeover fights, corporate governance issues continued to percolate through state and federal politics and into policymaking. Ultimately the two fundamental conflicts over governance regulation of the 1990s, the first between transparency and structural regulation and the second over litigation rules, would jointly shape reform in the post-Enron era.

One signal change in the politics of securities regulation and, by extension, corporate governance, was an increase in hostility (on the right) and skepticism (on the left) toward litigation as a means of enforcing legal norms. This struggle defined the second great conflict in the politics of corporate governance and securities regulation during the 1990s. Criticism of securities litigation began to intensify during the merger and acquisition boom of the 1980s and the subsequent recession and bankruptcies of the early 1990s.[13] Though couched in economic and technical legal terms, the core of this debate concerned the allocation of power in the corporation as much as it did abuses and inefficiencies of litigation. Over the course of the 1990s, political conflict over the scope, role, and litigious means of enforcing regulatory norms grew increasingly intense. By the end of the decade, anti-litigation forces inside government and out had not only passed pathbreaking securities litigation reform

---

13. See, e.g., Alexander (1991, claiming an increase in meritless securities litigation); compare Seligman (1996, arguing that no evidence of litigation rates or strike suits supports statutory restrictions on securities).

legislation but effectively redefined the politically acceptable limits of protecting shareholder interests. The policy pendulum decisively swung away from litigation-based enforcement of shareholder rights.[14]

Congressional Republicans had potent political reasons to pursue securities litigation reform with increasing fervor. First, crippling the securities plaintiffs bar would deny the Democratic Party its substantial financial backing. Second, not only was reform an excellent way to reinforce the support of managerial elites for the Republican Party but it provided a political wedge issue to appeal to socially liberal business elites in the high-tech industry. Accordingly, litigation reform attacked two important sources of Democratic funding and support while consolidating and potentially expanding the Republicans' business base.

By the early 1990s, the critics of securities litigation found both political parties increasingly congenial to their pleas for legislative relief. In response to rising litigation rates, the anti-litigation coalition expanded during the 1990s. The supporters of reform legislation included not only corporate managers, the traditional foes of securities litigation, but also securities and accounting firms, as well as the economically ascendant Silicon Valley firms that depended upon equity financing.[15] Split over litigation reform and seeking a more business-friendly political strategy and policy agenda, the Democrats sought to neutralize the issue by drafting moderate reform legislation in 1993 and 1994 that balanced the interests of corporations, shareholders, and plaintiffs' attorneys.[16] Driven by interest group loyalties, political calculation, and an increasingly hard-line ideological approach to policy, the Republican Party pushed for more substantial legal change. In 1993 the Republicans made securities litigation reform a component of their "Contract with America" campaign platform. After the 1994 "Republican Revolution," in which the right wing of the Republican Party took control of Congress under the leadership of Newt Gingrich, the party made good on its promise.

The Private Securities Litigation Reform Act of 1995

After three years of fierce political conflict and an epochal shift in the control of Congress, conservative congressional Republicans spearheaded the passage of the Private Securities Litigation Reform Act of 1995 (the PSLRA) over President Bill Clinton's veto.[17] This was the *only* successful override of a

---

14. See *Harvard Law Review* (2000).
15. Avery (1996, 339–54) and Kelleher (1998, 51–53).
16. Seligman (1996, 717–19).
17. Pub. L. No. 104-67, 109 Stat. 737 (1995).

presidential veto during Clinton's two terms in office. Intended to curtail the use of the courts and litigation for the prosecution of securities fraud claims, the PSLRA placed more stringent pleading requirements on securities fraud suits in an attempt to streamline the procedure for dismissing these suits before they entered the expensive discovery phase.[18] Its proponents hoped that the law would reduce the settlement value of, and thus the incentive to file, weak or meritless suits. The PSLRA reflected a sea change in American politics and policy characterized by a hardening of Republican opposition to and erosion of Democratic support for private litigation as an enforcement mechanism.

The act also reflected the struggle to find alternative enforcement mechanisms to replace private litigation. Its measures provided for three such alternatives: (1) the use of institutional investors to monitor plaintiffs' attorneys on behalf of all shareholders, (2) reliance on certified public accountants as informational intermediaries and monitors of corporate finances and performance, and (3) litigation by the SEC rather than private plaintiffs and attorneys. By highlighting the role of institutional investors and external auditors, the act represented a nascent structural turn in securities and corporate governance law based on the hope that private actors would perform governance and enforcement functions through institutional relationships and incentives under law. The growing importance of institutional investors was reflected in the PSLRA's creation of a "lead plaintiff" position (generally the shareholder with the largest stake) to police litigation, promote the swift disposition of meritless suits, and prevent collusive settlements.[19] The provision legally empowered institutional investors to act as a counterweight to the power of both plaintiff attorneys and corporate managers. Congress wishfully saw institutional investors as a less adversarial means of controlling conflicts of interest. This image of self-regulation by rival capitalists appealed to policymakers and managerial interests alike.

However, the PSLRA's lead-plaintiff provision produced unintended and paradoxical results. Institutional investors initially had little interest in intervening to terminate lawsuits.[20] The expense and unpredictability of litigation and the fear of potential liability to other shareholders displeased with their conduct as lead plaintiffs discouraged deep-pocketed institutional investors from curbing securities litigation. Instead, they used this new power to intervene with growing frequency to prevent plaintiffs' counsel from cutting opportunistic settlement deals with managers in meritorious cases, thereby

---

18. *Securities Regulation and Law Reporter* (1995).
19. PSLRA, § 27(a)(3)(A) & (B), 15 U.S.C. §§ 77z-1(a)(3)(A) & (B), 78u-4(a)(3) (A) & (B) (2006) (procedure and substantive criteria for appointment of "lead plaintiff"). This provision was inspired by an inventive 1995 law review article by Weiss and Beckerman (1995).
20. Grundfest and Perino (1997a, 1997b).

prolonging litigation and increasing the amount of final settlements and damage awards.

The PSLRA's use of auditors to detect fraud and the SEC civil actions to enforce the securities laws proved even less effective. Title 3 of the PSLRA, which contains the auditing and auditor disclosure provisions, failed to address the basic conflicts of interest in the management-auditor relationship that SEC Chairman Arthur Levitt would criticize in subsequent years, and it did not provide for an effective means of enforcement. Instead, during the late 1990s, auditing firms became—knowingly or unknowingly—instrumental in the manipulation or outright misrepresentation of corporate finances.[21] Auditor responsibilities under the PSLRA were enforceable by the SEC alone, not by private litigation, and only when auditors filed a report of suspected illegal activity. SEC civil and criminal actions authorized under the PSLRA failed to fill the enforcement gap left by securities litigation reform, as the stock market boom of the late 1990s sent the agency's workload spiraling upward, with its budget lagging far behind.[22] However, the PSLRA's primary purpose was not to advance structural regulation but to curb private litigation. And its passage reflected a clear political realignment antagonistic to securities litigation. The political constraints that precluded the adoption of litigation-driven enforcement mechanisms in securities regulation and corporate governance law would even withstand the post-Enron crisis.

The Securities Litigation Uniform Standards Act of 1998

The anti-litigation realignment became even clearer several years later. The federal character of American law and regulation raised the specter of a massive loophole for plaintiffs' attorneys. Critics of litigation asserted that any reduction in federal securities suits would be offset by the number filed in state courts. Federal law had not preempted securities regulation or private litigation at the state level, but both had been reduced to secondary status as the post-New Deal federal regulatory regime developed. The PSLRA's restrictions on private shareholder suits, however, raised the possibility that state court litigation of state law claims might become increasingly attractive to plaintiffs and their attorneys as federal courtrooms became less hospitable.

Spurred on by arguments—and at best ambiguous evidence[23]—that the PSLRA had pushed securities litigation into state courts, Congress passed the

21. See generally Coffee (2006, chaps. 2 and 9).
22. See 15 U.S.C. § 77t(f) (authorizing SEC actions for "aiding and abetting liability") and 15 U.S.C. § 78j–1(d) (SEC has exclusive authority to enforce auditor's duty to disclose fraud and penalize violations).
23. See Caiola (2000, nn. 186–90 and accompanying text).

Securities Litigation Uniform Standards Act of 1998 (SLUSA) to close the alleged loophole by preempting state securities fraud laws and granting federal courts exclusive jurisdiction over securities lawsuits brought under federal law.[24] This time the Republicans had support from a majority of Democrats in Congress, especially those in the California delegation, who were eager to cultivate and maintain high-tech industry support. Chastened by the PSLRA veto override and acutely sensitive to the political trends supporting litigation reform, the Clinton administration also signed on in support of the legislation.

The SLUSA centralized regulatory authority over securities markets in striking fashion. The political potency of the securities litigation reform agenda and the growing political power of anti-litigation constituencies overrode the sentiments and rhetoric of conservative neofederalism. Despite their centralizing effect, however, the PSLRA and SLUSA preserved the autonomy of state corporate law, including fiduciary duties and related derivative suits (known as SLUSA's "Delaware carve-outs"). Federal securities litigation reform thus generated opposing policy incentives: on the one hand, it invited further fragmentation of corporate governance law by increasing reliance on state fiduciary law and litigation; on the other hand, it promoted the encroachment of federal law on traditional core areas of state corporation law. This process of federalization would eventually become a central issue in corporate governance reform.

AFTER ENRON: THE SARBANES-OXLEY REFORMS

Finance Capitalism and the Politics of Reform

This tension between the fragmentation and federalization of corporate governance law heightened as American finance capitalism became enveloped in controversy fueled by scandals and systemic crisis in the aftermath of the late 1990s stock market bubble. Even at the nadir of the crisis, irresistible forces driving legislative and regulatory reform confronted immovable political constraints on policymaking. This combination of factors channeled reform efforts towards pro-shareholder structural regulation, but also contributed to the substantial flaws of the resultant reforms.

The euphoric dot-com bubble of the 1990s died a painful death, as bubbles always do. The Dow Jones Industrial Average fell by 25 percent between March 19, 2000, and July 19, 2002. Standard & Poor's 500 Index lost nearly 28 percent

---

24. Pub. L. No. 105-353, 112 Stat. 3227 (codified as amended at 15 U.S.C. §§77p, 77v, 77z-1, 78-4, and 78bb (2000)).

during the same period.[25] The Wilshire 5000 Index, among the most comprehensive of American stock indexes, fell by over 40 percent from a peak of $17.25 trillion on March 24, 2000, to $10.03 trillion on July 18, 2001.[26] The bursting of the stock market bubble and the sustained impact of corporate scandals and bankruptcies after the collapse of Enron in December 2000 wiped out approximately $7 trillion of market capitalization. According to one estimate, 17 percent of these losses, nearly $1.2 trillion, were attributable to the wave of corporate finance scandals that devastated investor confidence and perceptions of market integrity.[27]

The crash not only destroyed investors' portfolios but also revealed the manipulative and often outright illegal financial conduct of corporate managers, accountants, financial institutions, and attorneys. The collapse drained a swamp of misconduct, bringing into full view the prevalence and severity of the conflicts of interest, financial engineering, earnings management, deficient accounting, and other dubious financial practices and outright fraud of the boom years. In response, public confidence in the reliability of accounting and financial disclosure reached a new low, and the entire financial system came under suspicion of fundamental systemic corruption. Investor confidence in the securities markets collapsed along with stock prices. Massive finance scandals at Enron, Tyco, WorldCom, Global Crossing, Adelphia, and other major corporations, along with the enormous market losses, stoked the public's resentment against corporate and financial elites. Revelations of managerial fraud, looting, and empire building punctured the inflated cult of the CEO.[28] The abuses and improprieties of corporate managers also revealed the inadequacies of corporate boards of directors, auditors, and other informational intermediaries, as well as government regulation and regulators. In the harsh light of hindsight, boards of directors of defrauded, looted, and bankrupt firms appeared at best negligent and at worst corrupt.

The mass shareholding that had expanded during the bull market of the 1980s and 1990s, once a key societal support for pro-market policies, now fueled pervasive cynicism, resentment, and finally fury against business, financial, and political elites. Business and neoliberal deregulation lost their luster in both ideological and political terms. The legitimacy of finance capitalism itself appeared to teeter as the prestige and reputations of principal political and economic actors plummeted. Key informational intermediaries, particularly accountants and stock analysts, failed to protect the public interest and appeared mired in conflicts of interest. If Enron symbolized the culture of corporate fraud and board failure during the 1990s, its auditor, the accounting

25. Graham, Litan, and Sukhtankar (2002, 3).
26. Seligman (2003, 624).
27. Graham, Litan, and Sukhtankar (2002, 2).
28. For a scathing critique of managerial compensation in light of the crisis, see Bebchuk and Fried (2004).

firm Arthur Andersen, represented the spread of corruption to the self-regulating professionals entrusted to protect the public interest in transparency. Likewise, stock analysts were unveiled as shills for the investment banks that employed them, and their stock ratings were exposed as largely worthless and often deceptive.

The government did not escape the public's corrosive skepticism. The legacies of past political attacks on regulation and reform came back to haunt those who had endorsed or participated in them. Securities regulators and prosecutors had failed to deter, detect, or punish managerial misfeasance and malfeasance. Congress's litigation reform legislation had intensified the pressures on the SEC while starving it of resources. The SEC itself was chaired by an avowed skeptic of regulation, Harvey Pitt, known for his representation of accounting firms in private practice and as the lead counsel for the accounting industry in its attack on Levitt's drive to increase auditor independence in the late 1990s. During the 1990s, congressional opposition in both parties had also rolled back a proposal by the FASB to require expensing of stock options and an effort by the SEC to compel the separation of auditing and consulting services by accounting firms.

This erosion of governmental regulatory efficacy made governance self-regulation through the board's monitoring of management all the more critical. But directors turned out not to be watching the CEOs, and neither regulators nor shareholders were watching these passive boards. The wave of corporate finance scandals and bankruptcies that followed from these serial governance failures frayed public confidence in the soundness, stability, and fundamental integrity of the financial system and corporate governance regime.

Heightening the apocalyptic ambience of the period, Enron collapsed just after the terrorist attacks of September 11, 2001. The succession of post-crash scandals unfolded in the aftermath of that catastrophe. By the spring of 2002, the combination of the terrorist attacks and pervasive financial scandals led policymakers in and out of Congress to fear the possibility of a general collapse of the American and international financial systems.[29] By late June, some were also worrying that an international financial contagion had taken hold, in view of the double-digit losses sustained in the first half of 2002 by the American, British, French, and German stock markets.

"Investor confidence" became a de facto ideational construct, though a rather ambiguous metric, of political economic legitimacy. Perhaps for the first time in American history, the interests and perceptions of the investor class were viewed, however questionably, as largely coterminous with those of the citizenry at large. The idea that the backlash in response to scandal and

---

29. This perception was repeatedly stated in my interviews with congressional aides from both parties.

financial crisis had been driven, or at least colored, by anti-financier populism is a recurrent theme in American political and legal history.[30] Yet the post-Enron politics of reform was not so much anti-management or anti-financier as it was *pro-shareholder.* This reflected a substantial shift in the politics of corporate and financial regulation in the United States. Integrity and fairness of the markets, the adequacy of financial disclosure, and conflicts of interest in corporate governance were increasingly judged by the interests of shareholders rather than those of consumers, local communities, workers, unions, or small business. The post-Enron corporate governance crisis made clear that the legal rules, market and corporate structures, and regulatory enforcement that buttress shareholder interests and investor confidence had become crucial to the legitimation of the political economic order. Consequently, even as it altered them, corporate governance reform was designed to restore and reinforce the structural features of the American political economy, with its market-centered financial system, emergent preoccupation with shareholder value, and financially driven managerial style. From this perspective, corporate governance reform was an essentially conservative, not radical, response to crisis in a conservative era.

The Relative Autonomy of Reform Politics

These overwhelming external forces and events allowed policymakers a rare and short-lived period of relative autonomy from established interest group politics. The most severe legitimacy crisis of the American financial system and corporate governance regime since the Great Depression disrupted the grip of a conservative coalition that favored minimal regulation and had blocked pro-shareholder reforms during the 1990s. Yet growing public demand for reform remained unfocused and detached from any specific proposal, program, or policy agenda. Loosened constraints of interest group politics combined with generic public approval for reform increased the autonomy of Democratic legislators in fashioning a response to the crisis, despite their minority status. That response became the Sarbanes-Oxley Act of 2002.

Sarbanes-Oxley was the product of a political struggle between Democrats using financial scandals against the Republicans and Republicans seeking to delay or dilute the legislation in keeping with their loyalty to corporate supporters and their antiregulation ideological policy agenda. Given Republican control of the presidency and House of Representatives and the party's characteristic unity and discipline within the veto-prone structure of the federal government, substantial reform was possible only under crisis conditions that weakened interest group influence and made resistance to reform intensely unpopular. Democrats took advantage of the approaching midterm elections,

---

30. Roe (1991, 10; 1994).

an outraged public, and disgraced Enron executives closely linked to President Bush himself. Corporate governance reform in the United States was as much a product of historical contingency as of underlying structural changes in the economy.

Opponents of reform among interest groups and in the Republican Party hoped to ride out the scandals without any major legislative or regulatory initiative. Bush's senior economic policy aide, Larry Lindsey, argued that government should consider "the option of doing nothing" because "the markets are moving ahead . . . [and] already discounting the stock of companies that show accounting irregularities."[31] The debate within the administration was driven to an almost astonishing degree by concern over litigation.[32] A combination of neoliberal ideology and brutal political calculation, embodied first and foremost by the White House but widely shared in high Republican circles, precluded any reform proposal that might result in more or new forms of litigation. Former treasury secretary Paul O'Neill ran afoul of this axiom of partisan politics. He advocated requiring senior executives to certify the accuracy of corporate financial statements and reducing the liability standard for violations of disclosure rules from recklessness to simple negligence, which would have resulted in a potentially massive increase in the number of managers who might be found liable.[33] Not surprisingly, when word of this proposal was leaked, the opposition by business groups was unanimous. But O'Neill was a minority of one. The White House political staff, the senior economic advisers, and SEC Chairman Pitt were all deeply opposed to any liberalization of liability standards, even if the SEC were given sole enforcement authority and private litigation were barred.[34] They were likewise opposed to the creation of accounting "best practices" standards that would inform the certification of corporate accounts by both the CEO and the board audit committee and thus form a benchmark for an emerging negligence standard. Remaining well within the established securities regulation paradigm, Pitt maintained, "It's not the job of government to protect shareholders from bad management. We need to focus on quality of disclosure, not quality of judgment."[35]

Sensing political vulnerability from the spreading scandals, the Bush administration in March 2002 announced a ten-point plan to combat corporate corruption. House Republicans led by Michael Oxley, chairman of the House Finance Committee, quickly submitted a bill patterned after the Bush plan. The bill garnered little praise from commentators and the public, and much derision from congressional Democrats for its support by and weak restrictions on the accounting industry and its almost complete reliance on

31. See Suskind (2004, 230).
32. Ibid., 221–34, 238–39.
33. Ibid., 210–11, 225–31.
34. Ibid., 225–31.
35. Ibid., 228.

the SEC. The commission's chairman was becoming an object of ridicule and a symbol of the ineffectual administration and Republican response to the mushrooming crisis of corporate corruption. Congressional Republicans pressed forward with Oxley's bill in an attempt to frame the legislative debate and establish the party's bargaining position against the Democrats.[36]

Shortly after the Republicans began work on their bill, Senate Democrats, led by Banking Committee chairman Paul Sarbanes, began hearings on the scandals and potential legislative responses to the crisis. Because they were completely shut out of the Republican-dominated House legislative process, the Democrats had to channel their policy positions through the Senate, where they held a short-lived one-vote majority following Senator James Jeffords's defection from the Republican Party.[37] Of the numerous committees that held hearings on Enron and the unfolding corporate governance crisis, however, the staid Committee on Banking, Housing, and Urban Affairs, with jurisdiction over securities law and accounting issues, took the lead on accounting and corporate governance reform.[38]

The rhetoric of shareholder value filled the chambers of Congress. In the House, representatives sought to outdo one another in their denunciations of greed and corporate fraud and malfeasance. Democrats sought to seize the political mantle of reform and capitalize on the scandals by denouncing Republican deregulation ideology and systemic flaws in securities regulation and corporate governance. The Republicans set out to neutralize these attacks by adopting the rhetoric of shareholder value and investor confidence while framing the scandals as a matter of a few bad apples rather the product of structural flaws in regulation and corporate governance. Similar language permeated the Senate debates over corporate governance reform. Some Democrats sharpened this general argument into a slashing attack on the Republicans' domestic policy agenda, including litigation reform, which they presented as pro-management, anti-investor, and increasingly dangerous to economic stability. Republicans sought to parry the Democrats' attacks by using the same language of trust and investor confidence, though in more muted terms.

Legislative results accompanied this rhetoric of shareholder interests and investor confidence only because the crisis had generated an unusual—and temporary—interregnum of interest group politics. The few-bad-apples defense against reform became increasingly untenable as the scandals impli-

36. Interviews, current and former staff members, U.S. House of Representatives, Senate, and Department of the Treasury, Washington, DC, March 2004.

37. This majority was precarious, and the public's attention to and memory of financial scandals was short. Following losses in the November 2002 midterm elections, both the Democrats' control of the Senate and the public's fixation on corporate finance scandals were gone.

38. The Senate Judiciary, Commerce, Labor, Tax, and Investigations committees held hearings on issues raised by Enron and the crisis of corporate governance, but their jurisdictional competence was either too narrow or too peripheral to frame a comprehensive policy response.

cated ever-widening circles of financial, business, and professional elites. A disintegration of interest group influence and the rise of entrepreneurial political actors accompanied the reform politics of 2001–2.[39] Tainted by scandal, corporate managers, accounting firms, and investment banks were weakened within the legislative process. Corporate managers in particular lost prestige and influence in the wake of successive corporate scandals and the popular perception that they, as a class, had looted American corporations and stolen from their shareholders.

The institutional investor community remained split over legislative and regulatory reforms. Corporate pension funds and most mutual funds, which are either controlled by or beholden to corporate managers, did not press for reform. Large public employee and union pension funds, long involved in a largely nonregulatory and voluntarist form of corporate governance activism, shifted their policy preferences dramatically in support of increased regulatory stringency and intervention in corporate governance. The AFL-CIO and its member unions strongly supported governance reforms that would help protect their members' private pension investments, provide them with more information regarding the financial health of businesses, and curtail managerial power.[40] However, like other interest groups, institutional investors and organized labor wielded minimal influence on the content of the reforms.[41]

Business interests were also deeply divided over reform. The financial services sector could not agree on the proper extent of corporate governance reform and government regulation of business and markets. Its members depended on public faith in the integrity of the securities markets, but as privileged insiders they benefited from the status quo. Financial institutions and service providers were politically weakened not only by intrasectoral divisions but also by their alleged roles in numerous scandals—such as dishonesty and conflicts of interest in stock analysis, initial public offering and stock market manipulation, and the aiding and abetting of dishonest corporate executives.

The business community's divisions only widened as the corporate scandals deepened. A strong endorsement of reform to reverse crumbling investor confidence came from a panel of some of the most eminent business and financial leaders in the country, including former Federal Reserve chairman Paul Volcker, former SEC chair Arthur Levitt, John Snow (CEO of CSX, former Business Roundtable Chairman, and future treasury secretary), Andrew Grove (former CEO of Intel), John Biggs (former CEO of TIAA-CREF), Peter Peterson (Blackstone Group and former commerce secretary), and John Bogle (former chairman of the Vanguard group).[42] Leading investment firms understood the depth and seriousness of the crisis, and they had an enormous stake

39. Cioffi (2006a); *see also* Cioffi (2004b).
40. Interview, senior AFL-CIO official, Washington, DC, March 2004.
41. Interviews, Senate Banking Committee staff, Washington, DC, March 2004.
42. Hill and Michaels (2002); see also Rohatyn (2002).

in ensuring that it was contained—by regulatory reform if necessary. Likewise, the New York Stock Exchange came out in support of reform—also in order to calm investors and restore confidence.

The leading business lobbying groups, the Business Roundtable and the Chamber of Commerce, took opposing positions. The Chamber of Commerce, historically more ideological in its intense opposition to government regulation, fought a rearguard battle against the reforms. The Business Roundtable, whose membership of predominantly large public corporations had long been opposed to government intervention into corporate governance, remained moderately opposed but in the end, supported the Sarbanes-Oxley reforms. By late June 2002, the Business Roundtable's president, John J. Castellani, announced, "We've passed the critical mass, both from the standpoint of the political structure as well as the erosion of confidence of the capital markets in corporate America. . . . It bodes for quicker and more intensive action."[43]

The accounting industry, having much to answer for and fearing that it would lose even more with reform, fought strenuously against the legislation— even at the risk of further antagonizing the public—but was in no position to stem the tide of popular opinion and political momentum. The large accounting firms—down to the Big Four of PricewaterhouseCoopers, Deloitte Touche Tohmatsu, Ernst & Young, and KPMG after the indictment, collapse, and conviction (later reversed) of Arthur Andersen—and the accounting industry's trade association (the American Institute of Certified Public Accountants, AICPA) were tainted by association with scandal, fraud, and conflicts of interest. Each of the Big Four was implicated in scandals. The industry had lost its legitimacy as a profession. As the legislative process moved forward, some Republican staffers on Capitol Hill even told accounting industry lobbyists to stay away—their very presence was politically damaging.[44] By July 2002 one accounting industry representative speaking to a senior congressional aide expressed the views of many in an industry and profession besieged by scandal, bad press, and a plummeting reputation: "Just make it stop."[45]

With the discrediting of and divisions among economic elites and interest groups, the autonomy of policymakers increased. This left the reformers in the Democratic Party remarkably unconstrained by interest group politics and free to capitalize on the public's outrage in pushing the reform legislation. In contrast to the Republicans in both the House and Senate, Paul Sarbanes and a majority of his fellow Democrats were favorably predisposed toward reform. The Democrats' slim Senate majority gave Sarbanes the institutional power to frame and advance a specific and technical legislative agenda. The Democrats draped their concerns and proposals in the rhetoric of pro-shareholder

43. Stevenson and Mitchell (2002).
44. Interview, former senior Republican staff member, House Finance Committee, Washington, DC, March 2004.
45. Ibid.

fairness and regulatory reform that was overwhelmingly supported by public opinion. The Senate Banking Committee moved deliberately through the winter and more quickly during the late spring and early summer of 2002, as the scandals and the sense of financial crisis among the public and the political economic elite escalated.

By June 2002, reform politics had taken on a life of its own beyond the control of interest groups and even congressional party leaders. After cooling somewhat during the spring of 2002, the sense of panic and outrage spiraled upward again as the corporate financial and accounting scandals culminated in late June with the collapse of WorldCom, following disclosure of a multibillion-dollar accounting fraud. The WorldCom collapse finally broke Republican resistance to Democratic legislative reforms. Public demand for securities law and corporate governance reform had become as irresistible as the electoral dangers of resistance were obvious.[46] The Bush administration and much of the congressional Republican leadership sought to neutralize the scandals as a potent November 2002 election issue by supporting corporate governance reform and accepting only minor compromises from the Democrats as the price.[47] The legislation passed by overwhelming margins in both houses of Congress.

Structural Regulation within Political Constraints

The corporate governance crisis once again revealed the need for strong legal rules and regulatory institutions as the foundation of efficient markets and functional nonmarket corporate hierarchies.[48] Significantly, however, the law and the regulation it enabled did *not* loosen legislative restrictions on securities litigation, let alone create significant new causes of action.[49] Instead, the

46. See Stevenson and Mitchell (2002).

47. The Democrats gave up a potent campaign issue out of a combination of idealism and calculation. In part, they chose to pursue good public policy over tactical expediency. In interviews, Republicans as well as Democrats described the motivations for passing the act in these terms. Interviews, congressional staff, House Financial Services Committee, Washington, DC, March 2003, March 2004. They also needed to insulate themselves from charges of obstructionism and from appearing to play politics with the American economy. Even at the height of the corporate financial and accounting scandals, the Democrats received little credit from the public for their reform efforts. The scandals fostered an all-embracing public cynicism toward American economic and political institutions and elites that extended to both parties. Either party would have faced intense public hostility, and likely electoral losses, if it had appeared to be obstructing reforms or foiling the progress of the legislation.

48. See Vogel (1996) and Cioffi (2006a).

49. There were two modest exceptions to the constraints on litigious enforcement mechanisms. One was a private cause of action under section 306 against officers to recover profits from illegal insider trading of company securities during pension fund "blackout periods" (during which beneficiaries are not allowed to sell shares). The other was an extension of the statute of limitations for securities fraud claims, which had been substantially shortened by the Supreme Court. Republicans could live with these exceptions so long as the PSLRA's restrictions remained intact.

Sarbanes-Oxley Act relied on a combination of governmental enforcement and structural regulation to carry out its reforms. Political dynamics and constraints drove the legislation in these directions. Even at the height of the crisis, two fundamental constraints of partisan politics remained firmly in place. The first was the Republicans' intransigence over adding or expanding any new shareholder rights enforceable through litigation. Second, members of both parties recognized that reforms giving shareholders a more direct and enhanced role in nominating and electing corporate directors were off-limits.

Preservation of securities litigation reform was a nonnegotiable item for congressional Republicans and the Bush administration.[50] As a result, Sarbanes did not even raise the issue of private causes of action when drafting legislation. Nor did the legislative debate present a serious effort, let alone a credible threat, of rolling back the 1990s' legacy of restrictions on securities suits. The Republicans did not even have to fight over such issues. Driven by intense and rapidly shifting political pressures for reform, yet still constrained by the anti-litigation politics of the 1990s, the Sarbanes-Oxley reforms were in effect forced to experiment with structural regulation. This followed not only from the political logic of the situation but also from policymakers' practical assessment of the unfolding corporate governance crisis in 2002. Sarbanes and many of his Democratic colleagues believed that it was a structural crisis, rooted in accounting and conflicts of interest, and they fashioned, in part, a structural solution.[51]

Sarbanes-Oxley imposed a welter of new regulatory requirements and prohibitions on publicly traded corporations, directors, corporate managers, accountants, securities analysts, and attorneys (see table 4.1). The most important and innovative provisions were those creating the Public Company Accounting Oversight Board (PCAOB) and reforming internal corporate board and management structures to institutionalize improved corporate governance within the firm. The PCAOB was a new, private regulatory body, appointed by and under the oversight of the SEC, charged with regulating the accounting industry. Its creation displaced self-regulation by the accounting profession and effectively federalized accounting supervision and rule making. This consolidated the SEC's control over disclosure regulation to an unprecedented degree, power the Supreme Court later enhanced by conferring agency authority to replace boards at will.

50. Confidential interview, senior Treasury Department official, Washington, March 2004. Sarbanes needed the support of Republican senator Michael Enzi to report his bill out of committee, and the Democrats knew any attempt to expand the use or availability of private litigation was a deal killer for the Republicans. Confidential interviews, former and current congressional staff, Washington, DC, March 2003, March 2004.
51. Interviews, Dean Shahinian, senior counsel, and Vincent Meehan, counsel, Senate Committee on Banking, Housing, and Urban Affairs, Washington, DC, March 24, 2004.

TABLE 4.1: MAJOR FEATURES OF THE SARBANES-OXLEY ACT	
Regulation type	*Provision/Legal requirement*
Regulatory structure/ capacity	• Public Company Accounting Oversight Board (PCAOB) • Increase in SEC budget
Transparency and disclosure rules	• Heightened disclosure of corporate finances • Disclosure of "off-balance sheet" transactions • Disclosure of codes of ethics (and waivers by the board) • Disclosure of reconciliation of pro forma financial results with generally accepted accounting principles (US GAAP) • Real-time disclosure of material financial information and developments • CEO and CFO certification of accuracy of financial reports and adequacy/weakness of internal controls
Governmental enforcement and sanctions	• Increased criminal and civil penalties on executives for disclosure violations • SEC enforcement of third-party aiding and abetting liability • Extension of securities fraud statute of limitations
Structural regulation	• Auditing committee comprised entirely of independent directors • Qualified financial expert on audit committee • Direct responsibility of audit committee for the appointment, compensation, and oversight of outside auditors • Audit committee approval of all auditor services • Report by auditors directly to the audit committee • Managerial pay set by compensation committees of independent directors • Legal authority of board to hire its own counsel and consultants • Limitations on nonaudit services performed by the firm's auditor (and board approval of permitted services) • Development, implementation, and certification of adequacy of internal controls • Whistleblower protections

Sarbanes-Oxley also fulfilled Levitt's agenda for enhancing auditor independence, one that had been abandoned by his successor, by mandating the separation of auditing and consulting services. This could be considered a form of structural regulation—the structure in this case being one of markets and industries. However, the separation of auditing from consulting services is more accurately analogized to the enforced market segmentation reminiscent of the Glass-Steagall Act's division of commercial and investment banking. The analogy is all the more striking as Glass-Steagall had been formally repealed in 1999 after more than a decade of regulatory and sub rosa erosion by the Federal Reserve, SEC, and Treasury Department. With Sarbanes-Oxley, any doubts about the continuing importance of the regulatory state in an era of finance capitalism were dispelled.

The more innovative and pathbreaking provisions of the Sarbanes-Oxley Act were those using structural regulation to intervene in the *internal* structure and affairs of the corporation, crossing a line that had impeded the reformers of the 1970s. Whereas the PCAOB reinforced traditional transparency and disclosure regulation through expanded authority over the accounting industry, the structural regulation provisions of Sarbanes-Oxley represented an extension of federal law into the intrafirm governance of the corporation, in part by directly intervening in the composition, structure, and operation of corporate boards. These issues had been within the traditional preserve of state corporation law. Federal law had placed some rather minor restrictions on boards, such as the ban on interlocking directorates under the Clayton Antitrust Act and the requirement of a minimum percentage of independent directors on mutual fund boards under the Investment Company Act of 1940, but nothing approached those imposed by Sarbanes-Oxley. Although stock exchange listing rules, adopted under SEC pressure, had already imposed board independence and committee requirements, Sarbanes-Oxley strengthened these rules and represented a new level of federal intervention in intracorporate affairs, one that arguably gave the SEC statutory powers over board composition, structure, and qualifications for the first time.[52]

Sarbanes-Oxley required public firms to appoint an auditing committee comprised entirely of independent directors, and at least one member must be qualified as a financial expert under new SEC rules. The audit committee now has direct responsibility for the appointment, compensation, and oversight of the outside auditors. The auditors report directly to the committee, which must approve all auditor services and resolve any disputes between management and the auditors concerning financial reporting. Likewise, the boards of public firms must now put in place independent compensation committees that set managerial pay. Sarbanes-Oxley also enhances the more general institutional capacities of the board by giving it the legal authority to hire independent counsel and consultants.

Finally, sections 302 and 404 of the law required CEOs and chief financial officers to certify the accuracy of the firm's accounts and the adequacy of the firm's internal financial controls. Section 404 also requires that the firm's external auditor attest to the managers' assessment of the firm's internal monitoring and risk-management systems as adequate to prevent accounting

---

52. William Chandler and Leo Strine, both judges on Delaware's enormously influential Court of Chancery, note that the listing rules are a de facto component of federal securities regulation and, increasingly, of the federalization of corporate governance law more broadly (2003, n.12) They go on to argue, in the context of a defense of Delaware's corporation law and doctrine, that Sarbanes-Oxley does not expand the SEC's powers over firms' internal governance affairs or over exchange listing rules (n. 57). The statute's provisions regarding independent directors and board committees, at a minimum, suggest the opposite, but the question of how far the SEC's authority now extends remains open.

manipulation and fraud.[53] In practice, this provision compels a review and restructuring of intrafirm managerial, monitoring, and reporting structures and practices. No provision of the Sarbanes-Oxley Act has sparked more criticism than Section 404. Ironically, this section has also been a boon to accountants, who audit, assess, and sometimes consult on the design of risk-management systems. The law that targeted the accounting industry has in at least one way enriched it significantly.

By encroaching on the traditional subjects of state corporate law, the Sarbanes-Oxley reforms centralized and federalized key aspects of corporate governance. This unprecedented federalization departed from nearly two centuries of American federalism that had endured even through the zenith of the New Deal and the postwar expansion of the regulatory state.[54] This break with such an established allocation of policymaking power indicates both the growing importance of corporate governance issues and the political impact of the financial and governance scandals of 2001–2.[55] The federal reforms represented a potentially substantial expansion and centralization of regulatory authority in tension with the political underpinnings of corporate law federalism and the American governance regime's constitution of broad managerial autonomy within the private sphere.

Members of Congress were aware of the innovative nature of the reforms. They were also aware that the use of structural regulation afforded them a solution to the problem of enforcement as well as the rapidly eroding legitimacy of American corporate governance institutions. As one congressional staffer described it, these structural fixes would be "self-executing" with no need (or option) for litigation.[56] The operation of the institutional arrangement itself would be the enforcement. Congress was also cognizant of its deviation from well-worn customs of federalism that allocated corporate law to the states. Indeed, Oxley discussed the issue with his staff repeatedly.[57] However, even a majority of Republicans believed that the securities markets, and thus the governance framework that underpinned them, were preeminently national in scope and importance.[58] Federalism was again jettisoned when it

53. Although this provision is often identified with congressional, i.e., Democratic, regulatory overreaching, the idea for CEO certification and internal controls was proposed by President Bush's treasury secretary, Paul O'Neill. See Suskind (2004, 229–230, 238).

54. Despite numerous critics who have asserted that Sarbanes-Oxley did not substantially alter the legal terrain of corporate governance (e.g., McDonnell 2003), others have emphasized the importance of this change in the scope and balance of federal authority. See, e.g., Karmel (2005) (former SEC commissioner); Chandler and Strine (2003) (Delaware Chancery Court judges).

55. Cioffi (2006b).

56. Confidential interview, former senior staff member, Senate Banking Committee, Washington, DC, March 2004.

57. Confidential interviews, former Republican staff members, House Financial Services Committee, Washington, DC, March 2004.

58. Ibid.

got in the way of practical politics. Structural regulation under Sarbanes-Oxley thus represents both a stunning reversal of the anti-regulation agenda of the 1990s *and* a reaffirmation of that decade's anti-litigation politics.

The importance of structural regulation and board reform implicates the second powerful political constraint on the politics of corporate governance reform. Despite the significance and sweep of the reforms, Sarbanes-Oxley did not reform how directors are nominated and elected. The act left the very foundation of governance and managerial power largely under the control of managers. This is a striking omission. There are only intermittent references to the subject in the legislative record. Surprisingly, given its importance, there were but a few passing witness statements regarding board nomination and election rules, and congressional Democrats were almost entirely silent on the matter.[59] Representative John LaFalce, then the ranking Democratic member of the House Finance Committee and a fierce critic of managerial abuses, merely noted that Congress did not have to address the issue because the SEC was empowered to adopt rules governing the nomination and election of direc-tors.[60] Yet during this period the Democrats were attacking the SEC under Chairman Pitt as ineffectual and resistant to substantial reform. The subject of board nominations and elections was simply too explosive to broach.[61] Any attempt to reform board nomination and election rules would have mobilized the American managerial elite against the Democratic Party and shifted its support even more disproportionately toward the GOP. Because the Demo-cratic Party had become increasingly reliant on the support of at least sections of the managerial elite, this threat precluded a fundamental challenge to the institutional bases of its power. If a litigation provision would have killed reform, so too would one that threatened the legal and institutional founda-tions of the corporate power structure.

THE BUSINESS BACKLASH

Business discontent over corporate governance reform simmered almost from the date of the Sarbanes-Oxley Act's passage. Three general factors contrib-uted to the backlash: (1) the perceived burdens of the new law and regula-tions, (2) managers' hostility to regulatory constraints on their autonomy, and

59. See United States Senate, 2002, 1010–11, 1026 (comments by Sarah Teslik, executive director, Council of Institutional Investors). Interviews with congressional staff confirm that the issue did not come up in internal committee or partisan debates over the reform legisla-tion. Interviews, Washington, DC, March 2004.

60. U.S. House of Representatives, Committee on Financial Services, 2002, 55 (comments by Rep. LaFalce) However, LaFalce's bill, voted down by the House, did contain a provision requiring a nominating committee comprised entirely of independent directors.

61. This assessment was confirmed by a former senior Republican congressional aide. E-mail communication, February 1, 2005.

(3) the balance of partisan politics at the national level.[62] Initially muzzled by the public outrage over the Enron-era scandals and other abuses that continued to become public, over time hostility toward corporate governance reform by conservative critics and business interests became increasingly vocal and highly publicized. The rhetoric of the public debate over the wisdom and necessity of reform focused on the disproportionate financial burdens it threatened to impose on small and medium-sized firms and on broader notions of the competitiveness of American financial markets in attracting and retaining corporate listings.

Tracing the development of the business backlash suggests that antipathy to constraints on managerial autonomy drove the growing opposition to post–Sarbanes-Oxley reforms more than concerns over costs, efficiency, and competitiveness. This conclusion is at odds with much of the public and academic discourse on governance reform. Scholarly commentary rooted in neoclassical economics has almost universally condemned Sarbanes-Oxley and related reform measures for creating costs far in excess of their demonstrable benefits. As discussed below, these critiques have some merit, but they were often exaggerated and highly speculative. They were also often the product of intellectual, ideological, or opportunistic commitments to a theoretical framework that privileged private contractual ordering, self-regulating markets, and federalism-enabled "markets for regulation" despite the serious malfunctioning of the highly contractual and market-driven American corporate governance regime and financial system. Evidence for the broader criticism that governance reform has eroded the competitiveness of American securities markets, particularly with respect to the more lightly regulated London Stock Exchange, was, and is, equivocal at best. The post-Enron, post–Sarbanes-Oxley debate over reform was really a highly politicized conflict over the relationship of government and law to business, the corporate form, and finance. It was a struggle over power, authority, and the future of American finance capitalism dressed in the language of economics and policy analysis.[63] And to understand this debate and the stakes it raised requires an analysis of the business backlash and its political underpinnings.

62. Though the focus here is on federal politics, law enforcement actions at the state level played a significant role in reforming some aspects of the American financial system. State attorneys general, led by New York's Elliot Spitzer, became increasingly active in these areas and have often been the first to uncover and remedy an increasingly wide variety of financial improprieties throughout corporate America—often to the acute embarrassment of federal regulators. By far the most important exercise of state law enforcement power was Spitzer's pursuit of leading stock analysts and the banks that employed them for conflicts of interest in recommending stock picks to the public.

63. It is difficult if not impossible to determine whether, or to what extent, managers seek to maintain autonomy from the state for ideological and normative reasons or because that autonomy has allowed them to enrich themselves lavishly during the past thirty years. It is reasonable to infer that both ideal and material interests inform managerial policy preferences and that they tend to reinforce each other even under crisis conditions.

Beginning of the Backlash

Less than four months after the passage of the act, and days after the Republican gains in the 2002 congressional elections, Robert R. Glauber, chairman of the self-regulating National Association of Securities Dealers (NASD), advocated delay in implementing the new regulations as he spoke out against "unduly bureaucratic" solutions to securities analyst conflicts of interest on Wall Street and their "onerous" costs to the securities industry.[64] By Sarbanes-Oxley's first anniversary, little more than one year after the peak of the accounting scandals, a former head of the AICPA, fumed that the legislation represented "the criminalization of [corporate] risk taking, which is the same as criminalizing capitalism."[65]

A growing number of business representatives and neoliberal commentators had begun to voice what would become an increasingly familiar litany of complaints about reform:

- High compliance costs, including increased audit fees and "directors and officers" insurance premiums
- Reducing the number of qualified people willing to serve on boards
- Discouraging domestic firms from going public and inducing public firms to go private
- Discouraging foreign firms from listing on American stock exchanges
- Slowing investment and growth
- Encouraging excessive risk aversion by management

Managers found two other issues particularly objectionable: (1) the expensing of stock options under newly proposed accounting rules and (2) the difficulties and expense of complying with the internal control certification requirements of Section 404. However, none of these features of Sarbanes-Oxley triggered a broadly based political counterattack on corporate governance reform.[66] With the exception of increased directors and officers insurance and auditing fees, empirical and anecdotal evidence did not support the criticisms. Treasury Secretary John Snow dismissed them out of hand, and one leading corporate governance consultant ridiculed the complaints as a bunch of

64. White (2002).

65. Schroeder (2003, quoting Robert Elliott, a former KPMG partner and former head of AICPA).

66. Complaints that section 404 imposed excessive compliance costs on small and medium-sized public firms were well taken. However, repeated delays in applying the provision to these companies rendered much of the criticism speculative. Significantly, larger firms accepted section 404 with little protest, and many found it useful in streamlining their internal operations. Therefore, opposition to the section did not trigger a broad-based managerial backlash against Sarbanes-Oxley and corporate governance reform, though attacking it on the ostensible behalf of smaller firms became a potent rhetorical strategy.

"urban myths."[67] Even the increased auditing fees did not appear significant in the broader context of corporate cost structures.[68] Nevertheless, polls of corporate executives revealed growing managerial skepticism and outright hostility toward governance reform.[69] Rather than dying down as businesses internalized the new legal norms and practices, opposition intensified and organized.

A central question raised by this antireform backlash remains stubbornly difficult to answer: what triggered and motivated the increasingly aggressive and public attacks on post-Enron corporate governance reforms? The most prominent and controversial issues raised by critics appear insufficient to explain the timing, political development, or intensity of the backlash. Opposition to the mandatory expensing of stock options was concentrated in the high-tech industry—most business interests had long concluded that this battle had been lost and that expensing would come, probably sooner rather than later.[70] Continuing skepticism about lavish managerial compensation weakened opposition to proposed regulation requiring clearer disclosure of stock option awards. Finally, beginning in late spring of 2006, the exposure of widespread and systematic manipulation of stock option grants through "backdating"—which guaranteed that options would net recipients large returns and which implicated over one hundred publicly traded firms and many of those in the high-tech industry—all but eliminated significant resistance to increased regulation of stock option compensation.

Despite numerous complaints to the contrary, the fear of criminal prosecution of managers for improperly certifying corporate accounts or of increased civil liability is not a credible motive for the increased opposition to reform. Criminal prosecution of corporations and their managers has always been, and remains, rare. Nothing in the post-Enron legal environment indicates that corporate governance enforcement through criminal proceedings was ever seriously considered as a response to any but the most egregious cases of managerial fraud. Likewise, the probability that corporate officers and directors will be subject to civil liability has not increased significantly.[71] Suits for breaches of fiduciary duties have always been difficult to prosecute successfully, and federal reform did not alter state corporate fiduciary law. Further, Sarbanes-Oxley and other related regulatory reforms refrained from enhancing the role of private litigation and left securities litigation reform laws intact.

Perhaps most important, the section 404 internal monitoring requirements of Sarbanes-Oxley do not credibly explain the antiregulation backlash. No

---

67. Schroeder (2003, quoting Patrick McGurn of Institutional Shareholder Services).
68. Ibid.
69. PricewaterhouseCoopers (2003).
70. See, e.g., Norris (2004) and Spinner (2003b).
71. See Black, Cheffins, and Klausner (2006).

other provision has generated more publicized hostility and resistance than that section. First, the costs of compliance were indeed appreciable and were especially threatening to smaller firms with less financial capacity to absorb them—though the SEC delayed section 404's application to small firms for years. These smaller firms and their representatives therefore were intensely interested in minimizing a regulatory burden they perceived as falling unfairly upon them. They also made far more sympathetic protagonists in a political and public relations battle against reform because they were not associated with the profoundly destructive scandals and corporate collapses that had prompted reform in the first place.

Second, it was not at all clear that section 404 internal risk controls could pass a cost-benefit analysis—though it is exceedingly hard to perform such an analysis that accurately assesses the value of scandals prevented or the value added to the market by increased investor confidence. Auditing costs further increased the expenses of section 404 compliance. The law required accounting firms, so tainted in the Enron-era scandals, to audit the adequacy of internal risk controls and thus made them de facto compliance gatekeepers. This created a conflict of interest fueled both by the accounting firms' intense risk aversion after the prosecution-induced collapse of Arthur Anderson and the creation of the PCAOB, and by their financial self-interests in conducting more thorough, expensive, and profitable audits of intrafirm controls. Not surprisingly, audit costs were the primary driver of the escalating costs of section 404 compliance, far in excess of congressional and SEC predictions.[72]

Finally, section 404 compliance required managers to modify the internal structure of their business operations and thus infringed on the autonomy that had long been central to American managerial ideology. Managerial hostility to section 404 was (and remains) pronounced among the managers of smaller public firms, but this does not explain the broader backlash against corporate governance reform. Most managers of large publicly traded firms accepted the costs and burdens of section 404 compliance, and many saw the benefits (also difficult to capture in cost-benefit analyses) of improved managerial capacity through better internal monitoring.[73] The most politically powerful business interests were not intensely opposed to section 404 at the time of its passage, and it is implausible that its associated costs mobilized opposition to reform *after* large firms had already committed the front-loaded investment in compliance. Once internal control systems were in place, many of the costs and complaints generated by section 404 began to diminish.[74] Smaller

72. However, audit costs have risen from what may have been artificially low levels set by accounting firms using auditing as a loss leader for the sale of more lucrative consulting services. As auditing and consulting were split after the passage of Sarbanes-Oxley, it would be reasonable to anticipate that audit fees would rise to their market level.

73. *Wall Street Journal* (2004), Stone (2005), and Katz (2006).

74. Cf. Byrnes (2004), Roberts (2004), and *Economist* (2004).

firms in particular also benefitted from amendments of the SEC and the
PCAOB rules to reduce the complexity, prescriptiveness, and expense of section 404 compliance.

In sum, the attacks on corporate governance reform appear insufficient to
explain why powerful business and financial interests shifted from supporting
or acquiescing in reform to attacking it in an increasingly public way. But the
SEC's 2004 proposal to reform the rules governing shareholder voting and
board elections was another matter entirely.

Shareholder Nominations, Voting, and Control

Despite the appreciably growing criticisms of Sarbanes-Oxley and associated
reforms, the opposition at first remained subdued. The political terrain shifted
dramatically in mid-2003. An SEC proposal to change proxy rules to give
shareholders the (very limited) ability to nominate and elect corporate directors transformed passive resentment into a potent managerial backlash. This
was not the agency's first foray into controversial and significant regulation in
the post-Enron era. Following the passage of Sarbanes-Oxley, the SEC under
William Donaldson, Harvey Pitt's successor as SEC chairman, had engaged in
a historic run of rule making. The agency strengthened financial and proxy
vote disclosure, accounting rules, and stock exchange regulation. It extended
structural regulation directly to mutual funds in response to a series of fund
governance scandals, mandating board independence from fund advisers such
as Fidelity, Putnam, and Vanguard by requiring a majority of independent
directors on fund boards. The SEC also pushed into the opaque and largely
unregulated world of hedge funds by requiring their registration with the
agency—eliciting protests that this was the first step toward more comprehensive regulation. Under SEC pressure and with its approval, the stock exchanges
further stiffened their listing rules on board independence and use of independent board auditing, nomination, and compensation committees. In its
statutory oversight capacity, the SEC even had a hand in the promulgation of
the deeply resented PCAOB rules implementing the section 404 internal controls provision of the Sarbanes-Oxley Act.

None of these initiatives proved as controversial as the board nomination
rules proposed by the SEC in October 2003.[75] The rules would have allowed
institutional investors access to corporate proxies mailed to all shareholders
only after substantial delays and under exceptional conditions. The proposed
rules would have created a two-step, multiyear process to place shareholder
board nominations on the corporation's formal proxy ballots. First, at least
35 percent of voting shareholders would have had to withhold their support

75. Securities and Exchange Commission (2003b).

for a company's director candidate in an annual board election. If this criterion was satisfied, a group representing at least 5 percent of shares would have been able to nominate and run its own nominee(s) on the corporate proxy the following year. Even then, the proposed rules would have allowed dissident shareholders to elect no more than a minority of three directors in this fashion. This was almost certainly insufficient to substantially change the functioning of boards and suggested that corporate boards, however restructured, would remain ineffective as checks on managerial power.

Earlier, in May 2003, the agency had solicited comments on the subject from "interested parties" in anticipation of proposing a rule on the subject.[76] The reaction was immediate. Comments poured in from business groups, professional associations, corporate attorneys and law firms, institutional investment funds, and shareholder advocates. By the time the comment period closed on the proposed rules, the SEC had received over eighteen thousand comment letters, by far the largest number regarding any rule in the commission's history.[77] The vast majority of comments received were in support of the SEC's modest proposal, but letter-writing campaigns by shareholder groups were politically overpowered by the opposition from managers and business groups. The ferocity of this opposition indicates the extraordinary sensitivity of board nomination and election rules and the strength of the gathering managerial backlash. Whereas interest groups had been divided and weakened during the debate over Sarbanes-Oxley, they were now far more unified and mobilized. Managers, business groups, and allied organizations attacked the proposed rules as destructive of corporate efficiency and as an invitation to public and union pension funds to use their vast holdings to pursue special interest agendas. Both the Business Roundtable and the Chamber of Commerce publicly opposed the rules, with the latter threatening to sue if they were adopted. Many institutional investors, unions, shareholder and consumer advocates, and a number of state treasurers publicly supported the changes, but some argued that the proposed rules were too weak to make a practical difference in who oversaw the county's largest corporations.[78]

The conflict escalated in the run-up to the 2004 presidential election. Opponents intensified their attack on the proposed proxy rule while the Bush administration reportedly weighed in against it behind closed doors. The SEC commissioners themselves split over the issue, with the Democratic and Republican commissioners bitterly divided at two to two and Chairman Donaldson seeking a compromise that neither side supported.[79] By July 2004, he conceded that the SEC was deadlocked over the board nomination proposal.[80] Its fate would

76. Securities and Exchange Commission (2003a).
77. Securities and Exchange Commission (2004), Peterson (2004a).
78. Peterson (2004a).
79. Peterson (2004b).
80. Peterson (2004b, 2004c).

turn on the election. As soon as the November 2004 election ended in a Bush victory and an augmented Republican majority in the Senate, postmortems for the board nomination proposal started appearing in the news. Donaldson later conceded that it was the "wrong proposal," not worth pushing through on a split vote.[81] By January 2005, news items reported that the plan was dead. Corporate governance reform had reached its high-water mark.[82] The failure of the SEC's proxy rule proposal brought a brief era of reform to a close. The structure of corporate governance was left in a state that preserved the institutional foundations of managerialism. Under intense pressure from administration and congressional conservatives and business groups, his reform agenda criticized and blocked by increasingly hostile Republican SEC commissioners, Donaldson faced a deteriorating and untenable political position. He resigned in early June 2005. Within hours of the resignation, President Bush nominated Representative Christopher Cox—the principal author of the House draft of the PSLRA in 1995 and a vocal critic of regulation—to replace him.

Opposition by Committee

By mid-2005, the antireform backlash had reached self-sustaining critical mass. Managerial elites drawn from large, small, industrial, high-tech, and financial firms had become increasingly and more uniformly hostile to reform. In September 2006, a private group of experts, with the blessing of the Bush administration, formed the Committee on Capital Markets Regulation to evaluate the costs, benefits, and effects of the Sarbanes-Oxley Act and related corporate governance reforms and recommend ameliorative changes. Harvard law professor Hal Scott had begun putting the group together a year before, arguing that reforms had eroded the international competitiveness of American securities markets. The committee's charge was thus broader and more politically palatable than a reconsideration of Sarbanes-Oxley.

Reframing the issue of corporate governance reform as one of capital market competitiveness provided two related benefits. First, it justified the inquiry to range beyond the post-Enron reforms and into issues of litigation rates, class-action rules, white-collar criminal prosecution, the power and activism of institutional investors, shareholder rights, and state-federal regulatory relations. Of course, Sarbanes-Oxley and subsequent SEC regulatory policy were also on the agenda. In particular, and for good reason, internal risk-control regulation under section 404 was highlighted as a subject of the review. Second, framing criticisms of reform in terms of concerns over international competitiveness partially insulated the committee from attack. The

81. Personal communication, former SEC chairman William Donaldson, New Haven, CT, June 13, 2006.
82. See Peterson (2004d).

committee's charge presented its mission as championing the economic interests of the United States in a globalizing economy rather than as an effort to roll back popular reforms, and as an application of sober economic analysis—at once practical and objective—rather than a political or ideological agenda.

To many critics, the committee's composition suggested a political and ideological tilt to the right.[83] Its connections to the Bush White House were underscored by the endorsement of and coordination with Treasury Secretary Henry Paulson, Jr., and the background of its co-chairs, R. Glenn Hubbard, former chair of the Council of Economic Advisers during the Bush's first term, and Brookings Institution board chair John Thornton, who had reported to Paulson when the latter was CEO of Goldman Sachs.[84] The relationship between the committee and the administration was perceived as so close that many people in political circles started calling it the Paulson Committee.[85] The SEC was not represented, and the group's membership pointedly excluded any former regulators. Scott explained, "We generally tried not to include regulators. . . . We would not want to put people in the position who had formulated these rules in the past. They may have a lack of objectivity."[86] Notwithstanding that issues of regulatory policymaking and enforcement could be usefully elucidated by people with such experience, Scott's point implied its inverse: those who had to comply with corporate governance and securities regulation were likely to have a bias of their own against regulation. Nor were representatives of organized labor included on the committee, despite the fact that union pension funds had long been the most activist investors and that labor is a critical stakeholder in the corporation. Representatives of institutional investors and shareholder advocates were heavily outweighed by senior managers. Although there were several eminent academics among the membership, some of whom were known for moderate views on regulation, the makeup of the committee was immediately criticized as imbalanced and favoring those hostile to regulation and governance reform.[87]

The committee's interim report, released shortly after the November 2006 elections returned the Democrats to control of Congress, adopted a skeptical tone toward corporate governance and securities market regulation but also

83. See Labaton (2006a).
84. See CNNMoney.com (2006) and Norris (2006).
85. Labaton (2006a).
86. Norris (2006). In a further elaboration both odd for an academic and insulting to regulators, Scott said, "Anybody on this committee is in the real world and will bring with them real-world perspectives."
87. Ibid.; Johnson (2006); cf. *Economist* (2006b).

embraced a rather moderate set of recommendations.[88] Aside from its intellectual content, the report provides a useful window into the domestic political debate over American corporate governance and international finance capital more generally. The committee criticized the frequency, expense, and uncertainty of securities litigation and suggested further legal reforms to reduce all three. It also counseled restraint in using criminal enforcement in securities and corporate governance cases, especially in the case of large accounting firms where another prosecution-induced collapse of a remaining Big Four auditor would worsen the already troubling market concentration in international audit services for large public firms. Likewise, the report condemned the highly detailed and prescriptive form of regulation in the United States and favored a more principles-based regulatory approach that left more flexibility in choosing the means of compliance. Not surprisingly, it also recommended a more demanding cost-benefit analysis of an empirical, risk-based approach to regulation.

Surprisingly, the committee generally applauded the Sarbanes-Oxley reforms and, while criticizing the costs and defects of section 404, did not recommend any changes in the act. Rather, the report suggested that the SEC and PCAOB change their implementing rules to reduce compliance burdens by clarifying the rules and focusing on areas of greater risk to investors. Nor was the report a victory for managerialism. Among its key findings and recommendations was a warning that the United States risked falling behind foreign jurisdictions in the scope of shareholder rights. In particular, the committee recommended reinforcing shareholder sovereignty and the market for corporate control by strengthening shareholder voting rights regarding takeover defenses (though not executive compensation) and director nominations and elections—and it endorsed SEC action on these issues.

However, the committee's policy recommendations were not as important as the way in which the committee articulated its critiques of American corporate governance regulation. It took a subject that had been viewed in primarily domestic political and economic terms and presented it as a feature of economic globalization. The committee's report reflected a broader shift in the debate over corporate governance in terms of international competitiveness and national comparative advantage in financial services. It repeatedly stressed that American securities markets were becoming less attractive to foreign issuers just as foreign markets and financial sectors were becoming more developed and competitive. Above all, London, with its light regulatory approach and quickly growing AIM (a market for small cap firms) loomed as a threat to

88. Committee on Capital Markets Regulation (2006). The moderate, measured tone was surprising given the heated debate and rancor over Sarbanes-Oxley and corporate governance reform in a conference hosted by Scott at Harvard the prior spring. See Brayton (2005). Intense criticism of the post-Enron reforms also became common among law and economics scholars. For a particularly vituperative and exhaustive example, see Romano (2005).

New York as the preeminent international financial capital and to American financial firms as the dominant players in global finance.

The critical link in the competitiveness argument was that regulation was causing this loss of market share for new stock issues and thus in related financial services. Hence, the relative decline in New York as a financial center was portrayed as an absolute decline in attractiveness due to legal and regulatory conditions. Market share thus had little to do with the relative rise of foreign markets as they began to be better regulated, develop greater liquidity, and foster supportive sophisticated (and significantly cheaper) financial services sectors—outcomes that American government officials and commentators had advocated for years.

Echoed by the Bush administration, the argument that corporate governance reform threatened American international competitiveness became common currency in political debates, yet it was also subject to increased scrutiny and skepticism. Duke University law professor James D. Cox denounced it as "an escalation of the culture war against regulation."[89] Numerous commentators, including Commissioner Roel Campos of the SEC, quickly rejected the report's empirical and causal analysis and the implicit argument that globalization would force the United States to pursue deregulatory reform or else lose its financial edge to foreign markets.[90] Even the *Wall Street Journal*, a publication generally sympathetic to criticisms of regulation, critically reviewed the report's international competitiveness arguments and suggested that the transformation of global finance and the rapid development of domestic capital markets made stock markets closer to home increasingly attractive for foreign firms.[91] Paradoxically, the globalization of finance capitalism, in part through more stringent pro-shareholder corporate governance law, may increase the *financial* "home bias" of investors and firms as listed companies forgo the inevitable complications of a cross-national listing on an American stock market.

Notwithstanding the economic arguments advanced by the proponents and opponents of reform, the shifting balance of political power in Washington was the ultimate arbiter of corporate governance reforms and the backlash against it. Just as the Republican gains in 2004 had emboldened critics of the new legal rules, Democratic gains in 2006 cowed them. Even prior to the election, political conditions did not favor statutory changes that would be perceived by the public as soft on corporate fraud and it was clear that any policy changes would have to be made through regulatory agencies under greater administration control. The Democratic successes in the November 2006

---

89. Labaton (2006a).

90. See, e.g., Campos (2006).

91. Ip, Scannell, and Solomon (2007); and Ball (2007); see also *Wall Street Journal* (2004); and McDonald (2006a). Likewise, the *Economist* noted that many factors contributed to the relative decline of New York as the pre-preeminent international financial center, the most important being the development of capital markets around the world. *Economist* (2006a, 2006b).

elections solidified a political regression to the mean as politicians of both parties began to advocate a balance between ensuring corporate (or managerial) accountability and preserving economic efficiency.

The new focus on international competition for stock listings and financial services cut across party lines, as indicated by a McKinsey & Co. report jointly sponsored by the Republican (later Independent) mayor of New York, Michael Bloomberg, and New York Democratic senator Charles Schumer, which focused on preserving New York's position as the leading international financial center and echoed many of the points made by the Committee on Capital Market Regulation. However, politicians of both parties were reluctant to press the argument of international competitiveness too far and pursue substantial policy or legislative changes. The Bush administration and leading Democrats maintained exquisite balancing acts on corporate governance policy. Treasury Secretary Paulson greeted the report warmly and adopted a public position that governance reform had been necessary and useful, but he maintained his prior public position that Congress and the SEC needed to ensure a proper balance between investor protection and economic vitality and competitiveness.[92] President Bush himself invoked the competitiveness argument but then called Sarbanes-Oxley a success and merely in need of regulatory fine-tuning.[93] Democrats, who had sounded conciliatory about revisiting Sarbanes-Oxley in the run-up to the 2006 elections, hardened their position on regulatory retrenchment afterward but also maintained the need for "balance" in crafting regulations.[94]

Most business executives were hamstrung in the debate over corporate governance reform. While many repeatedly denounced excessive compliance costs, particularly those imposed by section 404, they were almost uniformly unwilling to call for a broader rollback of the reforms, fearing that this would send a negative signal to investors, regulators, and the public.[95] Many managers also simply disagreed with the fierce criticisms and dire predictions unleashed by those active in the backlash. Most businesses had quickly adjusted to the new regime and found its burdens manageable.[96] The review and ultimate relaxation of the section 404 implementation rules by the SEC and PCAOB further diminished the momentum of the backlash against governance reform.

Politicians and policymakers from across the political spectrum accepted Sarbanes-Oxley as a permanent and major feature of the business and regulatory landscape. Interest group politics had returned to its normal state, and the ire of business and financial elites focused once again on civil litigation and liability. Ironically, with litigation-driven means of enforcement off the

92. Taub (2006) and Paulson (2008).
93. McKinnon and Conkey (2007).
94. McDonald (2006b) and Labaton (2006b).
95. Glatner (2005).
96. KPMG Audit Committee Institute (2006) and Katz (2006).

policy table, continued concerns with corporate governance and managerial accountability reinforced the importance of structural regulation, without ameliorating its politically contentious character. This would become abundantly clear as conflict over reform flared again over the subjects of shareholder proxy proposals and board nominations—this time triggered by a federal court decision.

The Judicial Resurrection and Administrative End of Shareholder Nomination Rights

In late 2006 the Second Circuit Court of Appeals entered the arena of shareholder voting rights and restored the issue to center stage. Ruling in a case brought by the American Federation of State, County and Municipal Employees (AFSCME) Pension Fund against the insurance giant American International Group, whose legendary CEO, Hank Greenberg, had been ousted amid disclosures of accounting irregularities, the court held that the corporation could not exclude from the proxy ballot a proposal granting shareholders greater power to nominate candidates for the board of directors (and thus foster competitive board elections).[97] The ruling rejected the SEC's argument that management could exclude such proposals and the underlying managerialist policy of curtailing shareholder nomination proposals that the agency had adopted in 1990 at the end of the hostile takeover boom. The decision effectively reopened the issue of shareholder voting rights that had appeared closed with the failure of the SEC's shareholder nomination proposal two years earlier.

AFSCME v. AIG held out the promise of a new and more effective lever to achieve a measure of shareholder democracy through direct representation on corporate boards. It also presented a potential means to further strengthen the mechanisms of structural regulation in corporate governance left incomplete by Sarbanes-Oxley and the failure of the SEC's 2004 director nomination proposal. The precedent opened a potential new legal avenue for institutional investors to restructure firm governance and fundamentally alter power

---

97. *American Federation of State, County & Municipal Employees, Pension Fund v. American International Group, Inc.*, 462 F.3d 121 (2d Cir. 2006). The court's decision was quite technical, as is often the case in interpretations of proxy voting regulations. The court held that SEC Rule 14a-8(i)(8), 17 C.F.R. § 240.14a-8, does not empower managers to exclude shareholder proposals to alter board nomination procedures, though it does permit managers to exclude a shareholder proposal that "relates to an election for membership on the company's board of directors." The court adopted the SEC's original interpretation, dating to its promulgation in 1976, which codified the long-standing policy of prohibiting shareholders from using the corporate ballot to seek control over the board. The SEC began broadening this "electoral exclusion" in 1990 to cover proposals to alter *any* board election procedures. The Second Circuit rejected this later reinterpretation as inconsistent with the rule's original policy justification and thus not subject to judicial deference. See 462 F.3d 121, 126–30.

relations between management and shareholders, provided they could secure a majority of shareholder votes on both bylaw amendments and subsequent board elections. Despite the disappointing record of shareholder activists in winning proxy contests against management, the ruling did pose an unaccustomed and significant threat to managers, whose reaction to the SEC's director nomination proposal revealed their intense opposition to shareholder nominations and contested board elections. The fact that the decision had been issued by the Second Circuit further raised the stakes because so many major American corporations are either headquartered or incorporated in New York (located within the Second Circuit) and therefore could be sued there.

However, the administrative law basis of *AFSCME v. AIG*, ruling on the SEC's reinterpretation of its own rules rather than on statutory interpretation, rendered the ruling vulnerable to administrative reversal. The SEC could simply amend its proxy rules through an ordinary agency rule-making procedure to, in effect, reverse the court of appeals. The legal procedure was relatively straightforward; the politics was not. Institutional investors and shareholder advocates came to AFSCME's defense against critics of the decision and began advocating for greater nomination rights and competitive board elections. Public opinion still favored shareholders over managers, and the SEC now had to contend with a Democratic Congress more critical of pro-management policies. Further complicating matters, but also making the ultimate outcome obvious in advance, was the fact that one Democratic commissioner had resigned, leaving a solidly Republican majority at the SEC. Cox had been deft in reconciling the divisions that had so bedeviled William Donaldson. But the revival of the shareholder nominations issue would make maintaining this balance particularly difficult.

In yet another round of rule making, the SEC adopted an odd and highly unusual approach to the question. Instead of developing the agency's position and submitting it as a proposed rule for notice and comment, as is the norm in administrative rule-making procedures, the SEC proposed two irreconcilable rules regarding shareholder proposals and board nominations.[98] One, supported by the Democratic commissioners, resurrected much of the Donaldson shareholder nomination proposal from 2004. However, this rule contained two bitter, if not poison, pills. It allowed exclusion of advisory (precatory) shareholder proposals, which accounted for the substantial majority of all shareholder proxy proposals (particularly those on social issues), and it allowed companies to opt out of shareholder nominations by a vote of the board if permitted to do so under state corporation law. The other proposal, supported by the Republicans, directly reversed the Second Circuit ruling by reendorsing the SEC's post-1990 policy of rejecting such proposals. Temporizing, Cox voted in favor of both. The result was something of a referendum on corporate

98. See Securities and Exchange Commission (2007b, 2007c).

governance reform and shareholder activism—except that the votes, in the form of public comments, mattered little to the ultimate resolution.

Interest groups organized an unprecedented campaign to overwhelm the SEC with comments during the legally required notice and comment period. The SEC received nearly thirty-five thousand comment letters, the overwhelming majority of which condemned both proposals for restricting shareholder rights. The record number of comments conclusively established a pattern showing the increasingly public, politically salient, and controversial character of SEC rule making related to shareholder rights in corporate governance. From the 1992 proxy rule amendments to Regulation FD in 2000 to the shareholder nomination and voting amendments in 2003–4 to the 2007 joint proposed rules on shareholder proxy proposals, each rule-making proceeding had set a successive record for the number of comment letters received and indicated the increasingly bitter divides over securities regulation and the federal role in corporate governance. Figure 4.1 shows the extraordinary growth

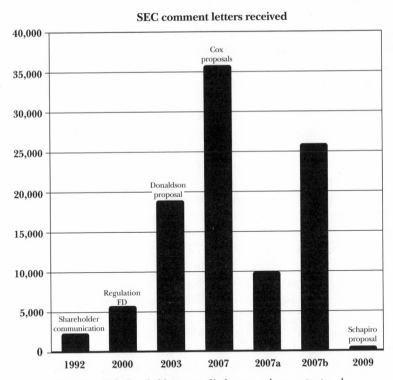

SEC comment letters received

Fig. 4.1: *SEC shareholder proxy disclosure and access proposals*

Source: SEC website. The two "Cox proposals" are 1) exclusion of shareholder proposals on director election processes (2007b) and 2) multiyear shareholder nomination procedure, coupled with exclusion of nonbinding shareholder proposals and opt-out from proposals on director elections (2007c).

in the number of comment letters received with respect to the most significant SEC proposals regarding shareholder power in corporate governance.

The SEC also held blue-ribbon roundtables on the complexities of the issue and the wide range of potential problems that might arise from contested nominations and elections. The debate over the AIG ruling and the new SEC proxy proposals centered on the possibility that expanded shareholder director nomination rights would politicize the corporation as labor and social investment groups took on a formal governance role and introduced stakeholder interests and non-economic agendas into the board room. Critics of expanded shareholder rights in board elections also raised the troubling possibility that hedge funds might borrow shares to vote in order to manipulate governance processes for their own gain to the detriment of other shareholders. From the critics' perspective, expanding shareholder rights to director nominations and contested board elections was fraught with risks and dangers on either side. On the one hand, they feared the potential incorporation of stakeholder representation into the American corporate governance regime, however far-fetched that outcome might be, would further widen the separation of *share* ownership and control. On the other, they feared that the market-driven short-termism of the American governance regime would reach its logical culmination in the complete severance of ownership and control via the purchase of voting power, and thus board seats, for short-term financial depredations.

In the end, however, the intellectual debate was window dressing. Following the resignation of Commissioner Roel Campos, a Democrat, the political die was cast with a Republican majority on the SEC. On November 28, 2007, the remaining commissioners voted to amend the proxy rules to allow exclusion of a shareholder proposal "[i]f the proposal relates to a nomination or an election for membership on the company's board of directors or analogous governing body or a procedure for such nomination or election."[99] The Cox SEC asserted that it was acting to restore legal certainty and a single authoritative statement of law by reinstating its prior interpretation of the rules. It thereby rendered the *AFSCME v. AIG* decision a dead letter.

Politics triumphed through the administrative process, but the fact that a highly respected and influential court had resurrected the issue of board nominations and that the Republican appointees on the SEC had to tread so carefully in re-endorsing their favored policy position against burgeoning opposition indicated that shareholder democracy (if not stakeholder representation), had become more highly politicized and its role in effectuating structural regulation had gained political support. Along with the broader questions concerning the juridical restructuring of the corporation and its governance, it was unlikely to disappear from the political stage.

99. Rule 14a-8(i)(8), 17 C.F.R. 240.14a-8(i)(8) (2007); see Securities and Exchange Commission (2007a, 16–17).

A merican corporate governance reform contains two intertwining dynamics. The first is that shareholder interests have grown steadily more powerful and ideologically influential in American politics during the past two decades. The rhetorical appeal of shareholder rights complemented the institutional imperatives of investor confidence, and both increasingly influenced policymaking conducive to the development and perpetuation of contemporary finance capitalism. Second, crises provide the conditions that allow critics and reformers to break through the bottlenecks and veto points of politics as usual but only for the usually brief duration of perceived emergency. As a practical matter, it follows that critics who argue that reform in the wake of financial crisis is too precipitous are also implicitly, if not explicitly, arguing against any meaningful regulatory response. Unfortunately, as indicated by the Enron-era scandals and the financial crisis of 2007–9, the American variant of finance capitalism has proven particularly vulnerable to recurrent and increasingly severe crises. Tendencies toward speculative excess followed by panic, the institutional flaws of corporate governance, and the pathologies of contemporary regulatory politics have combined repeatedly to produce combustible economic conditions that have prompted reforms only belatedly and usually in a form too limited to prevent the fire next time.

However, the politics of reform and regulatory innovation remains embedded in institutional structures that constrain choices and the way in which they are made in the present. Power relations within the political economy animate these constraints, and they are themselves the legacies of political, legal, and economic arrangements. The very structure of the federal government and pluralist interest group politics makes it exceedingly difficult to pass major reform legislation under ordinary conditions. In a fragmented and veto-prone political system, reform and institutional development proceeds in a pattern of punctuated equilibrium—a political and regulatory dynamic that mirrors the boom-bust cycles of an increasingly financially driven economy. During periods of sudden, episodic, and crisis-driven reform state actors possess increased policymaking autonomy as interest group alignments and power are destabilized.

Even under crisis conditions, structural and political constraints on policymaking do not disappear. Markets and the institutions on which they depend may fail, at times spectacularly, but the underlying dynamics of institutionalized interests and political constraints persist. Established patterns of interest group politics swiftly reassert themselves. Knowing this, state actors may be seen as discounting crisis and may internalize established political constraints for fear of antagonizing potent constituencies. This renders nonnegotiable matters implicating the fundamental interests of powerful groups—even when they are politically weakened. These interests are shaped over time by the institutional, legal, and regulatory context in which these actors operate. Hence, established forms of regulation are likely to be reproduced and strengthened in times of economic crisis. Bona fide regulatory innovation tends to conflict with established organizational forms and routines in the private sphere, institutional bases of power and authority, business models, and managerial strategies. True critical junctures, conditions severe enough to disrupt these tightly interwoven dimensions of economic life, are rare. In their absence, reform tends to recapitulate existing modes of regulation. The implication is that significant regulatory change and innovation are a sign of deeper crisis in the political economy and of more fundamental change.

The post–Enron-era reforms illustrate this argument. Corporate governance reforms in the United States display a pattern of punctuated evolution. Public and private actors adopt periodic legal and institutional changes within powerful, implicit, and largely unchallenged constraints. Senate Democrats never openly challenged the premises or policy commitments of securities litigation reform or managerial control over board nominations and elections. Hostility toward private litigation may have begun on the Republican right, but it achieved bipartisan support that placed firm political limits on any advances in regulatory policymaking. The relative success of Congress and the SEC in improving federal regulation of financial disclosure and the accounting industry contrasts with their failure to provide an adequate legal and institutional foundation for structural regulation premised on stronger boards, independent directors, and more active shareholders. Disclosure regulation was familiar to the American business and financial elite. It was in some ways essential for the preservation of the institutional and market conditions in which they operated. Even American organized labor, with its large pension fund holdings, sought to reinforce the regime of disclosure regulation that fosters market-driven finance capitalism.

In contrast, the inability of Congress and the SEC to carry structural regulation to its logical conclusion by giving shareholders a meaningful role in nominating and electing directors highlights the persistence of the basic institutional and interest group constraints on policymaking and reform politics in the United States. The Democrats in Congress, having become increasingly reliant on managerial elites for financial and political support, could not pursue a policy course that would rupture those alliances. Even had they been more ambitious and daring, they knew full well that the Republicans, because they controlled the House and the executive branch and had the ability to filibuster in the Senate, were in a position to thwart more radical reform and impose on their opponents the political costs of breaking with business interests. Financial interests, from Wall Street financial institutions to pension and other investment funds, from financiers and hedge fund operators to the millions of middle-class beneficiaries of institutional investors, have grown more influential in recent decades, but they have not yet displaced managerial elites in terms of political power.

Yet because of the enforcement problems created by political aversion to litigation, the trend toward structural regulation accelerated and has begun to encroach on managerial autonomy and power. Paradoxically, this emphasis on structural regulation led policymakers to tinker with some of the most basic and sensitive power relations in any capitalist society. In turn, this legal intervention in the structure of the corporation triggered resistance that revealed the political limits of reform. Even at the height of the corporate governance crisis, fundamental reform of corporate power structures, such as that implied by the SEC's shareholder nomination proposal, was politically impossible. By failing to address how boards are actually nominated and elected, the governance provisions of Sarbanes-Oxley, which relied so heavily on the independence of directors and board committees, were left with a weak foundation. The struggle over board nomination and election rules, along with the limited success of the business backlash against governance reform, reveals that corporate governance and structural regulation have become important foci of policy debate and contentious partisan political issues. It also shows the persistence of power relations and how quickly politics returns to normal after a crisis.

This restoration of ordinary interest group politics did *not* mean that policy or the policy debate over corporate governance regulation and reform returned to the status quo ante. The scandals, crises, and reforms of 2000–10 shifted the terms of debate over corporate and financial power in the United States. Corporate governance law and politics steadily shifted in favor of shareholders and structural regulation to protect their interests appears a firmly entrenched feature of American business and finance. Yet the struggle over power and authority within the corporation remains very much alive. This intensifying battle over corporate governance and its future has grown more politicized and divisive over time, not less. The financial crisis of 2007–9 and accompanying Great Recession clarified the fundamentally political character of these conflicts over reform and dispelled the notion that legal development follows an evolutionary path toward greater economic efficiency. This crisis, like others in recent decades, once again underscored the deficiencies in the American corporate governance regime. The criticisms of Sarbanes-Oxley and subsequent reforms as imposing excessive mandatory risk management practices and unduly interfering with the internal operation of corporations now seem quaint. Corporate governance is the once and future battleground over the balance of power within the American political economy.

CHAPTER 5

German Corporate Governance Reform

The Limits of Legal Transformation

T hroughout the 1980s and into the 1990s, Germany was commonly portrayed as lagging other advanced industrial countries such as the United States, United Kingdom, and even France in reforming its corporate governance regime and securities markets. Between 1990 and 2005, however, Germany's governance regime changed more than it had during the prior half century and arguably since the Industrial Revolution. This process of legal change has led some German commentators to speak of "permanent reform."[1] The resulting corporate governance regime has remained distinctively German, with a pronounced stakeholder orientation that distinguishes it fundamentally from the American model, but it is now far more protective of shareholders and designed to facilitate financial market development. Reforms have largely displaced self-regulation and federalist arrangements with formal law and regulatory centralization at the federal level. Legal change has substantially reallocated power within the corporation through forms of structural regulation.

Amid the sustained upheaval of domestic economic crisis, European integration, and financial globalization, partisan political strategies intersected with shifting interest group preferences to drive reform. In contrast to the more episodic and reactive course of reform in the United States, German governance reform was the product of sustained and deliberate governmental policy. This was all the more remarkable because the pro-shareholder content of these reforms represented a significant break with the subordination of shareholders in Germany's postwar governance regime. The German

1. See Noack and Zetzsche (2005); Zoellner (1994), and Seibert (2002).

government created the country's first federal securities regulator, steadily expanded its powers and jurisdiction, and ultimately consolidated all financial regulators within one powerful agency. It repeatedly overhauled federal company law (including passage of a controversial Takeover Act), eliminated capital gains taxes on the liquidation of cross-shareholdings, instituted a permanent Corporate Governance Commission, and continuously revised the official Code of Best Practices backed by legislation. A range of structural changes in company law increased the power of the supervisory board and shareholder protections. Litigation reform moderately expanded shareholders' ability to use lawsuits as an enforcement mechanism in corporate governance. German politicians and interest groups have pushed some corporate governance reforms in advance of and beyond those of the European Union (EU) while also successfully resisting other EU-driven reforms.

These developments have altered some of the core structural features of the German economic model, and at the same time they challenge some prominent academic theories of economic and regulatory reform. German corporate governance reform undermines theories of neoliberal convergence and path dependence alike. The country's governance regime retains its national distinctiveness, particularly with respect to employee representation, even as its legal and regulatory foundations have been transformed. Finally, it does not support the thesis that reform has been driven by EU policymaking and economic forces unleashed by European market integration. Neither EU politics nor supranational economic forces have displaced national politics and political governance. Instead, German corporate governance has developed into a new hybrid form that combines increased shareholder protections and rights with established mechanisms of ownership, control, and stakeholder incorporation. This chapter traces the juridical evolution of the German governance regime and presents a political explanation for its trajectory.

The genesis and content of these reforms can be understood only in the political economic context that produced them. By the 1990s, Germany's postwar economic miracle was over. Rising unemployment and slowing growth during the 1980s pointed to underlying problems in economic performance and adjustment. The country's vaunted model of organized capitalism appeared not only incapable of sustaining a high-growth, high-wage, and high-employment economy but also politically ossified and incapable of reform. After a brief post-reunification boom, economic growth slowed to less than 2 percent annually, and unemployment hovered near 10 percent. During the 1990s, large segments of the political elite and the German electorate began to lose faith in established economic arrangements at the same time that they became beguiled by the high rates of growth, job creation, booming stock markets, and innovative high-tech industries in the United States.

Making matters worse, the twin challenges of German reunification and European integration further strained the German economy and macroeconomic policy. Aside from the immense costs, profound errors in the economic reunification of West and East Germany exacerbated the country's woes. The absorption of a large working-age population without the skills or capital-intensive infrastructure needed to reach West German productivity levels yet bound by nationwide sectoral collective bargains exacerbated mass unemployment. Unification of the Eastern and Western currencies at a one-to-one ratio compelled tight, growth-throttling monetary policies in Europe to contain its inflationary impact. European monetary union constrained German deficit spending, under a stability pact imposed by Germany, despite domestic stagnation, high unemployment, and falling demand. Committed to the great project of European economic integration but embedded in entrenched political economic structures, German political elites were under intense cross-pressures to liberalize and preserve the established German model. The internationalization and continental integration of capital markets raised fears that Frankfurt—and Germany—would languish as a global financial center. Increasing competition and shrinking margins in the overbanked domestic market spurred the pursuit of higher profits and returns to capital by financial institutions. Under tightening macroeconomic and EU-driven political constraints, policymakers sought ways to encourage corporate and market restructuring to improve economic performance.

Segments of the German political and economic elite identified corporate governance reform as a way to advance corporate restructuring, improved economic performance, and European integration. Such reform, largely a matter of legal and regulatory change, would cost relatively little in terms of public spending; the costs would be political, not budgetary. The reform sparked considerable partisan and interest group conflict, as might be expected when changes in law and policy threaten to alter some of the most foundational power relationships in the political economy.

These reforms reveal three characteristics of the law and politics of corporate governance. First, reform is fundamentally a political process. State actors and partisan political strategies dominated the formulation of policy agendas and legislative proposals and alignment of interest group coalitions. Further, despite the progress of European economic integration, corporate governance reform reveals the primacy of national politics. EU initiatives were extraordinarily successful in areas of broad consensus, such as securities law, but were blocked by serious national conflicts, as in the areas of company and takeover law. Second, the reform process displayed a double movement from disclosure regulation to structural regulation (i.e., from securities to company law), and from changes in substantive law to the enhancement of enforcement mechanisms, whether they were administrative oversight, institutionalized bargaining, or litigation. Each movement was accompanied by increasing political conflict that helps explain the dynamics of reform over time. Finally, the Center-Left was the driving force behind the most controversial aspects of corporate governance reform and the chief advocate of shareholders over managers. The pace and depth of reform were dependent on the political strength of the centrists in the SPD. The collapse of the SPD-Green government gave rise not only to the Grand Coalition of the Christian Democratic Union (CDU) and SPD and a revitalized leftist politics but also to a more cautiously moderate course on reform.

GERMAN SECURITIES LAW REFORM

EU Integration and the German Political Economy

Three intertwined dynamics have driven German capital market regulation since the 1980s. First, the European Union's single-market agenda produced a bold legal harmonization program to integrate financial markets across the continent, and this implicated Germany's deep commitments to European integration.[2] Second, financial globalization, increasing domestic banking competition, and eroding profits drove large German financial institutions to endorse reform as a way of creating conditions that supported more market-driven business strategies. Third, state actors pursued corporate governance reform to advance their own partisan and programmatic ends: support for the EU and European economic integration, the formation and maintenance of interest group coalitions, and domestic corporate restructuring to achieve improved economic performance without substantial governmental expenditures.

Throughout the 1980s and the early 1990s, German banks and corporate interests alike opposed the liberalization and regulatory transformation of financial markets. EU directives recurrently focused on improved transparency, disclosure, and regulatory oversight of securities markets and listed companies to protect minority shareholders and promote stock market development. German corporate governance, however, had fostered a constellation of interests that disfavored financial transparency, and the banks at first resisted the EU agenda. Corporate managers and banks went so far as to fight a rearguard action against the adoption of insider trading legislation even after losing the battle against adoption of the EU insider trading directive that mandated its passage.[3] Likewise, they opposed legislation that would compel the disclosure of ownership stakes in corporations.[4]

---

2. For convenience, I use the term EU to refer to both the European Community and the European Union.
3. Confidential interview, Bundesverband für Deutsches Banken (BDB), Berlin, November 1999; interview, Josef Tobien, Deutsche Börse, Frankfurt, December 8, 1999.
4. Interviews, Markus Herdina and Helmut Achatz, Deutsches Aktieninstitut (DAI), Frankfurt, December 6, 1999.

Opaque financial arrangements and dealings gave managers, financiers, and dominant shareholders advantages they were loath to relinquish. Lax regulation inculcated expectations of financial privacy and substantial control on the part of blockholders. The prevalence of concentrated, family-dominated holdings personalized and intensified this expectation.[5] The practices of relational and universal banking tied major banks to traditional lending practices threatened by market-based financial services. Industrial managers not only recoiled from transparency that might jeopardize their relative insulation from shareholder pressures and regulatory oversight; they also established competitive strategies that relied on long planning horizons and stable financing to facilitate incremental improvements in design, product quality, and production techniques in Germany's core industrial sectors.[6] The relative opacity of the German financial system encouraged a symbiotic relationship between medium- to long-term corporate adjustment strategies and financial structures dominated by internal financing through retained earnings and bank debt. Managers could easily smooth earnings by drawing down on hidden reserves, while banks had enduring relations with firms that rewarded long-term financing with steady and predictable revenues.

Reform of securities and financial market regulation began with the EU's accelerating efforts to create a common market during the late 1980s and early 1990s. A central component of that agenda was, and still is, the construction of EU-wide capital and financial services markets, and one of the primary mechanisms for achieving this goal was the harmonization of financial market law. A series of EU directives promulgated by the European Commission (EC) advanced harmonization by requiring their implementation in member states' domestic law. The investment services directive, the banking directives, the insurance directive, the insider trading directive, and the transparency directive—to give only a partial list—reshaped the landscape of European law and the structural determinants of European finance. The EU's extensive progress on regulatory harmonization in financial market regulation sharply distinguished it from similar efforts in company law. Company law harmonization and the aspiration for a pan-European corporate form has been on the EC agenda since at least the early 1970s, but disputes over German board codetermination and takeovers either precluded agreement among the member states or repeatedly forced them and the European Commission into awkward compromises, as discussed below. In contrast, the member states struck agreements across a wide range of subjects in the area of financial markets law.

Cumulatively, EU directives were instrumental in the liberalization, harmonization, and integration of securities law through a proliferation of financial market laws that in many ways increased state intervention in the markets. The adoption of these directives peaked in the middle to late 1980s, followed

---

5. Ibid.
6. This point is made particularly well in O'Sullivan (2000) and Lazonick (1997).

by a major consolidation and rationalization initiative with the adoption of the investment services directive (ISD) in 1993.[7] The ISD placed the wide array of existing directives on securities markets and financial services in a broader programmatic framework to create an adequate regulatory and market infrastructure for a truly integrated European market in financial services. It harmonized and increased the minimum standards of financial regulation while cultivating the legal grounds for conducting cross-border financial services activities within the EU. The ISD also required the creation or strengthening of national regulatory authorities. The EU's great market-building project necessitated the expansion of member-state power.

Although the EU's financial market integration and legal harmonization agendas influenced German legal reforms, they were not the principal drivers of domestic reform. Nor did causation run unidirectionally from Brussels to Berlin (or earlier to Bonn). EU financial market integration and legal harmonization could proceed only with German support and faltered when it was lacking—as was made plain by the decades of conflict and deadlock over company law reform (discussed below). The EU reforms marked only a starting point for German corporate governance reform. For the most part, the politics of financial system and corporate governance reform in Germany were driven endogenously by changing domestic economic, interest group, and political conditions that led Germany to support parts of the EU agenda and to go beyond it in some respects. Moreover, EU law also left considerable discretion to the member states in the implementation of commission directives.[8] The EU's principle of "subsidiarity" and its post-1985 policy of "minimum harmonization" set the necessary and sufficient standards for market integration. But these normative constraints on EU promotion of legal harmonization and market unification favored greater reliance on mutual recognition and regulatory competition than on the imposition of detailed substantive law on member states.[9]

Economic Interests and the Politics of Financial Regulation

Initially, financial market reforms reflected Germany's continued commitment to European integration. The government of Helmut Kohl, the last led by those with personal memories of the Second World War, was deeply

7. See Investment Services Directive, Council Directive 93/22/EEC of May 10, 1993, on investment services in the securities field, OJ L 141 of June 11, 1993, amended by European Parliament and Council Directive 95/26/EC of June 29, 1995.

8. Article 189 of the Treaty of Rome states that a directive "shall be binding, as to the result to be achieved, upon each Member State, but shall leave to the national authorities the choice and form and methods." Treaty Establishing the European Community, March 25, 1957 (Treaty of Rome), art. 189 (new art. 249, as amended).

9. See Tison (1999, 8) and Timmermans (2003, 626).

committed to European integration. The leadership of the CDU under Kohl was willing to accept financial market and securities law reform as its necessary price. The CDU's coalition partner, the neoliberal Free Democratic Party (FDP), strongly favored pro-market liberalization, but Kohl was generally unwilling to alter the basic structural arrangements of the German economic model. He also had good reasons to be careful; there were fairly narrow limits to the economic and legal reforms that the Center-Right's supporters would bear.

By the early 1990s German politicians and policymakers were increasingly concerned about the competitiveness and efficiency of German financial markets and institutions in an environment of rapidly internationalizing capital markets. Dissatisfaction with the established financial market structure among important segments of the German financial sector had been growing since the middle to late 1980s. Managers of the most prominent financial institutions and officials of the private banks' peak association, the BDB (Bundesverband für Deutsches Banken), began to perceive competitive disadvantages of Germany's bank-centered relational finance system. Yet the financial sector remained uncertain as to what, if any, appropriate policy responses should be undertaken at the national level to increase the depth and development of securities markets.

By the mid-1990s, the policy preferences of major German banks and industrial firms had undergone a profound transformation. Rather than trying to thwart reform, the banks and the BDB pressed for passage of the Second and Third Financial Promotion Laws, which created the legal foundations for the marketization (or modernization) of German finance.[10] This dramatic change in position was driven by the banks' interests in finding more profitable lines of business and in maintaining Frankfurt's position as a financial center. The internationalization of financial markets and services broke open the cosseted, semiclosed national financial systems of the postwar era. Major German banks were exposed to greater foreign competition, particularly from American investment banks, but this presented them with potential opportunities that were more lucrative than their traditional lending and service lines of business. Traditional German relational banking imposed growing opportunity costs on the major banks by impeding their transition to a business model based on proprietary securities trading and selling sophisticated financial products and services. The banks sought a regulatory framework commensurate with American standards of transparency that would encourage the use

---

10. Second Financial Market Promotion Act (*Gesetz über den Wertpapierhandel und zur Änderung börsenrechtlicher und wertpapierrechtlicher Vorschriften, Zweites Finanzmarktförderungsgesetz*) of July 26, 1994, Federal Law Gazette, pt. I, p. 1749; Third Financial Market Promotion Act (*Gesetz zur weiteren Fortentwicklung des Finanzplatzes Deutschland, Drittes Finanzmarktförderungsgesetz*) of March 24, 1998, Federal Law Gazette, pt. I, p. 529. Interviews, BDB, Berlin, November 1999; Dr. Thorsten Pötzsch, Ministry of Finance, Berlin, October 29, 1999.

of more market-based finance and related services.[11] By the time the Third Financial Market Promotion Law was passed in 1998, the expansion of securities regulation was a matter of political consensus.[12]

The entry of American investment banks into the German market during the 1990s added to the domestic pressure for reform. They not only heralded unprecedented competition but also altered policy preferences within the financial sector. These foreign institutions became increasingly prominent in the BDB and in policymaking circles in German politics throughout the mid- to late 1990s.[13] Foreign banks have their own lobbying and policy association based in Frankfurt, the Association of Foreign Banks, but this group had relatively little impact on the substance of legislation and policy.[14] In part this was because the BDB accepted the most powerful and successful American financial institutions into the halls of power. In fact, by the late 1990s, Goldman Sachs had joined the inner circle of lobbying and policymaking at the BDB.[15] The Americans received a place at the bargaining table, and the German banks got the benefit of their experience and sophistication in both financial and regulatory matters.[16]

The enhanced political influence of the banks and the BDB contrasted with the diminished influence of the peak industry association, the BDI (Bundesverband für Deutsches Industrie), a redistribution of influence that continues to this day.[17] The BDI was plagued by more membership splits and greater ambivalence with respect to securities market and regulatory reform. When consensus is lacking, a peak association cannot speak with the unified and authoritative voice needed to influence the policy process. The BDI's membership ranged from major publicly traded multinationals to the small and medium-sized *Mittelstand* firms, and included a large number of privately held firms. These constituents had very different interests in the regulation of

11. Though interviewees frequently referred to "international standards," they almost always focused on American standards and frequently criticized the United States for seeking to unilaterally impose American transparency policy on the rest of the world.

12. Interviews, Helmut Achatz, DAI, Frankfurt, December 6, 1999; Dr. Thorsten Pötzsch, Ministry of Finance, Berlin, October 29, 1999.

13. Confidential interview, BDB, Berlin, November 1999.

14. Ibid. The AFB did not fail to influence policy for lack of trying, however. The association adopted a publicly vocal role in public policy debates. Ibid.; interviews, Dr. Thorsten Pötzsch, Ministry of Finance, Berlin, July 10, 2000; Lucy Shiels, Association of Foreign Banks, Frankfurt, December 10, 1999. However, its reliance on public pronouncements and policy statements reflects its relative weakness in the behind-the-scenes deal making among established national peak associations.

15. Confidential interview, BDB, Berlin, November 1999.

16. Ibid.; interviews, Jella Benner-Heinacher, DSW, Düsseldorf, December 9, 1999; Christa Frank, Deutsche Börse, Frankfurt, December 8, 1999; Josef Tobien, Deutsche Börse, Frankfurt, December 8, 1999.

17. Confidential interviews, Ministry of Finance, Berlin, July 2003, and BDB, Berlin, July 2007.

finance, and their divisions hobbled the BDI's efforts with respect to securities law reforms.[18]

During the early and mid-1990s, large publicly listed firms helped organize the Frankfurt-based DAI (Deutsche Aktien Institut) to advocate the improvement and modernization of German financial markets and increase industry's access to securitized finance. Though the DAI ostensibly represented the interests of listed firms, its constituencies also included the major banks and financial institutions. With a far more focused agenda and more unified membership than the BDI, the group became a leading lobbying group for reform of financial markets and their regulation.[19] Thus, by the mid-1990s, the most powerful financial and industrial firms in Germany had realigned their preferences in favor of a reform agenda that served their interests by favoring those of shareholders. With this shift in interest group politics, Germany became a supporter of the EU's capital markets and securities regulation agenda—albeit an initially cautious one. By the late 1990s, securities regulation reform would become a matter of uncontroversial consensus as Germany supported the streamlining of the EU's legislative process for securities and capital market regulation. This was known as the Lamfalussy process, named for the head of the so-called group of wise men convened to prepare the legal blueprint for integrated European markets for capital and financial services.

The Institutionalization and Expansion of Regulatory Authority

Whatever the earlier reservations of German political and economic elites over the EU's common market objectives, national politics became the primary driver of financial market reform policies over the course of the 1990s. This was evident when Germany created its first federal securities regulator in 1994. The ISD required a national authority to administer securities and financial services regulation but gave the member states broad latitude as to the form of such a body.[20] Within a year, Germany created the German Federal Securities Supervisory Office (Bundesaufsichtsamt für den Wertpapierhandel, or BAWe), a centralized federal agency that displaced the established federalist and self-regulatory structure and exceeded the minimum requirements of the ISD.

As the major banks' policy positions shifted, German securities law and regulation changed at an accelerating rate. This transformation led to the

18. Interviews, Dr. Thorsten Pötzsch, Ministry of Finance, Berlin, October 29, 1999; Josef Tobien, Deutsche Börse, Frankfurt, December 8, 1999.

19. Interviews, Markus Herdina, DAI, Frankfurt, December 6, 1999; Helmut Achatz, DAI, Frankfurt, December 6, 1999.

20. Investment Services Directive, Council Directive 93/22/EEC of May 10, 1993, on investment services in the securities field, OJ L 141 of June 11, 1993, title VI, art. 22, §§ 1–2.

emergence of a well-developed disclosure regime of securities regulation. Institutionally, the reform of German securities regulation entailed extensive centralization of regulatory authority over financial markets and services. The pivotal moment in German securities law reform was the passage of the landmark Second Financial Market Promotion Act in 1994. In a stroke, the act created a body of federal securities law, the BAWe, and the basis for administrative rulemaking in securities regulation.[21] The BAWe replaced the decentralized system of state-level exchange regulators with a centralized and nationally authoritative source of regulation and enforcement power. Though the exchanges and the Länder authorities retained a nominal regulatory role, the BAWe, like the SEC in the United States, became the primary agency charged with protecting the interests of investors.[22]

The BAWe's early history was marked by intense legislative activity and an extraordinarily rapid expansion of its jurisdiction and regulatory responsibilities. From 1994 to 1998, its mandate came to include a growing number of financial institutions and service providers, a widening array of substantive areas of regulation, and stronger enforcement powers. Like the SEC, the BAWe oversaw the filing of prospectuses, the disclosure and reporting of material information by public companies, insider trading, and the reporting of voting rights and ownership stakes. It also supervised financial services providers and took a lead role, in the absence of effective channels of private litigation, in investigating and bringing enforcement actions for suspected violations of securities rules. In order to address the historical fragmentation of German securities markets, as well as the internationalization of securities markets and related regulatory issues in a fragmented international system, the BAWe was charged with coordinating domestic regulation of German stock exchanges and cooperation with foreign securities regulators.[23]

The BAWe was empowered to formulate disclosure and market transparency regulations and interpretive guidelines. It was made responsible for monitoring the compliance of listed corporations with reporting requirements and "ad hoc disclosures" (analogous to the continuous duty of disclosure of American public corporations), which grew from under 1,000 in 1995 to nearly 3,500 in 1999.[24] Likewise, the BAWe took responsibility for monitoring compliance with disclosure requirements concerning changes in voting rights stakes in

---

21. See Securities Trading Act (*Wertpapierhandelsgesetz-WpHG*) of July 26, 1994, §§ 3–11, Federal Law Gazette, pt. I, p. 1749, promulgated as art. I of the Second Financial Promotion Act.

22. See ibid. §§ 4–7, 40.

23. See WpHG §§ 5–7, 19, 30, 36c.

24. See BAWe (1999, 27–29). Under the German ad hoc disclosure rules, information must be disclosed if it (1) is new and unknown to the public, (2) occurs within the issuer's sphere of activity, (3) is likely to affect the assets or financial situation or the general trading position of the issuer, and (4) is likely to exert significant influence on the stock exchange price. Securities Trading Act § 15.

listed companies (similar to those of the SEC's reporting requirements under the Williams Act). The agency was also charged with overseeing compliance of investment services firms with rules of conduct intended to protect individual investors from negligence, fraud, and underhanded practices in the brokering and dealing of securities. Finally, the BAWe became the lead enforcer of new prohibitions on insider trading, marking a sharp departure from prior (and ineffective) voluntary restraints without formal enforcement mechanisms.[25]

In contrast to the institutionally independent SEC, the BAWe was located within and answerable to the Ministry of Finance. Accordingly, it was subject to ministerial oversight and agenda setting in terms of policy development and the drafting of new regulations. Given this closer relationship between the BAWe and federal government, the steady growth of the agency's activism and scope of jurisdiction during the 1990s indicated broader policy priorities at the federal level.[26] Although it grew quickly to a staff of approximately 150 by the end of 2001, it remained a small agency by any standard.[27] In comparison, the SEC had 3,285 staff members (equal to 2,936 full-time equivalent positions) at the end of 2001. Like the SEC, the BAWe was chronically understaffed, partly because of its ever-expanding responsibilities and partly because it was difficult to recruit personnel away from the private sector as financial activity surged during the late 1990s.

The BAWe and federal regulation did not erode the role of the Länder so much as fill the vacuum they had left.[28] The result was analogous to the early development of the SEC: a centralized federal regulator ascendant over a fragmented federalist regulatory system and a consolidating national financial market structure. The Länder authorities and the stock exchanges themselves retained regulatory power over the listing rules that defined the conditions under which corporations could list on public exchanges.[29] The Frankfurt Börse, in particular, tightened its listing rules regarding disclosure and voting practices in response to increased competition from other major European exchanges for investment capital.[30] Foreign investors, listed firms, securities regulators, and even the head of the BAWe criticized this dual regulatory structure, but the problem of multilayered rules and regulatory authorities was

25. WpHG §§ 12–20; see BAWe (1997, 1998, 1999). The voluntary insider-trading Kodex was widely ignored and regarded as a failure. Interviews, Markus Herdina, DAI, Frankfurt, December 6, 1999; Hans-Werner Neye, Ministry of Justice, Berlin, November 11, 1999.
26. Interviews, Dr. Susan Bergstrasser, BAWe, Frankfurt, July 19, 2000; Nicole Krüger, BAWe, Frankfurt, July 19, 2000.
27. BAWe (1996, 1997, 1998, 1999); interview, Dr. Susan Bergstrasser, BAWe, Frankfurt, July 19, 2000; Nicole Krüger, BAWe, Frankfurt, July 19, 2000. Because the BAWe was merged with the other financial regulators in 2002 to form the BAFin (discussed below), figures after 2001 are not comparable, though staffing for securities regulation continued to climb.
28. Interviews, op cit. n. 27.
29. Interview, Dr. Susan Bergstrasser, BAWe, Frankfurt, July 19, 2000.
30. Interview, Josef Tobien, Deutsche Börse, Frankfurt, December 8, 1999.

moderated by the growing federal dominance of securities law and regulation.[31]

Liberalization did not figure in these legal reforms. Securities law reforms during the 1990s produced, first and foremost, a massive increase and centralization of regulatory authority and capacity. The second prevailing trend was the accelerating expansion of regulatory jurisdiction over a widening array of economic actors and activities. The predominant substantive norms developed during these two periods were transparency of financial status and governance structures and market integrity measures to ensure formal equality among investors. The paradox was that a deliberate policy of creating a more market-based financial system and maintaining Frankfurt's position as a global financial center compelled an unprecedented expansion of formal regulation and strengthening of federal regulatory capacity.

POLITICAL ENTREPRENEURIALISM, THE SOCIAL DEMOCRATS, AND CORPORATE GOVERNANCE REFORM

The Politics of the Control and Transparency Act

Consensus over corporate governance reform, evident in the area of securities regulation, broke down when the policy debate turned to issues of company law. The Kohl government balked at deeper governance reforms that threatened the established internal power relations of the corporation. Corporate managers nestled within the protective legal, blockholding, and cross-shareholding structures of "Germany AG" were (and are) a core constituency of the Center-Right Christian Democrats. They were divided over corporate governance reform, with a substantial number hostile to potential constraints on their autonomy and authority. Opposition was also intense among owners and managers of many small and medium-sized firms within the *Mittelstand*, often referred to as the backbone of the German economy, who feared that corporate governance reforms would disrupt their stable sources of credit. The FDP, Germany's sole liberal party, with historically close relations to major banks and the financial sector, had sought pro-shareholder company law reform for much of the 1990s but had been rebuffed and endlessly delayed by the more

---

31. Interviews, Dr. Susan Bergstrasser, BAWe, Frankfurt, July 19, 2000; Deutsche Börse, Frankfurt, December 1999. These criticisms triggered considerable controversy in Germany, but, like corporation law federalism in the United States, the system proved resistant to change.

traditionalist CDU.[32] Instead, the Center-Left SPD took up the corporate governance reform agenda, first in opposition and then in the governing SPD-Green coalition government under Chancellor Gerhard Schröder from 1998 to 2005.

The SPD's embrace of corporate governance reform produced the second politically pivotal moment in the reform process, the passage of the Control and Transparency Act (the KonTraG) in 1998.[33] The first reform of German company law since 1965, the KonTraG highlights how partisan political strategies and shifting coalitional alignments produced—and limited—reform. Company law reform added another, more politically contentious dimension to the broadening corporate governance policy agenda and one that would have to confront the structural legacies of Germany's postwar political economic model far more directly than the creation and expansion of federal securities law had done. This made it all the more remarkable that the era of the SDP-Green government, from 1998 to 2005, would be a period of unparalleled change in corporate governance law favoring shareholders and financial institutions—delivered by the Center-Left.

The KonTraG was a product as much of political strategy as of reformist zeal. While the SPD was still in opposition, Theodor Baums, a rising academic expert on company law and a vociferous advocate of corporate governance reform, approached Hans Martin Bury, an up-and-coming member of the SPD in the Bundestag, to advocate putting governance reform on the national political agenda.[34] Baums suggested that the SPD frame the issue by targeting excessive bank power in finance and corporate governance. By doing so, it could use the support of its venerably anti-bank left wing and unions to help mobilize a broader anti-financier populism that had been smoldering already as a result of various financial scandals. The policy would also be good for restructuring an economy that seemed stagnant. The SPD hierarchy saw this as a legislative strategy that could play well with their left wing and help establish the SPD as the party of economic modernization.

Taking advantage of the opportunity presented by economic crisis and shifting interest group preferences, the SPD could present itself as serious about restructuring the economy and enhancing economic democracy while outflanking the CDU by portraying it as the party of managerial interests and

---

32. The governing coalition had set up a working group on company law reform, but the CDU made no serious effort to address the issues of corporate governance and company law reform until the SPD proposal was made public. Interview, Dr. Rainer Funke, member of the Bundestag, FDP Bundesfraktion, Berlin, November 2, 1999. See also Ziegler (2000, 203–4) and Cioffi (2002).

33. Corporate Control and Transparency Act (*Gesetz zur Kontrolle und Transparenz im Unternehmensbereich*) of April 27, 1998, Federal Law Gazette, pt. I, p. 786.

34. Interview, Dr. Theodor Baums, University of Osnabrück, July 13, 1999.

an increasingly dysfunctional economic status quo.[35] In the process, the party sought to cultivate support within the financial sector and among middle-class investors to broaden its electoral appeal. This placed the CDU in a difficult position. It had long relied upon the support of business and financial elites that were increasingly split over corporate governance reform. The nonliberal conservatives of the CDU were wary of alienating the many corporate managers who were antagonistic toward pro-shareholder reforms, but they faced increased tension with the FDP over reforms the latter had long favored.

Centrist SPD leaders confronted resistance from segments of organized labor (particularly the rank and file) and traditionalist left-wing factions suspicious of Anglo-American "casino capitalism." In part, the centrists prevailed because the corporate governance policy agenda appealed to the long-standing ideological antagonism of the German Left toward the insularity, hierarchy, and conservatism of Germany's financial and corporate elite.[36] The centrists' victory in this policy debate (and Schröder's rise within the SPD) also indicated the growing recognition among union leaders that deteriorating economic conditions compelled some sort of reform agenda.

The draft legislation introduced by the SPD in the Bundestag mandated the divestment of the banks' equity stake in corporations and the total prohibition of bank voting of deposited shares, imposed a limit of five board mandates (seats) per person, and gave the BAKred, Germany's federal bank regulator, expanded authority to investigate the activities of banks in corporate governance. According to Baums, the SPD sponsors knew the proposed legislation had no chance of passage. The strategy was to get public attention and pressure the government to support a compromise bill in the Bundestag that would be tolerable to and in part supported by the banks.[37] The strategy worked remarkably well.

Under pressure from the SPD and the FDP, the CDU threw its support behind a compromise law. The banks and the BDB demanded substantial tax concessions in the event that they were forced to liquidate their equity holdings and bluntly warned that their voting of proxies for their brokerage clients was an unprofitable service that they would suspend if it were made any more expensive or cumbersome.[38] The CDU, FDP, and the banks thought that the

35. See Cioffi (2002) and Höpner (2003). For an excellent analysis of the Schröder government's attempts to create a shareholding culture in Germany during the late 1990s, see Ziegler (2000).

36. For a fine historical account of this ideological aspect of German social democracy in historical perspective, see Höpner (2003); see also Cioffi (2002).

37. Ibid. Although the Bundesrat had also worked on a company law reform bill, under German law the upper house has no veto over issues of company law and thus played virtually no role in the legislative process.

38. Ibid.

SPD attack on "bank power" was mere posturing.[39] The banks called the politicians' bluff, as anticipated by all sides. Neither the government nor the SPD wanted a serious conflict with the banks. Withdrawal of the banks from voting deposited shares, without some replacement, would result in fewer shareholders voting, more unpredictable shareholder votes, and less managerial accountability.[40] Nor were they willing to table a vastly more complicated and controversial tax reform agenda that would benefit the banks.[41] The government and Bundestag agreed to remove the provisions on compulsory divestments and the outright elimination of bank proxy voting.

Following these concessions in the political bargaining, the banks and the BDB fell surprisingly silent, even on the final provisions that diluted bank voting power.[42] Given the anti-bank sentiment that had driven corporate governance reform onto the political agenda, the BDB and the individual banks saw the benefits of keeping a low profile in the ongoing debate. But the major banks were also quietly supportive of the reform agenda to improve and deepen German securities markets.[43] They had already targeted financial services and the consulting business generated by these markets as their growth areas and had reconsidered their traditional role in corporate governance. Likewise, they acceded to modest limitations placed on the number of board mandates that could be held by one person. In the banks' view, large numbers of interlocking board mandates had generated increasingly bad publicity and conflicts of interest that hampered their transition to more market-based business models. In effect, the banks gave up what they no longer wanted. With the most controversial items removed from the agenda, the attack on bank power faded as the issues of financial transparency, the role of the board, and the use of new mechanisms of financing and compensation emerged as core concerns.

The CDU and FDP proposed a number of additional terms that sparked further controversy. One was a limit on the maximum size of supervisory boards. A second was an FDP attempt to bar or at least limit cross-shareholding among corporations. Both of these initiatives were blocked in short order.

39. Interview, Dr. Rainer Funke, member of the Bundestag, FDP Bundesfraktion, Berlin, November 2, 1999.

40. Interviews, Markus Herdina and Helmut Achatz, DAI, Frankfurt, December 6, 1999.

41. Moreover, the publicly owned Landesbanken own a large amount of corporate stock, generally in smaller but locally important firms. Many SPD politicians were not eager to see a law that broke the tight financial linkages that ensured stable credit and financing to firms in their jurisdictions.

42. Interviews, Markus Herdina and Helmut Achatz, DAI, Frankfurt, December 6, 1999; Marcus Becker-Melching, BDB, Berlin, November 11, 1999; Dr. Rainer Funke, member of the Bundestag, FDP Bundesfraktion, Berlin, November 2, 1999.

43. Interviews, Markus Herdina and Helmut Achatz, DAI, Frankfurt, December 6, 1999. A representative of the BDB also suggested that this was generally the case, though with reservations on the particulars of the reforms. Interview, Marcus Becker-Melching, BDB, Berlin, November 11, 1999.

Allianz and Munich Re, the German insurance giants, in particular fought against any mandatory abolition of their large and extensive cross-shareholdings. Compulsory divestment, as in the case of bank equity stakes, would force the insurers and a large number of other firms to incur huge capital gains tax liabilities. The CDU and FDP saw that the provision was likely to trigger potent opposition throughout corporate Germany and quickly dropped it.[44]

The proposed limitation on the size of the supervisory board entangled the legislation in the politics of codetermination. The limit was ostensibly justified on the grounds that a smaller board would be more cohesive and effective. However, diminishing the size of the board would reduce or eliminate the board seats granted to the unions that represented employees in these firms. The unions and the SPD therefore saw this proposal as an attack on codetermination and organized labor.[45] The heads of the German Federation of Trade Unions (Deutscher Gewerkschaftsbund, or DGB) and the more conservative white-collar union association protested to the Economic Ministry. Faced with intense opposition on an issue of great symbolic importance but little practical value, the CDU dropped the provision from the draft law.[46] Introducing shareholder primacy norms in corporate fiduciary law would have been seen as an assault on board codetermination and stakeholder governance. It was not even considered.[47]

The final KonTraG legislation addressed the subjects of bank power, the role and power of the supervisory board, auditing, share voting rights, stock options, and litigation rules.[48] The law weakened the influence of Germany's universal banks by forcing them to make a choice: if their holdings exceeded 5 percent of a corporation's stock, they could vote their own equity stakes *or* vote the proxy votes of the shares deposited by their brokerage customers. The law preserved the German bank-based system of proxy voting while encouraging a reduction in the size of bank blockholdings. The KonTraG also required that banks disclose all other board mandates held by their representatives, their ownership stakes in firms, and alternative ways for share depositors to exercise their votes. It strengthened the banks' statutory fiduciary obligation to vote proxies in the best interests of the average shareholder.

44. Interviews, Dr. Rainer Funke, member of the Bundestag, FDP Bundesfraktion, Berlin, November 2, 1999; Dr. Ulrich Seibert, Ministry of Justice, Berlin, July 5, 1999, and November 11, 1999.

45. Thus the unions would be caught in a dilemma: either they lost their board seats or they fought to keep their seats and risked alienating their rank-and-file employees. Interview, Dr. Roland Köstler, DGB and the Hans Böckler Stiftung, Düsseldorf, December 12, 1999.

46. Interviews, Dr. Rainer Funke, member of the Bundestag, FDP Bundesfraktion, Berlin, November 2, 1999; Dr. Ulrich Seibert, Ministry of Justice, Berlin, July 5, 1999, and November 11, 1999.

47. Interview, Dr. Rainer Funke, member of the Bundestag, FDP Bundesfraktion, Berlin, November 2, 1999.

48. A useful summary of the KonTraG's provisions is provided by the law's principal drafter, Ulrich Seibert (1999).

The KonTraG deployed structural regulation to strengthen the roles of the supervisory board and external auditors. Already a prominent feature of the German stakeholder governance regime, it was now used to increase the legal protection of shareholder interests. The law shifted the responsibility to hire and oversee the auditor and receive audit reports from the management board to the supervisory board. This reallocation of information and power enhanced the monitoring function of the supervisory board. The annual audit also had to include an assessment of risk management and monitoring systems. The law contained additional reforms to ensure the independence and reliability of auditors. The reforms of auditor rules and board responsibilities for external audits were strikingly similar to provisions of the American Sarbanes-Oxley Act passed nearly four years *later* in the wake of the Enron-era financial scandals. Germany, the alleged laggard in reform, leapfrogged American law and regulation—without the prompting of a serious fraud-driven financial crisis.

Other structural provisions addressed shareholder voting rights. The KonTraG imposed a one share–one vote rule that barred unequal voting rights among common shares. The KonTraG also abolished voting caps that limited the maximum number of votes by one shareholder. Conversely, the KonTraG prohibited the voting of cross-shareholding stakes above 25 percent (a blocking minority under German company law) in supervisory board elections to prevent managers from wresting control from shareholders by engaging in reciprocal voting with the managers of other firms. Overall, the law sought to weaken the control of managers, banks, and blockholders.

The KonTraG also incorporated distinctively Anglo-American corporate governance and financial concepts. For the first time, the law allowed stock repurchases as a way to raise share prices without incurring taxes and the use of stock options as executive compensation (though with strict limitations on their terms and exercise to prevent abuse). Finally, the KonTraG contained modest shareholder litigation reforms. It lowered the percentage of shares needed to demand the filing of a claim against supervisory and management board members on behalf of the corporation for gross breaches of the fiduciary duty of loyalty.[49] It also substantially raised the damages limitation on auditor liability.[50] However, the KonTraG did not otherwise alter the litigation procedures that effectively discouraged shareholder lawsuits and did not enable direct shareholder suits.

In addition to its legal innovations, the KonTraG represented an important political turning point that presaged the political strategy and policy agenda of the SPD when it came to power in a Red-Green coalition under Chancellor Schröder in late 1998. First, the centrists in the SPD embraced the

---

49. From 10 percent to 5 percent or 1 million DM of nominal capital.
50. From 500,000 DM to 8 million DM for listed corporations (2 million DM for unlisted companies).

cause of shareholders and assembled an interest group coalition in support. They had secured the support of the Left and labor and the quiet backing of the banks, and had succeeded in splitting the business community. Notably, shareholders were not an influential constituency in this coalition. Block-holders were largely hostile or ambivalent to reforms that threatened their means of corporate control. Smaller shareholders were too few and their advocacy groups too weak to matter much in the political calculus. Banks, however, were powerful and a prime target for cultivation by the SPD's dominant centrists. Further, the reform agenda now extended to company law and the structural attributes of the corporation, which were far more politically contentious than disclosure regulation under securities law.

Thus, politically and legally, the KonTraG inaugurated a new phase of reform. The era of Red-Green government ushered in an unprecedented series of legal changes, but it also would be marked by intense conflicts over the future of German capitalism and corporate governance. Within three years of the KonTraG's passage several developments would spark heightened conflict over corporate governance reform: (1) the hostile takeover of a Mannesmann, a major wireless telecommunications company, (2) major tax reforms designed to break up German cross-shareholdings, and (3) the proposal of an EU takeover directive. The KonTraG inadvertently mobilized political and economic elites against liberalization of takeover law, even as it set the stage for broader pro-shareholder corporate governance reforms.

The Mannesmann Takeover

The hostile takeover of Mannesmann in February 2000 sent a slow-motion shock wave through German politics.[51] Mannesmann was truly an exceptional case in German business. It was an old Düsseldorf-based metalworking and engineering firm that had made an extraordinarily successful transition to wireless telecommunications. The company found itself suspended between the traditional structures and practices of German corporate governance and the new norms of shareholder capitalism. Mannesmann had not adopted International Accounting Standards or US-GAAP, and it remained a diversified corporate group (*Konzern*) that improbably combined its old metalworking business with world-class wireless telecommunications. It was not listed on either the New York or London stock exchanges, and because of its origins in the steel sector, it was governed under full-parity Montan codetermination.[52]

51. Höpner and Jackson (2001) and Milhaupt and Pistor (2008) provide excellent detailed overviews and analyses of the Mannesmann takeover and its implications for German corporate governance.
52. Höpner and Jackson (2001, 25).

Yet Mannesmann had avidly pursued shareholder value. Its high share price had financed a series of strategic acquisitions that turned it into one of Europe's leading wireless telecommunications companies and an attractive investment for foreigners. By 1999, its stock market capitalization equaled 11.5 percent of the German blue-chip DAX index. It had no "main bank" (*Hausbank*) relationship (although the Deutschebank chairman, Josef Ackermann, was on its supervisory board), and its shares were widely held rather than locked up in blockholdings or cross-shareholdings. Foreign investors held approximately 80 percent of its stock, with Anglo-American institutional investors owning 19.2 percent.[53]

In November 1999, Vodafone, a smaller but aggressively acquisitive British wireless telecommunications corporation, launched a successful cross-border hostile takeover bid for Mannesmann. Chancellor Schröder issued a few critical comments regarding the incursion of Anglo-American capitalism into Germany, but he was roundly criticized for interfering in a market transaction and quickly withdrew from an active role in the matter. In fact, his half-hearted and unsuccessful intercession was seen by many as the end of Germany AG. After a four-month battle, Vodafone won shareholder support for its bid, and Mannesmann surrendered after its supervisory board approved generous management severance packages that would later trigger an extremely controversial criminal case.

For the first time, a successful hostile takeover had been launched against a major German corporation by a foreign firm. It provided striking evidence of the prominence American investment banks had achieved in Germany by the end of the 1990s. Mannesmann retained Morgan Stanley, Merrill Lynch, and J.P. Morgan as its advisers. Goldman Sachs and Warburg Dillon Read advised Vodafone. The Mannesmann situation also revealed surprising vulnerabilities to takeover within the German corporate governance regime, as German law barred takeover defenses, such as poison pills, common in the United States.[54] To some extent Mannesmann's vulnerability was a special case. Having no Hausbank relationships with Mannesmann, the major German universal banks did not defend the target company and at least tacitly supported the takeover.[55] The company's unusually dispersed and international shareholder base made Mannesmann atypically vulnerable to a tender offer bid.

53. Ibid., 25–26, table 5.
54. In some important ways German law was *more* favorable to the hostile bidder than was British law. Vodafone took advantage of German law by successively raising the bid price for Mannesmann shares, prohibited under British takeover rules, and certainly did not consider the legal defenses available under German company law insurmountable. Interviews, Dr. Roland Köstler, DGB, Düsseldorf, July 8, 2003; senior official, Hans Böckler Foundation, Düsseldorf, July 18, 2000; cf. Höpner and Jackson (2001, 44–45).
55. Interviews, Dr. Roland Köstler, DGB and Hans Böckler Foundation, Düsseldorf, July 18, 2000; senior official, Hans Böckler Foundation, 18, 2000; cf. Höpner and Jackson (2001, 44–45).

Notwithstanding supervisory board codetermination, employee representatives were primarily concerned with protecting the economic interests of workers (particularly those in the old steel sector subsidiaries), not with the independence of the firm as an ongoing enterprise.

Initially, the political and public response to the takeover bid was surprisingly muted. Takeovers remained unpopular with the public, but opponents of takeovers and economic liberalization failed to mobilize politically around the issue. Although Mannesmann's management fought bitterly, it did not seek aid from the government.[56] There was little of the widespread public outcry or union militancy that had accompanied the abortive ThyssenKrupp hostile takeover two years before or the near collapse of the Holzmann construction group that was avoided only by the reluctant intervention of Deutschebank under public and government pressure.[57] Though IG Metall opposed the takeover, it did not call for mass demonstrations against it.[58]

The public perception shifted, however, as it became clear that the deal was not the advertised merger of equals and that the German operations were no longer being directed from Düsseldorf. This represented a blow to German pride, a more serious blow to the economic heartland around Düsseldorf, and a looming threat to Germany's corporate elite. Germans began to see the specter of casino capitalism beneath the rhetoric of shareholder rights. An innovative company that had appeared to play by the new marketplace rules of shareholder value, high-tech innovation, and widely held stock was seen as having paid the price of its own existence. Even though *no* further hostile takeovers occurred in Germany, resentment and fear slowly festered.[59] Tax reform and a proposed EU takeover directive would make these sentiments politically combustible.

Tax Reform and the Unbinding of Germany AG

Webs of cross-shareholdings provided the glue that kept Germany AG intact and made takeovers difficult.[60] Firms and financial institutions refused to liquidate their stakes in other corporations so long as capital gains taxes were prohibitively high (over 50 percent). The Mannesmann takeover showed that the country's firms, at least those with dispersed share ownership, were now

56. See generally Höpner and Jackson (2001).

57. Cf. Ziegler (2000, discussing, inter alia, the ThyssenKrupp takeover attempt and eventual merger).

58. Interviews, Dr. Roland Köstler, DGB and Hans Böckler Foundation, Düsseldorf, July 18, 2000; senior official, Hans Böckler Foundation, July 18, 2000.

59. Numerous interviewees referred to the extent and intensity of antitakeover attitudes.

60. See discussion in chapter 3. Cf. Jenkinson and Ljungqvist (1999) and Köke (2001, empirical studies finding reduced chances of a change in control where there are complex extensive cross-shareholdings).

exposed to tender offers from outside the country. Less than six months later, tax reform legislation increased this vulnerability by eliminating capital gains tax impediments to unwinding protective cross-shareholdings.[61]

The tax reform law (*Steuerreform*) of July 2000, abolished capital gains taxes on the liquidation of cross-shareholdings. The Schröder government hoped this would invigorate German securities markets by increasing the proportion of shares traded (the "free float" of issued securities). Despite evidence that Germany's firms were now vulnerable to takeover, the government wanted to intensify financial market and shareholder pressures on German corporations to restructure and adjust to changing economic conditions. The capital gains tax reform signaled how central corporate governance reform had become to the SPD-Green government's political strategy and policy agenda. Strikingly, the Center-Left government with business support pushed the legislation through a resistant legislature over intense *conservative* opposition. The tax reform became a highly visible and controversial piece of the Schröder government's agenda, and fierce political maneuvering was required to push the legislation through the Bundesrat, where CDU representatives held the majority. Only shrewd bargaining and promises of additional federal transfers to strapped Länder governments secured its passage.

Economics did not drive the reform; politics did. The tax break on dispositions of cross-shareholdings was assailed by critics as a gift to business and particularly to the financial sector at the center of these cross-shareholdings. But this was, in part, the point. The Schröder government was cultivating support among the banks and the financial sector while driving a policy wedge to split business interests. After the resignation of the left-wing Oskar Lafontaine as finance minister and SPD chairman after only six months in office, there was little to impede the pro-finance and largely pro-business policy tack of the SPD centrists that dominated domestic policy.[62] With the weakening of the SPD's left wing, corporate governance reform joined employment policy, welfare spending, and pension reform at the core of an increasingly neoliberal economic program. The SPD-Green government advanced these policies not only to improve German growth and employment performance but also to pry constituencies from the CDU and FDP. By mid-decade, this strategy would fail spectacularly as the SPD split apart, hemorrhaged support, and lost power amid continued economic stagnation. An early indication that the SPD's political calculations were flawed came with the conflict over the EU takeover directive and German Takeover Act.

---

61. Cf. Holloway (2001).

62. Lafontaine never explained his reasons for resigning but, after three days of silence, he held a press conference in which he cryptically said, "If the team does not play well anymore, one must look for a new team." (BBC 1999). He made good on that veiled threat when he helped form the Left Party, which contributed to Schröder's election loss in 2005 and continues to cripple the SPD politically.

Taking effect in January 2002, the tax reform law quickly set off a wave of asset sales by banks and firms, though not a wholesale disintegration of cross-shareholdings.[63] The underdevelopment and relative illiquidity of Germany's capital markets constrained divestment of cross-shareholdings.[64] The international stock market crash of 2001–2 further slowed the disposition of stakes. Nevertheless, hostile takeovers became a more realistic possibility in the wake of the tax reforms, in part by creating liquidity. This looming threat altered the political terrain of corporate governance reform in Germany. The effects of this shift were felt both within domestic politics and in Brussels as the EU debated a long-awaited takeover directive. The result was the first defeat of a European Commission initiative in the European Parliament.

TAKEOVER POLITICS IN GERMANY AND THE EU

The EU Takeover Directive

The harmonization of company law has been a prominent item on the EU agenda since the 1970s.[65] In June 2000, the German government, which held the rotating presidency of the Council of the European Union, brokered a political bargain over a draft takeover directive. In June 2001, after further contentious negotiations over antitakeover defenses and greater consultation rights for employees, the European Commission submitted the draft directive for the required majority vote of the European Parliament.

The draft was the clearest and most far-reaching attempt to impose market-driven Anglo-American shareholder capitalism on the EU member states. Not surprisingly, it became one of the most divisive pieces of legislation ever to come before the European Parliament, sparking fierce opposition and unusual alliances. The most controversial provision and a focus of opposition, article 9, imposed a requirement of "neutrality" on directors and senior managers in responding to a hostile takeover bid; this would have prohibited corporate boards and managers from adopting post-bid defensive measures without shareholder approval. The controversy over board neutrality focused the political debate on the economic and social desirability of hostile takeovers. Despite signs of mounting opposition in the parliament, the council rejected a substantive amendment loosening the restrictions on defenses. Nonetheless, by June 2001, the EC and EU member-state governments, including Germany,

---

63. See Höpner and Krempel (2004).
64. See, e.g., Bushrod (2001b).
65. For a complete legislative history, see High Level Group of Company Law Experts (2002, 13–17).

had approved the draft directive. Yet political opposition to it was already brewing in Germany.

The threat posed by takeovers to vested economic interests mobilized powerful constituencies against the takeover directive. Over time, the hostile takeover of Mannesmann by Vodafone had steeled opposition to takeovers across a broad swath of German interest groups and voters.[66] German managers saw the directive as a threat not only to their positions but also to the independence and the comparative institutional strengths of German corporations. The managers of DaimlerChrysler, Volkswagen, BASF, and several German chemical companies led managerial opposition to the directive.[67] Volkswagen was a particularly effective lobbyist with the chancellor, who had recently sat on its supervisory board as premier of Lower Saxony.

The German industrial unions, a key pillar of support for the governing SPD, were adamantly opposed to the importation of Anglo-American takeovers. They had supported other corporate governance reforms that strengthened disclosure regulation and the role of the supervisory board but regarded takeovers as fundamentally more prejudicial to their interests and to German stakeholder governance. Organized labor saw the takeover directive as a means of decisively shifting power and income from employees to shareholders. German managers and labor thus formed a potent coalition across class and ideological lines to oppose the directive and its supporters in the financial sector and government.[68]

Prior domestic corporate governance reforms intensified German opposition to the directive.[69] Together, the KonTraG and tax reform legislation had eliminated the principal antitakeover defenses in Germany by imposing a one share–one vote rule and weakening control through cross-shareholding and bank proxy voting. In contrast, the takeover directive would have *allowed* golden shares, dual-class share structures, ownership pyramids, and cross-shareholding to shield companies in other countries, including France, Italy, the Netherlands, and Sweden, that allowed or encouraged them. This left German firms asymmetrically vulnerable to transnational takeover threats. Ironically, the draft directive also would have placed more stringent restrictions on takeover defenses than the United States did.[70] German firms would have been threatened with takeover by savvy American firms and financial institutions experienced in hostile takeovers. The only thing surprising about the broad-based opposition to hostile takeovers and the takeover directive in Germany was how belated it was and that it took the government by surprise.

---

66. See *Financial News* (2001).
67. See *Wall Street Journal Europe* (2001) and Simonian (2001).
68. Simonian (2001).
69. See Fithin (2001).
70. Cf. Betts and Hargreaves (2001).

The mobilization against the takeover directive forced the German government into a humiliating and unprecedented reversal of position in the European Council. Only a few weeks from completion of the political process, the government shifted its position to oppose the directive, generating accusations of betrayal from other EU governments.[71] Germany was isolated and outvoted fourteen to one on the conciliation committee draft. The opposition then moved to the European Parliament, which was faced with a stark choice between a neoliberal takeover framework and rejection of the draft directive and twelve years of work.

German Christian Democrat Klaus-Heiner Lehne was both the rapporteur for the directive in the European Parliament and the leader of the opposition to it. Hailing from the area near Mannesmann's home base in Düsseldorf, Lehne focused on the absence of a level playing field for takeovers and warned of an ensuing unfair and unscrupulous struggle for economic power through corporate control. While he was concerned that the takeover directive would put German companies at risk against other European and American companies, he framed his arguments in terms of a broader reallocation of corporate and economic power that would operate unequally across EU member states. These arguments appealed to a large number of European Parliament members. The issues stressed by Lehne dominated the debate.[72] Outside Germany, asymmetric strategic advantages in the market for control were especially worrying to firms in Italy and Spain under takeover threats from French companies, some of which had been recently privatized but were protected by state-created golden shares. Lehne also argued that European corporations would be at a disadvantage against better-defended American firms—a fear that reportedly was shared widely across Europe. The metaphor of the level playing field resonated much more in the European Parliament than did appeals to protectionism, let alone German economic nationalism.

Finally, the draft directive was perceived as posing a direct threat to national sovereignty and national models of capitalism. It would have disrupted the complicated and distinctive balance of interests worked out by the member states during the postwar period. The directive's neutrality requirement would trigger a norm of shareholder supremacy in takeover situations when the interests of shareholders, managers, and employees come into sharpest conflict. The potential disruptive effects of the directive were particularly serious for German board codetermination, which precludes shareholder primacy. Scandinavian countries such as Sweden, where neocorporatism is manifest outside and above the firm at the national and sectoral levels, were not as hostile to the directive as were Germany, the Netherlands, and Austria, where *internal* firm governance played a more central role in articulating and

---

71. See Hargreaves (2001) and Krause (2001).
72. See Hong (2001).

reconciling stakeholder interests. From the vantage point of organized labor, Social Democrats, and many Christian Democrats, the neutrality provision was not neutral at all but a decisive shift in the legal framework of corporate governance in favor of neoliberal shareholder capitalism and against nonliberal organized capitalism.[73]

In this light, it is not surprising that voting broke primarily along national rather than ideological lines.[74] In the European Parliament, the two major blocks, the Party of European Socialists (the Social Democrats with 181 members of parliament) and the European People's Party (the Christian Democratic block with 232 MEPs), both split along national lines. Only the liberals supported the conciliation committee compromise as a united block (52 MEPs) affiliated with the Liberal, Democrat, and Reform parties.[75] An opposition block of MEPs comprised of both Christian Democrats and Social Democrats, largely from Germany, the Netherlands, Austria, Spain, and Italy, rejected the directive.[76] The opponents were pointed in their comments, attacking the committee's draft as failing to provide for a level playing field in the market for corporate control despite ample warning of discontent over the issue in the European Parliament.[77] Members of parliament also stressed their resentment of and opposition to the perceived heavy-handed and inflexible attitude often shown by council and commission in the conciliation process.[78] In a sign of deep European divisions over takeovers and the role of EU law, the draft failed by a tied vote of 273 to 273 (with 22 abstentions).

The German Takeover Act, the EU Compromise, and the Mannesmann Trial

The backlash against the EU takeover directive spilled over into the debate on Germany's first takeover law. The Schröder government had made the same calculation in the domestic arena as it had on the European Commission: it backed a liberalizing reform of company law that would push Germany toward an active—and sometimes hostile—market for corporate control.[79] The Finance Ministry, the government, and the Bundestag had initially drafted the

---

73. Conversely, even in the United Kingdom, the source of the most unequivocal political support for the takeover directive, there were criticisms that the measure's imposition of more uniform legal standards would *weaken* shareholder protections under British corporate governance rules and derogate from the country's sovereignty (Tringham 2000).

74. Callaghan and Höpner (2005); see also Cioffi (2001, 2002).

75. See Hong (2001).

76. For an analysis of the voting patterns in the European Parliament, see Callaghan and Höpner (2005).

77. See Lehne (2001).

78. Ibid.

79. Interview, Oliver Wagner, BDB, Berlin, July 26, 2007; cf. Braude (2001b).

statute, duly endorsed by a government expert commission, in anticipation of implementing the EU takeover directive into domestic law.[80] The Mannesmann takeover and the mounting opposition to the draft EU directive changed all this.[81] A bureaucratic and technical drafting exercise became highly politicized as critics of liberalization started to appreciate the implications of the Mannesmann takeover and other corporate governance reforms. The government and its expert commission acknowledged the legacy of stakeholder governance by noting that the interests of workers as well as shareholders should be taken into account in responding to hostile bids, yet the proposed law contained no concrete protections for employee interests.[82]

Cross-class opposition to takeovers across the political spectrum drove the government to accept expanded managerial powers to adopt takeover defenses.[83] Led by managers and unions, the opponents effectively countered the large banks and shareholders groups favoring more neoliberal takeover rules and a hostile market for control.[84] Managers won greater leeway to adopt takeover defenses. Labor secured greater procedural and informational rights. However, given the intensity and political power of the opposition, the final legislation remained surprisingly takeover-friendly.

The German cabinet approved the Securities Acquisition and Takeover Act on July 11, 2001, one week after the rejection of the EU takeover directive.[85] The Bundestag approved the legislation in November 2001, and it became effective on January 1, 2002. The law imposes minimum bid disclosure rules, a mandatory takeover bid requirement once an acquirer's voting stake reaches a 30 percent threshold (preserving 25 percent blocking minorities), and a squeeze-out rule that allows a majority owning 95 percent or more of a corporation's stock to buy out the remaining minority shareholders.[86] The act also extends the BAWe's regulatory authority to cover corporate takeovers, including a thirteen-member advisory board with two seats reserved for representatives of organized labor.[87] The terms of a takeover bid, along with the

80. Interview, Dr. Hans-Werner Neye, Ministry of Justice, Berlin, November 11, 1999; Braude (2001a).
81. Betts (2002).
82. Chancellor Schröder obliquely supported this balancing of interests by warning that institutional investors should behave "responsibly" in takeover situations and that bidders should commit themselves to developing the acquired firms. Ibid.
83. See Bushrod (2001a).
84. See Braude and Hong (2001) and Barbier (2001a, 2001b).
85. Securities Acquisition and Takeover Act (*Wertpapiererwerbs und Übernahmegesetz*, WpÜG) of December 20, 2001, Federal Law Gazette, pt. I, p. 3822.
86. Hobday (2001). Mandatory bid rules are designed to distribute the control premium to all shareholders by requiring owners acquiring a control block (e.g., 30 percent) to then make an offer to the remaining shareholders on similar terms. Squeeze-out rules encourage buyouts by eliminating "hold-up" problems by shareholders who refuse to tender their shares and then demand a large premium for them afterward.
87. Securities Acquisition and Takeover Act §§ 4–9.

acquirer's post-takeover business plan, must be fully disclosed through publication and a filing with federal securities regulators.[88] The target's management is required to respond with a public report assessing the adequacy of the offer and the bidder's business strategy.

The Takeover Act, unlike the failed EU directive, contains a limited duty of neutrality.[89] However, the statute expands the latitude of management to seek shareholder authorization for specified defenses against a hostile takeover. These shareholder resolutions are valid for up to eighteen months and require a 75 percent supermajority vote, and the supervisory board must approve any deployment of these defenses.[90] Just as important, however, the duty of neutrality "does not apply to acts that would also have been performed by a prudent manager of a company not affected by a takeover offer, the [search] for a competing offer, *as well as acts approved by the supervisory board of the target company.*"[91] This provision grants the supervisory board potentially vast discretion to defend against takeover, similar to the reallocation of legal authority to the boards of American corporations during the 1980s. Moreover, the Takeover Act allows for a variety of antitakeover defenses (excluding poison pills), along with the ability to adopt a more highly leveraged capital structure unattractive to would-be acquirers.[92] The act does not fundamentally change the structure of fiduciary obligations. They are still owed to the enterprise, not to the shareholders. It maintains the jurisprudential foundations of stakeholder governance.

Far from recognizing shareholder primacy, the Takeover Act obliges both the offeror and the target's management to disclose information either to the works council or directly to the employees concerning the terms of the offer and its implications for the firm and employees and their collective representation.[93] Thus, the act makes use of and may reinforce the works council as an institution even as it expands the supervisory board's power. This use of the codetermined board and the works council within the disclosure procedures of the Takeover Act shows the resilience of the German institutional model and how stakeholder institutional arrangements can facilitate reform by mediating potential conflicts among stakeholder interests in the reform and practice of corporate governance.

Following the passage of the German Takeover Act, the European Union once again sought to fashion a uniform approach to takeover regulation, but

88. See ibid. §§ 11, 14.
89. "[T]he managing board of the target company may not perform any acts which might result in the success of the offer being prevented." Securities Acquisition and Takeover Act § 33.1.
90. Ibid. § 33.2.
91. Ibid. § 33.1 (emphasis added); see also Braude (2001a).
92. Under preexisting company law, poison pill defenses are generally regarded as an unlawful discrimination among shareholders and a violation of preemption rights.
93. See Securities Acquisition and Takeover Act §§ 10.5, 11.2.6.2, 27.

now the battle lines had hardened further and the council and European Commission were chastened by the debacle of 2001. At long last, in 2004, the EU adopted a takeover directive, but it was a heavily diluted and, in neoliberal circles, much criticized version of the law that had so inflamed passions three years earlier. In part, the European Court of Justice smoothed the way by ruling golden shares illegal under European treaty law.[94] But the German Takeover Act also provided a new, and decidedly lower, benchmark for harmonization. Most important, the directive gave the member states the ability to opt out of the "nonfrustration" rule and duty of neutrality, leaving it largely neutered. Most member states, including Germany, duly opted out of the provision, thereby preserving wide variation in the treatment of hostile takeovers across Europe and in national models of capitalism.

In Germany hostile takeovers remained almost nonexistent. The persistence of cross-shareholdings (despite reforms to encourage their dissolution), the power of unions and works councils, and the ability of companies to defend against bids likely discouraged them. However, there is one more factor that is less well recognized: the inability to make golden-parachute side payments to board members in takeover situations when they agreed to an acquisition. This became a common practice in the United States and helped drive takeovers in the presence of strong antitakeover defenses. Not so in Germany. Once again, the Mannesmann takeover played a pivotal role in this development.

In what might be regarded as the final revenge of Mannesmann's ghost, Düsseldorf prosecutors brought charges against the members of the compensation committee (*Präsidium*) of the defunct firm's supervisory board for criminal breach of trust (*Untreue*) for awarding themselves and members of the management board "appreciation" payments totaling over €57 million.[95] Those charged were among the most prominent people in Germany. They included Deutsche Bank CEO Josef Ackermann; Joachim Funk (Klaus Esser's predecessor as Mannesmann CEO); Klaus Zwickel, the head of IG Metal, the county's most important union; and Jurgen Ladberg, former head of the company's works council. Former Mannesmann CEO Esser, who received a €16 million payment, and another senior manager were tried as accomplices. The proceedings were complex, protracted, and extraordinarily controversial. German company law requires an appropriate relationship between managerial compensation awarded by the supervisory board and executive responsibilities and company performance, and breach of that duty can be punished criminally.[96] Framed in this way, the legal issues were hardly clear. Critics argued, with

---

94. Judgments of the Court of Justice in *Commission vs. Portugal,* 2002 E.C.R._I-4731; *Commission vs. France,* 2002 E.C.R. I-4781; *Commission vs. Belgium,* 2002 E.C.R. I-4809 (June 4, 2002).

95. See Gevurtz (2007) and Kolla (2004). Milhaupt and Pistor (2008, chapter 4) present a more detailed "institutional autopsy" of the case largely consistent with the analysis here.

96. See Stock Corporation Act § 87 (I) 1; Criminal Code § 266.

justification, that there were no ascertainable standards for assessing compensatory appropriateness and that this was particularly intolerable in a criminal case. Further, the defendants' supporters argued that the payments were more than justified by the recipients' creation of shareholder value by fighting and then negotiating a takeover that raised the purchase price by €50 *billion.*

The defendants' first trial ended in an acquittal in July 2004. The court ruled that the payments had violated fiduciary standards of company law but not the criminal code. After an appeal by prosecutors, the German Federal Court of Justice (Bundesgerichtshof), the country's highest court in non-constitutional cases, agreed that making the payments was a breach of the directors' fiduciary duties, but it reversed the acquittals and remanded the case for a new trial on the grounds that the record was sufficient to establish a criminal violation.[97] The court ruled that extracontractual payments could only be upheld as legal if they added value to the corporation *prospectively* and that the post-takeover awards were necessarily retrospective because Mannesmann had ceased to exist as a result of the defendants' actions. As the retrial began, the state prosecutors and defendants settled the case through rescission of the awards and imposition of substantial fines. This removed a cloud over the futures of some of the titans of the German economy but left in place a powerful legal deterrent to golden-parachute payments.

The trial played well with the general population, whose hostility to extravagant managerial pay was far greater than that seen in the United States or Britain. But the business and financial elite saw the trial as a manifestation of all they believed was wrong with the German economy: excessive egalitarianism, legalistic rigidity, hostility to restructuring, and excessive state and judicial interference in corporate affairs. Political conservatives, including the CDU's chairwoman, Angela Merkel, publicly attacked the prosecution as an assault on economic modernization. So long as the Mannesmann debate played out over questions of equality and distributional justice, it mirrored the broader conflict and uncertainties over economic reform and change in Germany. But there was a second and underappreciated practical aspect to the decision as well.

The absence of side payments to managers (at least those that had not been provided for in advance by contract) reduces the likelihood of takeovers. A critical lubricant of the merger and acquisition machinery of the liberal market economies was largely precluded by an atypical interpretation and harsh enforcement of German fiduciary law. German and American courts have recognized the inherent and intense conflicts of interest in takeover situations and adjusted fiduciary standards accordingly, but they have done so in

97. BGH, Decision of December 21, 2005, 3 StR 470/04, Neue Juristische Wochenschrift (NJW) 522 (2006), reversing and remanding Landgericht Düsseldorf, Decision of July 22, 2004, 28 Js 159/00. The Federal Court of Justice is Germany's highest court in nonconstitutional cases.

opposite ways. American fiduciary law tends to facilitate takeovers as in the shareholders' immediate interests. The rigid limitations on managerial side payments imposed by the German courts reinforced the fiduciary conception of the best interests of the corporation and the stakeholder tradition in German law. The Mannesmann ruling tends to push managers back into alignment with employee interests in resisting takeovers, whereas American and British law is far more tolerant of side payments that align managers with shareholders' short-term interests in accepting a takeover premium.[98] Going forward, the reformers would not only have to abide by the political constraints on the liberalization of the German political economy; they would also have to be mindful of potential resistance from the German courts.

THE CORPORATE GOVERNANCE CODE AND REGULATORY CENTRALIZATION

Policymaking by Commission

The Schröder government used corporate governance reform as a way of positioning itself in ongoing debates over German economic modernization and change, but the conflictual politics of takeovers revealed the limits of this agenda. Aware of growing political tensions over economic reform, the government sought to avoid fueling opposition to its corporate governance and financial market reforms. It did so by maintaining the balance of stakeholder power within firm governance and by increasing its reliance on policymaking by commission. Institutionally, it redoubled the centralization of policymaking and regulatory authority.

After a 1998 commission of the Bertelsmann and Hans Böckler foundations found that works council formation was lagging, the government passed codetermination legislation in 2001 that marginally expanded the powers of works councils and made them somewhat easier to form.[99] The law itself was not of great practical significance, but, like the incorporation of employee consultation in the Takeover Act, it indicated the continued political importance of organized labor and the attraction of the stakeholder model. The Social Democrats used the legislation to compensate the unions and the party's leftwing for supporting or acquiescing to far more important pro-business reforms of securities, company, tax, takeover, and pension laws. The law also reflected the labor movement's anxieties and shift in strategy. With union density sharply declining (if not collective bargaining coverage) and sectoral

98. Cf. Gervurtz (2007).
99. *Frankfurter Allgemeine Zeitung* (2001); Fickinger (2001a, 2001b). For a critical analysis, see Addison, Bellmann, and Wagner (2004).

bargaining yielding little but wage restraint, codetermination had become an increasingly important mechanism of labor power and organization.[100]

This maintenance of stakeholder power, in combination with increased shareholder protections, was displayed again as the government appointed two successive corporate governance commissions.[101] The commissions' composition replicated the interest group configuration of traditional peak association bargaining but allowed the government to select the group's membership. The first, in 2001, was charged with drafting a comprehensive code of best practices in German corporate governance. The commission chair, Professor Theodor Baums, insisted that the politically explosive subject of codetermination be excluded from the commission's deliberations on the grounds that it would destroy the consensus required on other important issues. The formation of a permanent government commission on corporate governance followed the release of the Baums Commission's report.[102] Impaneled in 2002, the standing Government Commission on Corporate Governance, known as the Cromme Commission after its chairman Gerhard Cromme (the former chairman of Thyssen-Krupp), made over 150 wide-ranging recommendations that largely followed the Baums Commission's recommendations.

The Cromme Commission's Code of Best Practice summarized existing mandatory terms of corporate governance law (in part to demystify German law to foreign observers), set out the best practices that firms would be generally expected to follow, and suggested additional voluntary practices. Many of the commission's recommendations proposed legislative changes that subsequently defined the policy agenda. These proposals included expanding disclosure and transparency; strengthening the role, obligations, and independence of corporate boards; improving external auditing; and modernizing corporate finance rules. The linchpin in the proposed legislative scheme was a proposed "comply or explain" rule that required firms to comply with best practices or explain via public disclosure why they had not. Most of the best practices targeted structural features of corporate governance, such as supervisory board powers, functions, and independence. The comply-or-explain rule and many of the commission's other recommendations were enacted quickly in the Transparency and Disclosure Act of 2002.[103]

100. Schulten (2001a, 2001b).

101. I am greatly indebted to Theodor Baums for this account of the German corporate governance commissions. Interview, July 9, 2003, Frankfurt.

102. Baums Commission, Report of the Government Commission on Corporate Governance, July 10, 2001. http://www.otto-schmidt.de/corporate_governance.htm; English summary at http://www.shearman.com/publications/cm_pubs.html; Cromme Commission (Government Commission of the German Corporate Governance Code), German Corporate Governance Code, adopted Feb. 26, 2002. http://www.corporate-governance-code.de/index-e.html.

103. See Transparency and Disclosure Act (TraPuG) (*Gesetz zur weiteren Reform des Aktien- und Bilanzrechts, zu Transparenz und Publizität* [*Transparenz- und Publizitätsgesetz*]), of July 19, 2002, Federal Law Gazette, pt. I, p. 2681.

Codetermination was conspicuously absent from the report. Once again, the commission's ground rules had placed supervisory board and works council codetermination outside the group's purview. This wariness reflected the extraordinary political sensitivity of the subject and, along with the works council reform, the broad popularity of codetermination among the electorate.[104] The government found its footing within a broader societal and political consensus.

The Corporate Governance Code and Transparency and Disclosure Act played off the political differences between transparency and structural regulation. The reform of securities law and passage of disclosure rules were characterized by consensus and deliberation. In contrast, structural regulation entailed fundamental changes in intracorporate power relations (through, e.g., reform of shareholder voting rights, takeover law, or codetermination) and generated more intense opposition. The comply-or-explain approach provided an opt-out that allowed companies to convert structural regulation into a less objectionable disclosure rule. This approach proved successful, and there was broad compliance with the code. The one prominent exception was disclosure of board compensation. Consistent and widespread refusal to disclose managerial pay finally prompted a legislative compromise that mandated disclosure of the total compensation of the management and supervisory boards.

Regulatory Centralization and the Centralization of Policymaking

In the area of securities regulation, where conflicts over corporate and economic power were far more muted, pro-market regulatory expansion and centralization proceeded with astonishing speed, exceeding that of the United States in some respects. In April 2002, the German Parliament further centralized financial regulation by consolidating all financial market and services regulation, including the regulation of securities markets, banking, and insurance. The law folded the BAWe within one massive agency, the German Financial Supervisory Authority (Bundesanstalt für Finanzdienstleistungsaufsicht, BAFin).[105] The consolidation of financial regulation within the BAFin was regarded as a functional necessity in a world in which the legal lines and conceptual boundaries between different forms of finance had largely dissolved. With this reform, Germany surpassed the United States in the centralization of financial services regulation.

---

104. This popularity endures. A 2004 opinion poll by the union-affiliated Hans Böckler Foundation found 89 percent of respondents thought works councils were beneficial and 82 percent did not want any weakening of supervisory board codetermination. Vitols (2005, 30).

105. Law on Integrated Financial Services Supervision (*Gesetz über die integrierte Finanzaufsicht*), April 22, 2002.

Compared with the endless turf battles characteristic of administrative politics in the United States, the formation of the BAFin was surprisingly smooth and uncontroversial. In part, this was due to the fact that universal banking in Germany had forced government regulators and policymakers to treat securities and banking issues in a more integrated way. Yet this regulatory centralization was also a product of the characteristic deliberation of the German political system. Once consensus is achieved among the relevant interest groups and peak associations regarding a given policy area, substantial policy initiatives and innovations can follow quickly.

While functional considerations led to regulatory centralization, conflicts over the government's reform agenda and chronic deadlocks within the established bargaining processes led to the *political* centralization of the policymaking process as well. The paralysis of the established consultative and policymaking machinery led the SPD government to rely on the use of expert commissions to formulate and frame policies.[106] Under Schröder's SPD, government commissions appropriated (or manipulated) the existing framework of centralized interest representation by handpicking representatives from peak organizations as well as experts, academics, and professionals, who were likely to reach a consensus on a given policy area close to the government's own position. This style of governance contained a contradiction: it relied on centralized peak associations for the representational legitimacy of expert commissions, but this policymaking by commission implicitly recognized the growing tendency of Germany's system of associational bargaining to produce impasse rather than consensus.[107] The proliferation of commissions was seen over time as manipulative and an implicit condemnation of both associational and political deliberation. The legitimacy of this favored means of policy formulation therefore grew increasingly fragile as deepening conflicts over reform weakened the political position of the Schröder government.

Corporate governance reform and the development of German finance capitalism could proceed only with continued political support. However, reform of the governance regime and financial system was part of a broader neoliberal economic policy agenda that was widely perceived by much of the Social Democratic base as contrary to their interests. Schröder's SPD struggled

---

106. For discussions of the German government's increasing use of commissions as a means of formulating policy, forging consensus, and avoiding deadlock among interest group and peak associations, see Zumbansen (2002); Baums (2001); cf. Heinze and Strünck (2003).

107. Some critics accused the government of using expert commissions to circumvent parliament. Government defenders counter, accurately, that parliament still must pass all legislation and that the commissions have not impaired democratic lawmaking. See *Economist* (2003) and Baums (2001). In contrast to corporate governance policy, the German Constitution circumscribes governmental intrusion into negotiations among the "social partners" in the area of labor relations. Accordingly, the government could not circumvent neocorporatist gridlock through commissions or the tripartite negotiations under the failed Alliance for Jobs (*Bundis für Arbeit*) early in Schröder's first term. See Streeck (2003).

on two fronts against the CDU and FDP opposition parties as well as its own left wing and restive industrial unions hostile to further reforms. By the federal elections of 2002, in which the CDU criticized the 2001 tax reforms as a giveaway to corporations and banks, the SPD's support had slid so far that the coalition just barely retained power. Economic policy contributed little if anything to Schröder's less-than-impressive victory. Instead of creating a new and enduring electoral coalition of workers and unions, the financial sector, and a growing constituency of middle-class investors, the Center-Left was eroding and fragmenting. The SPD leadership was especially frustrated, if not embittered, by the failure of their pro-finance and pro-business policies to generate more support from the financial sector in the 2002 elections.[108] The SPD's centrists had hoped to split business interests and recruit greater support from the financial sector. Instead, the bankers played the major parties off each other to get their favored policies.

The SPD-Green coalition continued to pursue corporate governance reform as part of a broader agenda of changes in tax, social welfare, employment, and pension policies. Corporate governance reform had the virtue of marshaling broad support on many policy points (especially in comparison with policy areas like labor market and social welfare reform). After the difficult struggle over takeover law, the ministries of Justice and Finance condensed the government's agenda into a ten-point plan for corporate governance reform in early 2003. The plan emphasized increased transparency, managerial accountability, and more effective mechanisms for the enforcement of shareholder rights. In its last two years, despite dwindling political capital, the Schröder government enacted much of this agenda. The continuity of corporate governance and financial system reforms under these conditions show that the relatively broad elite support for this agenda (or at least acquiescence) remained unaffected by the controversies surrounding many of the government's other economic policies.

TWO HARD CASES: THE EUROPEAN COMPANY AND LITIGATION REFORM

The most noteworthy and contentious reforms during the final years of the Red-Green coalition were the negotiation and implementation of the EU's European Company directive and pathbreaking changes in German shareholder litigation law. These reforms are critical test cases for the propositions that German corporate governance reform is, on the one hand, driven by EU

108. Confidential interview, senior adviser, Social Democratic Party, Düsseldorf, July 2003.

harmonization and, on the other, adopting aspects of American-style adversarial and adjudicatory enforcement mechanisms.[109] Each touches on extraordinarily sensitive subjects of corporate power. The adoption and content of each of these measures demonstrates the continued importance of national politics in the evolution of corporate governance and distinctiveness of the German governance regime. But the creation of the European company form also reveals the intensifying pressures on Germany to adapt to the policy dynamics and legal developments at the EU level.

The Ambivalence and Ambiguity of Litigation Reform

As discussed in chapter 3, with the exception of challenges to the conduct of annual general meetings, German law discourages lawsuits, and shareholder litigation has not played a significant role in corporate governance. This began to change, quite modestly, with parts of the KonTraG reform. The collapse of the once-soaring high-tech Neue Markt, the poor performance over time of the Deutsche Telekom stock following an enormous public offering, and several other corporate scandals during the first decade of this century increased the political salience of litigation rules.[110] Two far more sweeping reforms of shareholder litigation under securities law and company law took up proposals by the government's ten-point corporate governance agenda and the Baums and Cromme commissions. The laws were passed within two months of each other in late 2005. The very fact that Germany was experimenting with some liberalization of litigation rules was noteworthy. Increasing the capacity of shareholders (or any stakeholder for that matter) to enforce their rights or pursue their interests is by definition of vital importance. However, both these laws evinced deep ambivalence toward litigation and litigiousness. They embodied compromises between the recognition that litigation plays a necessary and inevitable role in a functional governance regime and the countervailing appreciation that it is also prone to inefficiency and rent seeking.

The 2005 amendments to the Stock Corporation Act (known by its German abbreviation, UMAG) created an analogue to the American derivative action that augmented the ability of minority shareholders to bring an action against directors on behalf of the corporation.[111] The UMAG cut the threshold for filing suit to 1 percent of shares or €100,000 and allowed shareholders to bring and control the suit directly (rather than by a court-appointed independent

109. See Keleman and Sibbitt (2004).
110. See Freshfields Bruckhaus Deringer (2005).
111. Law on the Improvement of Corporate Integrity and Modernization of Decision-Directed Suits (*Gesetz zur Unternehmungsintegritat und Modernisierung des Anfechtungsrechts*) (UMAG) of September 22, 2005, BGBI 1 2802.

representative).[112] The law also relaxed the "loser pays" rule for court costs and fees and allowed plaintiffs to seek reimbursement of costs regardless of the suit's outcome so long as the court upheld the action in a preliminary proceeding. However, the political controversy over the desirability of litigation also produced provisions designed to curb litigation and contain its costs. The law codified a version of the business judgment rule, already recognized by the Federal Court of Justice in 1997, and thus sanctioned a potent defense against all but egregious director conduct. In a compromise with the CDU-controlled Bundesrat, the law created a new preliminary procedure to test the substance of derivative suits and screen out "professional plaintiffs" to prevent abusive strike suits.[113] The legislation reflected an effort to rebalance the interests of shareholders and managers by carefully calibrating the practical availability of litigation.

But the UMAG reforms also took aim at lawsuits challenging decisions approved by the shareholders' general meeting—the most prevalent type of shareholder litigation and the single greatest source of litigation abuse. As noted in chapter 3, actions to challenge important business decisions on highly technical legal grounds had led to Germany's own problems with professional plaintiffs and strike suits. The UMAG created a preliminary proceeding to screen out strike suits within a relatively expeditious four months and curtailed the plaintiff's ability to extract quick lucrative settlements by blocking urgent business decisions through litigation. Significantly, these suits were commonly filed to block mergers, acquisitions, and capital increases, where time is of the essence. The reforms therefore supported more active markets for capital and corporate control (if not for hostile takeovers).

The 2005 securities law reforms (known as KapMuG) created a form of collective litigation that, though falling far short of the American class action, still represented a sharp break with the historically individualistic character of German shareholder litigation.[114] In part, this reform also derived from the government's pro-shareholder reform agenda. The Baums Commission had proposed a form of collective action as necessary for the effective protection of shareholders from material misrepresentations, and the Deutscher Juristentag, Germany's preeminent lawyers' association, had considered the issue in 2002.[115] Notably, each body concluded that collective actions were needed for the efficient conduct of securities litigation where individual claims were likely

112. Stock Corporation Act § 148. Dissident shareholders can also use an online shareholders' forum to solicit support to initiate action against directors. Ibid. § 127a.

113. See Lederer (2006, 1603–4) and Noack and Zetsche (2005, 1041–42).

114. Law on Model Proceedings in Capital Market Disputes (*Gesetz über Musterverfahren in kapitalmarktrechtlichen Streitigkeiten*) (KapMuG) of Aug. 16, 2005, BGBl. I, p. 2437.

115. Baums Commission, Report of the Government Commission on Corporate Governance, July 10, 2001, 88–90); Deutscher Juristentag (2002, Recommendation 1.15).

to be small, the number of claimants large, and the costs of litigation steep, but neither endorsed an American-style class-action procedure.

But the KapMuG was also the product of a serious setback in the attempt to create a German shareholder culture (*Aktienkultur*). The 1996 privatization of Deutsche Telekom had attracted a massive oversubscription for IPO shares, partially as a result of an unprecedented government advertising campaign. The government sweetened the public offering by guaranteeing the stock's value for a period of time (derided by some as shareholder capitalism with "training wheels"). These shares plummeted in value after the expiration of the guarantee period and the collapse of the global telecom bubble in 2001. Shareholders claimed that the company had overstated the value of its real estate holdings by €2.8 billion.[116] A single judge was submerged under approximately fifteen thousand individual suits filed by over 750 attorneys with no way to consolidate the proceedings or effectively vindicate shareholder rights.[117] After years of paralysis without a single final judgment, some plaintiffs filed an action with the Constitutional Court, claiming denial of fundamental justice under law. Although the court dismissed the claim, it called for experimentation with collective actions to address mass litigation and obliquely called on the legislature to enact appropriate reforms.[118]

The KapMuG created a procedure in which the first filed claim is certified as the "lead case" (*Musterverfahren*) once ten cases based on the same set of facts are filed. The common issues of law and fact are defined by the regional court and then, with the support of other claimants, adjudicated by the provincial court. If the action is dismissed, all claimants contribute to the costs of the lead case. The court's rulings on common factual and legal issues in the sample claim are binding on all other cases based on the same set of facts. There is no opt-in or possibility of opting out of the collective procedure. The lead case procedure was designed as a way of overcoming shareholder collective action problems, which grow more serious as ownership becomes more diffuse, as well as severe problems of judicial economy in mass litigation without re-creating what were seen as the lawyer-driven excesses of the American class-action system. Even so, the procedure was sufficiently controversial that the law was introduced literally as an experiment: it was drafted to expire on November 1, 2010, five years after its effective date, unless renewed.

The litigation reforms laws were the product of political compromise amid serious interest group conflict. Business interests, including the BDI and the BDB, were opposed in particular to derivative actions, but they were assuaged by the provisions curtailing litigation over decisions approved by the shareholders' general meeting and by the preservation of procedural obstacles

116. Baetge (2007, 7–9).
117. Ibid.
118. Ibid.

to bringing private suits.[119] The peak business associations were adamantly opposed to an even more fundamental reform of securities law that would have replaced the established intent standard with a negligence standard of liability in actions for material misrepresentation. The intensity of opposition forced the government to withdraw the proposed legislation. The managers and banks split over collective proceedings in securities litigation, with the BDB favoring a pro-shareholder litigation position as a way of further developing the capital markets yet opposing the importation of class-action procedures.[120] Shareholder groups and the plaintiffs' bar demanded the adoption of a true class action but did not have sufficient influence to sway the policy debate. The legislative outcomes suggest the waxing influence of the financial sector and the BDB, particularly in policy areas where managers (and thus the BDI) split over reforms.[121] Where the BDB opposed liberalization, as with derivative actions, the reforms were more modest and contained significant concessions to business.

Some commentators consider these litigation reforms a transformative moment in German corporate governance. Such extravagant claims are at best premature. Business interests may have brokered political deals over litigation rules that gave them more than they gave up. Lack of data precludes a more definitive assessment, but it appears that only a small number of derivative and collective actions have been brought.[122] Fiduciary duties are still vague, as they indeed must be in a stakeholder system that has as one of its primary functions the reconciliation of multiple opposing interests. Collective actions can serve as a shareholder sword if a lead case is successful, but they may be far more effective as a corporate/manager shield if it is dismissed.[123] If a lead case fails to establish an essential element of a claim, all other related cases likewise will be dismissed. But if the case succeeds, *all* remaining cases must still be tried individually as to noncommon issues such as reliance and damages.

Further, German procedural law is still largely antagonistic to litigation. Contingency fees are still not allowed in securities and corporate fiduciary cases, and there are no juries or punitive damages. Most important, there is still no American-style discovery in German litigation procedure. This poses a fundamental problem for proving cases and may make the lead case mechanism an even greater boon for companies by effectively shutting down litigation of

119. Interview, Oliver Wagner, BDB, Berlin, July 26, 2007.
120. Ibid.
121. Interview, Thomas Lorenz, BDB, July 26, 2007.
122. Interview, Olaf Müller-Michaels, partner, Hölster & Elsing, Düsseldorf, July 18, 2007; Borrego (2007).
123. *Cf.* Freshfields Bruckhaus Deringer (2007), citing a Regional Court's dismissal of a lead case against DaimlerChrysler alleging unlawful delay in disclosing the resignation of management board chairman Jürgen Schrempp. See OLG Stuttgart, 28.2.2007, BB 2007, 567. The Federal Court of Justice reversed, however, and remanded for further proceedings. Bundesgerichtshof II ZB 9/07, 25.2.2208, LMK 2008, 260596.

alleged disclosure violations by maintaining an informational vacuum. Lack of discovery also substantially tilts bargaining power toward management. Where expenses of litigation are lower for the corporation, plaintiffs have less leverage in settlement negotiations. There may be fewer strike suits under these rules, but there will also be fewer successful meritorious ones. Litigation reform may reframe the politics of litigation by inducing shareholder advocates to press for more of it in the future.[124] At present, this remains a matter of sheer speculation; the strenuous opposition by managerial interests and skepticism in the policy community toward litigation make such a move unlikely.

The Societas Europaea and German Company Law

The European Company, or Societas Europaea (SE), created a new pan-European corporate form that had been under consideration since at least 1970.[125] As such, it represented not only a singular development in European company law but also a potentially disruptive avenue of regulatory competition among national corporate governance regimes. Created by a 2001 EU regulation and thus directly applicable to the member states, the SE was also politically packaged with a directive on employee representation.[126] The EU's regulation-directive approach to the SE resolved two of the most difficult problems that had loomed over the European company law project: intractable conflict over codetermination and the practical impossibility of creating an entire body of company law that would provide enough legal certainty to encourage adoption of the form.

The political conflict over codetermination was addressed by the "supplementary" directive, which conferred limited employee informational and consultation rights and created a "special negotiation procedure" to address board-level worker participation and representation. Employees now have the right to be informed of material decisions and to consult as part of the decision-making process. Where 25 percent of the firm's employees have board codetermination rights, their representatives must consent to any change in board composition and structure. This provides a safe harbor for existing

---

124. See Freshfields Bruckhaus Deringer (2007, 29).

125. There are four ways to form an SE: (1) merger of existing companies from at least two different member states, (2) formation of a holding company owning existing companies from at least two member states, (3) formation of a subsidiary of existing companies from at least two different member states, and (4) conversion of an existing national company with an existing subsidiary in another member state. Reg. (EC) 2157/2001, art. 2(1)–(4).

126. Council Regulation 2157/2001 of October 8, 2001, on the Statute for a European Company (SE), 2001 O.J. (L 294) 1; Council Directive 2001/86/EC of October 8, 2001, Supplementing the Statute for a European Company with Regard to the Involvement of Employees, 2001 O.J. (L 294) 22.

forms of codetermination, defusing a politically explosive issue on which the European Company and harmonization of European company law had foundered for decades.[127] In addition, the SE regulation and directive leaves numerous and large gaps to be filled by the national company law of the jurisdiction where the company has its legal seat. This means that the SE adds a layer of law and regulation atop existing bodies of national company law, which it effectively appropriates to ensure requisite legal certainty and familiarity. Rather than displace national company law, the SE maintains much of that law's central importance. As a result, it may protect member-state company law more than threaten it. In effect, there are as many SE forms as there are member states. This helps explain why Germany agreed to the regulation-directive SE package and implemented the SE directive in late 2004—despite the CDU's brief delay of the legislation by wielding a veto in the Bundesrat.[128]

Agreement on the SE legislation can be understood only in light of the decade-long effort by the European Court of Justice (ECJ) to foster pan-European legislative competition over company law. In the famous *Centros* case and its progeny, *Überseering, Inspire Art*, and *Sevic*, the ECJ steadily, if not wholly, undermined the "real seat" theory of incorporation that required firms to incorporate under the law of the jurisdiction in which it maintained its headquarters.[129] Under the ECJ's expansive (and highly questionable) interpretation of the freedom of establishment and free movement of capital in the original EC Treaty of Rome, a corporation chartered in one member state may establish its headquarters and even do all its business in another member state. The member state in which the firm has its headquarters (its "seat") must recognize the foreign incorporation under the law of another EU state and register the firm to do business within its borders as it would a firm chartered under its own law. The ECJ stripped member states of their plenary power to regulate the internal governance affairs of firms headquartered within their territory via company law. This created the possibility of regulatory arbitrage, an EU-wide "Delaware effect," in which companies are incorporated, either initially or through reincorporation, in jurisdictions with permissive legal regimes engaged in a competition for charters and exerting pressures on all countries to adopt similar company laws. It is notable that this extraordinary change in European law came from the ECJ, the least democratically accountable EU institution. The ECJ forced the issue of company law competition

---

127. The proposed fifth directive on company law has never been adopted largely because of conflicts over codetermination.

128. European Company Implementation Act of December 28, 2004 (*Gesetz zur Einführung der Europäischen Gesellschaft*), Federal Law Gazette, pt. I, p. 3675.

129. Centros Ltd and Erhvervs-og Selbskabsstyrelsen, Case C-212/97 (1999) ECR I-1459; Überseering BV and Nordic Construction Company Baumanagement (NCC), Case C-208/00 (2002) ECR I-9919; Kamer van Koophandel en Fabrieken voor Amsterdam v. Inspire Art Ltd., Case C-167/01 (2003) ECR I-10155; Sevic Systems AG, Case C-411/03 (2005) ECR I-10805.

where political attempts at harmonization had failed for decades—and continue to fail, as evidenced by the suspension of attempts to adopt an EU one share–one vote "shareholder democracy" rule and a directive on transfer of corporate seat.[130]

Because it institutionalizes the stakeholder model in a stronger form than any other EU country does, Germany is arguably at greater risk of corporate flight under ECJ case law, either through transfers of the legal seat of existing firms or through the cumulative effect of new incorporations. The number of small, private start-up firms from other member states incorporating in the United Kingdom, the country with the most permissive company law in the EU, rose over 600 percent from 1997 to 2006, and of the 120,000 firms fitting this description, 48,000 were based in Germany.[131] The economic impact to date has been de minimis, and most such incorporations appear to be motivated by the United Kingdom's lower minimum capital rules rather than by escape from codetermination or other legal requirements.[132] Serious tax consequences have discouraged transnational reincorporation, particularly for large public companies.

The SE may make a race to the bottom in company law somewhat less likely by creating an avenue to consolidate multinational subsidiaries and merged enterprises in one legal entity, while maintaining much of the original home country's company law, rather than fully reincorporating in another jurisdiction. Of the forty-five SEs established as of July 2008, nineteen are headquartered in Germany. Five of Germany's most prominent firms have reorganized themselves as SEs: Alianz, Fresenius, BASF, Porsche, and MAN Diesel.[133] These companies have denied any motivation to escape board codetermination, aside from a stated desire to ensure more equitable representation for their multinational workforces, and all retain quasi-parity employee representation. But their conversion to the SE form is considered a warning sign in Germany of the growing pressure on the legal framework of the country's governance regime.[134]

The ECJ's erosion of the real-seat theory, the availability of the SE form, and increased conflict over board codetermination in Germany raised increasing concerns about the viability of German board codetermination. In 2004, German managers launched an unprecedented attack on codetermination, citing pressures of EU law and market integration.[135] But EU developments

130. See McCreevy (2007).
131. Becht, Mayer, and Wagner (2007).
132. Bratton, McCahery, and Vermeulen (2008).
133. See Worker-Participation.EU, http://ecdb.worker-participation.eu (database of established SEs as of July 2008, figures excluding SEs without operations or employees).
134. Interview, Prof. Uwe Schneider, Member, BAFin Takeover Panel and German delegate, OECD Steering Group on Corporate Governance, Darmstadt University, July 20, 2007.
135. Göhner and Bräunig (2004).

do not explain the attack or its timing. Their attack was not based on serious economic concerns (let alone data) or the state of EU law; it was the product of the specific political conditions at the end of the Red-Green coalition.

THE IMPLOSION OF THE SPD AND MERKEL'S GRAND COALITION

Collapse of the Red-Green Coalition

By 2004, Schröder and the SPD confronted growing tensions over economic and welfare state reform that opened into splits within the party and the reforms' failure to improve economic conditions. Following his extremely narrow victory in the September 2002 elections, Schröder's political position eroded nationally and within the SPD as growth slumped and unemployment climbed. The worsening economic conditions cast a particularly harsh light on the government's corporate governance and financial market reforms. The bursting of the Internet stock market bubble and the post-Enron market crashes spilled over into Germany as the Neue Markt, the Frankfurt Börse's answer to the American NASDAQ for the listing of new high-tech growth stocks, collapsed and eventually closed entirely. Steep declines in the DAX and main Frankfurt market segments restored Germans to their traditional risk aversion as they fled stocks for safer investments. The breadth, seriousness, and sheer sleaze of the Enron-era financial scandals undermined the reputation and appeal of the American model of finance and corporate governance.

Finally, intraparty conflict reached a peak over the government's "Hartz IV" reforms, which weakened employment protections and cut unemployment and other social welfare benefits, and its "Agenda 2010," which pursued increased economic competitiveness through further labor market liberalization and corporate tax cuts. Whatever the merits of the Hartz reforms and the broader agenda, it was clear that they were politically damaging to the SPD at a time of chronically high unemployment. By mid-2004 the party's popular support was collapsing below 30 percent, and its membership plummeted by over 150,000, particularly among workers and union members, including many long-time party activists.[136] The SPD's secretary, Franz Müntefering, sought to play the populist card against foreign (i.e., American and British) hedge funds in an April 2005 interview, memorably calling these investors "locusts" that stripped good firms of assets and left desolation in their wake. The rhetoric resonated, but it bore no relation to government policy.[137]

---

136. Prantl (2005).
137. Corbett (2005).

The entire political system was showing signs of intense strain as more of the electorate turned to the left in opinion polls, but Schröder and the SPD remained intransigently attached to a neoliberal, pro-business agenda. The center could hold no longer. Between mid-2004 and mid-2005, what had been the solid Center-Left for six decades shattered amid demonstrations and defections. Germany's proportional representation electoral system gave the Left an exit option, and in the spring of 2005 they took it. A leftist block led by experienced SPD members and dissident union members quit the SPD and formed a new Left Party in alliance with the largely Eastern ex-Communists to oppose further liberalizing reforms. Oskar Lafontaine, Schröder's ex-finance minister and current nemesis, stepped in to lead the new party.

The SPD was confronted with increasing tensions within its own ranks over the content of reform, which it tried and ultimately failed to contain. The conflicts over takeover law were a harbinger of even more intense discord over reform that would shatter the German Center-Left, doom the Schröder government, and transform the German party system. The CDU majority in the Bundesrat effectively blocked Schröder's reform agenda and impaired his capacity to govern. He was beset by growing divisions within the SPD and loss of support among the electorate. Following the SPD's devastating defeat in North-Rhine Westphalia and other Länder elections, Schröder called for the dissolution of parliament and an early parliamentary election for September 2005.[138] The early election was seen by some as a final desperate attempt to rescue political momentum for his reform agenda and by other observers as an act of preemptive political suicide.

The major parties framed the election as a stark choice between Schröder's reform agenda and the CDU's sudden embrace of a more radical form of neoliberalism under its new leader, Angela Merkel. The first party leader from the former East Germany, Merkel was hailed during the campaign as Germany's Margaret Thatcher. She relentlessly attacked the stakeholder model as the source of Germany's seemingly intractable economic and political crises and touted the market as the solution. The CDU's neoliberal turn was a stunning miscalculation. Although the party went into the election with a commanding lead in the polls, its support collapsed swiftly in response to its call for radical free-market reforms. Instead of resolving the political crisis, the election confirmed the divisions within the German polity and did much to make the political stalemate permanent. Both the SPD and the CDU fared poorly; neither was able to form a majority governing coalition with their favored coalition partners (the Greens for the SPD and the FDP for the CDU). The Greens, who had become increasingly liberal during their spell in power, lost votes as

---

138. This was a sensitive issue in Germany after the traumas of the Weimar period's endless and ultimately disastrous elections. This was only the second snap election in post–World War II history. The president and the Constitutional Court had to sign off on the dissolution and new elections, and both were criticized for allowing them to go forward.

well. But the election did usher in a political upheaval. The Left Party's emergence as a viable electoral competitor with nearly 9 percent of the vote fundamentally altered the logic of the party system in Germany. The FDP and the Left Party sapped votes from the Center-Right and Center-Left, respectively, indicating significant polarization and a serious legitimacy crisis (*Staatsverdrossenheit*) engulfing both Left and Right.[139]

The emergence of the Left Party and the neoliberal FDP's public refusal to join a coalition with the SPD forced the CDU and SPD into a Grand Coalition with Merkel as chancellor but with the SPD in control of most major ministries. With both the SPD and the CDU wary of the political unpopularity of further neoliberal reform, the arrangement ensured that the new government's economic policies would remain cabined within the narrow confines of consensus. The SPD in particular was paralyzed. It could no longer afford to move to the right on policy now that there was a viable competitor on its left to siphon away disillusioned voters. Accordingly, the SPD repudiated the Hartz IV reforms and much of the Agenda 2010. Yet the fear was that if it lurched to the left to recapture its old working class and union base, it would likely lose a portion of the middle-class votes that formed much of its contemporary base. The immobilizing political position of the SPD and the CDU's rapid retreat into a pragmatic defense of the social market economy resulted in extreme caution and minimal policy innovation. Merkel's Grand Coalition did not roll back Schröder's reforms, but it did not propose any major ones of its own. In the area of corporate governance policy, continued reforms focused on securities law, on which there was broad agreement among the political class and widespread indifference among the electorate. More controversial domestic reforms were out of the question.

The Attack on Board Codetermination

Amid the SPD's dramatic political collapse, board codetermination, long a taboo and untouchable feature of German corporate governance, had become a subject of debate. By 2004, the new European legal terrain, created by ECJ case law and the new SE corporate form, emboldened codetermination's critics and worried the supporters of the traditional stakeholder regime. The increasingly public conflict over the future of codetermination surfaced in a government commission appointed to study the issue and in the Deutscher Juristentag. The criticism had entered the core of German politics as well. Two of the peak business associations, the BDI and the BDA, formed a joint commission condemning Germany's strong form of quasi-parity codetermination and calling for a maximum of one-third of supervisory board seats for employee

---

139. See Sommer (2005).

representatives.[140] The business associations saw the growing disillusion, fragmentation, and political erosion of the Center-Left and took the opportunity to begin an assault on board codetermination, despite its status as a central institution and symbol of the stakeholder regime.

Chancellor Schröder, realizing that he needed to shore up support among labor and his party's Left, formed yet another expert commission to study the economic impact of board codetermination.[141] The goal was to respond to the anti-codetermination rhetoric of the BDA and BDI, and of much of the foreign and domestic business press, with empirically grounded, evidence-based analysis. An expansive literature on board codetermination had accumulated in the decades since 1976. Scholars overwhelmingly concluded that codetermination had at most a negligible impact on the economic performance of firms. But the evidence was to prove beside the point as the politics of codetermination and corporate governance intersected with the partisan politics leading to the dissolution of the Red-Green coalition.

Schröder had announced the formation of the Commission for the Modernization of Enterprise-Level Codetermination" before calling the 2005 snap election. At the same time, the CDU's newly radical, neoliberal policy agenda emboldened the critics of codetermination to escalate their attacks. Schröder was left in the difficult position of impaneling a commission on which consensus would be impossible. In an exceedingly shrewd move, he turned to Kurt Biedenkopf to chair the commission. Biedenkopf was one of the most prominent of the CDU's senior statesmen, having been the secretary general and deputy chairman of the party in the 1970s, a prominent member of the Bundestag, and premier of Saxony from 1990 to 2002. Biedenkopf also was a political and intellectual architect of codetermination as a way of securing labor peace and the legitimation of corporate capitalism during the 1970s. Thus he was unlikely to support the dismantling of one of his great accomplishments.

The codetermination commission revealed the limits of Schröder's policymaking by commission and the breakdown of associational politics. By 2005 the intensification of political conflict over economic reform in Germany left ever less room for consensus and compromise. Expert commissions cannot recreate the conditions for deliberation and agreement once their social and economic foundations have collapsed. Business and labor representatives were a mirror image of each other's intransigence. The representatives of the BDI and BDA, certain that a new neoliberal era was about to dawn, adopted a hard

140. See Göhner and Bräunig (2004, joint press release of the BDA and BDI).
141. This account is deeply indebted to conversations with Wolfgang Streeck, director of the Max Planck Institute for the Study of Societies and member of the government's Codetermination Commission, and Thomas Raiser, the author of the Deutscher Juristentag's (unadopted) report on the status of German codetermination.

line on rolling back codetermination. Labor's representatives, the heads of IG Metall and the DGB, did not acknowledge the EU's threat to codetermination. They believed they had defanged the new SE legislation with the addition of the employee representation directive, and they did not appreciate the potential for German firms to reincorporate under the ECJ's case law. Both sides saw the status quo as favoring them. Labor viewed the existing legal and institutional arrangements as entrenching their position. Managers viewed the political status quo as portending the imminent collapse of the Left and the long-awaited emergence of a neoliberal right. Each side would refuse to sign on to any report the deviated from these fixed positions.

The peak business associations' hopes for the second coming of Thatcher were crushed by the results of the September 2005 elections. Even though they could no longer even hope for a radical, neoliberal turn in government policy, the reality of an imminent Grand Coalition between the CDU and the SPD did not produce compromise, let alone consensus. The stalemate between labor and managerial interests continued, but Biedenkopf and the independent members of the commission had extracted a promise from Merkel that if the business and labor representatives refused to endorse the final report, it would be submitted without them. By the time the report was submitted to the new chancellor, now embracing a new centrist pragmatism, it was abundantly clear that any significant reform of codetermination would be politically impossible, and the report's voluminous summation of the existing research on the subject did not support one.

At approximately the same time, the Deutscher Juristentag was also the debating the future of board codetermination. That the most influential association of German lawyers was even discussing the previously sacrosanct subject indicated the extraordinary change in national politics and legal thinking at the beginning of the twenty-first century. Another indication of the intensification of conflict over codetermination was the open conflict that spilled over into the Juristentag deliberations. The body had often addressed politically and practically important legal subjects, but, virtually without exception, they reflected a pre-established collective consensus or compromise position on the jurisprudential and policy issues. Historically, the proceedings concluded with a clear majority vote among the members to adopt the official report prepared by an eminent legal academic along with commentaries by two or three other experts. As the discussion of codetermination began, it was apparent that there was no consensus, and just as on the government codetermination commission, there were no grounds for compromise. The divisions reflected conflicts between labor and capital, and between labor and corporate lawyers, that had been growing since the late 1990s as German quasi-parity board codetermination appeared to be an increasingly isolated outlier in EU and international corporate governance debates. These conflicts broke out into the open during the next decade.

Some areas of contention might have lent themselves to compromise, but the ultimate issue was the continued existence of quasi-parity board representation. The debate itself was largely dominated by arguments that been made for decades: codetermined boards were too large and inefficient, the law was too inflexible to respond to the needs of different types of businesses, the presence of employees limited trust and open discussion on the board, management was able to play employees and shareholders off each other, and codetermination imposed a discount on share prices. There were also a number of newer arguments that reflected the growing internationalization of major German corporations and the effects of EU law. The possibility of corporate migration out of Germany under the ECJ's case law and the availability of the SE form loomed large, especially following the reincorporation of Allianz as an SE. Further, codetermination now appeared increasingly parochial in that only German employees could vote for representation in firms that now often had as many, if not more, foreign employees. The stakeholder logic was turning on itself in an age of globalization.

Under these new conditions, several experts, including Thomas Raiser, the lead author of the codetermination report, made the argument that the implementation of board representation should be subject to greater negotiation. The unions rejected all these arguments and the policy recommendation that followed. They suspected that representation of foreign employees was a ploy to weaken codetermination by weakening German labor. They also suspected, with justification, that negotiations would be used to target the unions' board seats. Business interests, led by the BDA, wanted to limit codetermination to one-third of board seats, a demand Raiser found entirely unjustifiable. The report duly analyzed the empirical literature and, like the government commission, found that there were no serious problems caused by board codetermination and that minor reforms, such as negotiation over the implementation of codetermination and allowance for foreign employee representation, would suffice to update it. It also found that there were significant benefits of codetermination, including the counterbalancing of shareholder short-termism, stakeholder dialogue favoring longer-term planning perspectives, and labor peace. Neither side agreed to the characterization of the findings or the proposals.

For the first time in the organization's history, the vote on an official Juristentag report was abandoned. The report was thus tacitly rejected in the absence of a clear majority position. Codetermination was no longer a matter of consensus but was swept up in the deepening cleavages of German interest group politics. But this simply meant that the opposing sides had once again fought each other to a stalemate—a position manifested at the highest level by the Grand Coalition itself. Codetermination, which was once the unassailable symbol of stakeholder governance, had again taken on powerful symbolic importance. Now, however, it was a symbol of the unprecedented pressures and internal divisions weakening the postwar German corporate governance regime and economic model.

REFORM ON AUTOPILOT? THE PERMANENCE
OF CORPORATE GOVERNANCE REFORM

The extraordinary complexity of corporate governance reform in Germany is hardly surprising. That there was reform at all is more so. A system so institutionally and politically entrenched and comprised of such densely interwoven rules, institutions, and practices tends to resist and frustrate attempts to change it. Once reform begins, it is likely to become a multivalent process that alters and adjusts the many pieces of a complex system. This complexity is also a product of the political character of reform. The interest group dynamics change across legal and policy areas, making them difficult to trace and defeating attempts to reduce them to an elegant master narrative or causal pattern. Even so, the scope, depth, and duration of reform suggest the substantial change in political and economic realities in Germany. The relative decline in the power of the Left and labor and the increasing power of financial capital—and those who control it—have set off a fundamental and enduring transformation of the German corporate governance regime and political economy.

Little has been left untouched. The new juridical structures continue to balance the countervailing power of stakeholder groups, but the power relations among these groups have been altered in ways subtle and stark. Securities law and centralized regulatory authority over securities markets are now permanent features of the political and economic landscape and are likely to continue expanding well into the foreseeable future. The rapid development of disclosure regulation and takeover law has strengthened the position of shareholders and particularly of institutional investors. The strengthening of the board has extended reform into the central governance organ of the corporation. Litigation reform introduced new mechanisms of enforcement that had been unthinkable a decade earlier. Even where reform was thwarted, as in the area of codetermination and bank control over voting deposited shares, the old rules and institutions are situated in a different legal landscape that changes their practical significance and meaning. These changes have not compensated for the weakening of the banks' role in firm governance as the old relational model dies out.[142] Labor's weakness and the incipient decentralization of labor relations may further undermine the established governance structures and weaken another check on managers. Managers and

142. Interview, Oliver Wagner, BDB, July 26, 2007.

managerialism may have been the unintended winners in corporate governance reform.

The years of the SPD-Green government were unusually favorable to corporate governance reform. The collapse of that government and the party system in which it emerged substantially dissipated support for additional structural changes in the corporate governance regime. The Grand Coalition could act only within a narrow band of consensus. The SPD was forced into repudiating much of the liberalism of its reform agenda. The CDU returned to its more traditional nonliberal conservatism. Thus the political space for far-reaching reforms shrank drastically.

And yet corporate governance reform continued. Much of it was now focused on refinements in securities law and the implementation of EU directives. At the national level, the explosion of securities regulation since the mid-1990s made continued legislative and administrative changes inevitable as these regulatory systems matured and adapted to changing circumstances. More law led to more ongoing legal change and regulatory politics. Further, the EU's streamlined Lamfalussy process for financial regulation reform produced a regulatory boom at the European level. The success of this reform agenda reflected the relatively broad consensus on securities regulation and market integration among the member states. The central role of the EU within this less controversial area of corporate governance law also indicated its importance as an alternative policymaking channel to the highly constrained, if not paralyzed, avenues of national politics. But where national politics remained hostile to legal harmonization (e.g., rules governing shareholder voting rights and the mobility of corporations), EU-level legislation stalled.

Ironically, in 2007–8 the German economy experienced its best growth and employment performance in decades, just as the American model of finance capitalism fell further into disrepute with the spreading subprime mortgage and credit crisis. The credit crisis further eroded confidence in finance capitalism as it caused the collapse and forced the merger of several German *Landesbanken* with heavy exposure to American securities and derivatives. Deutsche Bank CEO Josef Ackermann was quoted in the press conceding, "I no longer believe in the market's self-healing power."[143] Horst Köhler, the president of Germany and former head of the International Monetary Fund, publicly seethed, "The only good thing about this crisis is that it has made clear to any thinking, responsible person in the sector that international financial markets have developed into a monster that must be put back in its place."[144]

The Merkel government took the lead in pressing for stricter international regulation of hedge funds and complex derivatives trading but had to settle

---

143. Wolf (2008), *Economist* (2008).
144. Benoit and Wilson (2008).

for more limited domestic hedge fund regulation.[145] The global credit crisis reinforced the centrality of law and regulation to the development of finance capitalism and virtually ensured another surge in the reform of corporate governance and financial regulation. The crisis-ridden character of finance capitalism has delegitimated the notion of self-regulating global financial markets and financial institutions, yet there is no credible means of achieving true international financial regulation. Consequently, the juridical structure of finance capitalism and corporate governance is more likely than ever to vary cross-nationally even as calls for international coordination and harmonization intensify.

145. See Barber Benoit, and Williamson (2008), Sims (2007), and Weiss (2006).

CHAPTER 6

Governing the Ruins

The Global Financial Crisis and
Corporate Governance

A CRISIS OF CORPORATE AND
ECONOMIC GOVERNANCE

On September 10, 2008, the Lehman Brothers investment bank collapsed. Unable to find short-term financing or a willing buyer in the absence of a government bailout or asset guarantees, one of Wall Street's largest investment banks was dragged under by enormous losses on mortgage-backed securities and related derivatives. The speed of Lehman's collapse, which was swiftly followed by the collapse of other major Wall Street banks, was breathtaking. Fear and uncertainty over the financial condition of major financial institutions around the world broke into open panic. Even prior to Lehman's fall, the global financial crisis that had begun in mid-2007 was the most serious since the 1930s. In September of 2008 a global economic collapse, a second Great Depression, became an imminent possibility. The American financial system was its epicenter. In the unprecedented government bailouts that followed, the United States, the driving force of neoliberal finance capitalism, embraced a perverse form of "lemon socialism," or finance corporatism, in which financial risk and losses were increasingly socialized while profits remained private.

The deepening crisis revealed the pervasive and egregious regulatory failures underlying the vast market failures and corporate collapses. The crisis struck the unregulated and least regulated areas of the financial system: mortgage lending practices and standards, the investment banks (or "broker dealers") and hedge funds of the "shadow banking system", securitized debt, derivatives, credit ratings agencies, leverage ratios, and bank asset valuation. The failures of the public and private sectors cannot be disentangled. At each weak point, opportunism and conflicts of interests took hold, metastasized, and engulfed the rest of the financial system. Deficiencies in corporate governance compounded manifold political and regulatory failures. Investors reaped high returns, heedless of growing and unsustainable risk; passive boards did not adequately oversee business strategies and risk management while approving huge, incentive-distorting managerial compensation packages. Prior reforms of corporate governance and financial regulation failed spectacularly.

This chapter examines the corporate governance implications of the global financial crisis, which was also a crisis of legitimacy for neoliberal corporate governance and finance capitalism. Systemically vital financial institutions failed while engaged in the ruthless and often reckless pursuit of profit maximization and shareholder value. An explanation of why they failed must go beyond denunciations of venal or inept management to account for the systematic and repeated failures of corporate governance in the context of finance capitalism. The juridical structure of finance capitalism and, within it, the juridical nexus of corporate governance fostered the conditions and pathological tendencies that created the crisis. A toxic combination of financial market deregulation (or nonregulation), pro-shareholder legal rules and governance arrangements, and managerialism produced a destructive and dangerously unstable form of macroeconomic ordering. Yet it was pro-shareholder corporate governance reforms that became central in the political debates and regulatory responses provoked by the crisis.

Given the enormity of the global financial crisis of 2007–9, the political, policy, and economic consequences will likely unfold far into the future. However, the general outlines of the crisis and the policy debates it has ignited confirm and extend the arguments developed in this book. I have argued that pro-shareholder corporate governance reform reflects the development of a broader political economic paradigm of finance capitalism and that these reforms are predominantly the political product of Center-Left parties in a coalitional alliance with the financial sector. I have also argued that corporate governance reform reflects an expansion of the regulatory state driven by the emergence of finance capitalism and that the resultant reform and juridification of corporate governance constitute the interests, normative commitments, and relative power of groups in nationally distinctive ways.

Together these arguments shed light on the causes of the financial crisis, as well as on the limitations of the policy proposals that politicians advanced in response to it. The global financial crisis left little doubt that we now live in the era of international finance capitalism. Many critics attributed the failings of this economic order, particularly in the United States, to the political Right's neoliberalism and pro-business bias. There is more than a little merit in this criticism, especially as applied to the Republican Party, but the Democrats and the SPD were deeply implicated and, in some instances primarily responsible, for the underlying regulatory policies and legal structures that contributed to the crisis. Consistent with the Center-Left's coalitional alignments, corporate governance reforms altered law and regulation in ways that benefited the financial sector (as did contemporaneous deregulation and nonregulation in the United States).

The global financial crisis intensified the dynamic of regulatory expansion and centralization associated with the political economy of finance capitalism. As argued in this chapter, pervasive regulatory failures and deregulation created the conditions for the crisis. Its severity indicates that finance capitalism requires a substantial regulatory state to save itself from self-destruction. Incentivizing the maximization of shareholder value exacerbated the dysfunctional dynamics of finance capitalism by fostering the short-termism, financial recklessness, and risk-intensifying executive compensation structures that contributed to economic crisis. It is ironic, then, that a principal regulatory response was pro-shareholder corporate governance reforms.

The expansion of shareholder voting rights and other controversial governance reforms, long sought by American investors and unions but opposed by a potent cross-sectoral alliance of corporate managers, were more politically palatable than more pressing financial system reforms stalled by intensive financial sector lobbying and partisan polarization in Congress. Germany passed managerial compensation legislation, while sidestepping regulatory issues raised by a banking sector less transparent and more highly leveraged than that of the United States. The most logical inference from this unexpected turn in reform politics is that large financial institutions retain disproportionate power in the politics of finance capitalism.

The emerging politics of reform may increase the divergence and importance of national variants of finance capitalism. The American response was to pursue further pro-shareholder and market-enabling reforms. The dominant German reaction to the crisis, focusing on issues of managerial compensation and the regulation of private equity and hedge funds, reflected a deep and widely held ambivalence toward the Anglo-American variant of finance capitalism. In each case, corporate governance reform proposals recapitulated or extended preexisting policy agendas, normative commitments, and regulatory approaches. These continuities were rooted in nationally distinctive constellations of interest group power and in the enduring effects of corporate governance law on institutional arrangements, normative expectations, and policy preferences.

Finally, the financial crisis intensified difficult problems of partisan conflict and political legitimacy. These difficulties were acute for both the Right and the Center-Left. Having supported pro-shareholder and market-oriented regulatory reforms, the Democratic Party and the Social Democratic Party were implicated in the destruction wrought by finance capitalism and programmatically constrained in responding to it. The parties' neoliberal drift and coalitional alliances with the financial sector in recent decades compromised a singular opportunity to draw on their historical identification with the interests of working people and the use of the regulatory state to constrain the power of financial and managerial elites. The financial crisis also created serious political problems for parties on the right. Neither neoliberal appeals to free-market principles and solutions nor more traditional sympathies and alliances with managerial elites hold much appeal to electorates when markets and managers have failed so abysmally.

In retrospect, for want of a compelling ideological or policy agenda on either the left or the right, the global financial crisis and Great Recession of 2007–9 may be viewed as a failed critical juncture. A critical juncture is not only a historical moment defined by the rupture of established political, economic, and institutional relations—criteria satisfied by the worst economic crisis since the Great Depression—it is also defined by the transformative outcomes that issue from these convulsive conditions. Whether or not the reforms undertaken amid the wreckage prove to be historically momentous, the crisis illuminated the juridical structure and power relations underlying finance capitalism.

The remainder of this chapter develops these arguments. The chapter begins by reviewing the causes and scope of the global financial crisis, focusing on how the crisis originated in the United States and spread through international markets and financial institutions. The next section examines how partisan and coalitional politics informed by neoliberal ideology produced the massive regulatory failures underlying the crisis. The following sections examine the role of corporate governance as a contributing cause of the crisis and the politics and substance of corporate governance reform in the immediate aftermath of the global financial collapse. The chapter concludes by analyzing postcrisis political difficulties and legitimacy crises afflicting the Democratic Party and the SPD and considers the troubling implications of these developments for the future of corporate governance reform.

THE GLOBAL FINANCIAL CRISIS: SECURITIZATION, CONFLICTS OF INTEREST, AND THE MARKET FAILURE OF SHADOW BANKING

The crisis that culminated in the financial panic of September 2008 had been brewing since early 2007, once mortgage defaults started to rise after the American real estate market peaked in late 2006. But the causes of the crisis originated much earlier. Beginning in the early part of the decade, financial institutions began to adopt an "originate and distribute" lending and securitization model that created a cascade of conflicts of interest and moral hazards of growing severity. Mortgage companies immediately sold the loans they issued to investment banks, which bundled and securitized them by slicing the cash-flow rights into "tranches" of securities (with declining priority of cash-flow rights to the underlying mortgage payments). By this feat of financial alchemy, investment banks aggregated individually risky mortgages into a series of debt securities, known as mortgage-backed securities (MBSs) or more generally as collateralized debt obligations (CDOs), with different risk profiles and matching interest rates.[1]

This process relied on the crucial assistance of ratings agencies and AIG, the world's largest insurance company, to make the "senior" tranches marketable. Ratings agencies, paid directly by the issuer banks, routinely underpriced the escalating mortgage risks underlying these securities and gave the top tranches AAA or equivalent ratings. With this seal of approval, other financial institutions and pension funds could buy the securities without triggering risk or capital reserve limitations under prevailing regulation and risk-management practices.

In addition, the London-based financial products unit of AIG became the world's largest issuer of credit default swaps (CDSs or swaps).[2] These unregulated derivatives functioned like insurance on securitized debt instruments, including CDOs. If the bonds defaulted, the holder of the CDS compensated the bondholder's loss. In AIG's case, CDSs did something even more valuable. Issuers and holders of CDOs could buy AIG CDSs on riskier, lower-tranche CDOs, and, through "ratings arbitrage," the insurer's coveted AAA credit rating effectively converted toxic debt into AAA investment-grade securities because AIG was ultimately liable for repayment.[3] Because derivatives were not subject to traditional insurance regulation requiring reserves to cover potential claims, the CDS trade was even more profitable—and dangerous.

The conflicts of interest that riddled this system drove its development and self-destruction. Mortgage lenders had an incentive to debase lending standards for loans they sold off immediately. The issuing banks externalized risks by marketing CDOs around the world, often through offshore subsidiaries that further insulated them from regulatory oversight and tax laws. They obscured the location and size of the residual risks of the lowest-rated tranches by placing them in off-balance sheet "conduits" or "structured investment

1. CDOs encompass a much wider array of securitized debt instruments, ranging from private equity loans to credit card debt. The crash in mortgage-backed CDOs also undermined the markets for these instruments, intensifying and broadening the credit crunch.
2. For an analysis of AIG's CDS business and collapse, see generally Sjostrom (2009), Dennis and O'Harrow (2008), and O'Harrow and Dennis (2008a, 2008b).
3. Nocera (2009).

vehicles" (SIVs). Conflicts of interest compromised the standards and review processes of the big ratings agencies (Moody's, Standard & Poor, and Fitch). Fund managers around the world seeking higher yields in an era of low interest rates, mistook (or ignored) systematically underpriced risk and fueled increasing demand for CDOs—satisfied by the packaging of ever-lower-quality mortgages into ever-riskier CDOs. The complexity and opacity of the CDS markets further obscured and in fact magnified systemic risk by creating impenetrable uncertainty over the size and location of potential liabilities and allowing massive, undisclosed one-way (unhedged) bets on future asset prices.

This system of debt securitization took in savings and channeled credit to the real estate market and pumped out debt securities. With government and corporate bond yields depressed in an environment of prolonged low central bank rates, investment funds seeking higher returns drove demand for CDOs. Surging market demand for CDOs and the cheap credit flooding the global financial system provided the capital to channel back into mortgage lending that sustained the great securitization machine and further inflated the real estate bubble. The securitization-lending cycle also contributed to a massive expansion of credit through the shadow banking system of largely unregulated investment banks, hedge funds, and derivatives issuers. This self-perpetuating cycle could continue only as long as real estate prices continued to rise and ensured low default rates on mortgages.

None of these parties acknowledged the dangers posed by an increasingly obvious real estate bubble. The end of the legal separation of commercial and investment banking in the United States allowed large commercial banks with investment banking units to join in the securitization boom. The participants in each link in this chain either possessed an illusory sense of security (or cynically ignored risks) based on flawed risk-management models that assumed ever-rising real estate prices, the risk-dampening financial alchemy of securitization, the accuracy of debt ratings, and the risk-spreading properties of derivatives. In July of 2007, as the securitized debt markets began to crash, Charles Prince, chairman and CEO of Citigroup (reliant on CDOs as one of the largest lenders to private equity funds) offered a revealing and ironic glimpse into the managerial mind-set at the peak of international finance:

> When the music stops, in terms of liquidity, things will be complicated. But as long as the music is playing, you've got to get up and dance. We're still dancing. . . . The depth of the pools of liquidity is so much larger than it used to be that a disruptive event now needs to be much more disruptive than it used to be. . . . At some point, the disruptive event will be so significant that instead of liquidity filling in, the liquidity will go the other way. I don't think we're at that point.[4]

4. Nakamoto and Wighton (2007).

The music stopped in the summer of 2007. Senior managers throughout the largest financial institutions and investment funds had failed to see imminent dire implications of the significant disruptive event that was already unfolding. Accelerating default rates on subprime mortgages during 2007 and 2008 triggered the collapse of the CDO market. In March 2008, Bear Stearns's heavy exposure to CDOs precipitated a collapse of market confidence and wiped out the bank's capital within days. The Federal Reserve Bank of New York arranged its acquisition at a fire-sale price by JPMorgan Chase by guaranteeing $30 billion of the collapsing investment bank's assets to sweeten the deal.

Lehman Brothers had bet that the CDO market would recover. The bankers bet wrong. The market fundamentals dictated a massive correction in real estate and CDO prices. They also misread the politics of the situation. Officials at the highest levels of the U.S. Treasury and Federal Reserve were shaken by the popular and political outcry against the Bear Stearns bailout and deeply concerned over the moral hazards of a second bailout.[5] They also believed, consistent with their faith in the self-correcting properties of markets, that other major financial institutions had largely unwound their more risky market positions to reduce their exposure to another bank failure.[6] In a controversial decision that is sure to provoke debate for decades, the officials decided to set a hard limit to government's intervention in the markets and let Lehman Brothers fail.

Lehman Brothers' failure set off a cascade of financial catastrophes. Its bankruptcy triggered billions in claims by a large number of counterparties holding swaps that AIG could not hope to pay. AIG had increasingly kept these swaps on its own books without any reserves or hedging against underlying defaults. Instead of spreading risk by selling off CDS issues, AIG had concentrated systemic risk within itself and then used the absence of regulation to obscure this fact.[7] As the financial markets crashed following Lehman's collapse, this concentration of risk amplified the financial crisis. Advocates of deregulated derivatives markets had claimed that they spread risk efficiently among sophisticated parties according to their ability and inclination to bear it, thus contributing to financial system stability. A long line of critics had countered that derivatives were too complex to be understood by even sophisticated financiers and fostered dangerous levels of systemic opacity and potential volatility. September of 2008 proved the critics correct.

Within weeks of Lehman's bankruptcy, the collapse and near collapse of some of the most preeminent American banks transformed the landscape of Wall Street. Bank of America bought Merrill Lynch at a distress price in

---

5. See Solomon et al. (2008).
6. See ibid.; Reddy and Hilsenrath (2008).
7. See Tett (2009) and Nocera (2009).

another government-brokered deal. Unable to continue as investment banks, Goldman Sachs and Morgan Stanley became bank-holding companies to qualify for government bailout funds. The Treasury and Federal Reserve effectively nationalized AIG and bailed out Citigroup and Bank of America, in the process becoming their largest investor. All these institutions and scores of others were propped up by unprecedented and controversial federal lending and asset guaranty programs.

International financial markets and institutions, heralded as a crowning achievement of economic globalization, became channels of contagion. Financial markets around the world seized in a classic liquidity crisis: liquidity is plentiful when it is not needed and evaporates when needed most urgently. Large, interconnected financial institutions and investment funds could find no buyers for CDOs at precisely the moment when they most desperately needed to sell assets to rebuild capital cushions and loss reserves. Mark-to-market accounting rules (adopted in the aftermath of the Enron-era accounting scandals) intensified the liquidity crisis by forcing financial institutions to book huge current losses on securities positions.

Overleveraged financial institutions around the world saw the value of their assets and capital bases evaporate along with liquidity in the asset and credit markets necessary for their survival. European banks, in particular, had invested heavily in CDOs, and many were even more overleveraged than American institutions. Trust, an essential element of any market system, dissipated among market participants, who were no longer confident of where the vast sums of bad debts were located and which institutions might be the next to fall. In a flight to safety, investors and institutions hoarded what cash or liquid assets they had. A chain reaction of financial panic swept the world as counterparty risks soared and credit contracted.

The liquidity crisis mutated into a systemic insolvency crisis, as the credit crunch froze short-term interbank lending and rendered otherwise solvent institutions incapable of financing continuing operations. As lending collapsed in the commercial paper market (short-term debt used by companies to fund operating expenses) and previously safe money market accounts crashed, the financial crisis spread to the "real" economy. The global economy approached the abyss.

In country after country, the imminent prospect of economic collapse forced central banks and governments to engage in unprecedented economic interventions. Coordinated and dramatic monetary easing by central banks failed to arrest the collapse. Central banks acted as lenders of last resort to provide the financing necessary to keep national economies on life support. Governments were forced to extend and expand deposit insurance and bail out their struggling financial institutions to contain and then halt what amounted to a global bank run. They engaged in massive multitrillion-dollar bailouts, "liquidity injections," asset and loan guarantees, partial or outright

TABLE 6.1: PROJECTED GOVERNMENT DEBT AND FINANCIAL STABILIZATION COSTS AS PERCENTAGE OF GDP, 2008–10

Country	Debt (est. 2010)	Growth of debt	Stabilization costs
United States	98	27	12.7
United Kingdom	73	21	9.1
Canada	77	13	4.4
Germany	87	19	3.1
France	80	13	1.8
Japan	227	30	1.7
Italy	121	15	0.9

Source: IMF (2009, 44, table 1.8) (stabilization costs = net cost of direct support to banks, estimated future costs of guarantees, and net cost of central bank liquidity provision).

nationalization of financial institutions, and direct lending to the private sector. After intense partisan political conflict in the shadow of the upcoming November election, Congress hastily passed the controversial $700 billion Troubled Asset Relief Program (TARP), with the Bush administration relying primarily on Democratic support.[8]

As of September 2009, the American government's support for the financial sector totaled $545.3 billion in expenditures (of which $72.9 billion had been repaid) and another $23.7 *trillion* in asset guarantees (representing the face value of the assets, not the likely costs).[9] Even more controversially, the Treasury used its guarantees of AIG's swaps, paying 100 cents on the dollar, as a conduit—out of public view and with little transparency or accountability—to channel *unrecoverable* bailout funds directly to some of the world's major financial institutions. The recipients included Goldman Sachs ($12.9 billion), Société Générale ($12 billion), Deutsche Bank ($12 billion), Barclays ($8.5 billion), Merrill Lynch ($6.8 billion), Bank of America ($5.2 billion), UBS ($5 billion), Citigroup ($2.3 billion), and Wachovia ($1.5 billion).[10] This list also begins to indicate the international scope of the crisis.

Table 6.1 sets out the bailout costs of the crisis. Unsurprisingly, it shows disproportionately large stabilization costs (funds committed directly to the financial system) borne by the United States and United Kingdom that are consistent with the greater financialization of their economies. The figures also indicate the severity of the crisis in Germany. Germany's highly leveraged large private banks and Landesbanken incurred huge losses on CDOs and other securities during the crisis.[11] The larger private banks had become far

8. Montgomery and Kane (2008).
9. SIGTARP (2009a, 137–38, table 3.4; 2009b, 31). The IMF's (2009) estimate of the ultimate costs was still $3.68 trillion ($1.85 trillion in asset purchase commitments, $1.83 trillion in guarantee commitments).
10. Walsh (2009).
11. See Gordon (2009).

more internationalized and exposed to securities market risks as they pursued more market-oriented business strategies. Since the 1990s, the Landesbanken, once the state-sponsored pillars of industrial policy, had suffered the EU-mandated withdrawal of state supports and responded by pursuing repeated ill-fated securities speculation strategies in search of higher returns to defray the higher costs of private capital and satisfy investor demands for increased shareholder value. The global financial crisis revealed not only the fragility of Germany's banks and their vulnerability to the collapse of securities markets, its negative shock to global demand also hit the broader export-driven economy especially hard, further worsening the banking crisis and the government budget deficit.

The teetering financial system revealed the fractured state of partisan and interest group politics in Germany. The CDU and SPD policy agendas were already narrowly constrained within their Grand Coalition. Cleavages within the financial sector and ideological divisions on both the right and left further hobbled government strategy and policymaking. In January of 2009, despite severe criticism of the government's ineffective bank stabilization fund passed in October 2008, the Social Democratic finance minister, Peer Steinbrück, adamantly refused to consider a bailout plan to address an anticipated $300 billion in bank losses.[12] By April, the severity of the crisis forced him to retreat, and he released a draft "bad bank" plan to take toxic assets off bank balance sheets.[13] Practical and political imperatives collided as the Grand Coalition government was attacked in the Bundestag from left-wing SPD and conservative CDU members. The government adopted a voluntary and diluted bailout program, valued at over $266 billion, which left the banks with ultimate responsibility for paying off losses on toxic debt securities after a period of twenty years.[14]

By the late summer of 2009, the threat of a second Great Depression had abated, but the consequences of the financial crisis and the Great Recession lingered, along with the deeply problematic political and regulatory implications of the crisis and the policy interventions used to contain it. Government policies across the industrialized countries recognized a class of financial institutions as too big to fail. The bailouts transformed the economics and politics of financial system regulation around the world. Although necessary in the face of imminent economic collapse, these changes in relationship between government and the financial system raised immense moral hazard problems and market distortions. After the decimating crisis and huge bank mergers of 2007–8, JPMorgan Chase and Goldman Sachs emerged as overwhelmingly dominant in investment banking, but the broader banking sector had become

12. *Deutsche Welle* (2009); Spiegel Online International (2009).
13. Donahue (2009).
14. See Benoit (2009).

vastly more concentrated as well—and created the conditions for its perpetuation. "Tier I" institutions (those declared systemically sensitive by regulators) accounted for two-thirds of all deposits.[15] Explicit or implicit guarantees of federal support lowered the costs of capital for these too-big-to-fail institutions and gave them a critical competitive edge.[16]

Across many of the advanced political economies, the structure and power relations of the emerging postcrisis order created profound political and regulatory problems. The resultant threats of increased systemic risk and massive rent seeking increased the importance of regulation and governance of large financial institutions. However, the systemic importance of large financial institutions, in the United States and abroad, enhanced their political power. They sought public funds and fought to shape—or kill—regulatory reform. The neoliberal paradigm of finance capitalism threatened to mutate into a dysfunctional form of finance corporatism. Financial regulation and corporate governance reform returned to the political spotlight across the industrialized countries but under political and economic conditions transformed by the magnitude of the crisis.

REGULATORY FAILURE, MARKET FUNDAMENTALISM, AND FAITH-BASED DEREGULATION

Perhaps no public event so encapsulated the intellectual and ideological dimensions of the crisis as the congressional testimony of Alan Greenspan, former chairman of the Federal Reserve Board, on October 28, 2008. During his terms as chairman, Greenspan had pursued and relentlessly advocated policies premised on the optimality of private ordering and self-regulating markets and a deep skepticism of regulation. Testifying before the House Committee on Oversight and Government Reform, Greenspan conceded that he had "made a mistake in presuming that the self-interest of organizations, specifically banks and others, were such . . . that they were best capable of protecting their own shareholders and their equity in the firms."[17] He noted that those who had shared those beliefs were now "in a state of shocked disbelief."[18] Greenspan lauded the sophistication of the "modern risk management paradigm [that] held sway for decades" but concluded that "[t]he whole intellectual

15. Cho (2009).
16. In 2007, large American banks (in excess of $100 billion in assets) paid 0.08 percent less interest in borrowing costs than smaller rivals; by late 2009 that advantage had quadrupled to 0.34 percent. Ibid. (using FDIC figures).
17. U.S. House of Representatives (2008, 33).
18. Ibid., 17.

edifice, however, collapsed in the summer of [2007] because . . . [the] models generally covered only the past two decades, a period of euphoria."[19]

Committee chairman Henry Waxman quoted a revealing statement Greenspan had made years earlier: "I do have an ideology. My judgment is that free, competitive markets are by far the unrivaled way to organize economies. We have tried regulation, none meaningfully worked."[20] Waxman pressed on, noting that Greenspan had had "the authority to prevent irresponsible lending practices that led to the subprime mortgage crisis" and had been "advised to do so by many others."[21] He pointedly asked Greenspan whether his ideology had led him to erroneous decisions. Greenspan replied, "To exist, you need an ideology." As for his own, "[Y]es, I found a flaw, I don't know how significant or permanent it is, but I have been very distressed by that fact."[22]

Treated in the press as a mea culpa of historic significance, Greenspan's testimony was actually more complex and ambivalent. His description of the previous twenty years as ones of financial euphoria was a damning statement about the nature of finance capitalism, but Greenspan also implied that the intellectual framework of neoclassical economics and "light touch" regulation had *not* crumbled, or might be easily rehabilitated. The flaw he now found in his economic ideology might yet prove insignificant in all but the most extreme and unusual economic conditions. The intellectual edifice of financial economic modeling and risk management had collapsed but only because analysts had used the wrong historical data. He also declared that the crisis was a freakish "once in a century credit tsunami" that, like a natural disaster, no one could foresee or avoid. We need not fear a repetition because exotic and imploding financial products and structures would be shunned by the rational investors of the future. Self-interest and market rationality would return to their proper foundational roles in the economic order.

Greenspan's concession that the self-interest of organizations had failed stood out in his implicit defense of finance capitalism. Corporate governance as a mode of private ordering and self-regulation of corporate affairs and systemic financial risks had failed along with organizational self-interest. The flaw in the system resided in the firm, not in the market. This diagnostic logic suggests that legal reform of corporate governance might be justified as a means of responding to the crisis even if more intensive financial market regulation were not.[23] This framing of the causes and implications of the financial

19. Ibid., 18.
20. Ibid., 34.
21. Ibid.
22. Ibid.
23. The concession also contained a revealing reification. Within the methodological individualism of neoclassical economics, the notion of organizational self-interest is problematic. Organizations do not have interests; the individuals and groups within them do. This reification avoids grappling with the destruction wrought by unbridled managerial and investor self-interest and the broader indictment of neoliberal deregulation it entails.

crisis sheds light on the prominence of corporate governance reform in post-crisis policy debates. But it also obscures the broader systemic defects that led to financial collapse.

Pervasive regulatory failures created the conditions for the global financial crisis. The consequent economic collapse represented the failure of the neoliberal ideology of self-regulating markets and policy agenda of regulatory minimalism that Greenspan had championed. The Fed's policy positions that central banks cannot identify or respond to asset bubbles before they burst, and the rejection of regulatory means of preventing or deflating them, reflected the blurring of economic theory into antiregulatory political ideology. Having rejected the crude weapon of interest rate hikes to deflate asset bubbles, policymakers were left with two main options: they could use regulation to eliminate the conditions that produced bubbles, or they could wait and cut interest rates to reinflate the economy after they burst. The Fed had regulatory means available to address dangerous forms of leverage and speculation by adjusting margin and capital reserve requirements, but it consistently refused to use these powers. Instead, it used loose monetary policy as a post hoc response to domestic and foreign financial crashes. Low interest rates increased liquidity and pumped up a bubble-prone economy, but unlike a direct Keynesian stimulus of consumer demand or business investment, the strategy stimulated demand indirectly by massively and unsustainably increasing private debt.

The Fed's rejection of regulation was not an isolated incident but a reflection of a much broader, and bipartisan, neoliberal trend in policy. Republicans had long championed financial deregulation, but during the 1990s leading Democrats in the Clinton administration and Congress appropriated much of this agenda as part of a broader effort to cultivate financial sector support. The Clinton administration and many congressional Democrats actively supported or acquiesced in both preemptive derivatives deregulation and the erosion of the legal separation of commercial banking from investment banking. Financial market and banking deregulation became a troubling and often obscured counterpart of the pro-shareholder policies and regulatory reforms embraced by the Democratic Party.

In 1998, Greenspan, Treasury Secretary (and former Goldman Sachs CEO) Robert Rubin, and the then assistant treasury secretary Lawrence Summers rolled back an attempt to regulate derivatives by Brooksley Born, then chair of the Commodities Futures Trading Commission.[24] In November 1999, Summers, having ascended to treasury secretary, joined by Greenspan, Levitt, and Born's successor as CFTC chair, William Rainer, issued a President's Working Group report that rejected warnings that unregulated derivatives trading posed enormous potential systemic risks and called for Congress to exempt

24. Faiola, Nakashima, and Drew (2008).

derivatives from. They argued that regulation would hamper beneficial financial innovations and that the self-interest of sophisticated parties, along with the efficiency of global markets, would provide adequate self-regulation.[25]

Phil Gramm, a Republican senator and a leading neoliberal critic of regulation who had deep ties to Enron, took the lead in Congress to foreclose any future regulation of derivatives.[26] Gramm drafted a bill, the Commodity Futures Modernization Act of 2000, that barred virtually all regulation of derivatives. He slipped it into an enormous omnibus budget bill with barely a murmur of dissent from congressional Democrats and none from the White House.

Large numbers of Democrats joined Republicans in accepting the steady erosion of the Glass-Steagall Act's separation of commercial and investment banking. The Clinton administration and a large majority of Democrats in Congress also supported the final repeal of Glass-Steagall by the Gramm-Leach-Bliley Act of 1999, which was pushed through to allow the formation of Citigroup as an immense and sprawling institution that encompassed investment banking, commercial banking, and insurance. Rubin left government in 1999 to become the vice chairman of Citigroup and would encourage the bank to become more deeply involved in issuing and trading securitized debt instruments like CDOs.

While Clinton-era law and policy left vast gaps and deep flaws in financial system regulation, regulatory enforcement withered further during the administration of George W. Bush. Under Chairman Christopher Cox, SEC enforcement actions declined at an accelerating rate from 2005 to 2008 as lengthy, burdensome, and contentious authorization and review processes systematically discouraged investigations of large financial institutions.[27] The dollar value of SEC penalties fell 39 percent in 2006, 48 percent in 2007, and 49 percent in 2008.[28] The number of enforcement attorneys declined more than 11 percent over this period.[29] By the time of Bear Stearns's collapse in March 2008, the SEC, once a jewel of the post–New Deal regulatory state and the bank's primary regulator, was deemed so marginal that it was barely included in the crisis management efforts led by the Treasury and Federal Reserve.[30] Finally, in December of 2008, the SEC's repeated failures to uncover the decades-long $50 billion Ponzi scheme by former NASDAQ chairman Bernard Madoff, despite having received explicit tips since 1999, focused attention on

25. See Summers, et al, 1999; see, e.g., Greenspan (2002).

26. See Lipton and Labaton (2008) and Lipton (2008).

27. See Adler (2009) and Scannell and Craig (2008); see generally Government Accountability Office (2008).

28. Farrell (2009).

29. Ibid.; GAO (2008).

30. Scannell and Craig (2008).

the decline of the agency.[31] The Madoff scandal, however, demonstrated problems beyond the ideological and politicized hostility of the Republican-dominated SEC leadership toward enforcement. The agency had been starved of resources by Congress for years, a trend only temporarily reversed in the aftermath of the Enron-era scandals. Antiregulatory sentiment (and arguably capture by the financial sector) went far beyond, and above, the SEC.

The fragmentation of the American financial regulatory system encouraged regulatory arbitrage and a downward pressure on oversight and enforcement. The multiplicity of banking regulators left gaps in the law that financial institutions used to escape supervision and restrictions altogether. Aside from these legal lacunae, fragmentation created perverse incentives for regulators to protect turf by engaging in a "race to the bottom." The Office of Thrift Supervision and the Office of the Comptroller of the Currency were particularly notorious for feeble enforcement. Financial institutions such as AIG strategically organized their corporate structures and financial products to evade regulation or to ensure that they were regulated by the least effective or most lenient (or captured) regulator. Interest group politics and the interests of congressional committees in retaining oversight of these ineffective overseers insulated them from abolition or consolidation.

Neoliberal deregulation and regulatory failure were not merely the products of cynical political servitude, bureaucratic self-interest, or capture by the financial sector. The prevalence of deregulation and light-touch regulatory approaches reflected a widely held belief in the self-regulating capacities of markets and firms. For example, Arthur Levitt, Clinton's SEC chair and a forceful advocate for regulation and investor interests, had joined the attack by the administration and the Federal Reserve on the effort by the Commodity Futures Trading Commission (CFTC) to regulate the derivatives markets, even though he had initially identified their risks and the need for some regulatory oversight.

The SEC's decision in 2004 to relax leverage restrictions on large investment banks also reflected the prevailing belief in the self-regulating capacities of firms and markets. As part of a political deal to head off stricter EU regulation of American investment banks, the banks' CEOs, including Goldman Sachs's Henry Paulson, who would become treasury secretary two years later, agreed to SEC monitoring in exchange for allowing the banks to use their own quantitative risk models to establish leverage levels—a form of self-regulation without the check or balance of formal enforcement power.[32] The vote was unanimous and uncontroversial and followed a meeting that lasted less than an hour.[33] Commissioners with long and distinguished records as zealous

---

31. See Appelbaum and Hilzenrath (2008).
32. Labaton (2008).
33. Ibid.

regulators approved the measure. The rule change led to the massive increase in average leverage ratios among major American investment banks and hedge funds from under 10:1 to approximately 27:1 at the height of the real estate and CDO bubble.[34]

This was hardly unique to the United States. European financial institutions, along with their subsidiaries and SIVs, were often even more heavily leveraged than American ones. When they were largely devoted to relatively safe traditional lending, their leverage ratios had not been a problem. But many of these banks (notably the German Landesbanken) did not have the accumulated institutional knowledge and expertise to negotiate the new world of market-driven finance and shadow banking. Market pressures drove them to boost shareholder returns by simultaneously increasing leverage and investing in CDOs and derivatives marketed (often deceptively) by U.S. and U.K. institutions.

The financial crisis was the product of incentives created by regulatory structures and the market opportunities and business models that these legal frameworks enabled. It was not a statistical fluke far out on the tail of probability. The endogenous processes by which the financial system self-destructed points out a serious—and often tendentious—error in characterizing the financial crisis of 2007–9 as an event that was essentially random, unforeseeable, and thus unpreventable. Firms and investment funds systematically exploited regulatory gaps and deregulation to pursue unsustainable business strategies. The structural, ideological, and partisan influences that weakened and stunted regulation from the 1990s on permitted the American financial sector to become a vast bubble machine and a rent-extracting enterprise and all but ensured a severe crisis.

The nonrandom, systemic character of the economic crises of 2007–9 compelled the recognition that structural and regulatory reforms were urgently needed. Popular outrage at the greed of financial actors, exemplified by soaring managerial compensation, and the immense economic destruction they had wrought once again fueled demand for regulatory expansion. Intriguingly, enhanced shareholder rights came to occupy a central place in the post-crisis push for legal reform. Underlying all these conflicts of interest and unsustainable debt-fueled financial activity was an incessant and intense pursuit of shareholder value and maximization of investment returns by managers. Outsized returns fueled the skyrocketing profits and managerial compensation in the financial sector. And yet shareholders were seen as a means of controlling managers and empowering them within corporate governance processes once again became an important avenue of reform.

34. See Tett (2009a, 134).

THE GOVERNANCE CRISIS BENEATH
THE FINANCIAL CRISIS

The global financial crisis was also, in an important sense, a crisis of the ascendant shareholder-centric corporate governance model. Governance flaws and distortions of managerial compensation were not merely a symptom of regime dysfunction but a key driver of economic disaster. The crisis would have been unlikely, if not impossible, had Wall Street firms remained private partnerships instead of becoming publicly traded corporations. One of the troubling paradoxes is that the pro-shareholder legal reforms adopted throughout the world intensified the incentives for short-termism, excessive risk taking, and managerial rent seeking. The crisis could not have become so devastating if corporate governance regimes had effectively protected and promoted the long-term interests of shareholders and stakeholders. The neoliberal conception of corporate governance and its imperatives to continuously maximize share prices became a source of structural weakness and intensified incentives for short-termism and recklessness by managers and investors alike. The central problems of corporate governance have become core vulnerabilities of finance capitalism.

At first blush, it seems odd that corporate governance contributed to the causes of a financial crisis so devastating to shareholders. After all, as argued throughout this book, the development of governance since the 1980s has strengthened the protection and position of shareholders. The growing influence of more-active institutional investors, increasing proportions of independent directors, and the alignment of manager and shareholder interests through incentive-driven managerial compensation have promoted the maximization of shareholder value. Moreover, the financial crisis of 2007–9 appeared to be less a product of firm governance failures than a profound market failure and systemic collapse.

Initial research indicates that pro-shareholder policies, practices, and boards, associated with "good" governance, were correlated with *worse* performance.[35] Pressure by boards to maximize shareholder value led to increased risk taking that produced higher returns during the debt bubble but greater losses during the crisis.[36] Likewise, initial studies of CEO compensation, the subject of so much public outrage and policy debate, indicate that bank performance during the crisis tended to be worse the *more* bank managers' compensation was aligned with shareholder interests.[37] The CEOs of large banks

---

35. Beltratti and Stulz (2009).

36. Ibid., 2–3. Not surprisingly, those that pursued traditional banking (with less leverage, more deposits, and more loans on their books) performed better.

37. Fahlenbrach and Stulz (2009, 3–4); cf. Erkens, Hung, and Matos (2009, 28–30, cross-national study finding correlation between increased losses and executive cash bonuses but not equity compensation).

generally held a large percentage of their personal wealth in the shares (and options) of their firms, and because they did not hedge or dispose of their holdings as the crisis approached, they lost much of it.[38] The evidence suggests that bank CEOs pursued the maximization of shareholder value, rather than short-term rent seeking, but did so via disastrous strategies.[39]

Managerial compensation and governance incentives in banking display particularly destructive tendencies toward intensifying risk.[40] Holding company structures common in banking and explicit or implicit governmental asset guarantees magnify risk taking. Holding companies incentivize senior managers to take risks by adding another layer of leverage, while limited liability shields them from losses in highly leveraged subsidiaries. In the presence of government asset guarantees, *shareholders also favor excessive risk* that increases potential returns because they discount losses that taxpayers will bear. These mutually reinforcing moral hazards will limit the effectiveness of corporate governance reforms that rely on shareholder empowerment to solve problems of excessive risk in financial institutions. Even with complete information and control, shareholders will opt for more risk than is socially optimal and systemically safe.[41]

The run-up to the global financial crisis of 2007–9 confirmed the dangers inherent in the combination of leverage, governance regimes that fostered short-term maximization of shareholder value, and managerial rent seeking. Urgent governmental responses to the global financial crisis did not diminish but intensified these perverse incentives. Governments expanded deposit guarantees, as in the United States, or adopted them where they had not existed previously, as in Germany. Crisis-driven policy responses also extended public guarantees from the traditional (and more highly regulated) banking sector to the shadow banking sector and to entirely new classes of unregulated debt and derivative instruments. Under these conditions, managers and shareholders will favor excessive risk taking when they benefit from the upside but can—or believe they can—dump toxic assets and catastrophic losses on taxpayers. The legacies of the crisis and government bailouts create incentives for greater concentration of national financial sectors and publicly underwritten speculation (gambling) that increases risk throughout the financial system instead of controlling it. Corporate governance reform can play an important role in escaping this incentive structure but only if policymakers recognize and address the problems inhering within the shareholder-centric model.

38. Ibid.
39. Fahlenbrach and Stulz are too quick to assert that bank executives could have cashed out or hedged their holdings as the crisis approached. Either move would have been a potent signal in an increasingly volatile market environment in which a bank's equity could disappear in hours. Selling shares might also have triggered insider trading allegations. It is possible that many bank CEOs did not anticipate the severity of the crisis, but that is still consistent with their pursuit of short-term, rent-seeking strategies.
40. Bebchuk and Spamann (2009).
41. Ibid.

These analyses raise the disturbing implication that pro-shareholder corporate governance may have fueled the crisis not because it failed but because it *succeeded*. The financial crisis casts doubt on the conception of good corporate governance premised on the maximization of shareholder value as a normative foundation and operational goal for a governance regime. This perspective on the crisis confirms the importance of corporate governance but raises questions concerning its potential to mitigate the crisis-prone character of finance capitalism. It also leads to a more critical view of the past and present politics of governance reform. As argued in prior chapters, pro-shareholder reform is a conservative regulatory agenda for a politically conservative age. Reforms designed to increase shareholder power without altering shareholder interests and time horizons, including those proposed in response to the financial crisis, must be viewed skeptically along with the political forces propelling them.

CORPORATE GOVERNANCE AND THE POSTCRISIS POLITICS OF REFORM

In the immediate aftermath of the global financial crisis and the collapse of Wall Street, there was a near universal expectation that a revival of the regulatory state would rapidly transform financial sectors and markets around the world. The regulatory responses to the crisis, however, were slow and relatively few. Excluding the dramatic, but largely ad hoc and temporary, government bailouts and central bank policies, there were few major changes in the law and regulatory structures that had so plainly failed between 2000 and 2009. As noted above, it is rather surprising that in both the United States and Germany corporate governance reforms were the primary legal reforms in response to the crisis. Reformers in both countries sought to strengthen boards and targeted managerial compensation practices and structures. The United States moved toward board nomination and election reforms that would upend the traditionally managerialist proxy voting rules. Germany passed a managerial compensation law tightening control of the supervisory board.

At the same time, governments and regulators in both countries, trying to control panic and prop up financial institutions, sought to dilute disclosure and accounting standards during a period when many financial institutions would otherwise have to expose huge losses and insolvency. In a reversal of the decades-long trend toward greater transparency and disclosure, the structural regulation of the corporation took precedence. However, despite the general similarities among them, these reforms had quite different political and economic implications in the United States and Germany. Germany's reforms effectively strengthened the codetermined board and the shareholders' meeting and thus could reinforce the stakeholder model and blunt managerial and political attacks on codetermination from the Right. The reforms pursued in the United States would further strengthen the shareholder-centric character of the governance regime.

Fighting the Last War or Rewriting the Rules of the Game?

The Obama administration avoided a direct challenge to the central role of finance and the power of large financial institutions in the American political economy. Its regulatory reform agenda, issued by Treasury Secretary Geithner, was viewed as so feeble that critics started to accuse the new administration of capture by Wall Street. The regulatory agenda called for the creation of a consumer financial products regulatory agency, consolidation of federal regulatory authority over financial markets and services, the effective dominance of the Federal Reserve over the regulatory structure as the primary systemic risk regulator, and the regulation of derivatives issuers and markets. Fiercely opposed by the financial sector, yet widely criticized as too timid and for giving too much regulatory power to the unaccountable and deeply ideological Fed, the financial reform agenda largely languished in Congress. The administration selectively and strategically intervened in regulatory policy but devoted its political capital to fierce political battles over its stimulus and budget packages, the handling of two wars, and a historic battle over health care reform. Aside from maintaining bailout policies needed to prop up the financial system, the White House left the SEC and congressional Democrats to pursue a postcrisis regulatory agenda.

Mary Shapiro, President Obama's appointee as SEC chair, quickly ushered in a sea change in corporate governance policy. The SEC proposed new proxy rules substantially stronger than the Donaldson shareholder nomination proposal and scrapped the Cox-era 2007 amendment allowing managers to exclude shareholder proposals to alter board election rules from the corporate proxy ballot. The proposal would require inclusion of shareholder nominations for up to 25 percent of board seats, provided the nominating shareholders held beneficial ownership of a sufficient number of shares for over one year (and through the board election) and were not seeking a change in control. Initially released in May of 2009 for public discussion and officially proposed in mid-June, the fact that the proxy access plan was one of the first major SEC rule-making proposals under the Obama administration indicated the high priority of governance reform.[42]

---

42. Securities and Exchange Commission, 2009 (proposal to amend Exchange Act Rules 4-11 and 4-8(i)(8)). The share ownership threshold varied by firm size: 1 percent for firms with net assets of $700 million or more, 3 percent for firms between $75 million and $700 million, and 5 percent for those with less than $75 million. Nominees had to be independent of

Policy debates over the expansion of shareholder rights with respect to proxy voting, board nominations, and director elections should be understood as part of a deeper and more enduring process of legal and institutional change. The prevailing direction of reform embodies a conception of firm governance as an explicitly representational, and quasi-political, process. In the shadow of the dramatic failure of self-regulating markets, the corporation had been reconceived, as advocated by reformers since the 1970s, as a self-regulating institutional form. In contrast with the New Deal's pronounced emphasis on market transparency and corporate disclosure, the boldest reform initiative in the wake of the financial crisis took the form of structural regulation to alter the core power relations within corporate governance.

The SEC's policy shift in 2009 represented a political breakthrough for shareholder activists who had been thwarted repeatedly during the Bush administration. It was also striking evidence that the Democratic Party leadership's shareholder empowerment agenda had become more central to its coalitional and regulatory strategies following the financial crisis. The policy change addressed the legal and institutional foundations missing from the Sarbanes-Oxley Act and other post-Enron reforms through another potentially far-reaching federalization of corporate governance law in furtherance of structural regulation.

In addition to the substance and timing of the proxy access proposal, agency personnel and organizational changes pointed to the high priority attached to governance reform by the SEC under Shapiro. She appointed Kayla Gillan, a staunch governance activist as the former general counsel of the California Public Employees Retirement System (CalPERS) and an original member of the PCAOB, to lead the proxy access effort.[43] In June of 2009, the agency created an Investor Advisory Committee, drawn largely from the ranks of corporate governance activists, to represent shareholder interests (and potentially, given some members' affiliations with organized labor, broader stakeholder interests as well) in SEC policymaking. The SEC specified shareholder voting and corporate governance as areas of special focus. In late 2009, Richard Ferlauto, the AFSCME pension fund's director of corporate governance and a principal architect of the union's *AFSCME v. AIG* proxy litigation, joined the SEC's Office of Investor Education and Advocacy.[44] Governance activists—long relegated to the political periphery—were now governmental insiders and playing an increasingly influential role in regulatory policy.

The embrace of shareholder democracy and structural regulation under the Obama administration and the Shapiro SEC proved predictably

---

management (as required by law and exchange rules), but did not have to be independent of the nominating shareholder(s) (e.g., a pension fund).

43. Scannell (2009).

44. Wilczek (2009).

controversial and politically contentious. The commissioners voted three to two in favor of the proxy access reform, with the Republicans voting against. Republican commissioner Troy Paredes denounced the rejection of the traditional enabling approach of American corporation law and fumed that the proposal would "work not only to displace private ordering and state law, but risk negating the impact of a shareholder vote" to opt-out of the federal rules and reduce shareholder access and power.[45] Seeking to limit further federal encroachment, Delaware had quickly amended its corporation law to allow shareholders to place proposals to alter board nomination and election bylaws on the company proxy ballot. Paredes advocated the new Delaware approach, but private ordering and the enabling approach of state law that had heavily favored managers for over a century had little traction with the new Democratic-leaning majority on the SEC in the wake of the financial crisis. Delaware's move was too little, too late.

As former SEC commissioner Joseph Grundfest observed, "The proxy access debate . . . is a knockdown, drag out political brawl" driven by partisan and interest group conflict.[46] He attributed the new push for pro-shareholder proxy access reform to the election of President Obama and the tipping of the partisan balance of power on the SEC toward the Democrats and their alliances with unions and public pension funds. In contrast to the circumstances surrounding the 2003–4 and 2007 proxy reform debates, political conditions in 2009–10 were less favorable to managerial interests. This partisan and interest group division was also evident in the SEC's approval in July 2009 of an amendment of the NYSE's listing rules that banned the long-established practice of "broker voting" in board elections. Broker-dealers had wielded full discretion in voting the unmarked proxies of shares held on deposit for retail investors—and they almost invariably did so in favor of management's recommendations. Activist pension funds and unions squared off against business groups, such as the Chamber of Commerce, that opposed the ban. The Republican commissioners voted against the rule, joining the business lobbies in arguing that it would empower institutional investors and effectively disenfranchise individual shareholders.

However, postcrisis corporate governance reform cannot be reduced so easily to a function of partisan control and interest group politics. As discussed in chapter 3, federalization of corporate law has been a perennial political issue for a century. Progressives have sought expanded shareholder voting rights and board reform repeatedly since the 1970s. Managerial interests have been powerful enough to block repeated reform attempts and have only gotten more influential since then, including within the Democratic Party. The twin shocks of the financial crisis and the 2008 elections transformed political and

45. Paredes (2009, 3).
46. Grundfest (2009, 16–17).

economic conditions, at least temporarily. The 2007 proxy rule amendments had attracted over thirty thousand comment letters. The far more consequential 2009 proposal received just over five hundred. Most observers regarded the reforms as inevitable. The comments skewed toward managers and representatives of large corporations, including prominent business lobbying groups like the Business Roundtable and Chamber of Commerce, and corporate law firms. Comments from large financial institutions were notably absent. However, the comments opposing the proposal betrayed a sense of fatalism and tended to pick apart the technical details and mechanics of the inevitably complex proposal and advocate delay and limited dilution.[47]

The Obama administration kept its distance from the debates over board elections and focused instead on an issue that resonated more with the populist mood of the public: management compensation. Seeking to exploit and inoculate itself from the public outrage over huge managerial bonuses paid by AIG and large banks following the government bailouts, Treasury Secretary Geithner met with Schapiro and held a press conference to publicize the administration's basic principles of executive compensation on the same day that the SEC released its proxy access proposal. In his statement, Geithner endorsed the SEC's "say on pay" proposal to allow shareholders to put nonbinding resolutions on compensation issues to a vote using company proxy materials. He did not once mention the SEC's board nomination and election proxy proposal.[48] The administration let the SEC and Congress take the lead—and the political fire—on the most contentious issues in corporate governance reform.

Congressional Democrats simultaneously advanced legislation to secure a new "Shareholders' Bill of Rights" that, in part, would confirm the SEC's statutory authority to regulate board elections in the likely event of a court challenge to the agency's jurisdiction.[49] Other provisions included (1) the annual election of directors, (2) majority voting for directors in uncontested elections, (3) nonbinding shareholder votes on compensation policies and packages, (4) mandatory "risk committees" of independent directors, (5) splitting the position of CEO and board chair, and (5) a new federal law of fiduciary duties imposed on investment advisers. Along with giving shareholders the power to nominate board candidates, the legislation would end the common practice of plurality voting that allows a single vote to elect a director to an uncontested

47. Even so, the complex issues raised by these comments and the advance of corporate governance legislation in Congress induced the SEC to delay final revisions and a vote on proxy access reform until 2010.

48. Geithner (2009).

49. Shareholder Bill of Rights Act of 2009, S. 1074, 111th Cong. § 4 (2009); Investor Protection Act of 2009, H.R. 3817, 111th Cong. § 2 (2009). These provisions would eliminate the litigation threat to SEC rule making under adverse case law. See *Business Roundtable v. SEC*, 905 F.2d 406 (D.C. Cir. 1990).

seat (currently, virtually all board elections are uncontested) and effectively bar the potent antitakeover defense provided by staggered boards.

The legislation was introduced by Senator Charles Schumer of New York, an important supporter of Wall Street and an assertive critic of Sarbanes-Oxley and federal regulation that might drive financial business and stock listings away from his state. Portions of the Schumer bill were also endorsed and advanced in the House by Financial Services Committee chairman Barney Frank as amendments to the Obama administration's far more modest Investor Protection Act. Though attacked by many Republicans as excessive government intervention in the private sector, the legislation moved through Congress more quickly than the rest of the Obama administration's regulatory reform agenda.

Taken together, the SEC's corporate governance reform proposals and related congressional legislation were a dramatic and arguably radical innovation in American corporate governance. But they also revealed continuity in the development and normative structure of American finance capitalism. The reform agenda embodied a faith in and commitment to the shareholder-centered model of corporate governance. As such, the proposed reforms were an extension of the political and juridical logic of the American corporate governance regime dating back at least to Adolph Berle and the New Deal.

In their broader political and economic context, these shareholder-empowering reforms offer a revealing view of the politics underpinning American finance capitalism following the global financial crisis. Pursuing fundamental corporate governance changes that eluded reformers of the Enron era and their predecessors proved easier politically than reducing the size, influence, importance, and speculative activities of the financial sector and the firms at its pinnacle. There are two distinct, though not necessarily contradictory, dynamics that explain the relative success (so far) of corporate governance reform compared with the imposing political difficulties faced by the broader agenda of financial system reform and re-regulation.

The first dynamic was the combined effect of the partisan shift in power and the SEC's capacity, as an independent agency, to act more quickly than Congress. A new reform-minded Democratic majority on the SEC took advantage of the upheaval of the financial crisis and used the independent agency's semi-insulation from political pressure to pursue shareholder-empowering governance reforms that had been blocked for decades. Aside from their belief in the merits of the policy, the commissioners' proxy reform proposals served the institutional interests of the SEC and the political interests of the Obama administration at a critical political moment. The SEC proposals strengthened the case for the agency's continued existence and autonomy, and would even expand its regulatory turf, after its marginalization and glaring regulatory failures during the Cox era. Its new activism undercut reform plans under both the Bush and Obama administrations to diminish the agency's authority or merge it with other financial regulators in a structure dominated by the Federal Reserve. The Obama administration and congressional Democrats, including those vulnerable to charges of capture by the financial sector, benefited from a visible federal commitment to reform without diverting political capital from their push for health care reform. From this perspective, corporate governance reform represented good, and politically cost-effective, public policy.

Interest group alignments and coalitional dynamics point to a second, far less charitable and optimistic, explanation of postcrisis reform politics that turns on the enduring and disproportionate power of the financial sector. The proposals triggered managerial opposition led by groups already aligned with the Republicans, but they provoked only a mild response from the financial sector, with more ties to the Democrats. In contrast, the financial sector fiercely resisted broader financial system reforms. The regulation of derivatives and derivatives markets, hedge funds and other institutions comprising the broader shadow baking system, ratings agencies, leverage ratios, and the systemic risks of too-big-to-fail institutions that posed potentially existential threats to the privileged position of the largest—and most dangerous—financial institutions and the interests of their senior managers. The consolidation of financial regulators and the creation of a strong and independent financial services consumer protection agency spurred intense opposition not only from the financial sector, but also from congressional committees whose members resisted any loss of jurisdictional turf that would threaten the power and campaign contributions generated by their legislative authority over regulators.

Muted opposition to the progress of corporate governance reforms thus may have reflected a political and legal bet by financial sector managers that enhanced shareholder powers within corporate governance would likely prove less constraining and threatening than other items on the postcrisis reform agenda. The managerial elite of the financial sector was well aware that fending off all legal reforms was politically impossible, and thus the pattern of their opposition and acquiescence reflected their priorities, which influenced the course and content of the reform process.[50]

However, there are reasons to question the effectiveness of the proposed corporate governance reforms in addressing some of the worst flaws and excesses of American finance capitalism exposed by the financial crisis of 2007–9. These concerns are raised by what is missing from the reform agenda and lead to a more critical assessment of the politics and functions of corporate governance. There is no consideration of moving toward a more stakeholder-oriented regime. Labor law reform, which was a prominent issue in

---

50. More speculatively, their appearance of resignation to corporate governance reforms may have reflected a collective judgment that these reforms could most easily be weakened after the fact by a powerful cross-sectoral mangerialist coalition.

many democratic campaigns in 2008, dropped off the political agenda—a development that indicates and reinforces organized labor's political marginalization. Even more telling, no reform proposals address the powerful incentives for myopic, short-term investment strategies that contributed to the financial crisis. If history is any guide, without lengthening investment time horizons and the depth of institutional investors' commitments to specific firms, their increased governance power will tend to reinforce and intensify demands for short-term maximization of share values, and their governance activism will tend toward a superficial and ineffective "box checking" approach based on formalistic best practices.

Increased shareholder power will be constructive only if the forms and incentives that constitute shareholding patterns are configured to promote long-term ownership and thus longer-term value creation by companies. The SEC's one-year holding requirement to gain access to the company proxy for purposes of board nominations is, at best, a modest gesture in the direction of extending shareholder time horizons. Long-term investment strategies and ownership stakes are a function of the *form* that institutional investment takes. Reforms to promote pension funds with long-term strategies or to discourage the short-termism of mutual funds and hedge funds are largely missing from political and regulatory agenda. In fact, investment and pension trends in the United States and other advanced industrial countries are moving in the opposite direction.

In the early 1980s, over 60 percent of workers were enrolled in a defined benefit pension plan, while just 10 percent had defined contribution plans.[51] By 2009, only 20 percent had defined benefit plans, and over 40 percent had defined contribution plans.[52] This shift represents a vast privatization and individualization of risk, and it reflects a steep decline in the types of pension funds that combined long investment time horizons with commitments to governance activism. The financial crisis devastated private pension plans and revealed the dangers of this vast privatization of risk, but it has only accelerated the shift to defined contribution retirement plans.[53] Yet, despite scattered calls to reverse the shift to defined contribution pensions, the subjects of retirement security and the governance repercussions of the dramatic decline in defined benefit pensions did not become part of the reform agenda.[54]

Rather than advancing long-term shareholding or financial security as a policy priority, postcrisis reform politics in the United States indicate that the financial crisis reinforced a number of distinctive market-driven features of the American financial and corporate governance order. Even as corporate takeovers, hedge funds, and private equity funds were condemned as contributing

51. *New York Times* (2009).
52. Ibid.
53. See Oxford Analytica (2009).
54. Cf. *New York Times* (2009).

to the crisis, they were used by policymakers as means of addressing the crisis and its aftermath. At a time when their legitimacy was plummeting, hedge funds and private equity funds received a governmental imprimatur as nimble, sophisticated agents of restructuring and as critical channels of finance.

Mergers and acquisitions played a prominent role in addressing the unfolding financial crisis from its inception, and, as private credit disappeared, one that was increasingly coordinated and financed by the federal government. Treasury Secretary (and ex-Goldman Sachs CEO) Henry Paulson, Federal Reserve chairman Ben Bernanke, and Federal Reserve Bank of New York president Timothy Geithner repeatedly relied on the highly developed merger and acquisition capacities of the American financial system in a series of ad hoc strategic responses to the serial collapse of major financial institutions. JPMorgan Chase acquired the wreckage of Bear Stearns and then the failing Washington Mutual retail bank. Bank of America (BofA) bought the bankrupt Countrywide (the largest and most infamous of the subprime lenders), and most notoriously, bought Merrill Lynch to prevent its imminent collapse from further inflaming the post-Lehman financial panic.[55] Not only did these financial-sector deals make use of the banks' acquisition skills, but they also reinforced the post–Glass-Steagall integration of investment and commercial banking.

Private equity funds also reemerged in the wake of the financial crisis to play a role in repairing the banking system. After much resistance and internal debate, the Federal Deposit Insurance Commission (FDIC) at first adopted bank resolution rules that sharply restricted the ability of private equity firms to acquire failed banks. This was done out of fears that the firms' short-term orientation would increase the price volatility of bank assets and that rapid flipping of acquired banks would disrupt the banking sector. The FDIC chair, Sheila Bair, had been almost unique among federal regulators in her fierce and outspoken criticism of the irresponsible and opportunistic short-termism prevalent throughout the financial sector during 2000–9 (a quality that estranged her from both the Bush and Obama administrations while making her irreplaceable). She enlisted public employee pension funds, known for their long-term orientation and governance activism, in efforts to recapitalize struggling banks, but the growing wave of bank failures overtook these efforts. Within months, Bair and the FDIC reversed course and loosened the acquisition rules to encourage private equity funds to bid for the growing numbers of failed banks and replenish its dwindling deposit insurance fund.

55. Under intense pressure from Paulson and Bernanke, who had control over bailout funds the bank desperately needed, BofA acquired the failing Merrill for $50 billion. The controversial deal, brokered and partially financed by more than $25 billion in federal funds, was so disastrous for BofA that it required two bailouts (totaling over $140 billion in capital injections and asset guarantees) and became the subject of securities fraud charges for the firms' failure to disclose to shareholders $3.6 billion in promised executive bonuses and more than $15 billion in losses.

The Obama administration rejected the nationalization of insolvent banks and "bad bank" plans used in most other countries for the containment of ·toxic assets. Instead, it followed the crisis-driven bailouts with a proposed Public-Private Investment Plan (PPIP) that would have used hedge funds and other institutional investors financed by heavily subsidized public loans to buy up—and determine a market price for—the huge inventory of CDOs and other toxic assets that remained on bank balance sheets. The politically and economically misconceived PPIP ended up playing virtually no role in cleaning up the financial system. However, the episode revealed that, far from seeking to transform the established and intensely market-driven character of the financial sector, the Obama administration preferred to maintain and make use of existing markets and the investment funds that populated them. This position was made even more explicit as the Obama administration joined the United Kingdom in resisting calls for increased hedge fund regulation led by Germany and France.

In each of these instances, the government relied on the distinctive adjustment capacities developed within the market-driven American financial order of earlier decades. Considerations of technocratic capacity shaped these strategies. The government, through the FDIC, was capable of resolving smaller bank failures. However, not only was the magnitude of the crisis overwhelming, but the Lehman disaster had also shown that larger financial institutions posed challenges of another order of magnitude. The expertise of American banks, investment funds, and an array of allied professional services in conducting mergers and acquisitions, structuring complex investment vehicles and securities transactions, and restructuring acquired companies gave the government ready access to private mechanisms for achieving rapid consolidation and restructuring of failing financial institutions. Conversely, without a significant tradition of state industrial policy or state ownership of commercial enterprises, the federal government had little experience or expertise in undertaking these activities and could hardly hope to develop them rapidly as the crisis unfolded. Governments enter crises empowered and constrained by the capacities history has bequeathed them. In the case of the financial crisis, those capacities for adjustment were located within the private sector and the prevailing political exigencies and coalitional alignments favored using them.

A New Egalitarian Governance or Return to the Social Market?

The German government's response to the global financial crisis was characterized by vociferous criticism of neoliberal finance capitalism and calls for strengthened regulation, resistance to bailout and stimulus packages, and much more modest domestic regulatory reforms. In part, this disjuncture between rhetoric and reform reflected the limitations of the Grand Coalition and the role of the EU as both a constraint on and a channel for domestic policymaking. However, the harsh rhetoric Berlin directed at the United States (and to a lesser extent Britain) was exceptional. Even before the financial crisis, German officials had been critical of American and British financial practices. Once it began, German leaders became extraordinarily confrontational, and at times openly contemptuous, in their criticisms of the United States on matters of regulatory and fiscal policy. The German-American conflict sprang from three distinct yet interrelated grievances.

First, the German government had for years warned of the dangers of the shadow banking system, particularly hedge funds, and called for stronger and more international regulation, but it had been ignored or actively resisted by American and British officials. German officials viewed the American failure to adequately regulate its own financial system as the proximate cause of the crisis and its neoliberal antipathy to regulation as a dangerous ideology that had imposed enormous costs on the rest of the world. Well before the crisis, neoliberal finance capitalism had sown controversy and discord in German politics and drawn criticism in high official circles—even as it penetrated the domestic financial sector and the government embraced pro-market and pro-shareholder reforms. The condemnation by Franz Müntefering, SPD chairman (and later vice chancellor in the Grand Coalition), of Anglo-Saxon investment funds as "locusts" exemplified this paradox.[56]

Chancellor Merkel was also critical of Anglo-American finance capitalism and weak regulation. Addressing the 2007 World Economic Forum in Davos, Switzerland, Merkel urged states "to minimise the structural risks in the international capital markets through greater transparency."[57] Pressing the message repeatedly in public and at Group of Eight (G8) meetings, the United Kingdom and the United States rejected out of hand Merkel's proposed tightening of disclosure regulation for investment funds. Peer Steinbrück, Merkel's SPD finance minister, ruefully recalled that the German proposals "elicited mockery at best or were seen as a typical example of the German penchant for overregulation."[58] Steinbrück became an especially sharp, and astonishingly undiplomatic, critic of the United States In an address to the Bundestag, he predicted that the international financial system would become "multi-polar" and, as a result of the crisis, "[t]he US will lose its status as the superpower of the world financial system."[59]

This tension between Germany and the United States sharpened as the crisis spiraled out of control in late 2008 and early 2009. In a series of emergency G20 summits, German demands for more stringent national and

56. Benoit (2007).
57. Vucheva (2008).
58. Ibid.
59. Woodhead (2008) and Benoit (2008).

international financial system regulation clashed with the Bush administration's laissez faire ideology.[60] Along with the French president, Nicholas Sarkozy, Merkel became the leading exponent of regulatory reform as the highest priority on the international agenda.[61] The German-French position increased tensions with the Obama administration as the Americans pushed for coordinated Keynesian stimulus measures and downplayed regulatory issues.[62] However, personal umbrage at being ignored and rebuffed does not alone explain Germany's position on financial regulation. There were compelling immediate and structurally determined reasons for the intensifying conflict between that country and the United States.

A second reason the German government's growing tensions with the United States as the financial crisis spread was that the damage to the domestic banking system was far worse than anticipated. Large segments of the German political and economic elites believed that American financial institutions had marketed huge sums of securitized debt and other complex financial instruments to German banks under questionable, if not fraudulent, pretenses. Hundreds of billions of dollars' worth of securities that had been sold to German banks as highly rated and safe assets turned toxic once the crisis hit. The facts revealed in light of the financial collapse indicated that there had been systematic misrepresentations in the securitization and marketing process, but there were few, if any, avenues of legal recourse.[63]

Finally, on a deeper level, the conflict between the two countries reflected their divergent forms of political economic organization and their very different normative, juridical, and institutional foundations. American officials, supported within the EU by the United Kingdom, had pressed for open financial markets and minimal regulation (aside from stock market regulation and corporate governance reform) and saw finance as an area of national comparative advantage. German elites, though divided, tended to see financialization as unproductive and increasingly dangerous. Outside the financial sector and a relatively small group of large internationalized firms, many managers, labor, and a growing proportion of the public had grown skeptical of neoliberal corporate governance and overtly hostile toward Anglo-American investment funds. The shareholder activism and takeovers practiced by hedge funds and private equity funds not only threatened the immediate interests of management and labor but also undermined the long-term stakeholder relationships and deeply held normative commitments that accounted for the success and legitimacy of the German economic model. Further, as international demand plummeted, the global recession triggered by the financial crisis imperiled Germany's export-driven economy—just as the economy had emerged from a

---

60. See Benoit (2008).
61. Samuel and Harnden (2009).
62. Sanger and Landler (2009).
63. Gordon (2009).

painful decade-long process of structural reform and firm-level adjustment. Anglo-American finance capitalism not only threatened the internal coherence and functionality of the German stakeholder model but now exacerbated the national economy's vulnerability to exogenous shocks in export markets.

As in the United States, German reforms during the financial crisis focused on corporate governance and tended to reinforce existing features of the governance regime. In August 2007, reflecting the continuing political controversy over locust investors, the legislature passed the Risk Limitation Act (*Risikobegrenzungsgesetz*) to strengthen disclosure rules and regulatory constraints on investors "acting in concert" in takeovers. Amending Germany's Takeover Act, the new law expanded the definition of concerted activity to include cooperation to influence the supervisory board or otherwise alter the corporation's business strategy, whether or not the cooperating shareholders actually vote their shares. If "acting in concert" is found, the shareholdings (now also including options to buy shares) are aggregated for purposes of triggering disclosure obligations and, if they amount to more than 30 percent of shares, mandatory takeover bid requirements. Violations of the law can be punished by suspension of the shareholders' voting and dividend rights. The law also requires corporations with more than one hundred employees to disclose any contemplated takeover attempt to the works council. The intended effect of the law was to weaken (largely foreign) activist investors, but its likely consequence is a strengthening of managerial autonomy from shareholder pressure short of a hostile takeover bid. A year later, the legislature passed an omnibus act to implement the EU's shareholder rights directive, which had been drafted with strong German governmental support.[64] The law continues the trajectory of German reforms by strengthening shareholder participation by use of Internet communications and proxy voting, a streamlined process for shareholders to authorize banks to vote proxies (or reassign them to shareholder associations), and by further limiting abusive shareholder litigation.

The major legal reform of corporate governance adopted directly in response to the financial collapse of 2008 targeted managerial compensation procedures and practices. Management and supervisory board pay had become increasingly controversial in Germany after the Mannesmann takeover, but disclosure regulation regarding compensation issues had been relatively weak and largely ineffective. The financial crisis transformed the political environment as concerns over rising inequality and takeover threats were compounded by the widespread belief that compensation practices were at the root of an increasingly corrupt and self-destructive form of capitalism.

---

64. Law Implementing the Shareholder Rights Directive (*Gesetz zur Umsetzung der Aktionärsrechterichtlinie*, ARUG), law of 30.07.2009 BGBl. I S. 2479; Shareholder Rights Directive 2007/36/EC of July 11, 2007, OJ L 184/17.

The financial crisis further reinforced the German government's renewed commitment to the principles of the social market economy after the long ascendance of neoliberal conceptions of finance and corporate governance. The German Corporate Governance Code was amended to expressly state that it "clarifies the obligation of the Management Board and the Supervisory Board to ensure the continued existence of the enterprise and its sustainable creation of value in conformity with the principles of the social market economy (interest of the enterprise)."[65] It elaborates that the "Management Board is responsible for independently managing the enterprise with the objective of sustainable creation of value and in the interest of the enterprise, thus taking into account the interests of the shareholders, its employees and other stakeholders."[66]

The Grand Coalition government began work on a management compensation law in September 2008, and by July 2009 both houses of the legislature had passed the Law on the Appropriateness of Management Board Remuneration (VorstAG).[67] The deepening financial crisis and looming September 2009 federal elections accelerated the political process, with the CDU fearful of being seen as impeding the regulation of managerial compensation and the SPD gesturing toward the Left with carefully calibrated populist appeals.[68] The law is superficially analogous to board oversight and approval of compensation in the United States, but it goes much further in regulating the process, criteria, and directors' obligations in setting managerial pay. The law restricts compensation structures that reinforce incentives for short-term maximization of shareholder value and excessive risk taking, and it mandates a set of institutional procedures and substantive standards to enhance the transparency of compensation and impose managerial incentives for long-term business strategies and sustained growth of the enterprise.

The entire supervisory board must now approve management board compensation packages.[69] Under the prior terms of the Corporate Governance Code, a board committee determined the details of compensation on a case-by-case basis, while the board as a whole set only general pay policies. The board is also now responsible for determining whether managerial compensation should be prospectively or retroactively reduced in the event of crisis or exceptional circumstances. Further, a cooling-off provision bars managers from taking positions on the supervisory board for a minimum of two years after leaving the management board.

In defining the supervisory board's duties, the law goes beyond procedure to mandate general substantive standards for the determination of the form

65. Corporate Governance Code § 1.
66. Ibid., § 4.1.1.
67. *Gesetz zur Angemessenheit der Vorstandsvergütung*, law of 31.07.2009 BGBl I, p. 2509.
68. Cf. *Legal Week* (2009).
69. The shareholders' meeting may hold a nonbinding vote on compensation packages, but it is not required.

and amounts of managerial compensation. The compensation must be proportionate to the individual's performance and to the pay scale within the company as a whole, but its appropriateness must also be assessed with respect to customary compensation practices in similar firms within the sector and geographic region. The board must give specific reasons for any deviation from these baselines.

The central concern underlying the VorstAG, however, was not the absolute level of compensation but the incentives created by its structure. Accordingly, to encourage long-term management strategies, compensation in the form of stock or options cannot vest in less than four years. Likewise, in an echo of the Mannesmann controversy, management compensation cannot rise as a result of extraordinary one-off events, such as assets sales, the realization of hidden cash reserves, a premium paid for shares in a takeover, or other external events (though it can be reduced on grounds of fairness in the event of extreme business reversals).

Finally, the VorstAG is exceptional in its emphasis on personal liability as a means of strengthening governance incentives and enforcing legal standards. The reallocation of compensation responsibilities to the entire supervisory board underscores the general legal obligations of board members imposed by the law. Though its effect may be more symbolic than real, the law underscores the importance and mandatory character of the new standards by expressly emphasizing the personal liability of supervisory board members for approving excessive or poorly structured compensation arrangements. The VorstAG also limits directors and officers insurance coverage of management board members by requiring a minimum deductible of 10 percent of the damages assessed or 150 percent of the manager's fixed annual pay.

Despite practical difficulties in applying vaguely defined criteria of individual merit and horizontal and vertical comparability, these standards capture the continued, or resurgent, importance of traditional conceptions of economic and corporate governance. The standard of horizontal comparability reinforces industry-specific patterns consistent with Germany's strong institutions of sectoral governance. More striking in light of the neoliberal trends of recent decades, the standard of vertical comparability legally enshrines the conception of the firm as a collective undertaking and a community of interests that must be protected from the corrosive effects of growing income inequality. The reform shifts managerial incentives toward the longer term by strengthening the supervisory board as an institution. As a result, the VorstAG also strengthens board codetermination. Employee representatives on boards will likely take a less generous view of managerial compensation and be more sensitive to threats of personal liability. An unintended consequence of compensation reform, therefore, may be an increase in conflict over the future of codetermination—or the rediscovery of its potential virtues.

THE POLITICAL TRAP OF FINANCE CAPITALISM AND THE CRISIS OF THE LEFT

Notwithstanding the corporate governance reforms that have taken place, the politics of finance capitalism appears ever more problematic as the severity of the financial crisis has underscored the need for additional reforms that national political systems have been unable to deliver. The allure of deregulation and laissez faire neoliberalism may be broken, or at least severely diminished, but aside from partisan choices in agenda setting, financial system reform faces imposing political and economic constraints. Even after these ideas have been declared bankrupt, the coalitional and structural power of the financial sector shapes the political process and the discourse of reform. The power of finance in determining economic health and the pivotal political role played by financial interests in partisan politics in both the United States and Germany have hobbled state capacities to pursue regulatory reforms. Governments have not been willing to contest the privileged position of the financial sector.

In each country, governments faced difficult economic and political constraints on their ability to respond to the financial crisis. Bailouts of the financial sector were controversial and difficult to negotiate, even at the depths of financial panic when the fate of the economy was at stake. Postcrisis regulatory reform has become in many ways even more difficult. Center-Left parties in particular are trapped in the political alignments cultivated in pursuing pro-shareholder and pro-financial market reforms. The financial crisis made those coalitional alliances and policy positions increasingly visible and damaging. The financial sector, led by large financial institutions, was the pivotal constituency in a politics of corporate governance reform that allowed it to play managers, labor, and shareholders off each other. Those alliances and the neoliberal turn in policy undermined public confidence in the Obama administration, while in Germany they tore apart the SPD and upended the country's party system.

There are compelling reasons to refrain from radical restructuring of the financial sector in the middle of a serious economic crisis. Any form of capitalism requires a solvent and functional financial system. Bailouts and regulatory forbearance, however politically unpopular, may be necessary to allow the repair of balance sheets and only thereafter the resumption of lending. These vital stages in recovery could be curtailed by the imposition of capital reserve requirements that increase with the size and systemic risks posed by banks, or by substantial restructuring of the financial sector through the breakup of too-big-to-fail institutions, or by the reimposition of the separation of investment and commercial banking. The risk is that a historic opportunity for reform may be lost and with it a last, best chance to avoid an even worse economic disaster in the future.

In the United States, the Obama administration has been notably reluctant to endorse, let alone pursue, fundamental reforms of the financial system. Partisan agenda setting helps explain the postcrisis politics of reform. Obama chose health care reform as the highest priority of his first term and the issue on which his administration, and the Democratic Party, lavished time and political capital. The diversion of resources and attention away from financial system reform reflected this choice. More importantly, however, coalitional politics and the persistence of neoliberal ideology within the Obama administration and the Democratic Party shaped this cautious approach to systemic reform and financial reregulation at the very moment when the Republicans' ostensible pro-business ideology appeared thoroughly discredited by the financial crisis and the disastrous record of the Bush presidency.

The government bailout of the banks without rapid regulatory reform reinforced the public's suspicion of state capture. The surviving financial firms dominated the financial sector even more completely than before the onset of the crisis. Treasury Secretary Timothy Geithner and White House economic adviser Larry Summers emerged as the most powerful, and visible, economic policy officials in the Obama administration, but they also personified the Democrats' appropriation of the financial deregulation agenda during the Clinton-Rubin years. As president of the New York Federal Reserve, Geithner was identified with the controversial bank bailouts during the worst of the financial crisis. Both he and Summers were widely viewed as unduly sympathetic to Wall Street interests and wedded to the neoliberal thinking that led to economic disaster and afterward impeded bolder reforms needed to prevent future financial crises and to reorient the Democratic Party's policy and coalitional strategies for the postcrisis era. After the triumphs of the 2006–8 election cycles, the perception that the Obama administration and the Democratic Party were tied to Wall Street and embraced policies that favored the interests of an increasingly loathed financial elite eroded the Democrats' popular support and fueled anger and cynicism within the electorate that corroded the legitimacy of the political economic order.

The White House chief of staff, Rahm Emmanuel, repeatedly noted that "a crisis is a terrible thing to waste," but institutional constraints, interest group politics, and the exigencies of a crisis situation limit a government's capacity to exploit such situations. Where party coalitions or institutional veto points require broad agreement on major policy changes, reform may be thwarted even if the ideas on which the prior regime rested are discredited. The structural importance of finance to the functioning of the economy is never as evident as when lending collapses during a financial crisis, conferring a paradoxical power in weakness that immunized it from substantial reform in the immediate aftermath of the crisis. The magnitude of the crisis caused by the financial sectors' reckless expansion of credit made its swift revival and the resumption of credit vital to economic recovery. The financial sector's *economic* weakness shielded it at precisely the moment when it was *politically* weakest. And even a weakened financial sector is a powerful force in American politics, especially when the reforms being considered pose an existential threat to the most profitable business activities of the largest and most influential of the surviving financial institutions.

The political trap in which the Center-Left finds itself ensnared is not unique to the United States. The gravity of the risks the Obama administration has taken on can be glimpsed in the paralysis of German policy in the wake of the crisis and the devastating SPD defeat in the September 2009 elections. The SPD's embrace of neoliberal economic reforms and the interests of the financial sector left it incapable of exploiting a financially driven economic crisis that, historically, would have provided the leading Left party with an extraordinary political advantage over the business-oriented Center-Right. Instead, the fracturing of the Left over issues of economic reform during the Schröder government preserved the CDU's feeble dominance of the Grand Coalition and then contributed to Right's victory in the 2009 elections and the formation of the first Center-Right government in over a decade.

The Grand Coalition of the CDU and SPD produced a stable government but one that was subject to drift and disagreement. To some extent, Merkel ameliorated conflict between the coalition partners with her retreat from neo-liberalism after the CDU's disappointing performance in the 2005 election that necessitated the Grand Coalition. Merkel swiftly recovered by moving back toward the center, essentially adopting Schröder's Neue Mitte strategy on the right by exploiting the residual appeal and legitimacy of the social market economy. The move was astute. The rupture of the Left over the Red-Green government's economic and social welfare reforms forced the SPD to move to the left to maintain its base. This opened a clear path to the center for the CDU.

Two slim areas of agreement between the CDU and the SPD, and among much of the electorate, were concern over soaring managerial compensation, as discussed above, and an antipathy toward hedge funds and activist investors. The Grand Coalition's consistent criticism of speculative finance and activist investors, such as hedge funds and private equity firms, reflected the political difficulties faced by the coalition partners, as well as the problematic relationship between market-driven finance and the German economic model. The SPD was trapped by its record of financial and corporate governance reform and its weakening appeal to its working-class base. Its reform agenda had facilitated the turn toward market finance and endorsed pro-shareholder positions that were arguably reflected in the German banks' strategic impera-tives to increase shareholder returns. Distinguishing between good and bad shareholders reflected the beliefs of many in the party, but it was also an attempt to wriggle out of the trap that the Neue Mitte had become. The SPD awkwardly positioned itself further to the left in response to the threat posed by the Left Party while remaining in the Grand Coalition. Its leadership revived the criticisms of hedge funds as locusts.

The CDU's position was much simpler. Its residual managerialism made activist investors, especially foreign ones, a natural target while allowing it to stoke and tap into the growing reservoir of popular hostility toward international financial elites and external pressures on the economic relationships that defined the social market economy. The CDU joined in these attacks (though with less rhetorical flair) and the Merkel government's postcrisis agenda in the G8 and G20 summits revived its earlier calls for stringent regulation of hedge funds—even though they had played a peripheral role in the financial collapse of 2007–8. However, hemmed in by EU rules allowing for the free flow of investment capital, and limiting discriminatory treatment of investors based in other EU member states, the government did not pursue legislation. Instead, Merkel advocated for regulation of investment funds at the international level with the same lack of success she had had earlier in the face of American and British opposition.

The September 2009 federal election finally dissolved the Grand Coalition and replaced it with the first Center-Right government in eleven years. Confidence in both of the major catchall parties had been eroding for years, resulting in the fracture of the SPD, the rise of the Left Party, and the growing fragmentation and incoherence of the party system that had necessitated the Grand Coalition. Both parties were tarnished by the years of infighting and drift and now by joint stewardship of an economic calamity. During the Grand Coalition, the SPD had regained some popular support by tacking to the left. But the party's candidate for chancellor, Foreign Minister Frank-Walter Steinmeier, had drafted the Schröder-era employment and social welfare reforms, and the SPD's association with neoliberal financial and labor market policies was more damaging than ever. The SPD suffered a crushing defeat, with its worst performance since the 1930s. This was of little satisfaction to the CDU, whose own performance was its worst in decades.

The CDU and the neoliberal FDP cleared a narrow majority to form a governing coalition, but the desultory campaign and the fractured popular vote hardly constituted a referendum on a radical turn toward neoliberalism. The CDU's post-2005 embrace of the social market economy clashed with the FDP's doctrinaire neoliberal ideology. However, if a neoliberal agenda cost the CDU in the 2005 elections, it was unlikely to repeat that error in the wake of a global financial crisis and recession attributed to neoliberal financialization. The public was already deeply cynical about the political and economic elites prior to the financial crisis. In 2007, opinion polls indicated that only 14 percent of respondents had confidence in the federal government; for business the figure was 11 percent.[70] Pro-shareholder policies and business practices were widely

70. Glabus (2007).

regarded as corrupt and antiworker.[71] The legitimacy crisis and paralysis afflicting the Center-Left was already becoming the burden of the Right.

Given the severity of the financial collapse and the Great Recession, perhaps the most astonishing feature of the crisis was the absence of reforms signifying a break with an economic order that had produced increasingly dangerous economic crises. The rise of finance capitalism fostered an expansion of law and regulation with respect to financial disclosure, market conduct, and shareholder rights. In light of the global financial crisis, it now appears that juridification and the expansion of the regulatory state were insufficient to constrain destructive financially driven behavior. Despite the obvious flaws of finance capitalism, political constraints in countries as different as the United States and Germany blunted efforts to reform finance and its power within the political economy.

The debt-driven finance boom of 2000–2007, unlike the 1990s equity-driven boom, bestowed few benefits on the broader population (excluding the dubious benefit of consumers cashing out inflated home equity). It reflected a massive transfer of wealth to the financial sector and to large financial institutions in the United States and United Kingdom in particular. The period did not witness a boom in any broader respect—from 2000 to 2007 employment and wages outside the financial sector stagnated, growth remained anemic, and economic inequality increased. Within the FIRE sector (finance, insurance, and real estate), firm profits, employment, and compensation spiraled upward far in excess of historical benchmarks. The stock market bubble and bust of the late 1990s generated high employment, growth in wages, and innovative and productive companies (along with the many failed ones) and helped create the fixed capital embodied in a valuable Internet and telecommunications infrastructure. The real estate and securitized debt bubble enriched financiers, produced an income distribution more skewed than that of the Gilded Age, and allowed a large number of Americans to live in houses they could not afford and finance consumption beyond their means for a few years before bringing down the global financial system.

Of course, it was not supposed to turn out this way. Finance capitalism was supposed to be increasingly efficient, productive, and stable. The financialization of the economy was supposed to spread and tame risk. Shareholder-centric corporate governance policy and practices were supposed to maximize long-term share and firm value while constraining managerial opportunism and controlling downside financial risks to shareholders and the economy. Instead, risks were both concentrated in major financial firms, which were increasingly vulnerable to a large systemic shock, and then magnified by

71. See Glabus (2006, 2007).

increasing leverage and enormous exposures to losses on debt-based derivatives. Underlying this dangerous mutation of the financial sector was a toxic combination of managerial short-termism fueled by pressures to maximize share prices, the perverse incentives created by ostensibly pro-shareholder compensation practices, and the inability or unwillingness of shareholders and boards to rein in managerial risk taking. The politics of finance capitalism and corporate governance played an important role in creating the conditions for the crisis, and the crisis had important implications for the future of reform.

The financial crisis of 2007–9 did not end the age of finance capitalism. Government bailouts of the financial sector around the world, the subsequent increase in financial-sector concentration, and the implicit, if not explicit, official recognition of the major financial institutions that survived as too big to fail provided perverse proof of this fact. Financial collapse exposed massive regulatory failures, particularly in the United States, and revealed the deep flaws in the neoliberal variant of finance capitalism. The crisis emanated from the major financial institutions of the world's leading neoliberal economies and spread globally through the least regulated domestic and international market segments. However, policy responses that rely primarily on the reform of corporate governance are unlikely to achieve the degree of systemic stability sought. The more thoroughgoing reforms that are needed might face political obstacles more daunting than the enormous practical difficulties.

CONCLUSION

Legal Form and the Politics of Reform

The global financial crisis of 2007–9 and the reform politics that it triggered in both the United States and Germany confirm the main arguments advanced in this book. The crisis not only demonstrated the increasing instability of modern finance capitalism, it also exposed the power relations underlying it. Pre-crisis patterns of deregulation and pro-shareholder regulatory expansion reflected, above all, managerial interests within large financial institutions. Post-crisis corporate governance reform initiatives indicated the increasing importance of structural regulation through shareholder empowerment, even as the crisis exposed the substantial flaws of the shareholder-centered firm governance and market-driven finance. The center-left parties' prior support of many pro-finance policies was implicated in the financial collapse, yet they persisted in advocating pro-shareholder reforms. However, the financial crisis and Great Recession also undermined support for the political right's neoliberalism and managerialism, which left American and German politics in an ideological vacuum amid serious legitimacy crises.

This chapter steps back from the details of policymaking and the intricacies of law to explain the broader patterns characterizing governance reform. Corporate governance reform illuminates the destabilization and reconstitution of the political economy in the age of finance capitalism. The global financial crisis of 2007–9 should leave no doubt that, for better or worse, this new form of international finance capitalism profoundly altered the political economy at the national and international levels. Financial systems became more market-driven in both market-based systems and in those that were historically bank-based and characterized by relational lending. The financial sector wielded more economic power and political influence as financial services and markets loomed larger in domestic economic policymaking. Shareholder value became, and has remained, a potent ideological rationale for economic reorganization and legal reforms. Finance capitalism, as it developed in the United States and spread around the globe, has proven to be dangerously crisis-prone and enduring. Thus an understanding of its structural evolution and political underpinnings is more important than ever.

The politics of reform since the early 1990s and following the crisis of 2007–9 should likewise leave no doubt that corporate governance regimes are integral to the operation and development of nationally distinctive variants of finance capitalism. The regulatory state is at the center of these emerging forms of organization, but increasingly intense political pressures for regulatory expansion are in tension with economic and interest group pressures for market and firm autonomy. This book has advanced the conception of corporate governance as a juridical nexus of company, securities, and labor relations law in order to examine the noncontractual foundations, and thus the regulatory politics, of governance regimes and finance capitalism. The increasingly marketized, financially driven, and shareholder-friendly form taken by contemporary capitalism relies to an ever greater extent on a juridical and regulatory infrastructure in place of social norms, trust-based relational ties, discretionary state authority, and neocorporatist bargaining.

Intensifying politicization inevitably accompanied this expanding and deepening juridification of corporate governance. The legal structures of national governance regimes reflected the patterns of political contestation that drove their evolution in response to political economic crises. Partisan and coalitional politics mediated the resulting struggles to balance the competing interests and claims of corporate stakeholders. They now shape the deep policy conflicts over how to address the profound threats finance capitalism poses to political and economic stability. Taken together, these political processes and legal reforms are creating varieties of finance capitalism, just as they produced varieties of industrial capitalism in an earlier age.

Corporate governance reforms in the United States and Germany display three significant common features that highlight the changing role of the state and law in the political economy. First, the regulatory state has expanded its role in ordering, overseeing, and facilitating the operations of financial markets and the conduct of market participants. Corporate governance reforms have consistently displaced self-regulation, increased the stringency and widened the scope of disclosure regulation, and strengthened shareholder rights. Second, these reforms have expanded the use of structural regulation to alter institutionalized power relations inside the corporation to increase shareholder protection while avoiding intrusive administrative oversight and litigious enforcement mechanisms. By creating, altering, and reallocating control rights and decision-making procedures and by monitoring structures within the corporation, the politics of reform has complemented disclosure with structural regulation through largely *self-enforcing governance processes.* Third, corporate governance reform has substantially centralized state regulatory authority. Reform not only expanded the scope and authority of the state but restructured it in ways that broke with historically entrenched patterns of federalism and regulatory fragmentation. The fact that such divergently organized political economies as the United States and Germany were both marked by these developments in regulatory policy and design suggests the depth of the political economic transformation entailed by the rise of finance capitalism.

Corporate governance reform serves two deep systemic functions in the political economy of finance capitalism that attracted the support of political and economic elites. First, the decay of industrial and macroeconomic management policies during the 1970s and 1980s and the more recent difficulties faced by neocorporatist arrangements have left the corporate firm as the primary site of economic activity and adjustment. Policies designed to intensify financial market and shareholder pressures on corporations have served to institutionalize, accelerate, and reinforce this mode of economic adjustment through firm-driven restructuring. Second, governance reform enhances investor confidence, which is the foundation of the securities markets. Reform thus furthers the development of markets favored by powerful segments of the financial sector and ties them into the coalitional politics of corporate governance.

This book presents the argument that corporate governance reform is the product of state actors framing policy agendas and realigning interest group coalitions in response to economic crisis. Changes in interest group preferences and alignments combine with shifts in partisan political strategies to expand legal protections for shareholders. Because the corporation and its governance are so bound up in legal rules and structures, reform is bound up in the politics of the regulatory state. The variation of partisan political strategies and interest group alignments with respect to the juridical components of corporate governance results in complex and nationally distinctive patterns of legal and regulatory change. Change in a domain of economic organization as politically sensitive as corporate governance is inevitably highly politicized. But disagreements abound over the character of this politics. The explanation of reform offered here privileges national politics and economic developments over international political and market pressures, political action over economic forces, and law and regulation over contractually constituted governance arrangements.

Rival theories cannot account adequately for the cross-national patterns of legal change or the important areas of persistent divergence observed in governance reform. Theories premised on the causal impact of the globalization of financial markets and international competition for scarce capital run into two problems. First, since the early 1990s, as financial markets globalized apace and reforms proliferated, capital grew cheaper and more easily available. Second, these theories point to a common, global cause, but variations in policy and regulatory outcomes reveal the insufficiency of such universalistic explanations. Likewise, explanations attributing reform to the impact of financial scandals and economic crises cannot account for variation in outcomes other than by resort to ad hoc distinctions among crises. Significant economic crises are generally endogenously generated and often politically rooted, and the underlying political dynamics of crisis will also shape the politics of reform.

Interest group theories contending that reform is the product of the changing interests or growing power of shareholders face insuperable theoretical and empirical shortcomings. Theoretically, shareholders face more daunting collective-action problems in the political arena than in the corporation. The empirical evidence simply does not support the claim that shareholders wield great influence or that politicians play such a passive role in the reform process. Nor can these theories adequately explain the political history of reform, including the complex interaction of public and private actors, the cleavages among and within interest groups, the partisan dynamics of the reform process, and the enabling and constraining effects of existing juridical and institutional arrangements.

Corporate governance reforms in the United States and Germany cast doubt on convergence theories predicting (or purporting to discern) the inexorable adoption of liberal market economic policies and institutions by historically nonliberal political economies. Likewise, they challenge stronger versions of the varieties-of-capitalism thesis suggesting that national institutional arrangements are path-dependent and that reform is of marginal importance. Yet rejection of neoliberal convergence and path dependence is, at best, an intermediate point in understanding the political economic changes that have swept over much of the world in recent decades.

This book argues that the strategic action of state actors in framing the policy agenda and mobilizing coalitional support has been the primary driver of corporate governance reform and that major financial institutions form the pivotal interest group in this coalitional politics. Understanding governance reform requires an analysis of patterns of legal change, the strategic behavior of state actors, and shifting coalitional alliances and partisan alignments in interest group politics. Different legal elements of national corporate governance regimes implicate distinct alignments of state actors and interest groups. State actors are central to processes of governance reform that vary not only *across* national political economies but *within* them. The juridical components of governance regimes change at different rates and to different degrees. The conceptualization of corporate governance as a juridical nexus helps to clarify this differentiation within the political dynamics of reform. Despite their integration within the regime, there is no single interest group coalition driving the reform process across all these areas of law and regulation.

Reform is shaped not only by the functional purposes of legal rules but also by their form. Transparency and disclosure regulation under securities law display the greatest degree of similarity and convergence. Structural regulation, the legal rules governing the corporate structure, employee representation (or its absence), and enforcement mechanisms that buttress governance rights remain widely divergent and nationally distinctive. The commonalities of reform reveal an emerging political economic paradigm of finance capitalism. The complexities of partisan and interest group politics have driven its development into nationally distinctive variants.

THE POLITICS OF CORPORATE GOVERNANCE REFORM

Political Preconditions of Reform

Corporate governance reform in the United States and Germany demonstrates the importance of three preconditions. First, changes in domestic economic conditions diminish the anticipated returns and/or increase the projected opportunity costs of retaining established economic strategies and practices. Changes in market structures, competitive pressures, and relative macroeconomic performance impose pressures to adjust on economic actors. When such changes rise to the level of full-blown economic crises, posing a realistic possibility of a severe economic downturn or political instability, their disruptive effects render established business strategies and forms of economic governance unsustainable. The more serious the crisis, the more likely that policymakers and interest groups alike will abandon attempts to reinforce existing legal frameworks and institutions and instead seek to replace them, in whole or in part, with new policies, laws, or practices.

Second, changes in the economic environment shift, or at a minimum destabilize, established interests and policy preferences of powerful interest groups. Economic crises sow fear, confusion, and uncertainty and therefore loosen interest group preferences and alignments on policy questions. Interest groups and constituencies become available for mobilization in new configurations in support of policy agendas. Crises disrupt established conceptions of economic organization, public policy, and law. They fuel demands for *something* to be done, but just what is often unclear, especially when a crisis involves technically complex economic and policy areas such as financial markets and corporate governance. The public may support the generic notion of reform to address pressing economic problems, but voters seldom have concrete ideas or informed preferences as to what reform should involve. Even sophisticated interest groups are often so uncertain or split by internal divisions that state actors become the essential proponents of reform.

Third, state actors must take advantage of these crisis conditions to frame legal reforms, mobilize political support, and press for their adoption. Economic crises open the political space for entrepreneurial policymaking by state actors and party strategists seeking to exploit the destabilization of interests and interest group alignments for partisan political gains. Given uncertainty and conflict over interests and policy preferences, state actors perform essential framing and coordination functions, in addition to their control over the lawmaking apparatus of the state. Crises do not *necessarily* foster reforms, but they do present new strategic opportunities for political actors that make reform possible. Changing economic conditions lead to reform when they destabilize or weaken a previously dominant coalition and when state actors succeed in fashioning a coalitional realignment, particularly when this leads to a shift in the identity and interests of the pivotal interest group(s) in support of legal and institutional change. Corporate governance reform in Germany and the United States satisfied each of these conditions but in very different ways and in the context of different types of economic crises.

Political Dynamics of Reform

In both the United States and Germany, a combination of structural economic problems and the inadequacy, or outright failure, of existing corporate governance arrangements created the conditions for reform. The collapse of the Bretton Woods international monetary regime in the 1970s destroyed the institutional foundations of semiclosed national financial systems and triggered the opening financial markets in all industrialized countries. This new market structure ultimately led the most powerful parts of the financial sector to favor market-facilitating legal reforms, including corporate governance reforms, deemed necessary for the maintenance and development of domestic capital markets and the financial services sector. Firms lost insulation from market competition and volatility as the maturation of international markets in goods and finance also limited the effectiveness of industrial policies, exchange rate manipulation, and Keynesian demand management. They would now bear the brunt of pressures for adjustment to sweeping changes in domestic and international economic conditions.

Notwithstanding the distinct character of economic difficulties in the United States and Germany, corporate governance reforms in both countries served to address problems of economic adjustment in a context of rapidly changing market and macroeconomic conditions. By protecting shareholder interests, reforms promoted ever-more-marketized financial systems and increased firm adjustment capacities through financial market and corporate governance regulation. Corporate governance reform had the added attraction of costing governments little and thus did not add to state fiscal strains.

The propensity of the new order of finance capitalism to produce periodic and increasingly serious financial scandals and crises increased the political pressures for reform.

In both countries, corporate governance reform was more the product of top-down policymaking by state actors than of bottom-up politics in which interest groups with clear preferences drove policy changes. State actors repeatedly played a pivotal role in framing and publicizing policy debates and agendas, working to mobilize and realign powerful interest groups and constructing interest group coalitions. They also exploited the divisions within these groups in assembling pro-reform coalitional alignments and neutralizing opponents. Shareholders, financial institutions, managers, and labor formed and re-formed coalitional alliances under the aegis of partisan politics that influenced the course and content of reform. In contrast to more statist countries where administrative bureaucracies had greater autonomy in policymaking, the political structures and legal traditions of the United States and Germany ensured that elected officials would play a more central role in shaping and adopting reforms. Hence partisan politics drove the process of legal change in corporate governance, with regulatory agencies taking on a secondary (though critically important) role. The reform process bore hardly any resemblance to the pluralist paradigm in which state institutions aggregate preferences and translate them into policy and law.

Significantly, the push for the most far-reaching reforms came from the Center-Left in both countries, and in both instances the Center-Left parties were in opposition when they began their efforts to mobilize powerful interest groups and public opinion in favor of reform. Corporate governance reform afforded both the SPD and the Democrats the chance to present themselves simultaneously as economic modernizers, anti-elitist populists, and allies of both minority shareholders (including the symbolically powerful, if politically feeble, individual shareholder) and segments of the increasingly powerful financial sector. Reform was consistent with both parties' historical conflicts with managerial interests and their skepticism toward self-regulating markets and laissez faire economic policies. Both parties had long advocated regulatory intervention in the private sphere to correct market failures, redistribute income, and redress the hierarchical asymmetries of private power. Although it seems paradoxical that the Center-Left would take up the cause of finance capital and shareholders, it is in some ways a logical extension of its longstanding commitment to and willingness to use the regulatory state to alter contractual and market outcomes.

A better understanding of the tensions between the historical ideological commitments of the Center-Left and its embrace of corporate governance reforms helps to illuminate the role of ideas in legal and policy change. Ideas are not merely epiphenomenal in the politics of reform. Some legal and economic theories are better suited than others to framing specific responses to particular policy problems. Legal and economic theories may also serve a political function by logically favoring the material interests and ideological biases of precisely those groups that state actors are seeking to mobilize in support of reform.

In the case of corporate governance reform, the ascendance of neoclassical theories of law and economics not only helped legitimate the move toward a more market-based form of finance and a shareholder-centric model of corporate governance but also provided clear policy prescriptions to achieve that end. This worked on the levels of ideological and interest group politics. As an ideological matter, shareholder protections, once widely viewed as primarily benefiting the economic elite, were reconceived as largely consistent with economic democracy, anti-elitism, egalitarianism, and fundamental fairness. Investor confidence, which has often functioned as a constraint of Center-Left policy preferences, was refashioned as a leading indicator of political economic legitimacy. The language and concepts of law and economics also facilitated the interest group politics underlying corporate governance reform by reconciling broad normative concerns with the narrower economic interests of powerful factions of the financial sector.

Yet these ideas and theories certainly did not overdetermine the policy agendas of corporate governance reformers. For every economic argument in support of regulatory reform, there is another diametrically opposed to state intervention in the private sphere. In fact, corporate governance reform departed from, and in some respects conflicted with, the contractualist prescriptions of much law and economics theory—at least in its most aggressively laissez faire forms. Legal changes in the corporate governance domain have tended to be intensively regulatory rather than contractually enabling, mandatory rather than permissive, and a political declaration of market failures rather than an endorsement of market rationality and efficiency. As economic reform during the 1990s and 2000–2010 enshrined the financial markets and the corporate firm as the primary sites of economic adjustment and innovation, legal change in governance regimes took the form of state intervention within both the securities markets and the internal structure of the corporation. Further, the economic and legal ideas underlying reform were hardly new; they were decades old. Neoliberalism, neoclassical economics, and American-style law and economics are thus better understood as more the product of politics and economic conditions than independent drivers of reform.

These general political preconditions of corporate governance reform leave the analysis at a highly abstract level. A causal explanation of the specific legal and regulatory changes that make up reform must look to the partisan and interest group politics underlying them. Variation in the degree of change across areas of law in the juridical nexus of corporate governance indicates the need for a more granular analysis of reform politics. This makes understanding the patterns of legal change in each country essential in framing the political analysis of reform.

PATTERNS OF CORPORATE GOVERNANCE REFORM
AND POLITICAL ECONOMIC ORDER

Common Characteristics of Reform

A central puzzle of corporate governance reform is posed by the patterns of legal and institutional change. Convergent tendencies in legal development coincide with the resilience of distinctive national features of governance regimes, while substantial reforms in some areas of law contrast with relative stability in others. Table 7.1 sets out the varying degrees of legal reform in the United States and Germany across the areas of law comprising the juridical nexus of corporate governance. The general trends toward stronger shareholder rights and protections, and thus a more shareholder-centered corporate governance regime, are clear. So are the wide variations in the reform of, and the enduring differences across, the juridical elements of these national regimes. The table indicates neither overarching convergence on the liberal market model of finance capitalism nor the stability born of path dependence. Instead, the reforms of the subareas of corporate governance law reflect more complex and issue-specific regulatory politics.

The salient policy and legal trends in corporate governance reform display important broad similarities across the American and German cases. Each case is characterized by increasing stringency of disclosure regulation, expansion of structural regulation to protect shareholder interests through board and auditing reform, regulatory centralization, and conflict over the role of litigation as a mode of enforcement. Policymakers in both countries strengthened disclosure rules to the benefit of shareholders in order to increase investor confidence and bolster domestic securities markets. Financial information had to be disclosed more quickly, comprehensively, and accessibly than ever before. In each case, legal rules were adopted or amended to limit the informational and rent-seeking advantages of corporate insiders, whether managers, large financial institutions, or controlling shareholders. Prohibitions of insider trading were strengthened and expanded in the United States, while in Germany they were adopted for the first time to replace ineffective voluntary self-regulation. Accounting rules were subject to much closer regulatory oversight and, in an indication of the importance of disclosure rules and principles to international financial markets, to accelerating efforts at international harmonization.

Structural regulation through the composition and legal responsibilities of the board along with internal monitoring and risk controls became increasingly important aspects of reform. In both countries, reform strengthened the board of directors (the supervisory board in Germany) as a mechanism of oversight and potential control over managers. Shareholder voting rights became the subject of intensified political conflict as the problems of conflicts

TABLE 7.1: DEGREE AND DIRECTION OF CORPORATE GOVERNANCE REFORM IN GERMANY AND THE UNITED STATES		
Area of law	*United States*	*Germany*
Securities law/disclosure regulation	Substantial pro-shareholder reform	Substantial pro-shareholder reform
Company law/structural regulation[a]	Moderate pro-shareholder reform with no stakeholder features	Moderate pro-shareholder reform with retained stakeholder features
Labor relations law[b]	No formal change (but substantial practical erosion in pro-labor efficacy)	No change in supervisory board codetermination; minimal pro-labor works council reform

[a]Including proxy voting regulation under American securities law.
[b]Relating to employee representation in governance structures and practices.

of interest and the structural allocation of power within the corporation became more acute. This structural turn in reform reflected a search for effective pro-shareholder governance mechanisms amid ambivalence or pronounced hostility toward private litigation as a means of enforcing shareholder rights. The corporate structure and allocation of control rights were modified for regulatory purposes to fulfill enforcement functions that would otherwise have been performed by litigation or administrative proceedings. Paradoxically, corporate governance reforms could only do so fulfill these functions through increasingly centralized legislative and regulatory authority and a blurring of the boundaries of the public and private spheres that were central to neoliberalism and neoclassical economic theory.

The distinction between prescriptive disclosure regulation and structural regulation also helps to explain the differences in the extent of reform across the areas of law examined here. Disclosure regulation mobilizes less managerial opposition than structural regulation. Transparency certainly creates constraints on managers and exposes them to intensified market pressures, but they also may benefit from the expanded financing options from a more market-based financial system. More important, the structural entrenchment of managerial authority enables managers to withstand these pressures or to command higher compensation and side payments for any loss in autonomy caused by enhanced shareholder power. Structural regulation reforms, altering the allocation of authority within the corporation—as in the cases of expanded shareholder voting rights and liberalization of takeover rules—directly threaten this source of managerial autonomy and entrenchment and therefore trigger broader and more intense political resistance.

Structural regulation tends to be located in company law and governance-related aspects of labor relations law, while disclosure regulation is primarily a matter of securities law. Hence it is not surprising that the former has undergone substantially more reform in comparison with the other bodies of law comprising the juridical nexus of corporate governance. A technical exception to this pattern is proxy voting regulation in the United States. Federal proxy voting rules are not only a form of structural regulation but also a rare instance in which federal securities laws, dating back to the New Deal era, directly encroach on the traditional subject matter of state corporation law. Consequently, attempts to significantly enhance shareholder power over managers through expanded voting rights have generally produced higher levels of conflict and opposition than proposals for more stringent disclosure rules. The resilience of German codetermination also demonstrates the greater intensity of conflict and resistance to reforms of structural regulation. The pro-labor regulation created by board codetermination was left unchanged, despite the attacks of peak business associations, not only because of its symbolic importance but because it helped labor reconcile pro-shareholder reforms with protection of employee interests.

Centralization of national regulatory authority was a critical dimension of corporate governance reform in both the United States and Germany. The American and German cases provide evidence that self-regulation and regulatory decentralization inadequately control conflicts of interest and agency costs within the corporation and financial markets. Weak disclosure and equity market regulation dampened the development of a market-based financial system in Germany and threatened Frankfurt's status as an international financial center. The feeble restraints of state corporation law on managerial conduct, the prevalence of conflicts of interest throughout the financial-services sector, and the decay of professional self-regulation by the accounting industry created the conditions for the corporate scandals and financial crises that shook the foundations of American capitalism.

In each country, building and restoring investor confidence required a concentration and expansion of regulatory authority at the federal level that broke sharply with historical forms of federalism. The American Sarbanes-Oxley reforms pushed back the long-established boundary between federal securities law and state corporation law with respect to the composition, structure, and responsibilities of the board. However, owing to the intense post–Sarbanes-Oxley political conflict over shareholder proxy voting rights, this shift was relatively modest and did not forge a sustained path of reform and regulatory development. German securities law reform largely displaced and absorbed the Länder-based market self-regulation that had prevailed for well over a century. The age of finance capitalism is also the era of regulation. And the regulatory state has undergone, and will likely continue to experience, a substantial transformative expansion in its responsibilities and capacities.

The German case is further complicated by the interplay of national and EU politics and legislation. Centralization has taken place on both the national and European levels. But the broad overview of corporate governance reform within the European Union shows that centralization through EU legal harmonization has gone much further and faster in the area of securities law, where there is widespread agreement on the strengthening of disclosure regulation, than in the area of company law, where consensus is lacking within and among the member states. Given broad agreement over reform in the area, the Lamfalussy process could streamline EU legislation in the area of securities law and regulation, in part by strengthening the role of and cooperation among national regulators. Consensus effectively centralized much legislative authority over securities law at the EU level, which in turn advanced regulatory centralization at the national level. In contrast, disagreements among the member states continue to limit the harmonization of company and labor relations law.

The exception to the primacy of national politics in corporate governance reform, particularly with respect to company law, is the case law of the European Court of Justice. Although their practical effects should not be exaggerated, ECJ rulings created the conditions for national legislative competition to attract the chartering of new and established firms and facilitated EU bargaining over a European corporate form. Criticism of codetermination has grown in Germany in no small measure because of the potential for reincorporation and the possibility of new firm formation outside the country under the ECJ's post-*Centros* case law. Judicial doctrine also made agreement over the SE, the European corporation, more attractive. However, despite the ECJ's best efforts, national divergence in company law persists, for example, in the areas of shareholder voting rights, board structure, transfer of the corporate seat, and codetermination. Even major legislative breakthroughs confirm these facts: the EU's new SE corporate form protected extant employee representation and incorporated much national company law in practice.

The Persistence of Divergence

In other respects the reform processes and outcomes in the two cases were strikingly different. Substantive policy outcomes and the order in which policy areas were addressed by the political process differed significantly. For all the substantial and almost exclusively pro-shareholder reforms undertaken in Germany from the early 1990s through 2009, the country has largely retained its stakeholder form of corporate governance. While the legal protection offered shareholders increased over this period, the institutionalized microcorporatism of the German corporation remained entrenched with the persistence of board codetermination and the modest strengthening of works councils. In contrast, the American corporate governance regime became increasingly shareholder-centered and market reinforcing. To the extent that reforms protected employees, they were protected as shareholders and pension beneficiaries, not as worker-stakeholders with a legally recognized representational status within firm governance. The issue never even appeared on the American policy agenda. The persistence of employee incorporation into the German stakeholder model of corporate governance was matched by the continued exclusion of employees from the institutionalized governance processes inside the American corporation.

Meanwhile, the American market for corporate control remained far more developed and imposed more intense constraints on managers than did the German market. The German microcorporatist stakeholder model constrained both managers and shareholders and reduced the plausibility and potential benefits of shareholder activism and corporate takeovers. As the cross-shareholding networks of Germany AG partially unwound, the number of mergers and acquisitions increased between 2000 and 2010. But very few corporate deals began, let alone ended, as hostile takeovers. The Mannesmann hostile takeover by Vodafone showed the possibility of launching a cross-border hostile takeover in Germany, but it proved an exceptional case. The subsequent prosecution of Mannesmann board members for approving golden-parachute bonuses to management effectively chilled further use of side payments to overcome managerial resistance in the face of takeover bids and made clear that Germany remained less than receptive to American-style takeover tactics and managerial compensation.

Moreover, American and German corporate governance regimes should not be caricatured respectively as representing a sharp distinction between a shareholder-centered and thoroughly market-driven model and a more institutionally constrained stakeholder-oriented one. Some of the differences between the two regimes run contrary to stereotype. In some respects, German shareholders enjoy substantially greater control rights than their American counterparts. German shareholders have long wielded more expansive rights, buttressed by litigation rules, to question management, receive information, and vote on important company policies and decisions in the shareholders' meeting. Under German shareholder voting and blocking minority rules, blockholders and large banks have far more influence over corporate governance and leverage over management than institutional investors in the United States. Germany reformed board responsibilities, external auditing, internal risk controls, and managerial compensation rules before the United States adopted analogous reforms—in some instances by years. Despite the increasing nominal independence of directors and belated board reforms, American managers have retained far more power over firm governance and fought fiercely—and so far successfully—to preserve it. If German corporate governance remains stakeholder-oriented, the American regime retains the stamp of managerialism.

Finally, American and German mechanisms of enforcement remain highly divergent in ways that reflect their respective traditional reliance on disclosure rules and structural regulation. Notwithstanding American anti-litigation reforms and moderate litigation liberalization in Germany, lawsuits are still far more prevalent and important in enforcing legal norms in the United States. The elective affinity between the American market-based financial system and corporate governance regime and its liberal rights-based legal system remains in place. In contrast, shareholder rights in Germany still favor the exercise of voice via the shareholders' meeting and are embedded in a microcorporatist governance structure in which they are counterbalanced by the rights and obligations of employee representation. Ideals of stakeholder representation and negotiation retain their potency in legal and popular conceptions of economic organization. Legal recognition and protection of plural constituencies, interests, and values favor forms of regulation with deep roots in German law and economic institutions that encourage negotiation rather than litigation.

Germany still does not permit class actions or contingency fees for plaintiffs' attorneys, retains its restrictive discovery rules, has no jury trials, and awards far more limited damages. Together these rules perpetuate substantial practical disincentives for litigation. Although litigation as an enforcement mechanism in American corporate governance has been curtailed by legislation and court rulings, it remains far more prevalent than in Germany. Despite recent reforms in that country to increase the efficacy of shareholder litigation, deep suspicion and resistance to litigious enforcement, often referred to as the "American disease," remains and has constrained pro-shareholder litigation reforms. Tellingly, reforms to create American-style shareholder derivative suits were adopted at the price of curtailing established avenues for challenging the decisions of the shareholders' meeting in court—precisely the one form of litigation that had proliferated in Germany.

Litigation rules and structural regulation are alternative modes of enforcing legal norms and vindicating social values, but they are being combined in new ways. These different approaches provide the legal infrastructure for distinctive governance regimes, but reforms since 2000 indicate that there are more degrees of freedom in altering the legal structure of corporate governance than often thought. Increasingly stringent disclosure regulation in Germany suggests that a stakeholder regime is compatible with greater financial transparency, just as legal strengthening of the board and institutional investors in firm governance may complement the American market-driven regime. Assuming that the balance of political power continues to favor financial capital, pressures to increase shareholder protections will almost certainly induce the expansion of structural regulation if litigation is substantially limited by law.

The differences in policy outcomes across the juridical components of corporate governance regimes also reveal the varying characteristics of reform (see table 7.2) Legal and institutional change is most commonly a process of "layering," to use Wolfgang Streeck and Kathleen Thelen's (2005) term. Corporate governance regimes, as complex integrated juridical frameworks, are

TABLE 7.2: CHARACTER OF LEGAL/INSTITUTIONAL CHANGE IN CORPORATE GOVERNANCE IN THE UNITED STATES AND GERMANY

Area of law	United States	Germany
Securities law/disclosure regulation	Displacement (litigation reform; auditing self-regulation; audit certification)	Displacement (federalization of Länder regulation and exchange self-regulation)
Company law/structural regulation[a]	Partial displacement/ layering (board independence, structure and duties; risk controls)	Layering (takeover law; "comply or explain" best practices, litigation reform)
Labor relations law[b]	Drift/exhaustion	Path dependence/drift

[a]Including board rules and proxy voting regulation under American securities law.
[b]Relating to employee representation in governance structures and practices, including board codetermination under German company law.

rarely if ever completely displaced. Specific elements may be displaced; law may expand to occupy previously unregulated economic space. But the new legal rules are the product of political forces shaped by received institutional arrangements and, once adopted, must be integrated within preexisting legal structures.

Corporate governance reforms in the United States and Germany shared a common normative and instrumental core, but did not eradicate the distinctive characters of these regimes. Reforms in both countries primarily advanced the common goal of increasing shareholder protections. Despite the compromises forced by managers (and to a lesser extent labor), reform altered preexisting juridical and institutional arrangements in ways intended to foster the self-reinforcing development of finance capitalism. However, by introducing these legal changes into very different political, economic, and juridical contexts, the reforms necessarily differed in their impact on the corporate governance regime as a whole. In the United States the reform of shareholder litigation, accounting, and disclosure rules limited well-developed mechanisms of enforcement and displaced long-established forms of private rule making and self-regulation with pro-shareholder structural regulation. Legal reforms altering the composition, structure, and election of the board partially displaced aspects of state corporation law and stock exchange self-regulation with federal structural regulation, but left the substrate of shareholder-centered governance intact. In Germany a new disclosure regime displaced Länder-based regulation and voluntary self-regulation. Company law reform explicitly modified parts of the existing structural regime and enhanced enforcement mechanisms to protect shareholders and encourage financial market development. But these reforms were layered upon an established and well-articulated regime of stakeholder-oriented structural regulation.

Last, corporate governance reform left the role of employees essentially untouched in both countries, a fact that had a different significance in each. In the United States it perpetuated the institutional drift and the near exhaustion of American labor law as its obsolescence fostered the continued decline of organized labor. In Germany the path dependence of board and works council codetermination reflected the greater strength of labor—though these arrangements now may be showing signs of decay and drift as union density and bargaining coverage decline and employers use works councils as a decentralizing alternative to sectoral negotiations.

CRISES, STATE ACTORS, AND COALITIONAL POLITICS

Coalitional models that posit a single dominant interest group alliance therefore fail to capture the political dynamics driving and constraining corporate governance reform. When there is no such alliance to set the agenda and drive reform politically, legal change becomes a significantly more complex process likely to produce ambiguity, internal contradiction, and incoherence in law and policy. Interest groups are not internally unified blocks with homogenous interests. The division and splintering of interest groups, along with uncertainty over their interests and preferences, play a critical role in shaping policy outcomes and legal change. A more realistic analysis must disaggregate both the stakeholder interest groups involved in the politics of reform and the elements of the legal structure they seek to change.

The variation in interest group alignments and alliances across different juridical elements of corporate governance also implicates the central role of state actors in orchestrating (or impeding) reform. Stakeholder groups themselves are often internally divided and, in times of crisis or economic stress, may be uncertain of their interests and policy preferences regarding highly complex and technical legal and policy issues. Under such circumstances, interest group alignments at the core of coalitional politics are often, ab initio, inchoate. They typically require the strategic intervention of state actors to overcome obstacles to coordinated, coherent, and effective group participation in policymaking and legal reform. Interest groups are thus subject to mobilization in multiple directions and vulnerable to divide-and-conquer strategies of state actors seeking to sideline potential opposition groups in complex strategies of coalitional politics. The more fractious and less well organized interest groups are, the more critical the role of state actors becomes in policymaking and reform. Counterintuitive as it may appear, state actors in the highly pluralist United States, often characterized as constrained within a "weak state," should play a *more* central role in corporate governance reform than actors in Germany's more organized political economy with its highly institutionalized and powerful peak associations. This is precisely what we see in the case studies.

Though state actors were important to the process of reform in Germany (particularly those in the SPD), actions by politicians and policy entrepreneurs within the U.S. Congress and the SEC were far more decisive in the formulation and adoption of reforms in the United States. But American state actors could push through substantial reforms only so long as interest groups and partisan opposition were weakened by conditions of economic crisis. Paradoxically, weak state capacity and the critical role of state actors in reform politics are logically consistent. If reform can occur only under conditions of interest group disability, state actors are the only agents available to drive it forward.

The different character of the economic crises in the American and German cases derived from the divergent political economic structures in each country and drove reform politics in different ways. In the United States reform was made possible by a severe *episodic* crisis and the consequent disabling of interest group and veto-point politics as usual. The corporate and market meltdowns of 2000–2002 and 2007–9 were the product of the country's market-driven financial and corporate governance regime. Once the crisis passed, opposition built up against continued reform and interest group politics began to revert to their normal veto-prone state.

In contrast, German corporate governance reform was the product of a *secular* economic crisis that created the conditions for a more enduring coalitional interest group realignment and thus for a reform process that lasted for over a decade. Germany's nonliberal political economic structure did not produce the dramatic market collapses or waves of corporate scandals seen in the United States, but it did contribute to the country's serious economic difficulties from the 1980s onward. Although German policymaking also suffered from institutional and partisan blockages, particularly in budgetary matters, its political structure did allow for a more prolonged and arguably more coherent reform process. The political collapse of the SPD in 2005 was the result of opposition not to governance reforms but to the welfare state and employment law portions of the Schröder government's Agenda 2010.

Analysis of the variation of interest group politics and partisan political strategies across the juridical components of corporate governance law clarifies both the patterns of conflict over reform and the persistence of divergent policy outcomes and regime structures. The following summary description of reform politics greatly compresses and simplifies the interest group breakdown and configurations but still captures a good deal of the complexity and fractiousness of interest group alignments on these policies issues.[1] Not only do

---

1. Certain groups are omitted from some tables on the grounds that they did not play a significant role in a given policy area out of indifference or ambivalence.

the groups in the categories used here have different interests with respect to different areas of corporate governance law, but the *intensity* of their interests varies as well.[2]

Tables 7.3 and 7.4 set out the shifting coalitional alignments in the German and American cases, respectively. As can be seen from table 7.3, interest group preferences and alignments in Germany changed across the areas of law. Several important patterns stand out. First, large financial institutions played a pivotal role in almost all areas of corporate governance reform. This point is reinforced by the observation that minority shareholders and shareholder groups have been and remain politically and economically weak as a legacy of Germany's bank-based financial system, the prevalence of public and unfunded company pensions, and undeveloped equity culture. Further, these institutions were deeply engaged in the policy debates, consistently favored market-facilitating reforms, and, in most cases, were largely successful in pursuing legislative reforms.

A second striking pattern was the consistent opposition of blockholders to pro-shareholder reforms and their repeated loss to reformist coalitions. These policy preferences were consistent with the efforts of blockholders to maintain their autonomy and control over the corporation, both of which were threatened by corporate governance reform. Transparency and disclosure regulation also intensified financial market pressures (through higher costs of capital, shareholder activism, or a takeover bid) on firms suspected of diverting excessive benefits to insiders. Structural regulation directly eliminated the tools of insider control, self-dealing, and diversion, such as passive or conflicted boards, compliant auditors, and unaccountable managers. Blockholders lost out politically for two primary reasons. First, large financial institutions, which were once among the largest blockholders in the domestic economy, defected when they shifted their preferences from maintenance of the traditional German financial model of opacity and long-term relational lending to supporting the development of financial markets and market-based financial services. Second, over time, the remaining blockholders began to see the potential benefits of well-developed stock markets that could give them the option of a more profitable exit. Accordingly, opposition to corporate governance reform among the old blockholders diminished, leaving those that remained even weaker and more politically isolated.

The final important pattern was the split among managers and in the policy positions taken by labor. Managerial elites split between the managers of large internationally oriented firms and those of smaller companies focused on the domestic market and suspicious that a more market-based financial system would impair their autonomy and access to capital. Managers of larger, publicly traded multinational corporations were interested in tapping

2. The significance of interest intensity is also discussed in Mabe (2004).

TABLE 7.3: GERMAN INTEREST GROUP ALIGNMENTS IN CORPORATE GOVERNANCE REFORM	
Proreform	*Antireform*
Securities law reform	
Large financial institutions and investment funds Shareholder associations Managers of large public firms Labor	Managers of small and medium sized enterprises (SMEs) Public banks and small private financial institutions Blockholders (ambivalent)
Company law reform (structural regulation/control rights)	
Large financial institutions and investment funds Shareholder associations Managers of large public firms Labor	Blockholders
Takeover law reform (neoliberal market for corporate control)	
Large financial institutions and investment funds Shareholder associations Managers of large public firms (split)	Labor Blockholders Managers of public SMEs Managers of large public firms (split) Small and medium-sized banks
Codetermination reform (weakening of supervisory board employee representation)	
Managers of public SMEs and large public firms Large financial institutions	Labor

Note: Takeover law is broken out because of the exceptional politics surrounding the EU takeover directive and German Takeover Act; codetermination reform is treated separately because of the distinctive conflicts over the issue.

international financial market and financial services and in accommodating Anglo-American norms of corporate governance and shareholder value. This faction of managers largely allied with large financial institutions in support of governance reform and, with the added support of organized labor, overcame opposition from blockholders and dissenting managers. The division among managers contrasted with the greater unity of organized labor. During the long period of reform examined here, labor maintained a de facto cross-class alliance with the financial sector mediated by the SPD. Organized labor backed reform from its early stages during the CDU Kohl government and strongly supported most of the SPD-Green government's subsequent disclosure regulation and company law reforms. This support was contingent on the maintenance and political insulation of codetermination and thus placed limits on the substance and politics of reform. Labor even acquiesced in the elimination of capital gains taxes on the sale of cross-shareholdings, though the reform was regarded as excessively generous to business. This support for reform did not extend to takeover law.

The area of takeover law reform is a special case. In fighting the SPD's heavily neoliberal takeover law proposals in the EU and at home, managers were more united and successful in their opposition; a significant number of managers of large, publicly traded firm allied with those from smaller firms and with organized labor to mobilize against a liberal market for control. The implicit labor-finance alliance broke down dramatically over the Schröder government's support for the EU takeover directive and its own domestic takeover law. Perceiving in takeovers a serious threat to German-owned industry and labor's powerful role in the German economic model, labor shifted its alliances to join with dissenting managers and blockholders in opposing the neoliberal vision of a market for corporate control. The conflict over the takeover law showed that labor's (and management's) acceptance of the Schröder government's embrace of finance capitalism was limited. Yet it was an exception to labor's general support for financial system and corporate governance reform.

The American case reveals salient issues and interest group alignments distinct from those seen in Germany (see table 7.4). In part these differences reflect the fact that the United States already had a well-developed market-based financial system and a more shareholder-centered corporate governance regime. Indeed, massive market and institutional failures within this regime would ultimately drive reform. Yet the pattern and processes of that reform also reveal the more conflictual and divisive politics in the United States. In comparison with the conflict between stakeholder- and shareholder-oriented governance models in Germany, American corporate governance reform inflamed the conflict between managerialism and shareholder primacy. The sides were more evenly matched and the political system even more immobilized than in the German case by partisan rancor, institutional veto points, and ferocious interest group resistance to reform. Reform in the United States was caught up in a very different set of conflicts in which financial and shareholder interests were in competition with other ideological and partisan goals. This is indicated by the vacillation and ambiguities of reform during the 1990s, when deregulation, anti-litigation reform, strengthened disclosure regulation, and experiments with pro-shareholder structural regulation were all tried with no coherent overarching policy agenda tying them together.

Reform in the United States did not display the unidirectional pro-shareholder trend seen in Germany. A central dimension of reform during the 1990s was an effort not to enhance shareholder protection but to curtail shareholder litigation. Congressional Republicans mobilized the support of corporate managers and the financial sector to support litigation reform. The prevalence and centrality of litigation as a mode of enforcement threatened these groups, creating the preconditions for a potent coalition that overcame the opposition of shareholder and labor groups. Litigation-driven enforcement was a legacy of postwar legal liberalism, and the collapse of that political-legal order not only put litigation on the policy agenda but generated political

TABLE 7.4: AMERICAN INTEREST GROUP ALIGNMENTS IN CORPORATE GOVERNANCE REFORM	
Proreform	*Antireform*
Securities litigation reform	
Managers of large public firms and SMEs Large financial institutions Investment funds (ambivalent and split)	Labor Investment funds (ambivalent and split)
Securities law reform (disclosure and accounting regulation)	
Investment funds Labor Large financial institutions (split)	Managers of SMEs Managers of large public firms Small financial institutions
Securities law reform (structural regulation)	
Investment funds Labor Large financial institutions	Managers of large firms Managers of SMEs Small financial institutions
Reform of shareholder voting and board elections (structural regulation)	
Investment funds Labor Large financial institutions	Managers of large firms Managers of SMEs Small financial institutions

Note: Shareholder litigation and voting rights reforms are broken out separately because of the distinctive political conflicts and alignments surrounding them.

constraints on litigation as a mode of enforcement that hardened into a broad bipartisan consensus. Likewise, managerial interests and portions of the financial sector (including the accounting industry) defeated attempts to tighten accounting regulation, despite its centrality to the transparency and disclosure regulation at the foundation of the American corporate governance regime.

These developments cut against shareholder interests and, as it turned out, the maintenance of functional, orderly markets. The structural incapacity of American government to engage in informed, deliberative, and constructive policy debate on major economic issues was reflected in the fact that little significant legal reform occurred even in the face of mounting concerns over the health of the American financial system and corporate governance. On issues implicating the fundamental allocation of political and economic power in the United States, legislation proved impossible in the absence of an extraordinary crisis.

The severity of the financial market and legitimacy crises in the wake of the stock market crashes of 2001 and the post-Enron corporate finance scandals broke through the partisan, institutional, and interest group gridlock of the 1990s. The interest group alignments set out in table 7.4 were marginal to the politics and substance of the Sarbanes-Oxley reforms and the administrative rule making that followed them. In the presence of multiple veto points and the absence of institutionalized interest articulation and negotiation, crisis-driven policymaking tends to be sudden and transitory. The urgency and delegitimizing effects of crisis conditions marginalize interest groups and opponents of reform but only for a relatively short period of time. Both aspects were evident in the post-Enron reforms. The belief that the American financial system was on the edge of collapse mandated immediate action; the fact that the crisis was caused by scandals implicating almost every major interest group in malfeasance, misfeasance, or negligent nonfeasance left no effective opponents to reform. Managers, accountants, Wall Street bankers, lawyers, and antiregulation conservatives lost legitimacy and power within the policy-making process during the crisis. These groups also splintered as insiders sought to preserve a system threatened with economic and political collapse and other factions sought to halt or minimize reform.

Shareholder groups strongly supported regulatory reform, but their influence was limited. Supporters of regulatory reform now included an overwhelming majority of institutional investors. The confident reliance on voluntarism and market power during the 1980s and 1990s proved an embarrassing failure as many in the corporate governance movement came to see regulation and formal enforcement as necessary (though not enough to press for rollback of litigation reforms). Organized labor (whose pension funds had long been at the forefront of investor activism) also strenuously advocated for reform. Although labor's positions reflected deeply rooted anti-managerialist sentiments, they were framed in terms of shareholders' rights and interests as successive financial crises cemented an alignment of labor and shareholders. The coalitional alliance was based on a conception of employees as shareholders, not as workers with interests in tension with those of investors and managers, let alone as stakeholders entitled to formal representation in corporate governance. Yet neither shareholders nor employees, constituencies hobbled by internal diversity and organizational weakness, were sufficiently powerful to drive reform. State actors in the form of congressional Democrats, and particularly those in the Senate, fulfilled that function.

A striking feature of the post-Enron period of reform was the resiliency of the deeper partisan and coalitional politics that had long constrained legislative and regulatory change. The Democrats' strategic choices implicitly assumed that the crisis would not persist and that power and interest group politics would return to the status quo ante (and thus guaranteed that result in a self-fulfilling prophecy). The Sarbanes-Oxley reforms can be viewed as a layering of a new pro-shareholder politics over the 1990s coalitional anti-litigation politics. The anti-litigation and pro-reform agendas were based on different coalitional alignments, but the pro-shareholder coalition did not fully displace the preceding managerialist one. The tacit assumption of interest group and coalitional resilience also influenced the form of the structural regulation adopted in the Sarbanes-Oxley Act. Reconfiguring the board of directors was a way out of the enforcement problem presented by the foreclosure of litigation remedies, but Sarbanes-Oxley was woefully incomplete in terms of restructuring power within the firm to make this form of structural regulation effective. The act did not alter the voting rights or procedures that insulated the corporation from actual shareholder representation through contested board elections.

Interest group and partisan politics *did* return to normal. The attacks on corporate governance reform began as soon as the crisis dissipated and then gathered momentum as a more organized backlash of managerial and financial elites. The attack morphed into an appeal to preserve the "competitiveness" of U.S. capital markets. In an attempt to mobilize a countercoalition for deregulation, the Bush administration was instrumental in publicizing the argument that precipitous overregulation was harming the competitiveness of American capital markets and the United States was losing financial business and corporate listings on domestic stock markets. This throwback to the framing and terminology of the 1990s convergence debates was largely a smokescreen.

The real issue was one of power—and the concern that regulation would reallocate it more fundamentally and dramatically toward shareholders. The SEC's proposal to grant shareholders extremely limited rights to nominate directors mobilized the full force of the business backlash. The ultimate failure of this reform demonstrated the power of the backlash coalition, through which managerial interests influenced the policy preferences of the financial sector. Business interests were split by sectoral cleavages, but the positional interests of managers spanned sectors. Reform of shareholder voting rights and board elections threatened the very core of these managerial interests in maintaining authority, autonomy, and power. And this threat mobilized managers in the financial sector into a managerialist coalition. If support for corporate governance reform was supplied by a cross-class coalition, opposition and backlash were led by a cross-sectoral alliance of managers.

The backlash failed to reframe the corporate governance policy agenda, let alone roll it back. The empirical weakness of the "competitiveness" arguments blunted their effectiveness. Many large financial institutions were at best lukewarm to the political backlash. They favored maintenance of investor confidence and wanted no adverse publicity as they made fortunes from a surging stock market, takeover deals, and the boom in securitized debt. Organized labor regarded the appeals to financial market competitiveness as a stalking horse for unconstrained managerialism and a form of neoliberalism harmful to pension beneficiaries and workers. Public opinion, though having cooled from the searing rage of mid-2002, was still hostile to and distrustful of managerial and financial elites tainted by abuse of stock options and soaring CEO pay. Predictably, the backlash movement almost entirely failed to advance its policy agenda.

Yet the rhetoric of competitiveness and deregulation reflected a politics much more deeply rooted in policy and political discourse than was indicated by the post-Enron backlash. Its increasingly malign effects became manifest in the financial crisis of 2007–9. The pervasive regulatory failures described in chapter 6 enabled the American housing market bubble and the securitization, systematic mispricing, and global distribution of what turned out to be worthless debt. While the economy sputtered for most of the population, the financial sector boomed on cheap debt, soaring real estate prices, and increasingly complex and opaque securities. The limits and systemic deficiencies of corporate governance reform earlier in the decade became obvious with respect to the efficacy of accounting standards, risk management, and shareholder oversight of corporate finances and managerial pay. Large Wall Street investment banks, the envy of international finance for decades, were the worst offenders in poor risk management, the securitization and distribution of risky debt, and in rewarding their managerial employees profligately for short-term profits earned by exposing their firms to immense and in the end inescapable risks. Not only did the flaws of the earlier legal reforms become apparent but so too did the devastating consequences of the consistent undermining of public and private enforcement of shareholder rights by conservatives in Congress, the courts, and the executive branch during the second Bush administration. The conditions were perfect for a global financial conflagration beginning in the United States and engulfing the world. This leads us to a final reflection on the politics of corporate governance in light of the catastrophic global financial crisis of 2007–9 and ensuing Great Recession.

The stock market crashes and scandals of 2000–2002 were serious but containable through legal reforms (and in part by monetary policies that contributed to the housing bubble) that left the autonomy and privileged position of major financial institutions largely intact. This allowed them to support, or at least acquiesce in, reforms that would aid the recovery of the financial markets. The crisis of 2007–9, in contrast, implicated the very foundations of modern finance capitalism and the too-big-too-fail institutions at its core. A commensurate regulatory response would pose an existential threat to the financial sector and the business models of the major firms that survived. Under these conditions, the most powerful segments of the financial sector defected from its prior role as the pivotal constituency in a pro-reform coalition. Without the financial sector's long-term support, as in Germany during the 1990s through 2005, successful reform would have to take the form it did after Enron: politically conflictual, flawed, incomplete, but above all rapid.

A number of lessons can be learned from earlier corporate governance reforms. First, increased transparency and disclosure are necessary but not sufficient to correct the profound structural problems of financial markets and corporate governance. Moreover, intrusive administrative oversight of financial institutions and market participants is likely to be impracticable (and probably undesirable). Litigation-driven remedies face intense political opposition in both the United States and Germany and are arguably inadequate to the task. Litigation as an enforcement mechanism is expensive, fails to adequately compensate investors, and, as a retrospective sanction, can hardly undo the kind of damage done by serious flaws in financial markets and corporate governance. Notably, the reforms adopted or considered in both countries in the wake of the crisis did not include any significant expansion of litigation rights.

Reform must impose structural regulation that strengthens the governance role of corporate stakeholders, particularly institutional investors and employees, not only in controlling risk but also in preventing its externalization by managers. To be effective, these reforms must go beyond granting shareholders more direct influence over the composition of the board to revisit pension policy in order to revitalize the kinds of defined benefit funds that provide more patient capital and play a more active role in corporate governance, as opposed to defined contribution plans that tend towards passivity, hyperdiversification, and speculation.

Second, the politics of reform in the wake of the credit crisis is significantly different from that which drove earlier governance reforms. In the past, the financial sector was a driver and beneficiary of a policy agenda favoring the development and reinforcement of finance capitalism. Now, in the shadow of massive public bailouts, that sector will be the target of reforms. The dire circumstances of the global financial crisis created the conditions for far-reaching, and perhaps transformative, change in contemporary capitalism and for the further development of distinctive national models of finance capitalism as the United States loses much of its prestige and political economic leverage over other countries.

Third, a lesson from the past is that timing and speed are of the essence in pursuing reform, especially in political systems such as that in the United States with multiple veto points and little institutional capacity for long-term policy deliberation. Reformers must act quickly not only to help restore investor confidence but also before interest group and institutional veto-point politics reasserts itself and freezes the governmental machinery of policymaking. This inevitably entails risks because legal changes made in haste can cause unintended negative consequences. But arguments against rapid reform amid crisis are often really rooted in self-interested or ideological opposition to regulation and reform in general. The SEC's success in strengthening shareholder voting power reflects not only its rule-making capacities as an independent agency but its speed in pushing proxy voting reforms while the crisis was at its nadir.

Finally, the depth of the crisis of 2007–9 should teach a lesson in humility. Economic theories and sophisticated statistical modeling techniques that cultivated false certainties and real hubris among the political and financial elites have betrayed their devotees. There is a pressing need for cross-national cooperation and learning in matters of corporate and economic governance. In comparison with the fragmented regulatory structure of the United States,

German-style consolidation of financial regulation is now a model for emula-
tion, though its failure to prevent the banks' huge losses on CDOs sounds a
note of caution. Likewise, Germany's advocacy of more comprehensive financial regulation appears prescient after regulatory arbitrage led to the collapse
of the largely unregulated shadow banking system. The structural attributes of
Germany's postwar stakeholder-oriented governance regime appear more
attractive in light of the growing inequality and engulfing economic crisis produced by the Anglo-American market-driven form of finance capitalism. Yet
the relative merits of divergent governance regimes and forms of finance capitalism do not and will not determine the real politics and political limits of
regulatory change. These limits appear all the more striking, and threatening
to political legitimacy, in the harsh light cast by the global financial crisis and
the Great Recession that followed it.

What might arise from the crucible of crisis may yet amount to a grand
experiment in the reform of political economic organization and corporate
governance. The defects of the German and American models are not hard to
identify, and crisis may still provide a rare opportunity to confront them. With
the declining power and appeal of the American economic model and no
international consensus emerging on a new paradigm to replace it, alternative
national and regional models of capitalism are more likely than ever to evolve.
We are likely to see plural forms of finance capitalism, just as we saw with managerialism during the era of postwar industrial capitalism. But this evolution
will be difficult, convoluted, and contentious. If the domestic and international
reforms ultimately adopted fail to address the deep and pervasive flaws of
finance capitalism that drove the global economy to the verge of utter collapse,
we face the prospect that these structural features will generate another, even
more destructive crisis that will not offer a second chance to pursue reform.

REFERENCES

Abdelal, Rawi. 2007. *Capital Rules: The Construction of Global Finance*. Cambridge, MA: Harvard University Press.

Adams, Edward S. and John M. Matheson. 2000. "A Statutory Model for Corporate Constituency Concerns." *Emory Law Journal* 49(4): 1085–1135.

Addison, John T., Lutz Bellmann, and Joachim Wagner. 2004. "The Reform of the German Works Constitution Act: A Critical Assessment." *Industrial Relations* 43 (2): 392–420.

Adler, Joe. 2009. "In Reports on Failures, Regulators Also Fail." *American Banker*, April 15.

Allen, William T., Jack B. Jacobs, and Leo E. Strine, Jr. 2002. "The Great Takeover Debate: A Meditation on Bridging the Conceptual Divide." *University of Chicago Law Review* 69 (3): 1067–1100.

Alexander, Janet Cooper. 1991. "Do the Merits Matter? A Study of Settlements in Securities Class Actions." *Stanford Law Review* 43: 497–598.

American Law Institute. 1994. *Principles of Corporate Governance*. Philadelphia: American Law Institute.

Andrade, Gregor, Mark Mitchell, and Erik Stafford. 2001. "New Evidence and Perspectives on Mergers." *Journal of Economic Perspectives* 15: 103–20.

Aoki, Masahiko. 1994. "The Japanese Firm as a System of Attributes: A Survey and Research Agenda." In *The Japanese Firm: The Sources of Competitive Strength*, ed. Aoki, Masahiko and Ronald Dore, 11–40. Oxford: Oxford University Press.

Appelbaum, Binyamin, and David S. Hilzenrath. 2008. "SEC Didn't Act on Madoff Tips." *Washington Post*, December 16, sec. A, 1.

Aranow, Edward Ross, and Einhorn, Herbert A. 1959. "Proxy Regulation: Suggested Improvements." *George Washington Law Review* 28: 306.

Assmann, Heinz-Dieter. 1990. "Microcorporatist Structures in German Law on Groups of Companies." In *Regulating Corporate Groups in Europe*, ed. David Sugarman and Gunther Teubner, 317–54. Baden-Baden: Nomos Verlagsgesellschaft.

Avery, John W. 1996. "Securities Litigation Reform: The Long and Winding Road to the Private Securities Litigation Reform Act of 1995." *Business Lawyer* 51: 335.

Bainbridge, Stephen M. 2008. *The New Corporate Governance in Theory and Practice*. Oxford, UK: Oxford University Press.

Ball, Yvonne. 2007. "Do Tough Rules Deter Foreign IPO Listings in U.S.?" *Wall Street Journal*, Eastern edition, February 20, sec. C, 3.

Barber, Lionel, Bertrand Benoit, and Hugh Williamson. 2008. "Merkel Urges Eurozone to Show Way over Market Rules." *Financial Times*, June 11.

Barbier, Hans D. 2001a. "Germany's Intricate Web." *Frankfurter Allgemeine Zeitung*, July 9.

Barbier, Hans D. 2001b. "Schröder's Quandary." *Frankfurter Allgemeine Zeitung*, English edition, February 7.

Baums, Theodor. 1992. "Corporate Governance in Germany: The Role of Banks." *American Journal of Comparative Law* 40 (2): 503–26.

——. 2001. "Reforming German Corporate Governance: Inside a Law Making Process of a Very New Nature—An Interview with Professor Dr. Theodor Baums." *German Law Journal* 2 (12). http://www.germanlawjournal.com/article.php?id=43.

Baums, Theodor and Bernd Frick. 1998. "Co-determination in Germany: The Impact of Court Decisions on the Market Value of Firms." *Economic Analysis* 1 (2): 143–61.

Baums, Theodor, and Kenneth Scott. 2003. "Taking Shareholder Protection Seriously? Corporate Governance in the United States and Germany." Working Paper 199, Institute for Banking Law, Johann Wolfgang Goethe University.

BAWe (Bundesaufsichtsampt für den Wertpapierhandel). 1997. Annual Reports.

——. 1998. Annual Reports.

——. 1999. Annual Reports.

BBC. 1999. "Excerpts from Oskar Lafontaine's Statement." Media World Watch/BBC Monitoring, March 15. http://news.bbc.co.uk/1/hi/world/monitoring/296803.stm.

Bebchuk, Lucian Arye. 2007. "The Myth of the Shareholder Franchise." *Virginia Law Review* 93 (3): 675–732.

Bebchuk, Lucien Arye, and Jesse Fried. 2004. *Pay without Performance: The Unfulfilled Promise of Executive Compensation*. Cambridge, MA: Harvard University Press.

Bebchuk, Lucien Arye, and Mark J. Roe. 1999. "A Theory of Path Dependence in Corporate Governance and Ownership." *Stanford Law Review* 52(1): 127–70.

Bebchuk, Lucian Arye, and Holger Spamann. 2009. "Regulating Bankers' Pay" Discussion Paper 641, John M. Olin Discussion Paper Series, Harvard Law School.

Becht, Marco, Colin Mayer, and Hannes F. Wagner. 2007. "Where Do Firms Incorporate?" Working Paper 70, European Corporate Governance Network.

Beltratti, Andrea, and René M. Stulz. 2009. "Why Did Some Banks Perform Better during the Credit Crisis? A Cross-Country Study of the Impact of Governance and Regulation." Working Paper 2009-03-012, Fisher College of Business.

Benoit, Bertrand. 2007. "German Deputy Still Targets 'Locusts.'" *Financial Times*, February 14.

——. 2008. "US 'Will Lose Financial Superpower Status.'" *Financial Times*, September 25.

——. 2009. "Berlin Forced to Dilute Bad Bank Scheme." *Financial Times*, May 18.

Benoit, Bertrand, and James Wilson. 2008. "Köhler Attacks Markets 'Monster.'" *Financial Times*, May 14.

Berger, Suzanne, and Ronald Dore, eds. 1996. *National Diversity and Global Capitalism*. Ithaca: Cornell University Press.

Berle, Adolf A., and Gardiner C. Means. 1932. *The Modern Corporation and Private Property*. New York: Macmillan.

Betts, Paul. 2002. "Europe's Capitalists Survey a Level Playing Field." *Financial Times, May 31*, 13.

Betts, Paul, and Deborah Hargreaves. 2001. "No Way In." *Financial Times*, May 2.

Black, Bernard S., Brian R. Cheffins, and Michael Klausner. 2006. "Outside Director Liability." *Stanford Law Review* 58: 1055–1159.

———. 1995. *Ownership and Control: Rethinking Corporate Governance for the Twenty-First Century.* Washington, DC: Brookings Institution.

Blair, Margaret M., and Lynn A. Stout. 1999. "A Team Production Theory of Corporate Law," *Virginia Law Review* 85: 247–328.

Block, Dennis J., Nancy E. Barton, and Stephen A. Radin. 1998. *The Business Judgment Rule: Fiduciary Duties of Corporate Directors.* 5th ed., vol. 1. New York: Aspen.

Bok, Derek C. 1971. "Reflections on the Distinctive Character of American Labor Laws." *Harvard Law Review* 84 (6): 1394–1463.

Borrego, Anne Marie. 2007. "Germany: A Taste of Class Actions." *American Lawyer* 29 (1): S7.

Boyer, Robert. 2000. "Is a Finance-Led Growth Regime a Viable Alternative to Fordism?" *Economy and Society* 29 (1): 111–45.

Brand, Donald R. 1988. *Corporatism and the Rule of Law: A Study of the National Recovery Administration.* Ithaca: Cornell University Press.

Bratton, William W. 1994. "Public Values, Private Business, and U.S. Corporate Fiduciary Law." In *Corporate Control and Accountability: Changing Structures and the Dynamics of Regulation,* ed. Joseph McCahery, Sol Picciotto, and Colin Scott, 23–40. Oxford: Clarendon.

———. 1993. "Self-Regulation, Normative Choice, and the Structure of Corporate Fiduciary Law." *George Washington Law Review* 61: 1084–1129 (April).

———. 2007. "Is the Hostile Takeover Irrelevant?: A Look at the Evidence," Working Paper, Georgetown Law Center.

Bratton, William W., and Joseph A. McCahery. 2004. "The Equilibrium Content of Corporate Federalism." Georgetown Law and Econ. Research Paper 606481, Georgetown Law Center.

Bratton, William W., Joseph A. McCahery, and Erik P.M. Vermeulen. 2008. "How Does Corporate Mobility Affect Lawmaking? A Comparative Analysis." Working Paper 91, European Corporate Governance Institute.

Braude, Jonathan. 2001a. "Germany Approves New Takeover Code." *Daily Deal,* July 11.

———. 2001b. "Germany to Swallow Poison Pills." *Daily Deal,* November 14.

Braude, Jonathan, and Victorya Hong. 2001. "Takeover Directive Divides Germany." *Daily Deal,* May 23.

Brayton, Colin. 2005. "At Harvard, Hard Words on New Rules." *New Market Machines,* March 14.

Bushrod, Lisa. 2001a. "Buyouts: Still Awaiting a Boom." *European Venture Capital Journal,* November 1.

———. 2001b. "Germany and Takeover Codes," *European Venture Capital Journal,* November 1.

Buxbaum, Richard M. 1987. "Juridification and Legitimation Problems in American Enterprise Law." In *Juridification of Social Spheres: A Comparative Analysis in the Areas of Labor, Corporate, Antitrust and Social Welfare Law,* ed. Gunther Teubner, 241–72. Berlin: Walter de Gruyter.

Byrnes, Nanette. 2004. "Sarbanes-Oxley: The Struggle to Catch Up." *Business Week,* November 15.

Caiola, Eugene P. 2000. "Comment: Retroactive Legislative History: Scienter under the Uniform Security Litigation Standards Act of 1998." *Albany Law Review* 64: 309–59.

Calio, Joseph Evan, and Rafael Xavier Zahralddin. 1994. "The Securities and Exchange Commission's 1992 Proxy Amendments: Questions of Accountability." *Pace Law Review* 14: 459.

Callaghan, Helen and Martin Höpner. 2005. "European Integration and the Clash of Capitalisms: Political Cleavages over Takeover Liberalization." *Comparative European Politics* 3: 307–32.

Campbell, John L. 2004. *Institutional Change and Globalization*. Princeton: Princeton University Press.

Campos, Roel C. 2006. Speech by SEC Commissioner: Remarks before the Consumer Federation of America Financial Services Conference, U.S. Securities and Exchange Commission, Washington, DC, December 1.

Cary, William L. 1974. "Federalism and Corporate Law: Reflections upon Delaware." *Yale Law Journal* 83: 663–705.

Chandler, William B. III, and Leo E. Strine, Jr. 2003. "The New Federalism of the American Corporate Governance System: Preliminary Reflections of Two Residents of One Small State." *University of Pennsylvania Law Review* 152 (2): 953–1005.

Charkham, Jonathan P. 1994. *Keeping Good Company: A Study of Corporate Governance in Five Countries*. Oxford: Clarendon.

Cho, David. 2009. "Banks 'Too Big to Fail' Have Grown Even Bigger." *Washington Post*, August 28.

Cioffi, John W. 2000a. "Governing Globalization? The State, Law, and Structural Change in Corporate Governance." *British Journal of Law and Society* 27 (4): 572–600.

———. 2001. "The Collapse of the European Union Directive on Corporate Takeovers: The EU, National Politics, and the Limits of Integration." BRIE Discussion Paper, Berkeley Roundtable on the International Economy.

———. 2002. "Restructuring 'Germany, Inc.': The Corporate Governance Debate and the Politics of Company Law Reform." *Law & Policy* 24 (4): 355–402.

———. 2004a. "Review of Mark J. Roe, The Political Determinants of Corporate Governance: Political Context, Corporate Impact." *American Journal of Comparative Law* 52: 763–70.

———. 2004b. "The State of the Corporation: State Power, Politics, Policymaking and Corporate Governance in the United States, Germany, and France." In *Transatlantic Policymaking in an Age of Austerity*, ed. Martin Shapiro and Martin Levin, 253–97. Washington, DC: Georgetown University Press.

———. 2006a. "Building Finance Capitalism: The Regulatory Politics of Corporate Governance Reform in the United States and Germany." In *The State after Statism: New State Activities in the Age of Globalization and Liberalization*, ed. Jonah Levy, 185–229. Cambridge, MA: Harvard University Press.

———. 2006b. "Corporate Governance Reform, Regulatory Politics, and the Foundations of Finance Capitalism in the United States and Germany." *German Law Journal* 7 (6): 533–62.

———. 2007. "Revenge of the Law? Securities Litigation Reform and Sarbanes-Oxley's Structural Regulation of Corporate Governance." In *Creating Competitive Markets: The Politics and Economics of Regulatory Reform*, ed. Martin Levin, Martin Shapiro, and Mark Landy, 60–82. Washington, DC: Brookings Institution Press.

———. 2009. "Adversarialism vs Legalism: Juridification and Litigation in Corporate Governance Reform." *Regulation & Governance* 3: 235–58.

Cioffi, John W., and Martin Höpner. 2006a. "Das Parteipolitische Paradox des Finanzmarktkapitalismus: Aktionärsorientierte Reformen in Deutschland, Frankreich, Italien und den USA." *Politische Vierteljahresschrift* 47 (3): 419–40.

———. 2006b. "The Political Paradox of Finance Capitalism: Interests, Preferences, and Center-Left Politics in Corporate Governance Reform." *Politics & Society* 34 (4): 1–40.

CNNMoney.com. 2006. "Sarbanes-Oxley Faces Changes from U.S. group." September 12. http://www.cnnmoney.com.

Coffee, John C., Jr. 1988. "The Uncertain Case for Takeover Reform: An Essay on Stockholders, Stakeholders and Bust-Ups." *Wisconsin Law Review*: 435–65.

———. 1989. "The Mandatory/Enabling Balance in Corporate Law: An Essay on the Judicial Role." *Columbia Law Review* 89: 1618–91.

———. 1991. "Liquidity versus Control: The Institutional Investor as Corporate Monitor." *Columbia Law Review* 91: 1277–1367.

———. 2006. *Gatekeepers: The Professions and Corporate Governance.* Oxford: Oxford University Press.

Committee on Capital Markets Regulation. 2006. "Interim Report of the Committee on Capital Markets Regulation," November 30.

Congressional Oversight Panel. 2009. Special Report on Regulatory Reform. http://cop.senate.gov/documents/cop-012909–report-regulatoryreform.pdf.

Corbett, Deanne. 2005. "The Year of the Locust." *Deutsche Welle*, May 19.

Cox, James D., and Randall S. Thomas. 2009. "Mapping the American Shareholder Litigation Experience: A Survey of Empirical Studies of the Enforcement of the U.S. Securities Law." Law & Economics Research Paper 09-10, Vanderbilt University Law School.

Culpepper, Pepper D. 2010. *Quiet Politics and Business Power: Corporate Control in Europe and Japan.* Cambridge: Cambridge University Press.

Deeg, Richard. 1992. "Banks and the State in Germany: The Critical Role of Subnational Institutions in Economic Governance." PhD diss., Massachusetts Institute of Technology.

———. 1999. *Finance Capitalism Unveiled: Banks and the German Political Economy.* Ann Arbor: University of Michigan Press.

Dennis, Brady, and Robert O'Harrow, Jr. 2008. "A Crack in the System." *Washington Post*, December 30.

Deutsche Welle. 2009. "Finance Minister Steinbrueck Rules out 'Bad Bank' for Germany." January 19.

Deutscher Juristentag. 2002. "Recommendations" (64th Conference of German Jurists, Section on Economic Law). *Neue Zeitschrift für Gesellschaftsrecht* 5: 1006.

Donahue, Patrick. 2009. "Steinbrueck Drafts German 'Bad Bank' Financial Rescue Plan." Bloomberg, April 11.

Dore, Ronald. 2000. *Stock Market Capitalism: Welfare Capitalism: Japan and Germany versus the Anglo-Saxons.* Oxford: Oxford University Press.

Economist. 2001. "Farewell, fair disclosure?" February 8.

———. 2003. "The Grind of Consensus." August 30.

———. 2004. "404 tonnes of paper." December 16.

———. 2006a. "Down on the street." November 23.

———. 2006b. "What's Wrong with Wall Street." November 23.

———. 2008. "Fixing Finance." April 3.

Edelman, Lauren B., and Mark C. Suchman. 1997. "The Legal Environments of Organizations." *Annual Review of Sociology* 23: 479–515.

Edwards, Jeremy, and Klaus Fischer. 1996. *Banks, Finance, and Investment in Germany.* Cambridge: Cambridge University Press.

Eisenberg, Melvin. 1989. "The Structure of Corporation Law." *Columbia Law Review* 89: 1461–1525.

———. 1999. "The Conception That the Corporation Is a Nexus of Contracts, and the Dual Nature of the Firm." *Journal of Corporation Law* 24: 819–36.

Erkens, David, Mingyi Hung, and Pedro Matos. 2009. "Corporate Governance in the 2007–2008 Financial Crisis: Evidence from Financial Institutions Worldwide." Finance Working Paper 249/2009, European Corporate Governance Institute.

Estreicher, Samuel. 1994. "Employee Involvement and the 'Company Union' Prohibition: The Case for the Partial Repeal of Section 8(A)(2) of the NLRA," *New York University Law Review* 69: 125–61.

Fahlenbrach, Rüdiger, and René M. Stulz. 2009. "Bank CEO Incentives and the Credit Crisis." Working Paper 15212, National Bureau of Economic Research.

Faiola, Anthony, Ellen Nakashima, and Jill Drew. 2008. "What Went Wrong." *Washington Post*, October 15.

Farrell, Greg. 2009. "Cox Regime at SEC under fire." *Financial Times*, May 7.

Fickinger, Nico. 2001a. "Time for a Little Back-Scratching." *Frankfurter Allgemeine Zeitung*, English edition, February 13.

———. 2001b. "Workers' Council Legislation Gets to Parliament." *Frankfurter Allgemeine Zeitung*, English edition, April 5.

Financial News. 2001. "Hostile Bids Give Way to Millennium Sensitivities." June 11.

Fithin, Caspar. 2001. "European Union: Takeover Tensions." In *Perspective, The Oxford Analytica Weekly Column*. 24 May.

Fligstein. Neil D. 1990. *The Transformation of Corporate Control.* Cambridge, MA: Harvard University Press.

Fligstein, Neil D., and Jennifer Choo. 2005. "Law and Corporate Governance" *Annual Review of Law Social Science* 1: 61–84

Frankenberg, Günter. 1985. "Critical Comparisons: Re-thinking Comparative Law." *Harvard International Law Journal* 26: 411–55.

Frankfurter Allgemeine Zeitung. 2001. "Reorganization of Workers Councils Approved." June 22.

Franks, Julian, and Colin Mayer. 1998. "Bank Control, Takeovers, and Corporate Governance in Germany." *Journal of Banking and Finance* 22: 1385–1403.

Frenchman, Robert S. 1993. "Comment: The Recent Revisions to Federal Proxy Regulations: Lifting the Ban on Shareholder Communications." *Tulane Law Review* 68: 161–94.

Freshfields Bruckhaus Deringer. 2005. "Securities Litigation—A View from Germany." Berlin.

———. 2007. "Class Actions and Third Party Funding of Litigation: An Analysis across Europe." Berlin.

Galaskiewicz, Joseph. 1991. "Making Corporate Actors Accountable: Institution-Building in Minneapolis-St. Paul." In *The New Institutionalism in Organizational Analysis*, ed. Walter W. Powell and Paul J. DiMaggio, 293–310. Chicago: University of Chicago Press.

Geithner, Tim. 2009. "Statement by Treasury Secretary Tim Geithner on Compensation." United States Department of the Treasury Press Release, TG-163, June 10.

General Accounting Office of the United States. 2002. "Report to the Chairman, Committee on Banking, Housing, and Urban Affairs, U.S. Senate, Financial Statement Restatements: Trends, Impacts, Regulatory Responses and Remaining Challenges." GAO-03-13, October 2002.

German Panel on Corporate Governance. 2001. *Corporate Governance Rules for Quoted German Companies: Summary of Recommendations.* Sherman and Sterling, LLP Trans. Cologne: Verlag.

Gevurtz, Franklin. 2007. "Disney in a Comparative Light." Working Paper, McGeorge School of Law.

Glabus, Wolfgang. 2006. "'Excessive, Brazen and Tasteless'—Why Germans Are Angry at Their Top Managers." *Atlantic Times,* November.

———. 2007. "Rebellion against the Elite: *Germans Distrust Politicians and Managers." Atlantic Times*, February.

Glatner, Jonathan D. 2005. "Here It Comes: The Sarbanes-Oxley Backlash," *New York Times*, April 17.

Göhner, Reinhard, and Klaus Bräunig. 2004. "Modernizing Codetermination." Press Release by the BDA and BDI, Berlin.

Goldberg, Arthur J. 1972. "Debate on Outside Directors," *New York Times*, October 29, F1.

Goldschmid, Harvey J. 1973. "Symposium, The Greening of the Board Room: Reflections on Corporate Responsibility." *Columbia Journal of Law and Social Problems* 10: 17–28.

Goldthorpe, John H., ed. 1984. *Order and Conflict in Contemporary Capitalism*. Oxford: Clarendon.

Gordon, Greg. 2009. "Goldman Left Foreign Investors Holding the Subprime Bag." McClatchy Newspapers, November 3.

Gordon, Jeffrey N. 1989. "The Mandatory Structure of Corporate Law." *Columbia Law Review* 89: 1549–98.

Gourevitch, Peter. 1996. "The Macropolitics of Microinstitutional Differences in the Analysis of Comparative Capitalism." In *National Diversity and Global Capitalism*, ed. Suzanne Berger and Ronald Dore, 239–59. Ithaca: Cornell University Press.

Gourevitch, Peter, and James Shinn. 2005. *The Politics of Corporate Governance Regulation*. Princeton: Princeton University Press.

Graham, Carol, Robert E. Litan, and Sandip Sukhtankar. 2002. "Cooking the Books: The Cost to the Economy." *Brookings Policy Brief* 106, August.

Greenspan, Alan. 2002. Remarks before the Society of Business Economists, London, September 25.

Grundfest, Joseph A. 2009. "The SEC's Proposed Proxy Access Rules: Politics, Economics, and the Law." Working Paper 64, Rock Center for Corporate Governance, Stanford Law School.

Grundfest, Joseph A., and Michael A. Perino. 1997a. "Securities Litigation Reform: The First Year's Experience: A Statistical and Legal Analysis of Class Action Securities Fraud Litigation under the Private Securities Litigation Reform Act of 1995." Unpublished report, February 27. http://securities.stanford.edu/report/psira_yr1/.

———. 1997b. "Securities Litigation Reform: The First Year's Experience." *Annual Institute on Securities Regulation* 29 (1): 241–95.

Hacker, Jacob. 2005. "Policy Drift: The Hidden Politics of US Welfare State Retrenchment." In *Beyond Continuity: Institutional Change in Advanced Political Economies*, ed. Wolfgang Streeck and Kathleen Thelen, 40–82. New York: Oxford University Press.

Hall, Peter. 1986. *Governing the Economy*. Oxford: Oxford University Press.

Hall, Peter A., and Daniel Gingerich. 2004. "Varieties of Capitalism and Institutional Complementarities in the Macroeconomy: An Empirical Analysis." Discussion Paper 04/5, Max Planck Institute for the Study of Societies.

Hall, Peter A., and David Soskice. 2001. Introduction to *Varieties of Capitalism: The Institutional Foundations of Comparative Advantage*, ed. Peter A. Hall and David Soskice. Oxford: Oxford University Press.

Hansmann, Henry, and Reinier Kraakman. 2000. "The End of History for Corporate Law." In *Convergence and Persistence in Corporate Governance*. ed. Jeffrey Gordon and Mark J. Roe, 33–68. Cambridge: Cambridge University Press.

Hargreaves, Deborah. 2001. "Germany Backs Out of EU Corporate Takeover Accord." *Financial Times*, May 1.

Hart, David M. 2004. "Business Is Not an Interest Group: On the Study of Companies in American National Politics." *Annual Review of Political Science* 7: 47–69.

Harvard Law Review. 2000. "Class Action Reform: An Assessment of Recent Judicial Decisions and Legislative Initiatives." 113: 1806–27.

Heinze, Rolf G., and Christoph Strünck, Contracting out Corporatism: The Making of a Sustainable Social Model in Germany," paper delivered at the Progressive Governance Conference, London, July 11–13, 2003.

Helleiner, Eric. 1994. *States and the Reemergence of Global Finance: From Bretton Woods to the 1990s*. Ithaca: Cornell University Press.

High Level Group of Company Law Experts. 2002. "Report on Issues Related to Takeover Bids," Brussels, January 10, http://ec.europa.eu/internal_market/company/docs/takeoverbids/2002-01-hlg-report_en.pdf.

Hilferding, Rudolf. 1910/1981. *Finance Capital: A Study of the Latest Phase of Capitalist Development*. Trans. Morris Watnick and Sam Gordon. London: Routledge and Kegan Paul.

Hill, Andrew, and Adrian Michaels. 2002. "Big Names in Bid to Revive Faith in Business." *Financial Times*, June 19.

Hill, Jonathan. 1989. "Comparative Law, Law Reform and Legal Theory." *Oxford Journal of Legal Studies* 9(1): 101–15.

Hirschman, Albert O. 1970/1981. *Exit, Voice, and Loyalty: Responses to Decline in Firms, Organizations, and States*. Cambridge, MA: Harvard University Press.

Hobday, Nicola. 2001. "German Takeover Law Seen as Buyout Boost." *Daily Deal*, November 14.

Holloway, Nigel. 2001. "The End of Germany AG." Forbes, June 11.

Hong, Victorya. 2001. "Vote on European Takeover Law Heats Up," *Daily Deal*. July 2.

Höpner, Martin. 2003. "European Corporate Governance Reform and the German Party Paradox." Working Paper 03.1, Max-Planck-Institute for the Study of Societies.

Höpner, Martin and Gregory Jackson. 2001. "An Emerging Market for Corporate Control? The Mannesmann Takeover and German Corporate Governance." Discussion Paper 01/4, Max-Planck-Institute for the Study of Societies.

Höpner, Martin, and Lothar Krempel. 2004. "The Politics of the German Company Network." *Competition and Change* 8 (4): 339–56.

Horowitz, Morton J. 1992. *The Transformation of American Law, 1870–1960: The Crisis of Legal Orthodoxy*. New York: Oxford University Press.

Hurst, James Willard. 1970. *The Legitimacy of the Business Corporation in the Law of the United States, 1780–1970*. Charlottesville: University Press of Virginia.

Hyde, Alan. 1993. "Employee Caucus: A Key Institution in the Emerging System of Employment Law." *Chicago-Kent Law Review* 69: 149–93.

IMF (International Monetary Fund). 2009. "Global Financial Stability Report: Responding to the Financial Crisis and Measuring Systemic Risks, Summary Version." April.

IMF Fiscal Affairs Department. 2009. "The State of Public Finances: Outlook and Medium-Term Policies After the 2008 Crisis." March 6.

Investor Responsibility Research Center. 1996. *Board Practices 1996: The Structure and Compensation of Board of Directors in S&P 500 Companies*. Washington, DC: IRRC.

Ip, Greg, Kara Scannell, and Deborah Solomon. 2007. "In Call to Deregulate Business, a Global Twist; Onerous Rules Hurt U.S. Stock Markets, But So Do New Rivals," *Wall Street Journal*, January 25, A.1.

Jackson, Gregory. 2001. "The Origins of Nonliberal Corporate Governance in Germany and Japan." In *The Origins of Nonliberal Capitalism: Germany and Japan in Comparison*, ed. Wolfgang Streeck and Kozo Yamamura, 121–99. Ithaca: Cornell University Press.

——. 2003. "Corporate Governance in Germany and Japan: Liberalization Pressures and Responses during the 1990s." In *The End of Diversity? Prospects for German and Japanese Capitalism*, ed. Kozo Yamamura and Wolfgang Streeck, 261–305. Ithaca: Cornell University Press, 2003.

——. 2009. "Understanding Corporate Governance in the United States: An Historical and Theoretical Reassessment." Report to the Hans-Boeckler-Foundation.

Jenkinson, Tim J., and Alexander P. Ljungqvist. 2001. "The Role of Hostile Stakes in German Corporate Governance." *Journal of Corporate Finance* 7: 397–446.

Jensen, Michael C., and William H. Meckling. 1976. "Theory of the Firm: Managerial Behavior, Agency Costs, and Ownership Structure." *Journal of Financial Economics* 3: 305–60.

Johnson, Carrie. 2006. "Report on Corporate Rules Is Assailed: Panel's Business Ties Spark Outcry." *Washington Post*, December 1, D1.

Kagan, Robert A. 1991. "Adversarial Legalism and American Government." *Journal of Policy Analysis & Management* 10: 369–406.

———. 1997. "Should Europe Worry about Adversarial Legalism?" *Oxford Journal of Legal Studies* 17 (2): 165–83.

———. 2001. *Adversarial Legalism: The American Way of Law*. Cambridge, MA: Harvard University Press.

Kamba, W. J. 1974. "Comparative Law: A Theoretical Framework." *International and Comparative Law Quarterly* 23: 485–519.

Karmel, Roberta S. 2005. "Realizing the Dream of William O. Douglas—The Securities and Exchange Commission Takes Charge of Corporate Governance." *Delaware Journal of Corporate Law* 30: 79–144.

Katz, David M. 2006. "Happy Birthday, Sarbox!" July 28. http://CFO.com.

Katzenstein, Peter J. 1987. *Policy and Politics in West Germany: The Growth of a Semisovereign State*. Philadelphia: Temple University Press.

———. 1985. *Small States in World Markets: Industrial Policy in Europe*. Ithaca, NY: Cornell University Press.

Keleman, Daniel R., and Eric C. Sibbitt. 2004. "The Globalization of American Law." *International Organization* 58 (1): 103–36.

Kelleher, Leslie M. 1998. "'Substantive Rights' (in the Rules Enabling Act) More Seriously." *Notre Dame Law Review* 74: 47–121.

Klages, Philipp. 2007. "The Contractual Turn: How Legal Academics Shaped Corporate Law Reforms in Germany." Paper presented at the Annual Meeting of the Law and Society Association. Humboldt-University, Berlin. July 25.

Kitschelt, Herbert, Peter Lange, Gary Marks, and John D. Stephens, eds. 1999. *Continuity and Change in Contemporary Capitalism*. Cambridge: Cambridge University Press.

Köke, Jens. 2001. "Control Transfers in Corporate Germany: Their Frequency, Causes and Consequences." Discussion Paper 00-67, Centre for European Economic Research, Mannheim, Germany.

Korn/Ferry International. 1993. 20th Annual Board of Directors Study. New York.

KPMG Audit Committee Institute. 2006. "Audit Committees Refocus on Setting Their Agenda, Now That Section 404 Compliance Is in Place, ACI Survey Finds." *Directors & Boards*, July.

Kraakman, Renier R., Paul Davies, Henry Hansmann, Gerald Hertig, Klaus J. Hopt, Hideki Kanda, and Edward B. Rock. 2004. *The Anatomy of Corporate Law: A Comparative and Functional Approach*. Oxford: Oxford University Press.

Krause, Klaus Peter. 2001. "Shareholders May Soon Have the Right to Block Takeovers in Advance." *Frankfurter Allgemeine Zeitung*, May 8.

Kübler, Friedrich. 1987. "Juridification of Corporate Structures." In *Juridification of Social Spheres: A Comparative Analysis in the Areas of Labor, Corporate, Antitrust and Social Welfare Law*, ed. Gunther Teubner, 211–40. Berlin: Walter de Gruyter.

Labaton, Stephen. 2006a. "Businesses Seek Protection from Litigation." *New York Times*, October 29.

———. 2006b. "Dodd's Balancing Act to Get Tougher." *New York Times*, November 22.

———. 2008. "Agency's '04 Rule Lets Banks Pile Up New Debt." *New York Times*, October 3.

La Porta, Raphael, Florencio Lopez-de-Silanes, and Andrei Shleifer. 2006. "What Works in Securities Laws?" *Journal of Finance* 61: 1–32.

Lazonick, William. 1997. "Finance and Industrial Development: Japan and Germany." *Financial History Review* 4: 113–34.

Lazonick, William, and Mary O'Sullivan. 2000. "Maximizing Shareholder Value: A New Ideology for Corporate Governance." *Economy and Society* 29: 13–36.

Lederer, Philipp. 2006. "A Comparative Analysis of the Liability of Non-executive Directors in the UK and of Members of the Supervisory Board in Germany." *European Business Law Review* 17 (6): 1575–1613.

Lee, Orlan. 1983. "Freedom of Speech vs. Loyalty to the Firm and Co-Workers: Issues Involving Co-Determination, Employee Participation in Management, and Labor Peace in German Decisions on Dismissal for Injecting Partisan Politics into the Workplace." *Journal of International Law and Policy* 16: 45.

Legal Week. 2009. "Questions Raised as Politics Hits German Pay Law." June 25.

Lehmbruch, Gerhard. 2001. "The Institutional Embedding of Market Economies: The German 'Model' and Its Impact on Japan." In *The Origins of Nonliberal Capitalism: Germany and Japan in Comparison*, ed. Wolfgang Streeck and Kozo Yamamura, 39–93. Ithaca: Cornell University Press.

Lehne, Klaus-Heiner. 2001. "Takeover Agreement Rejected after Tied Vote." Report on Takeover Bids—Proposal for a 13th Council Directive (Press Release), Doc.: A5-0237/2001, July 3–4.

Levitt, Arthur, with Paula Dwyer. 2003. *Take On the Street: How to Fight for Your Financial Future.* New York: Vintage.

Levy, Jonah, ed. 2006. *The State after Statism: New State Activities in the Age of Globalization and Liberalization.* Cambridge, MA: Harvard University Press.

Levy, Jonah, Robert A. Kagan, and John Zysman. 1999. "The Twin Restorations: The Political Economy of the Reagan and Thatcher 'Revolution.'" In *Ten Paradigms of Market Economies and Land Systems*, ed. Lee-Jay Cho and Y. H. Kim. Seoul: Korea Development Institute, 1999.

Levi-Faur, David. 2005. "The Global Diffusion of Regulatory Capitalism." *The Annals of the American Academy of Political and Social Science* 598 (1): 12–32.

Levi-Faur, David, and Jacint Jordana, eds. 2005. *The Rise of Regulatory Capitalism: The Global Diffusion of a New Order.* Newberry Park, CA: Sage.

Licht, Amir N. 2001. "The Mother of All Path Dependencies: Toward a Cross-Cultural Theory of Corporate Governance Systems." *Delaware Journal of Corporate Law* 26: 147–205.

Lipton, Eric, "Gramm and the 'Enron Loophole'." *New York Times*, Nov. 17, 2008.

Lipton, Eric, and Stephen Labaton, "Deregulator Looks Back, Unswayed." *New York Times*, Nov. 17, 2008.

Loss, Louis. 1961. *Securities Regulation.* 2nd ed., vol. 1. Boston: Little, Brown.

Lütz, Susanne. 1998. "The Revival of the Nation-State? Stock Exchange Regulation in an Era of Globalized Financial Markets." *Journal of European Public Policy* 5 (1): 153–69.

———. 2000. "From Managed to Market Capitalism? German Finance in Transition." *German Politics* 9 (2): 149–71.

———. 2005. "The Finance Sector in Transition: A Motor for Economic Reform?" *German Politics* 14 (2): 140–56.

Lütz, Susanne, and Richard Deeg. 2000. "Internationalization and Financial Federalism: The United States and Germany at the Crossroads?" *Comparative Political Studies* 33 (3): 374–405.

Lütz, Susanne, and Dagmar Eberle. 2007. "On the Road to Anglo-Saxon Capitalism? German Corporate Governance Regulation between Market and Multilevel Governance." Research Paper 4/2007, Comparative Law and Political Economy Working Paper Series, Osgoode School of Law, York University.

Mabe, William. 2004. "Globalization and Corporate Governance—The Effect of Capital Mobility on Financial Disclosure Laws in Developed Countries." Paper delivered at the American Political Science Association annual meeting, September.

Marens, Richard. 2004. "Waiting for the North to Rise: Revisiting Barber and Rifkin after a Generation of Union Financial Activism in the U.S." *Journal of Business Ethics* 52 (1): 109–23.

McCraw, Thomas K. 1984. *Prophets of Regulation: Charles Francis Adams, Louis D. Brandeis, James M. Landis, and Alfred E. Kahn.* Cambridge, MA: Belknap Press of Harvard University Press, 1984.

McCreevy, Charlie. 2007. Speech by Commissioner McCreevy at the European Parliament's Legal Affairs Committee, European Commissioner for Internal Market and Services, SPEECH/07/592, Brussels, October 3.

McDonald, Elizabeth. 2006a. "Stock Market Brawl." Forbes, November 2. http://www. Forbes.com.

——. 2006b. "Waiting On Sarb-Ox Reform." Forbes, November 9. http://www.forbes. com.

McDonnell, Brett H. 2003. SOx Appeals, University of Minnesota Law School Legal Studies Research Paper Series, Research Paper No. 04-7 (draft dated December 18, 2003). http://ssrn.com/abstract=497422.

McKinnon, John D., and Christopher Conkey. 2007. "Bush Gives Hope to Foes of Sarbanes-Oxley Law; President Offers Political Cover for Easing Burden on Business, but Joins Executive-Pay Critics." *Wall Street Journal,* February 1, A 4.

Milhaupt, Curtis J., and Katharina Pistor. 2008. *Law and Capitalism: What Corporate Crises Reveal about Legal Systems and Economic Development around the World.* Chicago: University of Chicago Press, 2008.

Millstein, Ira M. 1998. *Corporate Governance: Improving Competitiveness and Access to Capital in Global Markets, A Report to the OECD by the Business Advisory Group on Corporate Governance.* Paris: OECD.

Minow, Nell. 1991. "Proxy Reform: The Case for Increased Shareholder Communication." *Journal of Corporation Law* 17: 149.

Mitchell, Mark L., and J. Harold Mulherin. 1996. "The Impact of Industry Shocks on Takeover and Restructuring Activity." *Journal of Financial Economics* 41: 193–229.

Montgomery, Lori, and Paul Kane. 2008. "Lawmakers Reach Accord on Huge Financial Rescue." *Washington Post*, September 28.

Moran, Michael. 1991. *The Politics of the Financial Services Revolution: The USA, UK, and Japan.* New York: St. Martin's.

Mülbert, Peter O. 1998. "Bank Equity Holdings in Non-Financial Firms and Corporate Governance." In *Comparative Corporate Governance: The State of the Art and Current Research,* ed. Klaus J. Hopt, Hideki Kanda, Mark J. Roe, Eddy Wymeersch, and Stefan Prigge, 445–564. New York: Oxford University Press.

Müller-Jentsch, Walthier. 1995. "Germany: From Collective Voice to Co-Management." In *Works Councils: Consultation, Representation, and Cooperation in Industrial Relations,* ed. Joel Rogers and Wolfgang Streeck, 53–78. Chicago: University of Chicago Press.

Nakamoto, Michiyo, and David Wighton. 2007. "Citigroup Chief Stays Bullish on Buyouts." *Financial Times,* July 9.

New York Times. 2009. "From Here to Retirement." Editorial, January 26.

Noack, Ulrich, and Dirk Zetzsche. 2005. "Corporate Governance Reform in Germany: The Second Decade." *European Business Law Review* 16 (5): 1033–64.

Nocera, Joe. 2009. "Propping Up a House of Cards." *New York Times,* February 28.

North, Douglas. 1990. *Institutions, Institutional Change and Economic Performance.* Cambridge: Cambridge University Press.

Norris, Floyd. 2004. "On Two Continents, Companies Ask Politicians for Accounting Favors," *New York Times*, June 18.

———. 2006. "Panel of Executives and Academics to Consider Regulation and Competitiveness." *New York Times*, September 13.

Nussbaum, Artur. 1935. "American and Foreign Stock Exchange Legislation." *Virginia Law Review* 21 (8): 839–75.

O'Brien, Richard. 1992. *Global Financial Integration: The End of Geography*. London: Pinter Publishers.

O'Harrow Jr., Robert, and Brady Dennis. 2008a. "The Beautiful Machine." *Washington Post*, December 29.

———. 2008b. "Downgrades and Downfall." *Washington Post*, December 31.

Organization for Economic Cooperation and Development, Ad Hoc Task Force on Corporate Governance. 1999. *OECD Principles of Corporate Governance*. Paris: OECD.

O'Sullivan, Mary. 2000. *Contests for Corporate Control: Corporate Governance and Economic Performance in the United States and Germany*. Oxford: Oxford University Press.

Oxford Analytica. 2009. "US/UK: Market Crash Accelerates DB Pensions Decline." June 22.

Paredes, Troy A. 2009. "Statement at Open Meeting to Propose Amendments regarding Facilitating Shareholder Nominations." May 20. www.sec.gov/news/speech/2009/spch052009tap.htm.

Paulson, Henry M. 2008. Remarks by Treasury Secretary Henry M. Paulson on the Competitiveness of U.S. Capital Markets. Economic Club of New York, November 20. http://www.treasury.gov/press/releases/hp174.htm.

Peterson, Jonathan. 2004a. "SEC Split on Aiding Investor Challenges." *Los Angeles Times*, March 8.

———. 2004b. "Shareholder Plan a Flash Point for SEC." *Los Angeles Times*, July 13.

———. 2004c. "Shareholder Proposal Is Stalled at SEC." *Los Angeles Times*, October 9.

———. 2004d. "Will There Be a Shift at the SEC?" *Los Angeles Times*, November 4.

Pierson, Paul. 2004. *Politics in Time: History, Institutions, and Social Analysis*. Princeton: Princeton University Press.

Pistor, Katharina. 2006. "Legal Ground Rules in Coordinated and Liberal Market Economies." In *Corporate Governance in Context: Corporations, States and Markets in Europe, Japan, and the United States*, ed. Klaus Hopt, Eddy Wymeersch, Hideki Kanda, and Harald Baum, 249–80. Oxford: Oxford University Press.

Polanyi, Karl. 1944/1957. *The Great Transformation: The Political and Economic Origins of Our Time*. Boston: Beacon Press.

Pontusson, Jonas. 2005. *Inequality and Prosperity: Social Europe vs. Liberal America*. Ithaca: Cornell University Press.

Porter, Michael. 1990. *The Competitive Advantage of Nations*. New York: Free Press.

Pound, John. 1993. "The Rise of the Political Model of Corporate Governance and Corporate Control." *New York University Law Review* 68: 1003.

Powell, Walter W. 1991. "Expanding the Scope of Institutional Analysis." In *The New Institutionalism in Organizational Analysis*, ed. Walter W. Powell and Paul J. DiMaggio, 183–203. Chicago: University of Chicago Press.

Prantl, Heribert. 2005. "Fraying at the Edges. Social Democracy Has Lost the Link to Its Original Constituency." *Atlantic Times*, August.

PricewaterhouseCoopers. 2003. "Senior Executives Less Favorable on Sarbanes-Oxley, PricewaterhouseCoopers Finds." *Management Barometer*, July 23. http://www.barometersurveys.com/.

Prigge, Stefan. 1998. "A Survey of German Corporate Governance." In *Comparative Corporate Governance: The State of the Art and Current Research*, ed. Klaus J. Hopt, Hideki

Kanda, Mark J. Roe, Eddy Wymeersch, and Stefan Prigge, 943–1044. New York: Oxford University Press.

Rajan, Raghuram G., and Luigi Zingales. 2004. *Saving Capitalism from the Capitalists: Unleashing the Power of Financial Markets to Create Wealth and Spread Opportunity*. Princeton: Princeton University Press.

Reddy, Sudeep, and Jon Hilsenrath. 2008. "The Government Stood Firm. Was It the Right Call?" *Wall Street Journal*, September 15.

Roberts, Dan. 2004. "Sarbanes-Oxley Compliance Costs Average $5m." *Financial Times*, November 12.

Roe, Mark J. 1991. "A Political Theory of American Corporate Finance." *Columbia Law Review* 91: 10–67.

———. 1993. "Takeover Politics." In *The Deal Decade: What Takeovers Mean for Corporate Governance*, ed. Margaret Blair, 321–53. Washington, DC: Brookings Institution.

———. 1994. Strong Managers, *Weak Owners: The Political Roots of American Corporate Finance*. Princeton: Princeton University Press.

———. 1995. "Path Dependency, Political Options, and Governance Systems." In *Comparative Corporate Governance: Essays and Materials*, ed. Klaus J. Hopt and Eddy Wymeersch, 165–84. Berlin and New York: Walter de Gruyter.

———. 1996. "From Antitrust to Corporate Governance? The Corporation and the Law." In *The American Corporation Today*, ed. Carl Kaysen, 102–27. New York: Oxford University Press.

———. 1998. "Codetermination and German Securities Markets." In *Comparative Corporate Governance: The State of the Art and Current Research*, ed. Klaus J. Hopt, Hideki Kanda, Mark J. Roe, Eddy Wymeersch, and Stefan Prigge, 361–72. New York: Oxford University Press.

———. 2003a. "Delaware's Competition." *Harvard Law Review* 113: 588–646.

———. 2003b. *The Political Determinants of Corporate Governance: Political Context, Corporate Impact*. Oxford: Oxford University Press.

Rogers, Joel. 1990. "Divide and Conquer: Further 'Reflections on the Distinctive Character of American Labor Laws." *Wisconsin Law Review* 1: 1.

Rohatyn, Felix G. 2002. "The Betrayal of Capitalism." *New York Review of Books*, February 28.

Romano, Roberta. 1987. "The Political Economy of Takeover Statutes." *Virginia Law Review* 73 (1): 111–99.

———. 2005. "The Sarbanes-Oxley Act and the Making of Quack Corporate Governance." *Yale Law Journal* 114: 1521–1611.

Ruggie, John Gerard. 1982. "International Regimes, Transactions, and Change: Embedded Liberalism in the Postwar Economic Order." *International Organization* 36: 379–415.

Sadowski, Dieter, Joachim Junkes, and Sabine Lindenthal. 2000. "The German Model of Corporate and Labor Governance." *Comparative Labor Law and Policy Journal* 22: 33–66.

Samuel, Henry, and Toby Harnden. 2009. "G20 Summit: Barack Obama Conciliatory over Nicolas Sarkozy's Walkout Threat." *Telegraph*, UK, March 31.

Sanger, David E., and Mark Landler. 2009. "In Europe, Obama Faces Calls for Rules on Finances." *New York Times*, April 2.

Scannell, Kara. 2009. "Corporate News: Policy Makers Work to Give Shareholders More Boardroom Clout." *Wall Street Journal*, March 26.

Scannell, Kara, and Susanne Craig. 2008. "SEC Chief under Fire as Fed Seeks Bigger Wall Street Role." *Wall Street Journal*, June 23.

Schattschneider, E. E. 1963. *Politics, Pressure, and the Tariff*. Hamden, CT: Archon Books.

Schroeder, Michael. 2003. "Corporate Reform: The First Year: Cleaner Living, No Easy Riches; Critics Say Sarbanes-Oxley Law Hobbles Stocks, Chills Risk Taking, But Upshot Is Far Less Dramatic." *Wall Street Journal,* July 22.

Schulten, Thorsten. 2001a. "Government Adopts Draft Bill on Reform of Works Constitution Act." *European Industrial Relations Observatory On-Line,* DE0103221N, March 20. http://www.eiro.eurofound.ie/2001/03/inbrief/DE0103221N.html.

——. 2001b. "Reform of Works Constitution Act Proposed." *European Industrial Relations Observatory On-Line,* DE0102242F, February 9. http://www.eiro.eurofound.ie/2001/02/feature/DE0102242F.html.

Schwab, Stewart, and Randall S. Thomas. 1998. "Realigning Corporate Governance: Shareholder Activism by Labor Unions." *Michigan Law Review* 96: 1018–94.

Securities Regulation and Law Reporter. 1995. "Congress Overwhelmingly Passes Bill to Reform Private Securities Litigation." 27: 1899.

Seibert, Ulrich. 1999. "Control and Transparency in Business (KonTraG): Corporate Governance Reform in Germany." *European Business Law Review* 10 (1–2): 70–75.

——. 2002. "Aktienrechtsreform in 'Permanenz'?" *Die Aktiengesellschaft* 47 (8): 417–40.

Seligman, Joel. 1996. "The Private Securities Reform Act of 1995." *Arizona Law Review* 38: 717–37.

——. 2003. *The Transformation of Wall Street.* 3rd ed. New York: Aspen.

Shapiro, Martin. 1972. "From Public Law to Public Policy, or the 'Public' in 'Public Law.'" *Political Science & Politics* 5: 410–18.

Shleifer, Andrei, and Lawrence H. Summers. 1988. "Breach of Trust in Hostile Takeovers." In *Corporate Takeovers: Causes and Consequences,* ed. Alan J. Auerbach, 33–68. Chicago: University of Chicago Press.

Shonfield, Andrew. 1965. *Modern Capitalism: The Changing Balance of Public and Private Power.* Oxford: Oxford University Press.

SIGTARP (Special Inspector General, Troubled Asset Relief Program). 2009a. Quarterly Report to Congress, July 21.

——. 2009b. Quarterly Report to Congress, October 1.

Simonian, Haig. 2001. "Berlin Bows to Pressure." *Financial Times,* May 2.

Sims, G. Thomas. 2007. "Germany Fights Lonely Battle to Rein In Hedge Funds." *International Herald Tribune,* May 17.

Sjostrom, Jr., William K. 2009. "The AIG Bailout." *Washington and Lee Law Review* 66: 943–91.

Smith, Rogers M. 1988. "Political Jurisprudence, The "New Institutionalism," and the Future of Public Law." *American Political Science Review* 82 (1): 89–108.

Solomon, Deborah, Dennis K. Berman, Susanne Craig, and Carrick Mollenkamp. 2008. "Ultimatum by Paulson Sparked Frantic End." *Wall Street Journal,* September 15.

Sommer, Theo. 2005. "Voters Have Lost Confidence. Germans Believe That No Future Government Will Solve the Country's Problems." *Atlantic Times,* August.

Soskice, David. 1991. "The Institutional Infrastructure for International Competitiveness: A Comparative Analysis of the U.K. and Germany." In *The Economics of the New Europe,* ed. A. B. Atkinson and Renato Brunetta. London: Macmillan.

——. 1999. "Divergent Production Regimes: Coordinated and Uncoordinated Market Economies in the 1980s and 1990s. " In *Continuity and Change in Contemporary Capitalism,* ed. Herbert Kitschelt, Peter Lange, Gary Marks, and John D. Stephens, 101–34. Cambridge: Cambridge University Press.

Spiegel Online International. 2009. "German Banks Are on the Edge of the Abyss," January 23. www.spiegel.de/international/business/0,1518,603181,00.html

Spinner, Jackie. 2003. "FASB Chief Says Congress Is Meddling." *Washington Post,* June 4, 2003, p. E03.

Sporkin, Stanley. 1977. "A Bill of Rights for Investors," *BNA Securities Reporter*, May 11, G1–G2.

Steinmo, Sven, Kathleen Thelen, and Frank Longstreth, eds. 1992. *Structuring Politics: Historical Institutionalism in Comparative Analysis*. Cambridge: Cambridge University Press.

Stevenson, Richard W., and Alison Mitchell. 2002. "Parties Maneuver over Risks in Growing Business Scandal." *New York Times*, June 28.

Stone, Amey. 2005. "SOX: Not So Bad After All?" *Business Week*, August 1.

Strange, Susan. 1996. *The Retreat of the State: The Diffusion of Power in the World Economy*. New York: Cambridge University Press.

——. 1998. *Mad Money: When Markets Outgrow Governments*. Ann Arbor: University of Michigan Press.

Streeck, Wolfgang. 1984. "Co-determination: The Fourth Decade." In *International Perspectives on Organizational Democracy*, vol. 2, ed. Bernhard Wilpert and Arndt Sorge, 391-422. London: John Wiley & Sons.

——. 1990. "Status and Contract: Basic Categories of a Sociological Theory of Industrial Relations." In *Regulating Corporate Groups in Europe*, ed. David Sugarman and Gunther Teubner, 105–45. Baden-Baden: Nomos Verlagsgesellschaft.

——. 1991. "On the Institutional Conditions of Diversified Quality Production." In *Beyond Keynesianism: The Socio-Economics of Production and Full Employment*, ed. Wolfgang Streeck and Egon Matzner, 21–61. Brookfield, MA: Edward Elgar.

——. 1992. "Codetermination after Four Decades." In *Social Institutions and Economic Performance: Studies of Industrial Relations in Advanced Capitalism*, ed. Wolfgang Streeck, 137–68. London: Sage.

——. 1997. "German Capitalism—Does It Exist? Can It Survive?" In *Political Economy of Modern Capitalism*, ed. Wolfgang Streeck and Colin Crouch, 33–54. London: Sage.

——. 2003. "From State Weakness as Strength to State Weakness as Weakness: Welfare Corporatism and the Private Use of the Public Interest." MPIfG Working Paper 03/2, Max Planck Institute for the Study of Societies (March).

Streeck, Wolfgang, and Kathleen Thelen, eds. 2005. *Beyond Continuity: Institutional Change in Advanced Political Economies*. Oxford: Oxford University Press.

Streeck, Wolfgang, and Kozo Yamamura, eds. 2001. *The Origins of Nonliberal Capitalism: Germany and Japan in Comparison*. Ithaca: Cornell University Press.

Summers, Clyde W. 1993. "Employee Voice and Employer Choice: A Structured Exception to Section 8(A)(2)." *Chicago-Kent Law Review, Symposium on the Legal Future of Employee Representation* 69: 129–48.

Summers, Lawrence H., Alan Greenspan, Arthur Levitt, and William J. Rainer. 1999. "Over-the-Counter Derivatives Markets and the Commodity Exchange Act: Report of the President's Working Group on Financial Markets." November 9.

Suskind, Ron. 2004. *The Price of Loyalty: George W. Bush, the White House, and the Education of Paul O'Neill*. New York: Simon and Schuster.

Taub, Stephen. 2006. "Paulson: Regs Went Too Far." August 1. http://www.cfo.com/article. cfm/7244995.

Tett, Gillian. 2009. *Fool's Gold: How the Bold Dream of a Small Tribe at J.P. Morgan Was Corrupted by Wall Street Greed and Unleashed a Catastrophe*. New York: Simon & Schuster.

Teubner, Gunther. 1985. "Corporate Fiduciary Duties and their Beneficiaries: A Functional Approach to the Legal Institutionalization of Corporate Responsibility." In *Corporate Governance and Directors' Liabilities: Legal, Economic, and Sociological Analyses on Corporate Social Responsibility*, ed. Klaus J. Hopt and Gunther Teubner, 149–77. Berlin: de Gruyter.

Thelen, Kathleen A. 1991. *Union of Parts: Labor Politics in Postwar Germany*. Ithaca: Cornell University Press.

———. 2002. "How Institutions Evolve: Insights from Comparative-Historical Analysis." In *Comparative-Historical Analysis: Innovations in Theory and Method,* ed. James Mahoney and Dietrich Rueschemeyer, 208–40. Cambridge: Cambridge University Press.

Tiberghien, Yves. 2007. *Entrepreneurial States: Reforming Corporate Governance in France, Japan, and Korean.* Ithaca: Cornell University Press.

Timmermans, Christiaan. 2003. "Harmonization in the Future of Company Law in Europe." In *Company Law and Financial Markets,* ed. Klaus J. Hopt and Eddy Wymeersch. New York: Oxford University Press.

Tison, Michel. 1999. "The Investment Services Directive and Its Implementation in the EU Member States." Working Paper 1999-17, Financial Law Institute, Universiteit Ghent.

Tringham, Melanie. 2000. "Bid Battles Under Attack." *Times of London,* December 21.

Turner, Lowell. 1991. *Democracy at Work: Changing World Markets and the Future of Labor Unions.* Ithaca: Cornell University Press.

U.S. House of Representatives. 2008. The Financial Crisis and the Role of Federal Regulators. Hearing before the House Committee on Oversight and Government Reform, 111th Cong. Preliminary Transcript. October 23.

U.S. House of Representatives, Committee on Financial Services. 2002. Corporate and Auditing Accountability, Responsibility and Transparency Act of 2002. Report No. 107-60, 107th Congress, 2d Session, March 13.

U.S. Senate. 2002. Legislative History of the Sarbanes-Oxley Act of 2002: Accounting Reform and Investor Protection Issues Raised by Enron and Other Public Companies. Hearings before the Committee on Banking, Housing, and Urban Affairs, Volume II, 107th Congress, 2nd Session, March 5, 6, 14, 19, 20, 21, 2002, S. HRG. 107–948.

Vagts, Detlev F. 1966. *"Reforming the 'Modern' Corporation: Perspectives from the German." Harvard Law Review* 80: 23.

Vitols, Sigurt. 2001a. "The Origins of Bank-Based and Market-Based Financial Systems: Germany, Japan, and the United States." In *The Origins of Nonliberal Capitalism: Germany and Japan in Comparison,* ed. Wolfgang Streeck and Kozo Yamamura, 171–99. Ithaca: Cornell University Press.

———. 2001b. "Varieties of Corporate Governance." In *Varieties of Capitalism: The Institutional Foundations of Comparative Advantage,* ed. Peter A. Hall and David Soskice, 337–60. Oxford: Oxford University Press.

———. 2005. "Prospects for Trade Unions in the Evolving European Corporate Governance System." European Trade Union Institute for Research, Education, Health, and Safety, Brussels.

Vogel, Stephen K. 1996. *Freer Markets, More Rules: Regulatory Reform in Advanced Industrial Countries.* Ithaca: Cornell University Press.

Vucheva, Elitsa. 2008. "France: Laissez-Faire Capitalism is Over." *Business Week online,* September 29. http://www.businessweek.com/globalbiz/.

Wallman, Steven M. H. 1999. "Understanding the Purpose of a Corporation: An Introduction." *Journal of Corporation Law* 24(4): 807–18.

Walsh, Mary Williams. 2009. "A.I.G. Lists Firms It Paid with Taxpayer Money." *New York Times,* March 16.

Wall Street Journal. 2004. "Long and Short: Corporate Regulation Must Be Working—There's a Backlash." June 16, C1.

Wall Street Journal Europe. 2001. "Takeovers? Nein!" Review & Outlook, May 30.

Weir, Margaret, Ann Shola Orloff, and Theda Skocpol, eds., *The Politics of Social Policy in the United States.* Princeton: Princeton University Press.

Weiss, Elliott J., and John S. Beckerman. 1995. "Let the Money Do the Monitoring: How Institutional Investors Can Reduce Agency Costs in Securities Class Actions." *Yale Law Journal* 104: 2053–2128.

White, Ben. 2002. "Wall Street Sees Chance to Put Off Reforms." *Washington Post*, November 8, E1.

Wiedemann, Herbert. 1980. "Codetermination by Workers in German Enterprises." *American Journal of Comparative Law* 28: 79.

Wiess, Bettina. 2006. "Acting Globally, Regulating Locally? Hedge Funds Are Viewed with Suspicion in Germany." *Atlantic Times*, March. http://www.atlantic-times.com/archive_detail.php?recordID=454.

Womack, James P. 1991. *The Machine That Changed the World*. New York: Harper Perennial.

Wilczek, Yin. 2009. "SEC Reflects 'Culture Shift' in Move to Shareholder Responsibility, Advocate Says." *Securities Regulation & Law Report* 41(47): December. 7. http://corplawcenter.bna.com.

Woodhead, Michael. 2008. "Angela Merkel: The Woman Who Saw the Crisis Coming." *Sunday Times* (UK), October 12.

Yamamura, Kozo, and Wolfgang Streeck, eds. 2003. *The End of Diversity? Prospects for German and Japanese Capitalism*. Ithaca: Cornell University Press.

Zetzsche, Dirk. 2004. "Explicit and Implicit System of Corporate Control—A Convergence Theory of Shareholder Rights." Center for Business and Corporate Law Research Paper, Heinrich-Heine-University, Düsseldorf, September 23. http://papers.ssrn.com/sol3/papers.cfm?abstract_id=600722.

Ziegler, J. Nicholas. 2000. "Corporate Governance and the Politics of Property Rights in Germany." *Politics and Society* 28(2): 195–221.

Zoellner, Wolfgang. 1994. "Aktienrecht in Permanenz." *Die Aktiengesellschaft*, 336–42.

Zumbansen, Peer. 2007. "Varieties of Capitalism and the Learning Firm: Corporate Governance and Labour in the Context of Contemporary Developments in European and German Company Law." *European Business Organization Law Review* 8: 467–96.

———. 2002. *"The Privatization of Corporate Law?* Corporate Governance Codes and Commercial Self-Regulation." *Juridikum* 132–40 (March).

Zumbansen, Peer and Daniel Saam. 2007. "The ECJ, Volkswagen and European Corporate Law: Reshaping the European Varieties of Capitalism." *Comparative Law and Political Economy Research* Paper No. 30/2007, Osgoode School of Law, York University.

Zweigert, Konrad and Hein Kötz. 1998. Introduction to *Comparative Law*, 3d ed. (Tony Weir trans.). Oxford, UK: Clarendon Press.

Zysman, John. 1983. *Governments, Markets, and Growth*. Ithaca: Cornell University Press.

CASES

Germany

ARAG/Garmenbeck, 135 BGHZ 244 (April 21, 1997).

BGH, Decision of 21 December 2005, 3 StR 470/04, Neue Juristische Wochenschrift (NJW) 522 (2006), reversing and remanding Landgericht Düsseldorf, Decision of 22 July 2004–28 Js 159/00.

Codetermination Case, 50 BverfGE 290 (1979), European Commercial Cases, vol. 2, pp. 324–86 (1979) (complete English translation).

OLG Stuttgart, 28.2.2007, BB 2007, 567, reversed and remanded, BGH II ZB 9/07, 25.2.2208, LMK 2008, 260596.

United States

American Federation of State, County & Municipal Employees v. American International Group, 462 F.3d 121 (2d Cir. 2006).

Aronson v. Lewis, 473 A.2d 805 (Del. 1984).

Blue Chip Stamps v. Manor Drug Stores, 421 U.S. 723 (1975).

Business Roundtable v. SEC, 905 F.2d 406 (D.C. Cir. 1990).

Central Bank of Denver v. First Interstate Bank of Denver, 511 U.S. 164 (1994).

Chiarella v. United States, 445 U.S. 222, 232 (1980).

Clapper's Manufacturing, 186 NLRB 324 (1970), enforced, 458 F.2d 414 (3d Cir. 1972).

Cort v. Ash, 422 U.S. 66 (1975).

CTS Corp. v. Dynamics Corp. of America, 481 U.S. 69 (1987).

Dirks v. Securities & Exchange Commission, 463 U.S. 646 (1983).

E.I. du Pont de Nemours & Co., 311 N.L.R.B. 893 (1993).

Electromation, *Inc.*, 309 N.L.R.B. 990 (1992), enforced sub nom. *Electromation, Inc. v. NLRB*, 35 F.3d 1148 (7th Cir. 1994).

Fibreboard Paper Products Corp. v. NLRB, 379 U.S. 203 (1964).

First National Maintenance Corp. v. NLRB, 452 U.S. 666 (1981).

Ford Motor Co. v. NLRB, 441 U.S. 488, 498 (1979).

JI Case Co. v. Borak, 377 U.S. 426 (1964).

Kardon v. National Gypsum Co., 69 F. Supp. 512 (E.D. Pa. 1946).

Moran v. Household International, Inc., 500 A.2d 1346 (Del. 1985).

NLRB v. Borg-Warner Corp., 356 U.S. 342 (1958).

Paramount Communications v. Time, 571 A.2d 1140 (Del. 1989).

Piper v. Chris-Craft Industries, Inc., 430 U.S. 1 (1977).

Revlon, Inc. v. MacAndrews & Forbes Holdings, Inc., 506 A.2d 173 (Del. 1986).

Santa Fe Industries v. Green, 430 U.S. 462 (1977).

Smith v. Van Gorkum, 488 A. 2d 858 (Del. 1985).

Superintendent of Insurance v. Bankers Life & Casualty Co., 404 U.S. 6, 13 (1971).

TSC Industries v. Northway Inc., 426 U.S. 438, 449 (1976).

Unitrin v. American General Corp., 651 A.2d 1361 (Del. 1995).

Unocal Corp. v. Mesa Petroleum Co., 493 A.2d 946, 955 (Del. 1985).

European Union

Centros Ltd and Erhvervs-og Selbskabsstyrelsen, Case C-212/97, 1999 E.C.R. I-1459.

Commission vs. Belgium, Case C-503/99, 2002 E.C.R. I-4809.

Commission vs. France, Case C-483/88, 2002 E.C.R. I-4781.

Commission vs. Portugal, Case C-367/98, 2002 E.C.R. I-4731.

Kamer van Koophandel en Fabrieken voor Amsterdam v. Inspire Art Ltd., Case C-167/01, 2003 E.C.R. I-10155.

Sevic Systems AG, Case C-411/03, 2005 E.C.R. I-10805.

Überseering BV and Nordic Construction Company Baumanagement (NCC), Case C-208/00, 2002 E.C.R. I-9919.

STATUTES, REGULATIONS, AND REGULATORY MATERIALS

Germany

Amendment of the Securities Trading Act by article 2 of the Law Implementing the EC Deposit Guarantee Directive and Investor Compensation Directive of 16 July 1998, BGBl. I 1842.

Amendment to the Securities Trading Act by article 3 of the Third Financial Market Promotion Act (*Gesetz zur weiteren Fortentwicklung des Finanzplatzes Deutschland, Drittes Finanzmarktförderungsgesetz*) of 24 March 1998, BGBl. I 529.

Amendment to the Securities Trading Act by article 2 of the Law Implementing EC Directives for the Harmonisation of Regulatory Provisions in the Field of Banking and Securities Supervision (*Gesetz zur Umsetzung von EG-Richtlinien zur Harmonisierung bank- und wertpapieraufsichtsrechtlicher Vorschriften*) of 22 October 1997, BGBl. I 2518.

Amendment to the Securities Trading Act by Article 16 of the Judiciary Notification Act and the Act Amending Cost Law Provisions and other Laws (*Justizmitteilungsgesetz und Gesetz zur Änderung kostenrechtlicher Vorschriften und anderer Gesetze*) of 18 June 1997, BGBl. I 1430 (JuMiG).

Baums Commission (Government Panel on Corporate Governance). 2001. Report of the German Government Panel on Corporate Governance (*Bericht der Regierungskommission "Corporate Governance—Unternehmensführung—Unternehmenskontrolle—Modernisierung des Aktienrechts"*) ("Corporate Governance—Corporate Management—Corporate Control—Modernization of Corporate Law"). German Parliament Document 14/7515. July 10. http://www.ecgi.org/codes/code.php?code_id=45.

Codetermination Act (*Gesetz über die Mitbestimmung von Arbeitnehmern*) of 4 May 1976, BGBl. I 1153, as amended 28 October 28 1994, BGBl. I 3210 (MitbestG).

Codetermination Act for Employees in the Mining and Iron and Steel Industry (*Gesetz über die Mitbestimmung der Arbeitnehmer in den Aufsichtsraten und Vorstanden der Unternehmen des Bergbaus und der Eisen und Stahl erzeugenden Industrie*) of 21 May 21 1951, BGBl. I 347 (Montan-MitBestErgG).

Corporate Control and Transparency Act (*Gesetz zur Kontrolle und Transparenz im Unternehmensbereich*) of 27 April 1998, BGBl. I 786 (Gesetz vom 27.4.1998, BGBl. I, S. 786 vom 30.4.1998) (KonTraG).

Cromme Commission (Commission of the German Corporate Governance Code), German Corporate Governance Code, adopted 26 February 2002, as amended thereafter (available at http://www.corporate-governance-code.de/index-e.html).

European Company Implementation Act (*Gesetz zur Einführung der Europäischen Gesellschaft*) of 22 December 2004, BGBl. I 3675.

Law Implementing EC Directives for the Harmonisation of Regulatory Provisions in the Field of Banking and Securities Supervision (*Gesetz zur Umsetzung von EG-Richtlinien zur Harmonisierung bank- und wertpapieraufsichtsrechtlicher Vorschriften*) of 22 October 1997, BGBl. I 2518 (effective 1 June 1998).

Law on the Improvement of Corporate Integrity and Modernization of Directed Suits (*Gesetz zur Unternehmungsintegritat und Modernisierung des Anfechtungsrechts*) of 22 September 2005, BGBl. I 2802 (UMAG).

Law on Model Proceedings in Capital Market Disputes (*Gesetz über Musterverfahren in kapitalmarktrechtlichen Streitigkeiten*) of 16 August 2005, BGBl. I 2437 (KapMuG).

Prospectus Act (*Verkaufsprospektgesetz*) as announced on 9 September 1998, BGBl. I 2701, as last amended by article 2 of the Act on the Further Promotion of Germany as a Financial Centre (Third Financial Market Promotion Act) of 24 March 1998, BGBl. I 529.

Second Financial Market Promotion Act (*Gesetz über den Wertpapierhandel und zur Änderung börsenrechtlicher und wertpapierrechtlicher Vorschriften, Zweites Finanzmarktförderungsgesetz*) of 26 July 1994, BGBl. I 1749.

Securities Acquisition and Takeover Act (*Wertpapiererwerbs und Übernahmegesetz*) of 20 December 2001, BGBl. I 3822 (WpÜG).

Securities Trading Act (*Wertpapierhandelsgesetz*) of July 26, 1994, promulgated as article I of the Second Financial Promotion Act (*Gesetz über den Wertpapierhandel und zur Änderung börsenrechtlicher und wertpapierrechtlicher Vorschriften, Zweites Finanzmarktördnungsgesetz*), BGBl. I 1749 (WpHG).

Stock Corporation Act (*Aktiengesetz*), 1965 BGBl. I 1089 et seq.

Third Financial Market Promotion Act (*Gesetz zur weiteren Fortentwicklung des Finanzplatzes Deutschland, Drittes Finanzmarktförderungsgesetz*) of 24 March 1998, BGBl. I 529.

Works Council Constitution Act 1952 (*Betriebsverfassungsgesetz* 1952) of October 1952, BGBl. I 681, as amended 2 August 1994, BGBl. I 1961.

Works Constitution Act of 1972 (*Betriebsverfassungsgesetz*) of 15 January 1972, BGBl. I 13.

Works Council Constitution Act (*Betriebsverfassungsgesetz*) of 23 December 1988, BGBl. I 1, ber. 902, as amended 19 December 1998, BGBl. I 3843.

United States

Delaware General Corporation Law, 8 Delaware Code Ann. §§ 101–398 (2010).

Employee Retirement and Income Security Act of 1974 (ERISA), 29 U.S.C. §§ 1001–1461 (2006).

Financial Services Modernization Act of 1999 (Gramm-Leach-Bliley Act), Pub. L. No. 106–102, 113 Stat. 1338 (2006).

Labor Management Relations Act (Taft-Hartley Act of 1947), 29 U.S.C. §§ 141–197 (2006).

Labor Management Reporting and Disclosure Act (Landrum-Griffin Act of 1959), 29 U.S.C. §§ 401–531 (2006).

National Labor Relations Act (Wagner Act of 1935), 29 U.S.C. §§ 151–169 (2006).

National Securities Markets Improvement Act of 1996, Pub. L. No. 104-290, 110 Stat. 3416, 15 U.S.C. § 77r (2006).

New York Stock Exchange, Inc., Order Approving Proposed Rule Change, Exchange Act Release No. 13,346, 42 Fed. Reg. 14,793, 14,794 (March 16, 1977).

Private Securities Litigation Reform Act of 1995, Pub. L. No. 104-67, 109 Stat. 737 (1995), amending title I of the Securities Act of 1933, 15 U.S.C. 77a et seq. (2006).

Sarbanes-Oxley Act of 2002, Pub. L. No. 107-204, 116 Stat. 745 (2002).

Securities Act of 1933, 15 U.S.C. § 77a-77aa (2006).

Securities and Exchange Act of 1934, 15 U.S.C. §§ 78a-78mm (2006).

Securities and Exchange Commission. 2009. Proposed Rule: Facilitating Shareholder Director Nominations, Exchange Act Release No. 60,089, 74 Fed. Reg. 29,024 (June 18).

———. 2007a. Final Rule: Shareholder Proposals Relating to the Election of Directors, Exchange Act Release No. 34-56914, IC-28075, 72 Fed. Reg. 70,449, 17 C.F.R. 240.14a-8(i)(8) (Dec. 6).

———. 2007b. Proposed Rule: Shareholder Proposals, Exchange Act Release No. 34-56160, 72 Fed. Reg. 43,466 (July 27).

———. 2007c. Proposed Rule: Shareholder Proposals Relating to the Election of Directors, Exchange Act Release No. 34-56161, 72 Fed. Reg. 43,488 (July 27).

———. 2004. SEC Comments on Proposed Rule: Security Holder Director Nominations. Release Nos. 34-48626; IC-26206. January 7. http://www.sec.gov/rules/proposed/s71903.shtml.

———. 2003a. Notice of Solicitation of Public Views Regarding Possible Changes to the Proxy Rules." Release No. 34-47778. May 1.

———. 2003b. Proposed Rule: Security Holder Director Nominations. Exchange Act Release No. 34-48626; IC-26206, 68 Fed. Reg. 60,784. Oct. 23.

———. 2000. Final Rule: Selective Disclosure and Insider Trading (Regulation FD), Exchange Act Release Nos. 33-7881, 34-43154, IC-24599, 65 Fed. Reg. 51,715, 17 C.F.R. 240.10b5-1 & 2, 243.100-103 (Aug. 24).

———. 1992. Final Rule: Regulation of Communications among Shareholders, Securities and Exchange Commission, Exchange Act Release Nos. 34-31326, IC-19031, 57 Fed. Reg. 48,276, 48,283 (Oct. 22).

———. 1978a. Proposed Rule: Shareholder Communications, Shareholder Participation in the Corporate Electoral Process and Corporate Governance Generally, Exchange Act Release No. 14,970, 43 Fed. Reg. 31,945, 31,947 (July 24).

———. 1978b. Withdrawal of Proposed Rule: Shareholder Communications, Shareholder Participation in the Corporate Electoral Process and Corporate Governance Generally, Exchange Act Release No. 15,384, 43 Fed. Reg. 58,533 (Dec. 14).

———. Rule 14a-8, 17 C.F.R. 240.14a-8 (April 1, 2009).

Securities Litigation Uniform Standards Act of 1998, Pub. L. No. 105-353, 112 Stat. 3227 (codified as interspersed subsections of 15 U.S.C. §§ 77–78).

Sherman Antitrust Act, 15 U.S.C. §§ 1–2 (2006).

Williams Act, 15 U.S.C. §§ 78m(d)–(e), 78n(d)–(f) (2006).

European Union

Council Regulation on the Statute for a European Company (SE), 2157/2001, 2001 O.J. (L 294) 1, 8.10.

Council Directive Supplementing the Statute for a European Company with Regard to the Involvement of Employees, 2001/86/EC, 2001 O.J. (L 294) 22, 8.10.

Insider Trading Directive, Council Directive 89/592/EEC of 13 November 1989 coordinating regulations on insider dealing, 1989 O.J. L334/30.

Investment Services Directive, Council Directive 93/22/EEC of 10 May 1993 on investment services in the securities field, 1993 O.J. L 141 of 11 June 1993, amended by European Parliament and Council Directive 95/26/EC of 29 June 1995.

Thirteenth Council Directive on Company Law concerning Takeover Bids, 1989 O.J. C 64, 14.3.

Thirteenth Council Directive on Company Law concerning Takeover Bids, European Commission's Amended Proposal, 10 September 1990, 1990 O.J. C 240, 26.9.

Thirteenth Council Directive on Company Law concerning Takeover Bids, Second Proposal for a Thirteenth Directive on Company Law concerning Takeover Bids, 1996 O.J. C 162, 6.6.

Thirteenth Council Directive on Company Law concerning Takeover Bids, Third Amended Proposal for a Thirteenth Directive on Company Law concerning Takeover Bids, 1997 O.J. C 378, 13.12.

Treaty Establishing the European Community, March 25, 1957 (Treaty of Rome), art. 189.

INDEX